common in literature, and shows how literature imbues such material with social, moral, and intellectual significance. He reveals the ways we take this process into ourselves, on the subconscious level, making the writer's transformation happen in our own minds, so that it becomes "a dream dreamed for us." He then shows how all the components of a work—plot, structure, characters, and style—build toward organic unity and combine their effects with our own quest for meaning. In the second part of the book, Mr. Holland uses his model of literary response to increase our understanding of a variety of well-known but puzzling literary phenomena.

Norman N. Holland is Professor of English at the State University of New York at Buffalo, and Chairman of the Department. He is the author of *The Shakespearean Imagination* and *Shakespeare and Psychoanalysis*. He is also an affiliate member of the Boston Psychoanalytic Institute.

The Dynamics of Literary Response

The Dynamics
of Literary Response

NORMAN N. HOLLAND

New York OXFORD UNIVERSITY PRESS 1968

For my mothers and fathers

Preface

This is not a book of literary criticism. One might call it meta-criticism or even infracriticism, but I suspect actual instances will do more to explain this book than fashionable prefixes. Here are some statements by critics, both past and present:

> As in a city when the evil are permitted to have authority and the good are put out of the way, so in the soul of man, as we maintain, the imitative poet implants an evil constitution, for he indulges the irrational nature which has no discernment of greater and less, but thinks the same thing at one time great and at another small—he is a manufacturer of images and is very far removed from the truth.

> A tragedy, then, is the imitation of an action that is serious and also, as having magnitude, complete in itself; in language with pleasurable accessories, each kind brought in separately in the parts of the work; in a dramatic, not in a narrative form; with incidents arousing pity and fear, wherewith to accomplish its catharsis of such emotions.

> From this account of [the metaphysical poets'] compositions it will be readily inferred that they were not successful in representing or moving the affections. As they were wholly employed on something unexpected and surprising they had no regard to

that uniformity of sentiment, which enables us to conceive and to excite the pains and the pleasure of other minds.

The Poet thinks and feels in the sprit of the passions of men. How, then, can his language differ in any material degree from that of all other men who feel vividly and see clearly? It might be *proved* that it is impossible. But supposing that this were not the case, the Poet might then be allowed to use a peculiar language, when expressing his feelings for his own gratification, or that of men like himself. But Poets do not write for Poets alone, but for men. Unless therefore we are advocates for that admiration which depends upon ignorance, and that pleasure which arises from hearing what we do not understand, the Poet must descend from this supposed height, and, in order to excite rational sympathy, he must express himself as other men express themselves.

My endeavours should be directed to persons and characters supernatural, or at least romantic; yet so as to transfer from our inward nature a human interest and a semblance of truth sufficient to procure for these shadows of imagination that willing suspension of disbelief for the moment, which constitutes poetic faith.

Poetry succeeds because all or most of what is said or implied is relevant; what is irrelevant has been excluded, like lumps from pudding and "bugs" from machinery. In this respect poetry differs from practical messages, which are successful if and only if we correctly infer the intention. They are more abstract than poetry.

In the process of composition, as every poet knows, the relation between experience and language is always dialectical, but in the finished product it must always appear to the reader to be a one-way relationship. In serious poetry thought, emotion, event must always appear to dictate the diction, metre, and rhyme in which they are embodied; vice versa, in comic poetry it is the words, metre, rhyme which must appear to create the thoughts, emotions, events they require. . . . Again, while in serious poetry detectable padding of lines is fatal, the comic poet should appear openly and unashamedly to pad.

In the last passage, W. H. Auden argues that the comic poet must "pad"—and, being a fine comic poet himself, he speaks with considerable authority. Yet he flatly contradicts Cleanth Brooks and W. K. Wimsatt in the passage immediately preceding. They point rather to the traditional notion that poetry must have organic unity. One might ask, though, whether they really mean that poetry succeeds "because" everything in it is relevant. Would they say, If everything in a poem is relevant, it is successful? And if so, why? Their statement rests, as does Auden's, on some unspoken assumption about the relationship of poetry to the mind of man.

Plato, at least, is far more explicit in the first passage quoted, his well-known objection to poetry as an imitation of imitations which stimulates the passions in an unhealthy way. Yet, aside from a sort of behaviorist description of the way people laugh and cry at fictions, Plato offers no explanation of the way poetry achieves these remarkable effects, so sharply different from the self-restraint he asks of us in everyday life. The last phrase of Aristotle's definition of tragedy is at least in part an answer to Plato: tragic poetry arouses pity and fear in order to purge them, and the medical metaphor of catharsis implies that this is healthy. Yet here, too, and in the passages from the *Politics* which gloss the key term, catharsis, there is no clear statement as to how poetry arouses emotions or what it does with them once they are aroused.

In the next three statements, Dr. Johnson criticizes the metaphysical poets for not heeding "that uniformity of sentiment which enables us . . . to conceive and to excite the pains and the pleasure of other minds." In the same vein, Wordsworth argues against poetic diction on the grounds that a poet "in order to excite rational sympathy . . . must express himself as other men express themselves." Both writers are assuming that a poet, to affect other men, must not choose either exotic images or exotic words, for they will somehow grate upon a sort of common human nature. Coleridge, however, implies just the opposite in his famous sentence dealing with the "willing suspension of disbelief"—the supernatural and romantic can be treated in such a way as to transfer human interest and procure poetic faith.

All these passages, in short, and, of course, a great many others, ranging from famous statements of principle to casual comments on particular writings, proceed from certain psychological assumptions about the impact of poetry and fiction on men's minds. Sometimes these assumptions are explicit, but more often they are not; and almost never does the critic make any attempt to validate them—they are simply held forth as commonsensical, intuitively valid, obvious on their face. Inevitably, the critical conclusions that rest on them are the weaker for this deep-rooted uncertainty.

It is the aim of this book to explore these psychological assumptions and to develop a model for the interaction of literary works with the human mind. How do we willingly suspend disbelief? What is the role of plain statement as against poetic diction? How do we "identify" with literary characters? What part does "organic unity" play in our response? How does literature "mean"? Can literature teach? Is the moral effect of literature good or bad —indeed, is there a moral effect at all? These are some of the questions this book tries to answer.

Ambitious though such a book may be, it is by no means the first to try to understand the literary experience psychoanalytically. There are at least two excellent books to which my indebtedness is far too great to be conveyed by mere footnotes: the late Ernst Kris's *Psychoanalytic Explorations in Art* and Simon O. Lesser's *Fiction and the Unconscious*. Kris's is a rigorous, technical study, written for the psychoanalytically informed, offering exact psychoanalytic formulations of many of the issues here presented in a literary way. Addressed more to a humanistic than a psychoanalytic audience, Lesser's pioneering work provides a full and many-sided study of the problems raised here. Flexible and humane, his book is indispensable to any study of our experience of literature. I should also mention another book: Marion Milner's *On Not Being Able To Paint*. From the quite different viewpoint of the visual artist it deals with many of the questions this book raises. Nevertheless, I was encouraged to find in Mrs. Milner's book confirmation for many ideas I had already had, as well as stimulus to new ones.

Kris's and Lesser's books are fine work, subtle, comprehensive, and correct. To venture into a field already so well explored would be presumptuous indeed, had I not something to add. First, I have broadened the scope of the inquiry to deal more extensively with poetry, theater, and film than they do. Second, I have structured the problem of literary response around such familiar entities as character, meaning, form, and the like rather more than they did; my aim is to coalesce the many, many components of response in the mind to a relatively few observable elements in the literary text. The result has been, I hope, to produce a more sharply focused and manageable model of our response. Finally, instead of starting out with psychological generalizations, I have tried, whenever possible, to derive general principles from the close analysis of particular literary texts. As an aid to the general reader, a glossary of some of the psychoanalytical terms used appears at the end of the book.

To say why I regard working with particular texts as so necessary and why, therefore, I regard psychoanalytic psychology as the only psychology useful for studying literary response involves me in a brief apologia. Like most critics my age, I was enormously influenced and pleased by the so-called "New Criticism" (already not so new by the time we came to it). I and, I am sure, many of my contemporaries felt we were seeing literature in ways that had never been possible before. We were less concerned with the terminological furors that engaged the first New Critics than with the close examination of particular texts for plot parallels, repeated images, figures of speech, structure, myths, points of view, and so on. We sought them out with enthusiasm and diligence and something of the excitement that the generation of biologists must have felt who were first able to use the microscope.

Often our intense and minute examinations seemed too precisely drawn—certainly many older scholars complained of them. And yet, if my own experience holds true for other critics, we all discovered in our different ways that literary works, even of a very crude kind, had an almost unbelievable fineness of form and structure. In even a *Saturday Evening Post* story, each episode can be shown to fit the idea that informs and shapes the story as a whole, while in a Shakespearean play a skilled critic can easily show the relevance of each individual line to the informing principle.

Just what these discoveries amounted to, however, was not always clear. In some way, the act of discovery itself seemed to enhance our experience of literature and that of the audience we wrote for or taught, though just exactly how this enhancing took place was by no means clear. Similarly, the things discovered must have had something to do with response, but just what?

This question of response affected me more than it evidently did others, because of another concern of mine—comedy or, more specifically, "the comic sense of life" which I once thought was a useful antidote to what then seemed to me the pomposity of Unamuno's phrase, "the tragic sense of life." Accordingly, I devised a course called "The Cosmic Sensibility"—promptly dubbed by my students "The Cosmic Sensitivity"—perhaps because I was particularly interested in that special lightening of the spirit that comedy evokes as its characteristic response. Over a decade or so, after looking at that comic transcendence mythically, religiously, thematically, I began to think about it psychologically.

I had already considered the various theories of laughter and come to the conclusion that Freud's was the only one that made any sense to me as a literary critic—that is, which led me back to that close analysis of a text which seemed to me then (and now) the *sine qua non* of literary understanding. Other theories were deductive rather than inductive. Bergson, for example, argues that we laugh when we suddenly find something mechanical encrusted upon that which is organic, pliable, and living. It is not difficult to look for and find this trope (and others) in many comic works, but once you have looked at the work and plugged it into the formula, "mechanical encrusted upon living," that is all you can do. With Freud's much more complicated theory, I found I was constantly driven back to the joke itself to see the coaction of its particular features and details. I came to wonder if psychoanalytic psychology could offer a theory for literature in general, not just jokes. Thus the book began.

This is a book that tries to answer the basic question confronting the textual critic: What is the relation between the patterns he finds objectively in the text and a reader's subjective experience of the text? As the above quotations show, this is a question that confronts all critics all the time. Everyone who thinks about literature faces the task of establishing a conceptual bridge between objective and subjective views of literature. I have suggested some of my subjective concerns; in fairness, I should now set out some of the objective assumptions that inform this book.

First, I propose to talk about literature primarily as an experience. I realize that one could talk about literature as a form of communication, as expression, or as artifact. For the special purposes of this book, however, literature is an experience and, further, an experience not discontinuous with other experiences. For example, Erving Goffman's well-known study *The Presentation of Self in Everyday Life* shows, from the point of view of the sociologist, how social mannerisms look very like drama. Such a sense of literature as continuous with other human experiences suits the social scientist well, for he is steadily faced with the problem of reconciling objective observation with subjective experience. It is an attitude rather less prevalent among students of literature than it should be.

Second, I do not use "literature" as a value term, a medal to be awarded to those works that please me. For whatever my definition is worth, I call something literature to the extent it responds to being looked at literarily, that is, by the kind of close verbal analysis the last thirty years of criticism have taught us. Thus, advertising, Pepys's diary, cinema, doggerel, and pulp all fall within the term to the degree they respond to a search for plot parallels, repeated images, and the rest. Often, these things on the periphery of literature proper will raise literary issues in a more direct way than works within the academic canon do. For example, a joke is a literary text that evokes a highly specific psychological and physiological effect; jokes evidently tap the sources of affect more immediately than lyrics do. Advertising and propaganda pose the question, How does literature teach? more directly than any respectable literature can.

Third, my method. I propose to describe works of literature objectively, as so many words on a piece of paper or spoken aloud. Then, I shall describe psychologically my own response to that objective stimulus and look for points of correspondence between the text objectively understood and my subjective experience of the text. My conclusions will always involve, then, two kinds of proposition: one the kind of thing a textual critic says; the other the kind of thing a psychoanalyst might say; and, always, an assumption that the two propositions are related (an assumption that I hope the first and third chapters will justify).

Inevitably this book must mingle subjectivity and objectivity, for that is its task: to build a conceptual bridge from literary texts objectively understood to our subjective experience of them. One can analyze literature objectively, but how or why the repeated images and structures shape one's subjective response—that is the question this book tries to answer. I shall have to rely rather heavily on my own responses, but I do not mean to imply that they are "correct" or canonical for others. I simply hope that if I can show how my responses are evoked, then others may be able to see how theirs are. As with most psychoanalytic research, we must work from a case history, and in this situation, the case is me.

Sometimes, I am sure, my experience will coincide with yours. There is, after all, generality even in the high subjectivity of literary responses. We would all agree, I suppose, that *Hamlet* is a better play than *Titus Andronicus* or that *Crime and Punishment* is darker than *Bleak House*. If I can discover why they are so for me, then perhaps I will have discovered why they are so for you—the stimuli, after all, are the same. At other times, you may feel that my response is idiosyncratic—so be it. The important thing is that we be as candid as we can, I in my assertions, you in your disagreements. To that end, I have tried throughout to use "I" and "you" and "we" with some care, to keep these three levels of discourse clear: subjective, objective, and "commonly experienced."

Implicit in all these other assumptions is my belief in close study of the text and in psychoanalysis. I think we can—and should—talk, at least initially, about literary works as purely formal entities, as they exist on the page or in the theater without reference to author's intention, value, historical background, or anything except the text itself and some dictionary knowledge. Certainly, much discussion of literature in the last decade has proceeded this way and with considerable success. To go from the text as an object to our experience of it calls for a psychology of some kind—I have chosen psychoanalytic psychology, because it takes as its data subjective states. It is the only general psychology I know that can talk about an inner experience with as much detail and precision as a New Critic can talk about a text. Since our task demands that we map objective texts into subjective responses, this approach is absolutely necessary. I am well aware of the many objections that are made to psychoanalysis—they seem to me, however, to rest on an extraordinary variety of misconceptions. Looked at intellectually or experienced subjectively, either way, it seems to me, psychoanalytic psychology offers a more valid and comprehensive theory of inner states than any other.

Validation is a highly troublesome issue in this as in any other psychoanalytic study because of the subjectivity of the data. I would like to think this book presents the Truth (with a capital T) about literary response, but, in the nature of the case, that is not possible. What this book creates is an hypothesis, but it is at least a testable hypothesis, unlike most literary theories. A psychologist skilled in designing experiments could confirm or deny the conclusions reached here, and I have suggested at the end of the book some possible ways of testing the model.

Finally, beneath and beyond these objective assumptions, I must confess to a bias or trait that colors them all. You may have noticed it already, and you may want to discount it at various points in the text. For me, the need to see and understand is very strong. To put the matter as exactly and with as much ambiguity as possible, I need to be sure that I am understanding all that I am seeing. And I can only hope you will be able to share this trait with me for the duration of this book, for, as we shall see, that is the way we inwardly experience books.

My indebtednesses in this book are many and far-reaching. I have mentioned above three writers of psychoanalytic aesthetics whose influence permeates this book. Three other writers, non-psychoanalytic, have influenced me more than my footnotes can indicate. Robert E. Lane in his *The Liberties of Wit: Humanism, Criticism, and the Civic Mind* takes literary critics to task for what sometimes seems an almost willful refusal to use ordinary systematic procedures of classification, theory, testing, or methodology. Morse Peckham's astringent *Man's Rage for Chaos: Biology, Behavior, and the Arts* applies behaviorist and perceptual psychology to a wide range of aesthetic problems; I am indebted to him not only for his attitude of open inquiry but for a number of specific insights. Similarly, Northrop Frye in all his writings has cleared the air of a great deal of obscurantist smog. If even a part of these writers' clarity and honesty has carried over into this book, I shall be most pleased.

I am heavily indebted to my fellow members of the Group for Applied Psychoanalysis and the Boston Psychoanalytic Society and Institute for the opportunity to present and discuss some of the ideas that follow. Dr. Elizabeth Zetzel and the late Dr. Joseph J. Michaels were of particular help. A number of friends and colleagues have read all or part of the manuscript and been kind enough to provide me with comments and critique: C. L. Barber, Albert S. Cook, Frederick C. Crews, Gordon Globus, A. R. Gurney, Jr., Louis Kampf, Simon O. Lesser, Bruce Mazlish, Morse Peckham, R. Robert Rogers, Andrew Silver, Irving Singer, Taylor Stoehr, Ruth Sullivan, William I. Thompson, Abraham Zaleznik. They have done much that the crooked shall be made straight, and the rough places plain. Over the years, my students, at M.I.T. and also at Stanford, Fisk University, and the State University of New York at Buffalo, have provided a great many helpful comments and corrections for which this is an all too abbreviated notice. I am particularly grateful to the Rockefeller Foundation for the chance to air my views as a Visiting Scholar at Fisk.

A number of the chapters that follow I have published separately in earlier versions or in parts. To the editors of the journals and books in which they appeared, I am doubly grateful: for having published them in the first place; for letting me use them now. Their appearance in earlier versions engendered editorial comment and, sometimes, scholarly controversy that led me to useful revisions and rethinking. I am indebted to the National Council of Teachers of English and Richard Ohmann, editor of *College English*, where part of Chapter 1 originally appeared; to Herbert Weisinger of the *Centennial Review* in which an earlier version of Chapter 3 was published; to Michael Wolff, editor of *Victorian Studies*, and to George Levine and William Madden, editors of *Victorian Prose as Art*, for segments of Chapter 4 and 5; to Frederick Morgan of the *Hudson Review* for segments of Chapters 6 and 7; to Richard Dyer MacCann, editor of *Cinema Journal* (formerly *Journal of the Society of Cinematologists*), where the nucleus of Chapter 8 first appeared; to Leonard Manheim of *Literature and Psychology* where segments of Chapters 4, 5, and 7 were published; to Maurice Beebe, editor of *Modern Fiction Studies*, for an earlier version of Chapter 8; to Sheridan Baker of the *Michigan Quarterly* where the prototype of Chapter 10 first saw the light of day.

I am grateful as I have been before to Mr. Sterling Lord of the Sterling Lord Agency. Whitney Blake of the Oxford University Press proved the kind of editor authors pray for. Mr. Clive O'Connor, Miss Susan Maycock, Miss Anita Sansone, Mrs. Susan Brooks, Mrs. Hilda Ludwig, Mrs. Miriam Scott, and Mrs. Virginia White helped ably and amiably in the final production of the manuscript.

To my wife, I owe far more in editorial, moral, and imperturbable support than any dedication can indicate.

Amherst, New York   N. N. H.
September 1967

Contents

I The Model Developed

1   Literature as Transformation

The Muse is an enigmatic lady. Ever since Aristotle we have tried to penetrate her mysteries, yet still she eludes us. Still we ask as Aristotle did: What is our emotional response to a literary work? What arouses it? What dampens it? Why do men enjoy seeing mimeses of the real world? How is it that literature can make painful things give pleasure? How does literature affect morality?

Later critics have added to the questions. Coleridge, in particular, raised the most puzzling issue of all: the "willing suspension of disbelief." Somehow, when we are engrossed in a literary work, we lapse into the same state of mind as the embezzler in the joke:

> The young executive had taken $100,000 from his company's safe, lost it playing the stock market, and now he was certain to be caught, and his career ruined. In despair, down to the river he went.
>
> He was just clambering over the bridge railing when a gnarled hand fell upon his arm. He turned and saw an ancient crone in a black cloak, with wrinkled face and stringy gray hair. "Don't jump," she rasped. "I'm a witch, and I'll grant you three wishes for a slight consideration."
>
> "I'm beyond help," he replied, but he told her his troubles, anyway.
>
> "Nothing to it," she said, cackling, and she passed her hand before his eyes, "You now have a personal bank account of $200,000!" She passed her hand again. "The money is back in

the company vault!" She covered his eyes for the third time. "And you have just been elected first vice-president."

The young man, stunned speechless, was finally able to ask, "What—what is the consideration I owe you?"

"You must spend the night making love to me," she smiled toothlessly.

The thought of making love to the old crone revolted him, but it was certainly worth it, he thought, and together they retired to a nearby motel. In the morning, the distasteful ordeal over, he was dressing to go home when the old crone in the bed rolled over and asked, "Say, sonny, how old are you?"

"I'm forty-two years old," he said. "Why?"

"Ain't you a little old to believe in witches?" [1]

The Muse always tricks us that way. Whether she has inspired a joke or a great tragedy, she tricks us as the witch tricked the young executive. In Coleridge's terms, we willingly suspend our disbelief. We agree, as it were, not to doubt that a witch could magically create a bank account—or at least not to doubt that a worldly executive would so believe.

Why do we suspend disbelief? Presumably, for the same reason we do most things in this world, to gain pleasure. Then, behind the question Coleridge raised, How does the Muse induce us not to disbelieve, stands the deeper Aristotelian puzzle, What is the pleasure literature gives us? Curiously, that question takes us to what might seem the least pleasurable part of literature—its moral significance or, more generally, meaning.

Literature means, we would all agree. But how? We might all disagree. A great many critics and philosophers have wrestled with "the meaning of meaning" in ordinary discourse. We can, however, make our question somewhat simpler if we narrow it and ask only what we mean by literary meaning above and beyond the meanings of everyday speaking and writing. Further, a psychoanalytic approach to literary works has, I think, something special to contribute to this gnarled question, because it can describe quite exactly the special pleasure of literature.

"A theme," Frank O'Connor has said, "is something that is

worth something to everybody." By "theme," here, I think O'Connor means, roughly, "plot plus meaning of the plot," for he goes on:

> The moment you grab somebody by the lapels and you've got something to tell, that's a real story. It means you want to tell him and think the story is interesting in itself. If you start describing your own personal experiences, something that's only of interest to yourself, then you can't express yourself, you cannot say, ultimately, what you think about human beings.[2]

Freud noticed this same limitation on the writer and concluded, "The writer softens the egotistic character of [his] daydream." How? That, said Freud, is the writer's "innermost secret, . . . the essential *ars poetica*." [3]

Freud's answer is at least as mysterious as the Muse herself, but Freud knew no New Critics. He had not been exposed, as, for example, modern college students have, to thirty years' accumulation of academic explications. If he had, he would have been all too aware that literature means, and it means in a general, not a personal way. O'Connor's phrasing leads to a definition: literary meaning is a statement of what in the literary work is of sufficient generality to be "worth something to everybody."

Uusually, meaning in this sense takes the form of statements like "*School for Scandal* is a play about the tension between appearance and reality," or "The theme of 'Pied Beauty' is the relationship between the permanent, universal, and ideal and the particular, various, and transitory." Meaning thus becomes a reader's attempt to state a universal proposition derived from the text, not so much a "moral" as an idea or quality that informs and permeates the whole. Northrop Frye, for example, contrasts narrative movement within a poem to "The meaning of a poem, its structure of imagery, [which] is a static pattern." [4] In my own teaching and writing, I have found it helpful to think of literary meaning spatially—as an idea that all the particular details of a work are "about," a "point" to which all the individual words or events in a literary work are relevant, not unlike the "point" of a joke. In a standard handbook for students, Frye suggests a similar procedure as basic to all critical analysis:

> The primary understanding of any work of literature has to be based on an assumption of its unity. However mistaken such an assumption may eventually prove to be, nothing can be done unless we start with it as a heuristic principle. Further, every effort should be directed toward understanding the whole of what we read, as though it were all on the same level of achievement.
>
> The critic may meet something that puzzles him, like, say, Mercutio's speech on Queen Mab in *Romeo and Juliet*, and feel that it does not fit. This means either that Shakespeare was a slapdash dramatist or that the critic's conception of the play is inadequate. The odds in favor of the latter conclusion are over-whelming: consequently he would do well to try to arrive at some understanding of the relevance of the puzzling episode. Even if the best he can do for the time being is a far-fetched or obviously rationalized explanation, that is still his sanest and soundest procedure.
>
> The process of academic criticism begins, then, with reading a poem through to the end, suspending value-judgments while doing so. Once the end is reached, we can see the whole design of the work as a unity. It is now a simultaneous pattern radiating out from a center, not a narrative moving in time. The structure is what we call the theme, and the identifying of the theme is the next step . . . . the theme is not something in the poem, much less a moral precept suggested by it, but the structural principle in the poem.[5]

Meaning in literature—Frye's "poem" is representative of all literature—goes beyond meaning in ordinary discourse to the extent the literary work is shaped and structured by such a central idea.

As a practical matter, it seems to me, most of what we think of as literary analysis is a process of successive abstraction. The skilled reader organizes the details of the text into recurring images and themes. Essentially, he abstracts repeated or contrasted words, images, events, or characters into categories. Some special critics may think in Marxist or psychoanalytic or Swedenborgian terms, but most use categories from everyday discourse. In *Hamlet*, for example, critics will speak of images of disease, incidents of broken rituals, or characters who do as against characters who talk.

If a critic wishes to go as far as he possibly can in this process —many critics, of course, don't—he further re-classifies this first level of abstractions (usually called themes) into a final level consisting of a very few basic terms which the work as a whole is "about." One might, for example, see *Hamlet* as "about" the imperfection that comes between idea and fact. If such a set of terms states the universal intellectual content of the work, if this is its "meaning," then a reader should be able to move from these three very general terms to less general themes like disease, ritual, word-and-deed, and from them back to the text itself. He should be able to see particular manifestations of one or another of the general terms (imperfections, idea, fact) at any point in the text—or else his generalizations from the text left something out.

The technique is a powerful one, as thirty years of "new critical" explications testify. Yet, as anyone knows who has practiced "close reading" or "explication" with students, it often seems overly intellectual, even sterile, certainly far removed from the roots of our pleasure in literature.

By contrast, psychoanalysis seeks out those roots by looking in literary works not so much for a central "point," as for a central fantasy or daydream, familiar from couch or clinic, particular manifestations of which occur all through the text. *Hamlet*, Freud told us sixty-seven years ago, expresses an oedipal fantasy, and all its incidents, imagery, and characters come together around this one issue.

Thus, both a "new critical" reading and a psychoanalytic reading will arrive at something central to a work, some general entity represented at any given point in the text by particular language. What, then, is the relation between these two central entities, one a statement, the other a fantasy? Most critics, I think, would say they are simply two different ways of looking at the text, each valid in its own way, as would be the Marxist or Swedenborgian interpretations. I would like to suggest that, on the contrary, the psychoanalytic reading has a very special relation to any other reading.

Consider, for example, our joke. A modern critic, looking at the joke simply as a literary production, would notice the repeated references to numbers and money. The joke's "incidental imagery" consists of "$100,000," "playing the stock market," "In addition," "slight consideration," "personal bank account of $200,000," the "money," the "company vault." Key phrases are: "What is the consideration I owe you?" "You must spend . . ." "worth it." All these quantifications culminate in the numbering of the young man's years, and one would abstract them as comparing values, distinguishing something from nothing.

The basic metaphor is the bargain. The old woman who can give everything, herself lacks youth and sex. The young man has these two things though he has lost everything else—and they bargain with each other and seem to exchange. As against the motif of exchange stand the un-bargains: the young executive's having "taken $100,000" and lost it "playing"; the witch's not delivering what she promised. Looked at only from the point of view of conscious, intellectual content, the point of the joke seems to be that the young man who thought he would get away with something for nothing or "for a slight consideration," "certainly worth it," finds instead that he has been had for nothing, or for a few magic gestures. More exactly, the joke contrasts what the young executive expected with what he got. He expected to get something (money) for nothing (sex), but he finds he has given something (sex) for nothing (promises of money).

If this analysis of the "point" is correct, if we have found those few terms to which everything else in the joke is related, we should be able to understand the young executive's "character" through this "meaning." Looking at the story realistically, we could say that the young executive's character—to the limited extent we see it in this joke—is that of a man who tries to get what he can of this world's comforts, paying nothing or as little as possible. He is a man who wishes to take into himself what he can. It is fitting, then, that his "punishment" is to be taken in by someone else, for it is a truth well known to confidence men (and artists) that the easiest man to gull is one trying to get something for nothing. Again, looked at realistically, he is quite sensible to believe and make love to the witch. Having lost everything, he has nothing left to lose. Like a Kierkegaardian knight of faith, he is perfectly right to make the leap into acceptance and trust. His character, in other words, is one particular manifestation of the informing idea of the whole, expecting something for nothing. The joke, in short, is quite moralistic—it punishes the young executive for trying to get something for nothing. And in playing a rather cruel trick on him, it plays a trick on us.

That formulation, however, raises a question more fundamental than meaning. If the joke tricks and fools us, how, then, does it give pleasure? It must give pleasure, or else we would not willingly suspend our disbelief.

I can remember quite vividly, the first time I heard the joke, a fleeting but highly gratifying thought that flashed through my mind when the old lady appeared, did her magic, and made everything right: Oh, if only it were so, if only there were magical people to solve all problems! The punch line quite abruptly deprived me of that fantasy—and yet I laughed and felt pleasure.

What had happened was the feeling from the last line, "I was fooled," had become a reassurance, somehow, not a disappointment. Midway in the joke my feelings toward the old woman changed. At first, she was a powerful parent-figure who would make all well. But then she became quite repulsively seductive. As a result, the feeling "I was fooled" became reassuring: there really are no all-powerful parent-figures who are also frighteningly grabby and seductive and sexual.

It is not hard to recognize a nurturing mother-figure in the crone who magically offers "sonny" all the sustenance he needs at the moment he needs it most. Her repulsiveness in the joke evokes the right feeling, namely, that she is sexually inappropriate, an "old crone on the bed." It is all right to take wish-fulfillment from her, but "distasteful" to make love. The image of taste and her own toothless mouth suggest a fearful fantasy about a mother taking into herself (into her mouth-like genitals) instead of giving into the mouth of her child. The mother-word "sonny" appears at the safe moment—when she lets us know that she is not going to behave like a mother.

In short, the joke gave me pleasure by the way it handled an oedipal fantasy (and I assume that, with appropriate variations, the same mechanism gave pleasure and reassurance to others). This parental reading of the joke gets confirmation from a variant that also went the rounds. Instead of a witch, a devil appears and the "slight consideration" is a night of homosexual love. The variant develops the same conflict between our succoring and our sexual ideas of a parent, but this time it is the father (seen in terms of the negative oedipus complex).

The primary level of the joke's fantasy is oedipal, but underneath that fantasy there is an oral motif. The joke works with a feeling of trusting and expectation that most of us have experienced consciously, but all of us have experienced before we were conscious of ourselves as such. Like Freud and other analysts, Erik Erikson locates its origins in infancy in the period when a child is dependent on its mother for its oral needs, and he shows how that trust leads to "identity." "Basic trust in mutuality is that original 'optimism,' that assumption that 'somebody is there,' without which we cannot live." Identity begins with that nurturing other because the child does not conceive of himself as a separate being until he can trust and await his mother as a separate being.[6] When he accepts her as separate, he has realized he is separate.

In this joke about expectancies and bargains and living or not living up to them, it is surely not difficult to see "mutuality" and "basic trust." We could think of the young executive as suffering oral frustration—his world no longer supports him. When the deprivation the young man suffers makes him feel he can no longer trust his world, he resolves to give up his identity by destroying himself in the engulfing waters of the river. His sense of trust in the old lady leads him instead to an engulfing world of magic, and he becomes a trusting child again. He is "taken in." Figuratively, he is duped; sexually, he is taken into the "toothless" mouth of the crone's genitals. We could even say the hero has a kind of death-and-rebirth through magic: a submerging of his self (from a "bridge") into an underworld of matriarchal magic, then a disillusioning re-emergence into rationality and the real world at the end. He acts out again oral fusion followed by an infant's discovery of his own identity. That is the infantile fantasy the joke works with. On a more realistic level, the young man accepts the witch as real the same way a brainwashed prisoner believes in his keeper; this parent-figure evokes in him the sense of basic trust one associates with a mother at the very moment he most needs that trust to regain his hold on life and his own identity.

At first, the joke reassures us by means of a series of displacements, not unexpectedly, for an exchange or bargain resembles a displacement: both shift attention or concern or, here, valuation from one thing to another. The first words of the joke, for example, shift our attention from the executive's wrongdoing onto his suffering. We pity him rather than condemn him, and we enlist the witch as our aide. At least at first, she, too, seems to pity rather that punish him (just as the story as a whole concerns the seduction of a superego). The "big" concerns of the joke should be the vanished career and the lost money, but these are rendered vaguely and abstractly. The first visual images the joke gives us are the bridge railing and the gnarled hand. In effect, the joke has displaced our attention from the theft and loss to the exchange with the witch. The taboo he broke by stealing becomes quite masked over by the witch's breaking the oedipal taboo.

More exactly, the story displaces the executive's wrongdoing (getting something for nothing) onto the parental witch. Similarly, it displaces our credulity in believing the story at all onto the young executive who believes the witch's story. Then, trust becomes dangerous when the witch becomes sexual. So the punchline undoes both these displacements—we are reassured, we disbelieve again, and we laugh.

To sum up, the story worked with an oral-oedipal fantasy that at first gave pleasure, then anxiety, then pleasure again. The plot and form of the joke served as the defensive ways of handling this fantasy, and the meaning or "point" of the joke turned out to be its intellectual or conceptual transformation. That is, being deprived for expecting something for nothing is simply an intellectual version of the original fantasy: the loss involved in getting mother sexually as against orally. We can call the joke's meaning a transformation analogous to a sublimation, for it makes the unconscious fantasy intellectually, morally, and socially acceptable and even pleasurable; more technically, it makes the fantasy ego-syntonic.

Meaning, then, in one of its aspects, is analogous to the sublimation of an infantile fantasy. Other aspects we shall see in other chapters, but the thesis here is: the meaning of the joke, its point or informing idea, has two levels. The first, conventional literary meaning, states the way the elements of the story are all relevant to an intellectual idea: "getting something for nothing." The second, a psychoanalytic statement, shows how the elements of the story, understood as having unconscious meanings ("toothless mouth" as genitals), are all relevant to a particular unconscious fantasy: being nurtured by a mother as against making love to her. The joke's meaning, then, is not simply a "point" which a static configuration of elements is "about." Rather, its meaning is a dynamic process: the joke transforms the unconscious fantasy at its heart into intellectual terms.

Is this notion of transformation true only for jokes? Or is it true for literature in general? We can test this concept of meaning-as-transformation against a work of literature that bears a striking resemblance to our joke: the Arthurian tale of Chaucer's Wife of Bath.

Mastery ("maistrie") is the point about which the three phases of the story come together, specifically, "maistrie" between man

and woman—who shall be boss? The Tale begins when a knight
blithely rapes a girl (thus depriving her of her right to say no—her
"maistrie"). Haled before King Arthur, he is condemned to be beheaded (no "maistrie" in that), but then the queen and the other
ladies wear out the king's resistance and get him a reprieve (their
"maistrie"). The queen offers the knight his life if he will return
in a year and a day to tell her "What thyng is it that wommen
moost desiren," [7] and the knight duly sets off on the second phase
of the story, his quest for an answer.

Until the very last day, he has no success, but on that day he
comes upon a fairy ring in the woods, which disappears and leaves
there a particularly revolting and horrible old woman: "A fouler
wight ther may no man devyse." He tells her his troubles, and she
agrees to tell him the secret provided he will grant her the next
boon she asks. The knight agrees, she tells him the secret, and the
knight and the crone return to the court, where the knight makes
his answer to the queen.

> "My lige lady, generally," quod he,
> "Wommen desiren have sovereynetee
> As wel over hir housbond as hir love,
> And for to been in maistrie hym above.
> This is youre mooste desir, thogh ye me kille.
> Dooth as yow list; I am heer at youre wille."

In short, women want "maistrie," and, though he has saved his
head, the knight's passive position suggests the amount of maistrie
he himself has already lost. He loses still more when the crone
holds him to his bargain. She asks him to marry her, thus beginning the third phase of the Tale.

Downcast by his predicament, the knight does marry the old
woman, but,

> Whan he was with his wyf abedde ybroght;
> He walweth and he turneth to and fro.

His grizzled bride twits him with impotency, and he replies that
she is loathly, old, ill-born, and poor. The nuptial couple then em-
bark on one of Chaucer's famous digressions, this time on the na-

ture of true nobility or "gentilesse." She points out that poverty is
a Christian virtue, that true nobility comes from Christ, that the
old deserve respect and finally, that since she is old and ugly, she
will never cuckold him. But as though her arguments were not
enough, she offers him a choice; either she will be foul and old, but
true, or she will be young and fair, and unfaithful—choose.

The knight, no doubt somewhat worn down by all the things
that have happened to him, gives up:

> "My lady and my love, and wyf so deere,
> I put me in youre wise governance . . .
> I do no fors the wheither of the two;
> For as yow liketh, it suffiseth me."
> "Thanne have I gete of yow maistrie," quod she,
> "Syn I may chese and governe as me lest?"
> "Ye, certes, wyf," quod he, "I holde it best."

And the ladies have won "maistrie" for the third and final time.
Gleefully, the crone announces she will be both young and true.
The wedding night proceeds with Chaucerian pace and vigor:

> She obeyed hym in every thyng
> That myghte doon hym plesance or likying,

and they lived happily ever after.

If my own feelings of disgust at the relationship between the
young knight and the old crone are any clue, the Wife of Bath's
Tale builds on the same sense of taboos broken as does the joke.
Raping the girl breaks one taboo (as the young executive's embez-
zling did). But we are not as repelled by those violations as we are
at the knight's being asked to perform sexually for the old crone.
This stronger revulsion has its roots in another, much deeper
taboo, that against sexual relations with a member of one's parents'
generation, a taboo ultimately derived from oedipal fears. And, lest
this seem too schematically Freudian, it is well to remember that
the first words the knight addresses to the old crone are, "My leeve
mooder," my mother dear (l. 1005).

It should be no surprise, then, that breaking these sexual taboos
produces a variety of threats of bodily injury leading to bodily de-

ficiency, helplessness, or loss—that is, threats analogous to castration. The knight's head is threatened first. Then, when the crone demands marriage, he feels his whole body lost: take all my goods, he begs her, "and lat my body go." Finally, his body trapped in marriage, it tosses and turns while he is unable to perform sexually. She asks,

> "Why fare ye thus with me this firste nyght?
> Ye faren lyk a man had lost his wit."

The loathly lady refers to the medieval tradition that lunatics were impotent—in doing so, she makes clear the sexual nature of the threats to the knight: bodily or mental loss, leading both to loss of sexual power and to impotency in the sense of general helplessness. Cutting off the head, loss of self-determination, loss of sanity—all symbolize the basic threat of loss: castration.

The phallic significance of the threat that the knight will be beheaded shows in the Wife's phrasing, too. The knight was condemned "and sholde han lost his heed," his head. Just five lines before, he had attacked the maid, and, said the Wife,

> maugree hir heed,
> By verray force, he rafte hire maydenhe[e]d;

that is, despite her resistance, by very force, he ravished her maidenhood or maidenhead (the word does double service in Middle English). The rhyme points to the pun: the knight's head corresponds to the maid's "heed," her power to resist, as well as to the "he[e]d" or "hood" in "maidenhood," her state in the world. In effect, the phallus means the power not to have others force their will on a helpless you which in turn means the intactness of your position in the world—a very irritating idea to the wife, who, as her Tale and Prologue amply show, resents the domination of the male and would rather have the phallus at her own beck and call.

What then does woman have instead? She has a secret, a hidden place. A man tries to poke into things; the knight, as inquisitive as Aristotle, "seketh every hous and every place." He comes upon a secret dance and hopes to learn some wisdom from it, but it disappears, and the old crone tells him, "Sire knight, heer forth ne lith no wey," you cannot penetrate here. You can only get at woman's secret if woman will bestow it on you—as the crone does. Even then, she performs her magical transformation behind the bed-curtain, and only after she has become young and beautiful does she invite the knight, "Cast up the curtyn, looke how that it is." And at that moment the knight is finally given her secret: "Dooth with my lyf and deth right as yow lest." Woman's secret place indeed contains the secret of life—and death (in her feared aspect), and the knight is taught he can only get to that secret place if it is freely opened to him—he cannot force his way by rape.

To state rather bluntly the fantasy at the heart of the story, it begins with phallic sexuality, conceived of as a kind of rape in which both woman and man lose something. He may be castrated, she, rendered passive and helpless. The Wife's Tale converts this phallic relationship to a regressive, oral one in which the man yields sovereignty (and his phallus) to the woman as a son might yield to his nurturing, all-powerful mother. Then, from this oral passivity, the last few lines of the Tale carry the couple to genital mutuality, albeit orally tinged by language as appropriate to an infant as to a bridegroom: "a bath of blisse."

In brief, then, the Tale starts with phallic, aggressive sexuality, regresses to a more primitive relation between taboo mother and passive son, and finally progresses to genital mutuality (though dominated by the woman—if you will obey me, I will give you pleasure). From the point of view of the Wife's own psychology, we could say she is compensating for her own missing phallus by setting herself up as a trap, threatening her successive husbands, in order to coerce them into giving up their phallic power to her. For us, the story builds on a fear of sexuality as phallic aggression leading to helplessness or loss, and the Tale deals with that fear by regression to oral passivity. But this jargon simply states the psychological underpinnings to what the story is very explicitly about:

abandoning "maistrie" in favor of mutual submission. In a relationship between a man and a woman, which shall have "maistrie,"
that is, which shall dominate the relationship? "Maistrie" itself? Or
passivity leading to mutual giving?

As this tangled syntax suggests, though, perhaps "maistrie" is not
as accurate a term as we might wish. Clearly, it is the theme that
binds together the three phases of the tale, but will it also bring
into a meaningful totality the Wife's digressions? There are four in
all, if we let the term include anything in the tale that is too long
for its narrative function: the Wife's introduction, setting the Tale
"In th'olde dayes of the Kyng Arthour," when there were elves instead of (as in the Wife's day) friars; the telling of the tale of
Midas' ears; the very long "pillow talk" about "gentilesse"; and, finally, the Wife's seven-line prayer that ends the Tale.

The Wife's introduction sets the Tale in an ancient, pagan time
when the land was full of "fayerye," and

> The elf-queene, with hir joly compaignye,
> Daunced ful ofte in many a grene mede.

Now, says the Wife, the omnipresent friars have replaced these
pagan powers. Thus, the Wife has set up some of the basic themes
that run through her Tale: the contrast between man and woman,
elf-queen and Christian God; the contrast between old and new,
the two generations that will be represented in the knight and the
loathly lady; the issue of masculine or feminine control, the elf-
queen, powerful with respect to "Kyng Arthour," as against the
friar who begs, but also, the Wife suggests, is given to assaulting
lonely ladies he meets (thus costing them "maistrie").

The Wife's second digression tells the story of King Midas' ears.
He had, under his long hair, asses' ears, which he hid from everyone's sight except his wife's. There is something wrong with his
body, something under the hair, something only his wife knows,
and that something wrong shows he is an ass. Again, I think, we
get implications of male helplessness and impotence. The asses'
ears are erect and hornlike. They may suggest Midas is cuckolded

(unmanned, castrated); at the same time, they may also be defensive against fears of castration—not only am I not missing anything, I have two extra.

Either way, however, it is the woman who wins. Midas asked and she swore that she would never tell what she had seen, but she couldn't stand not telling it—this is the reason the Wife gives for telling the story: some woman was bound to give the knight the secret he needed to save his head. So, Midas' wife went down to the water's edge and whispered, "Myn housbonde hath longe asses erys two!" And ever after, the reeds whisper the same—so Ovid says, but not the Wife, for that is not the relevance of her digression.

In Ovid, the story is told of the king's barber, but, for the Wife, the story shows woman's ability to humiliate and dominate man by means of her power over his vulnerable body. The story also suggests the maternal quality of this power, for it demonstrates not only woman's power over man, but also the giving, outpouring quality of woman—she is unable to keep her secret to herself. That quality contrasts with Midas' efforts to hide and withhold the secret. (Later, the Wife will complain of men "[niggard] of dispence.") Moreover, this quality of giving is an irresistible compulsion, not unlike the source of life itself, that outruns and escapes masculine efforts to master it by authority. (There may be the faintest hint of a mythic ancestry through Ovid for her dichotomy —Dionysus was the ass-headed god, ever-dying, and the wife is not unlike Venus in her giving out and animating the forces of nature, the reeds.)

The Wife gives Ovid as her authority, saying he tells King Midas' story "amonges othere thynges smale." She thus links Ovid with verbal and rather trivial knowledge (why reeds sound the way they do), while her own telling links it to everyone's experience (that women cannot keep a secret), to the immediate context of the Tale (the knight will surely learn the secret), and, indeed, to her own lengthy and hardly discreet Prologue. Similarly, Midas' wife speaks from experience—she has actually seen the ears. In

short, the Wife's second digression further builds the antithesis between man and woman on which her Tale depends: woman as giving, man as withholding; woman linked to sight and experience,
man, either Midas or Ovid, to verbal authority.

The "pillow talk" and the final prayer, the Wife's third and
fourth digressions, make a pair. The third begins when the knight
complains on his wedding night that his bride is not only low-born
but "so loothly and so oold also." She replies that true nobility
("gentilesse") comes not from high birth or riches but "cometh
fro God allone," citing Dante, Seneca, and Boethius for her authorities. She turns to poverty: it is godlike, for Christ himself was
poor, and she gives another battery of authorities, Seneca, Juvenal,
"and othere clerkes." As for old age, even if there were "noon auctoritee . . . in no book," one would know that men should be
courteous to an old man "And clepe hym fader," call him father.
(If I may be psychoanalytic, since one should call an old man father, what should one call an old woman?) Finally, as for her ugliness, that guarantees her chastity and fidelity. Again, in psychoanalytic terms, the loathly lady is identifying, quite explicitly, the revulsion at her ugliness with a sexual taboo. Since her remarks immediately before tended to identify her with a mother, we can see
a relation between two kinds of revulsion: revulsion at sexual relations with a member of an older generation; revulsion at sexual relations with one's mother—and the revulsion guarantees chastity.

Be that as it may, one thing is clear: the loathly lady goes
through 112 lines of more or less ecclesiastical argument, before she
offers the knight his choice. She makes the knight hear about "gentilesse." In the same way, the second two phases of her Tale, the
Quest and the Wedding Night, give the knight first the verbal
knowledge of "maistrie," then the actual experience of giving it up.
And the whole form of Prologue and Tale contrast Dame Alice of
Bath's lengthy and authoritative disquisition upon marriage and
"maistrie" with stories that transform those two verbal abstractions
into the fullness of experience.

In other words, the Wife's Tale sets up another contest, parallel to the contest between male and female: the contest between, in the first words of her Prologue, "experience" and "auctoritee." By and large, we are to identify men with "auctoritee," the tyrannical husbands, the raping knight, the punishing Arthur, and the various clerkly authorities, Solomon, Ptolemy, Boethius, or Ovid. Women —the queen, the loathly lady, the Wife herself—express experience, fertility, and life, as in the Wife's lovely, if pagan, reminiscence: "I have had my world as in my tyme."

The Wife's closing prayer, her last digression, follows directly upon the knight's experience of "gentilesse" as an alternative to "maistrie." The Wife prays, first, for husbands meek, young, and "fressh abedde"—in other words, "giving" husbands. She asks, second, that women have "grace" to outlive them. While the Wife's penchant for variety is sufficient, no doubt, to explain such a wish, it would also be well to remember that the loathly lady is old and somewhat supernatural and also a somewhat murderous mother: she is wishing the son-husband's death. At a still less conscious level, the Wife's prayer makes explicit the knight's child-like feeling toward the benevolent mother the Wife and the loathly lady become, namely, that while his own existence is precarious, she will go on forever; she is the tower of security; she will be "there." The Wife prays, third, that Jesus will shorten the lives of those that will not be governed by their wives (with, again, the unconscious murder-wish that those who do not obey their powerful mothers may die). Finally, she rounds out her symmetrical prayer by asking for a plague on "olde and angry nygardes of dispence," husbands who are stingy and will not give.

In short, the Wife of Bath's Tale sets up a fundamental contrast: between masculine, verbal, limiting authority or "maistrie" and feminine submission to the plenitude of experience. In so doing, she sets also the keynote for the three themes of the "Marriage Group" identified by Kittredge: rhetoric, "gentilesse," and, of course, marriage. Rhetoric she identifies with masculine verbalism and "auctoritee," true gentilesse with "experience" and the feminine giving up of "maistrie." And our analysis of the digressions in the Wife of Bath's Tale suggests that a better way than "maistrie" of stating the idea that informs the story is: Which shall have "maistrie"—the imposition of "auctoritee" or submission to "experience"?

This statement of the idea that informs the Tale (and much of the Prologue) gives still another digression relevance: "the wordes bitwene the Somonour and the Frere." Those two worthies represent Mother Church in precisely these two aspects: the Summoner imposes ecclesiastical authority; the Friar begs and is at least supposed to be passive and submissive.

The Wife's Tale purports to prove that if life is to be a contest of authorities, woman will very likely win and man will very likely be unmanned. If, however, man submits to the dominance of a motherly woman, both will gain. The boy-gets-girl ending seems to me a little hard on masculinity, but, all things considered, a happy ending. I am pleased that an old crone becomes a Playmate. And mutual submission and giving seem to me a good thing, even, perhaps, a Christian thing, as hinted by Sir Walter Scott's comment: "What was a mere legendary tale of wonder . . . in the verse of Chaucer reminds us of the resurrection of a skeleton, reinvested by a miracle with flesh, complexion, and powers of life and motion." [8] As the loathly lady says when the knight complains of her skeletal qualities,

> I koude amende al this,
> If that me liste, er it were dayes thre,
> So wel ye myghte bere you unto me.

I could amend all this—my poverty, ugliness, low birth, and age —if it pleased me to do so, within three days, provided you bear yourself properly to me. "Dayes thre" suggests to me some doubtful, but perhaps not totally irrelevant associations.

The loathly lady explicitly compares herself to Christ when she claims her "gentilesse" from Christ, not men. She is poor, she says, just like Christ. The analogue that comes most readily to my mind is Flaubert's "The Legend of St. Julian the Hospitaller." There, the saint welcomes a loathsome leper to his hut. When he can love and bed with and embrace this most repulsive of human beings, he finds he is embracing Christ. The leper is, of course, not the radiant, triumphant Christ of the Transfiguration (not until the end of the story); he is the "man of sorrows" of Isaiah 52 and 53: "His visage was so marred more than any man, and his form more than the sons of men." "He hath no form nor comeliness; and when we shall see him, there is no beauty that we should desire him." "We did esteem him stricken, smitten of God, and afflicted," even as the knight regards his bride. "A fouler wight ther may no man devyse." Her phrase, "dayes thre," would mark the difference between the Christ of the Cross, despised and rejected of men, and the Christ triumphant of the Resurrection. Man's submission to Christ transfigures him, even as the knight's submission transfigures the loathly lady.

If "dayes thre" would have triggered the same associations in the Wife's hearers that it does in me, then her Tale achieved complexities indeed. But it wouldn't have. Professor D. W. Robertson, Jr., has been kind enough to show me how the Tale uses a heroine well known in medieval stories. The loathly lady, he writes,

> belongs . . . to a common medieval type (also represented by the Wife herself) that can conveniently be described as "The Old Whore," related to Ovid's Dipsas, to La Vieille in the *Roman de la Rose*, and to a number of other figures of the same kind. Specifically, she promises her victim, "I shal fulfille youre worldly appetit" [1. 1218]. . . . The fulfillment she offers, moreover, blatantly disregards the lessons of her preceding discourse, which emphasizes the advantages of (1) virtue, (2) voluntary poverty, and (3) wisdom (the quality honored in old age). The young man is obviously interested in the pleasures of the flesh instead. As soon as the lady has obtained the "maistrie," her victim considers her to be young and fair and true.
>
> To understand this "miracle," it is necessary to know something of medieval moral philosophy. The Old Woman, like the Wife herself, represents the "feminine" element in man (i.e., the senses as distinct from the reason, the flesh as distinct from the spirit, etc.). When this element is given the "maistrie," the

victim becomes blinded by his own desires so that he cannot discern even the most obvious truths. Thus, for example, a medieval proverb runs, "He who loves a frog thinks the frog to be Diana." The "miraculous" elements in the story generally should be translated into events that can and do ordinarily take place. We do not, that is, ordinarily encounter "foure and twenty" ladies in a dance who suddenly become a disappointing old hag. We do, however, sometimes discover that the parade of luscious wenches we pursue either in fact or imagination turns out not to be very attractive. To make the "luscious wench" attractive again, all that is really necessary is that we submit to her. That is, whether the "luscious wench" seems to be fair and true or simply another manifestation of fallen Eve, old and ugly, depends entirely on ourselves. The "oldness" of the old whore, incidentally, is not altogether a matter of history, but is related to the "oldness" that Christians are supposed to cast off at baptism (e.g., see Rom. 6: 4–6) and periodically thereafter in penance.[9]

In short, to her first audience, the devious Wife has managed to represent as a good thing (and perhaps even as *caritas* itself) a quite un-christian submission to old Eve. If "dayes thre" tipped off a medieval hearer to anything, it was simply that submission to the loathly lady acts as a mocking alternative to and parody of man's proper submission to Christ. The parody, if parody it be, is all the more delicious in that so rigorous a feminist as Dame Alice has quite naturally cast God as a woman.

If the Tale embodies this parody, it becomes one more instance of Chaucer's reinterpreting pagan joys into at least the possibility of Christian values, as in the cruiselike pilgrimage itself or that "Aprille" with its amorous birds but restless pilgrims. The Tale as a parody illustrates not only Alisoun's perverse ability to turn conventional churchly views topsy-turvy;[10] it also shows in a larger and less parodic sense a basic pattern of medieval literature. That is, medieval narrative moves not in a pattern of conflict and resolution but in a hierarchy of values:[11] the low—submission to "worldly appetit"—has at least the potential of becoming the high —submission to Christ. After all, lechery was the least of the seven deadly sins.

There is, however, still another dimension of "meaning" in the
Wife of Bath's Tale. Chaucer's sources for it are of two types. In
the English group, evidently derivative, loving the loathly lady
leads to sovereignty in marriage. In the earlier, Irish group, loving
the loathly lady leads to a tanist's sovereignty in the kingdom. In
either case, the loathly lady would seem to derive from some Persephonic figure deep in the Celtic twilight, some combination of
crone and virgin, spring goddess and destroyer, who gives to the
year-king who wins her the power to rule.

In the Irish sources, notes Professor Sigmund Eisner, "Her
loathly form represents winter." "The original meaning of the marriage. . . . was a seasonal myth—the worldwide belief in marriage
between the sun and the earth. The sun, by cohabiting with the
earth, insured the earth's customary bounty." In the English
sources, the choice is between the lady's being loathly by day or
loathly by night, but the implications of day or night match those
of spring or winter, and, Eisner concludes, "The prototype of the
Wife of Bath's heroine traveled even more widely than Alice herself. Originally, she was the earth goddess who annually married
the solar deity." [12]

At a less primitive level, if man submits to the life-and-death
power of woman, both gain. If not, both lose. And the Persephonic
level fits not only Professor Robertson's reading (submission to the
old Eve) and the Wife's concern with phallic loss as against a son's
giving in, but also her contrast between imposition of authority
and submission to experience—the fertile, giving power of women,
be they earth goddesses or just worthy ladies of Bath.

But, as the Friar would surely say at this point, "This is a long
preamble of a tale!" Our theme is literary meaning, of which we
have seen several different kinds in the Wife of Bath's Tale. From
a purely analytic, "new critical" point of view, the story contrasts
dominance by verbal or other masculine authority to submission to
feminine or other experience. For a modern reader—this modern
reader, anyway—that submission seems good: it makes an old

crone into a lovely maiden. But as so often for modern readers of medieval literature, what the story means to us ironically reveals our moral and spiritual distance from our forebears. In terms of the traditional allegory pointed out by Professor Robertson, the story contrasts proper Christian values with submission to the Old Whore of "worldly appetit," beautiful (or transfigured) only because man is foolish enough to believe in her. Still more mythically, submission to the Persephonic life-and-death power of woman leads to mutual strength rather than mutual loss (as in the sources studied by Professor Eisner). Psychoanalytically, the reader replaces the danger of phallic woundings, rape, beheading, wearing asses' ears, helplessness, mental impotency or sexual—by submission to a mother's nurturing but also murderously powerful love.

Clearly, meaning is not simply "there" in the text; rather it is something we construct for the text within the limits of the text. And even inconsistent readings may be appropriate: my "modern reader's meaning" may be just as right for some readers as Professor Robertson's interpretation is for Chaucer's first audience.

If you are a critical relativist (as I am on Mondays, Wednesdays, and Fridays), you will simply accept each of these different readings as valid to the extent it brings all the elements of the story together to a single "point." If you are a critical monist (as I am on Tuesdays, Thursdays, and Saturdays), you will carry one step further the process of successive abstraction that led us to these several meanings. You will abstract these various kinds of meaning, the modern reader's meaning, the medieval allegory, the Persephonic myth, and any other interpretations that may turn up subsequently, all together into one abstraction that covers all these possible meanings: perhaps, "Chaucer's Wife of Bath's Tale is a study in authority and submission." *

---

* It is not difficult to demonstrate that any verbal text, taken as a series of discrete words or events, can be recursively classified into a final, single "meaning." Any two things can be logically related: an elephant is like a Rembrandt in that neither is a wastebasket; they are both in the class of non-wastebaskets.

The point is, all these meanings are similar, as we can see if we
set them down in a chart:

	AUTHORITY	SUBMISSION
Modern reader's meaning	Masculine, verbal restraint	Feminine giving and receiving
	Imposition of "auctoritee"	Submission to "experience"
	Secular "gentilesse" (restricted to the nobility)	Christian virtues (possible for all)
	Rejected "man of sorrows"	Christ believed in
Medieval meaning	"Worldly appetit" rejected	The Old Whore adored
	Authority of reason and spirit	Submission to senses and flesh
Mythic meaning	Repulsive woman and powerless man	Persephone and the ruler
Psychoanalytic meaning	Phallic wounding	Oral submission

The story asks, Which will it be? Which of these two modes shall
have "maistrie" over the other? And the story comes out trium-
phantly for the right-hand side—submission (though that may be
good or evil depending on the reader's values). Either way, though,
the question and the answer shape and inform the story's incidents

---

One could go on to relate all the elements of a literary text into such classes,
and one could classify classes until one arrived at a very small number of
classes to one or another of which all elements in the text would be related.

This is, of course, a trivial demonstration. As a practical matter, the elements
in a literary text tend to group in classes that represent familiar literary themes:
art and nature, appearance and reality, mind and matter, time and eternity,
male and female, and so on. As a purely logical matter, however, any number
of these traditional themes can be grouped into a unitary "meaning." It is
possible. Whether it is desirable is another matter. Most professional critics
feel more comfortable with separate themes, not pushing for a final, central
statement of meaning to which each and every element of the text is relevant.
Either way, however, implicit in any literary text is some grouping, be it full
or partial, into meaningful themes. Either way, then, a literary text implies a
transformation toward meaningfulness.

and its language. Either way, the story has a theme or themes that are "of sufficient generality to be 'worth something to everybody.'"

Our process of successive abstraction seems sound enough, but it does not explain why Chaucer might have grabbed somebody by his medieval lapels to tell him the story nor why the story has engrossed five centuries of readers (even some modern readers who quite misinterpret it). I claimed at the outset that the psychoanalytic meaning had a special relation to all other meanings. It does so, because the fantasy psychoanalysis discovers at the core of a literary work has a special status in our mental life that moral, medieval, or Marxist ideas do not. These are conscious and adult and intellectual. Fantasies are unconscious, infantile, and fraught with emotion. Fantasies are what make us grab somebody by the lapels. Ideas do so only if they are the later representatives of fantasy. The crucial point, then, in this analysis and in the chart of meanings is: the psychoanalytic meaning underlies all the others.

At the heart of this story we experience a child's fantasy: if I am phallicly aggressive and do not submit to my mother, she will castrate me. Fantasies such as this were once all too real to us and a mass of evidence from couch and clinic shows they still provide much of the steam and pattern in our adult lives. If so, then the recognition of the fantasy level in this story points to a very general concept of literary meaning. That is, meaning is not a statement, but a process. The fear, if I do not submit to mother, she will castrate me, becomes in our conscious reading of the story the pleasure of submitting instead of coercing (whether as individual readers we value that pleasure in modern, medieval, or mythic ways).*

The story "means" in that it transforms its unconscious fantasy

---

* I think, for example, we tend to value experience over Scriptural authority, equal partnership as against authority in marriage, and (some of us anyway) the pleasures of the here-and-now to the traditional values of religion. To a medieval audience, however, Professor Robertson says, "He who allows his wife to dominate him will be served as the Wife of Bath seeks to serve her husbands; he who allows the flesh to dominate the spirit will find it a tyrant like the wife; and, finally, he who disregards the spirit of the Scriptures in favor of experience will find himself enslaved to the Old Law, unredeemed by the 'freedom wherewith Christ hath made us free.'" [13]

into social, moral, intellectual, and even mythic terms. Meaning is not a static set of relevancies, but a dynamic process of transforming one kind of relevancy, unconscious, to another, conscious. Sometimes, as in the Wife's Tale, the transformation reverses the unconscious fantasy, making what is fearful desirable. Other stories, like the *Playboy* joke, are more like a sublimation, making illicit wishes conform to moral demands. But all stories—and all literature—have this basic way of meaning: they transform the unconscious fantasy discoverable through psychoanalysis into the conscious meanings discovered by conventional interpretation.

We can represent this transformation, this special status of psychoanalytic "meaning," graphically. We begin with a text which is, ultimately, a discrete collection of words:

xxxxxxxxxxxxxxxxxxxxxxxxxxxxxxxxxxxxxxxxxxxx

The text has a direction; it begins, progresses, and ends. But a skilled reader also gives the text meaning by making connections between all the parts of the text, regardless of direction or position. He makes it, in Frye's phrasing, "a simultaneous pattern radiating out from a center, not a narrative moving in time." As I see it, the skilled reader abstracts recurring images, incidents, characters, forms, and all the rest into certain themes. In the Wife's Tale, for example, he finds themes of male-female, withholding-giving, words-experience, old-young, and so on. We can represent this abstraction into themes as a kind of "stretching" of the text:

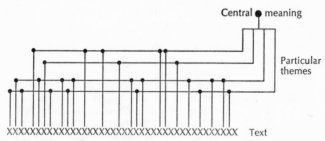

Some readers might then take the final step of abstracting all these several themes into a single, central, nuclear "meaning" such as "authority and submission."

If psychoanalytic themes and meaning were like the rest, they would fit simply as one particular grouping into this general picture. But the fantasies the psychoanalytic reading discovers have a special status: infantile, primitive, bodily, charged with fear and desire, we know from clinical evidence they involve the deepest roots of our cumulating lives. Nor can they be abstracted as other meanings can, by the commonsensical, "square" categories of ordinary experience or logic. Rather, they come together by the curious, abrupt groupings known as primary-process thinking: condensations, displacements, symbolizations, projections, splittings, klang associations, and the like. We need therefore to represent the psychoanalytic reading and the primary-process connections among its themes in a special, pre-logical way:

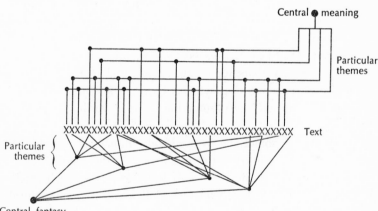

Consciously, we arrive at the psychoanalytic reading by a process not unlike our approach to other kinds of meaning. We abstract images, incidents, characters, forms, and the rest into certain psychological themes: man-woman, mother-child, castration-gratification, coercion-submission, and so on. It is more necessary than in ordinary reading to pull these together into the central fantasy known from clinical evidence: if I am phallicly coercive, mother will castrate me; if I submit, she will gratify me. It is more necessary to think the psychoanalytic reading through to its ultimate form, because it is this ultimate form of the fantasy that generates our response. It is from such deep and fearful roots of our most personal experience that literature gets its power and drive.

We shall return to this picture again and again, for it represents in at least a concise and, I hope, a helpful way "the dynamics of literary response." We shall, however, have to develop it further, for a number of things are missing. Most important, we have been able so far to represent only the text, not the reader. If he appears at all, he is only the invisible agent of this "stretching" of a discrete collection of words. We have talked about meaning, but not form (which will appear in Ch. 4). Especially lacking is an account of the role of language (Ch. 5).

But we have made a beginning. We have been able to see at least a major force in the pleasure we get from literature. Literature transforms our primitive wishes and fears into significance and coherence, and this transformation gives us pleasure. It is this transformation of deep personal feelings that Freud called, "the innermost secret," "the essential *ars poetica*" in which the writer "softens the egotistical character of the daydream." It is this act of meaning that transmutes in laymen's terms, "something that's only of interest to yourself" into "something that is worth something to everybody."

What is worth something to everybody, though, is not the general statement that informs the literary work, the "moral" of the story, but our pleasure in the act of transformation which reaches that moral (or social, intellectual, religious, or philosophical) theme. Fantasy gives force to conscious meaning, but conscious meaning mollifies and manages our deepest fears and drives. If we wish to see literature in its fullness, then, we must deal not with conscious meaning alone or unconscious alone, but the transformation of each into the other. As so often in literary matters, either-or must give way to both-and, the point not only the loathly lady makes, but even the ferociously charitable Wife of Bath herself.

2   A Dictionary of Fantasy

People have fantasies. That quite commonplace, extraliterary fact is one of two postulates on which this book rests. The other is also an empirical observation: whatever their sect, literary critics find central or core ideas that permeate and inform the literary work—this is what we mean when we say literary works have "organic unity." Psychoanalytic critics find a core of fantasy; other kinds of critics find cores of social, biographical, political, philosophical, moral, or religious meaning.

Given these two postulates, we can begin to build. People have dreams and daydreams in which they gratify wishes and impulses, experience or allay fears. People have had and will have such fantasies all their lives. They must, in order to act, for one must imagine an action to perform it. Fantasies, moreover, occupy a special prior and primitive place in our mental life, and, therefore, a psychoanalytic reading of a literary work in terms of fantasy also has a special status. It is not simply a reading parallel to other readings from ideologies, Marxist, Swedenborgian, Christian humanist, or whatever; it is the material from which other such readings are made.

Psychoanalysis is not an ideology. Rather, it is clinical and experiential, and the fantasy it discovers in a literary work provides a base for our experience of that work just as fantasies—projections, imaginings, anticipations—provide a base for our experience of life itself. They are the stuff of childhood from which adult thinking grows. Even in adult life, as dreams clearly show, unconscious infantile fantasies provide the force behind mature, conscious wishes. That, then, is the special and wonderful thing about literature: it does for us in an intense, encapsulated form what we must do for ourselves as we mature in life—it transforms primitive, childish fantasies into adult, civilized meanings.

The vast literature on the kinds of fantasies people are likely to have (either as wish fulfillment or anxiety mastery) enables us to set up a kind of dictionary of the fantasies we can expect to find literature transforming. And here we come upon the strange and astonishing farrago of wishes, impulses, complexes, and fears that people so often dismiss as "psychoanalysis." We should remember, though, that when we speak of particular impulses and particular defenses against them, we are very close to the immediate data of couch and clinic. These are not "constructs" or "hypotheses" or "intervening variables" but things that many people have directly observed in dreams, in children's play, and in the psychoanalyses of both children and adults.

A child develops, according to psychoanalytic observations, in a series of phases, customarily distinguished by the part of his body or family which gives the child most pleasure—or conflict—at the time. For our purposes, we can enlarge the customary five phases and list seven: oral, anal, urethral, phallic, oedipal, latent (or latency, during which the child renounces his oedipal wishes), and genital (the period of puberty and after). Of course, children do not behave so neatly as adults with schemes might wish. Phases overlap, and no one phase excludes the others from importance. Indeed, in normal development, these phases cumulate, so that successful mastery of conflict in one is a precondition for development in the next. Unresolved conflicts will persist, finding expression in the new idiom of the next stage. It is common, in clinical psychoanalysis, to trace the influence of early issues even to the end of life. As the twig is bent, so grows the tree.

Because these phases cumulate, we begin to develop a life style quite early. One can see recognizable personality types in any kindergarten class, and by the time we reach latency or puberty, we have become quite individual. As a result, we cannot say very much about the role the fantasies of latency and puberty play in our response to literature. They do play an important part, but fantasies at this level of maturity, and, *a fortiori*, in the adulthood beyond, are far too various to be generalized about. Our dictionary must be confined to oral, anal, urethral, phallic, and oedipal fantasies—beyond them, no dictionary is possible.[1]

Psychoanalysts, psychiatrists, and psychologists, however, when they discuss the fantasies embodied in literary works, like to use terms like narcissism, masochism, homosexuality—clinical entities for adults which are more familiar to the practicing therapist. The therapist, except in psychoanalysis proper, is less likely to be concerned with the childhood roots of adult personality. As a literary critic, though, I much prefer to look at the fantasies in literary works through what we know of the fantasies typical of the various libidinal phases associated with child development. Needless to say, both types of description are close to clinical observation (though of different kinds). And neither contradicts the other: the libidinal phases of childhood have in them the seeds of the adult clinical entities.

Admittedly, it sounds odd to describe so-and-so as "an anal writer" or a given work as "an oral story" or a "phallic poem." Nevertheless, I prefer the phasic descriptions, for the reference of literature to the child suggests the universality of its appeal better than does referring to the more individualized adult. Also, developmental notions reveal the organic continuity of literary works. Plays and stories usually reach from the most primitive oral fantasies to complicated oedipal ones, just as, clinically, a man's earliest experiences of loss or anxiety provide a style for their later equivalents. Because an approach to literature through libidinal phases suggests such a continuing style, one can often see strikingly direct and pervasive connections between the writer and his work, between his literary style and his life style. A writer may never live out the adult masochistic fantasies embodied in his works, but the libidinal level of childhood conflict at the root of those literary fantasies will necessarily show in his life. Erikson, for example, has repeatedly shown this kind of continuity in his biographical studies.

Most important, though, and as we shall now see in some detail, notions like orality and anality lead us directly to images, which are, for the literary critic, probably his richest source of insight. In general, I think, an approach to literature in terms of adult syndromes reveals things about plot and character, but an approach through the libidinal phases opens up the additional possibility of talking about language, a topic all too often missing in psychological studies of literature.

The earliest phase is that period in infancy when our life revolves around what goes in and what comes out of the mouth, the oral phase. The key transaction in this developmental phase is "self-object differentiation." As Freud describes it,

> An infant at the breast does not as yet distinguish his ego from the external world as the source of the sensations flowing in upon him. He gradually learns to do so, in response to various promptings. He must be very strongly impressed by the fact that some sources of excitation, which he will later recognize as his own bodily organs, can provide him with sensations at any moment, whereas other sources evade him from time to time— among them what he desires most of all, his mother's breast —and only reappear as a result of his screaming for help. In this way there is for the first time set over against the ego an "object," in the form of something which exists "outside" and which is only forced to appear by a special action.

> In this way, then, the ego detaches itself from the external world. Or, to put it more correctly, originally the ego includes everything, later it separates off an external world from itself. Our present ego-feeling is, therefore, only a shrunken residue of a much more inclusive—indeed, an all-embracing—feeling which corresponded to a more intimate bond between the ego and the world about it.[2]

To reword Freud, the very young child does not distinguish "out there" from "in here." Only by being able to wait for, expect, trust in, the reappearance of a nurturing other, does he begin to sense that there is a world which is not a part of himself. Only by recognizing that other as a being separate from himself does he recognize himself as a bounded entity.

In literature, this earliest phase appears as fantasies of losing the boundaries of self, of being engulfed, overwhelmed, drowned, or devoured, as in Poe's stories of being buried alive. But these fantasies can also be of a benevolent merger or fusion, as when Chaucer's bridegroom gets a "bath of blisse." Both the *Playboy* joke and the Wife of Bath's Tale reveal their oral basis by the presence of an all-powerful, maternal woman.

Often, when literary works ask us to enter an environment explicitly labeled as fantastic, we are being asked to merge orally into that new world, be it of romance, fairytale, utopia, or science-fiction. We must "trust" this new world as we would a nurturing mother, take it in and be taken into it. Sometimes, the eat-or-be-eaten quality of the fantasy becomes quite explicit as in "Hansel and Gretel" or Golding's *Pincher Martin* where the hero finds himself shipwrecked and starving on a mid-Atlantic rock which turns out to be his own tooth.

Freud notes adult experiences that stem from this earliest oral fusion and merger. "Normally," as adults, "there is nothing of which we are more certain than the feeling of our self, of our own ego. This ego appears to us as something autonomous and unitary, marked off distinctly from everything else."

> There is only one state—admittedly an unusual state, but not one that can be stigmatized as pathological—in which it does not do this. At the height of being in love the boundary between ego and object threatens to melt away. Against all the evidence of his senses, a man who is in love declares that "I" and "you" are one, and is prepared to behave as if it were a fact.[3]

Not unnaturally, the child comes to link (as so many metaphors do) love with food: "Honey, you're sweet," or, as Shakespeare calls it, "eating love." "There is no love," says Shaw's Jack Tanner, "sincerer than the love of food."

There is another state in which the adult feels fusion, Freud admits (though evidently "one that can be stigmatized as pathological"), the "oceanic feeling" of the mystic. We would expect, then, to find poems and stories about love or about religious mysticism based on fantasies of oral merger. But such fantasies can appear in almost any context:

> O for a beaker full of the warm South,
>   Full of the true, the blushful Hippocrene,
>   With beaded bubbles winking at the brim,
>   And purple-stained mouth;
>   That I might drink, and leave the world unseen,
>   And with thee fade away into the forest dim.

Not only the final line but the very ambiguity of the word "mouth" (the beaker's or Keats's?) carries out a typical fantasy and mood of fusion with an environment, devoured and devouring.

Because the oral phase occupies the earliest period when self and object are still not clearly differentiated, this first phase is important for establishing our ability to trust external realities, especially other people. It is important, too, for establishing what we might call our abilities to do nothing, to be passive, to wait. These traits can become too overdone in the adult personality: typically, the malingerer, the addict, the alcoholic, have been disturbed in this first phase of orality, and stories about them tend to show its traces. Erikson describes the basic issues of the oral stage as getting and giving in return; these personalities are disturbed in this modality. In West's *Miss Lonelyhearts*, for example, the hero perceives the demands of others upon him as though they were devouring him; for him, as for Christ his mentor, to give unto others is to be devoured oneself. "Body of Miss L, nourish me."

In the first half of the oral stage, the child is passive and dependent. At about the age of six months, he becomes able to put things in his own mouth or spit them out—the child also learns to bite. The first half of the oral phase is therefore known as the passive part; the second half as the sadistic part, because one of the characteristic oral wishes is the desire to incorporate into oneself both the wished-for and the feared contents of the mother's body, an aggressive return to the original at-oneness. The child's putting things in his mouth really means making them a part of himself (incorporation, a precursor of introjection and identification). By making them a part of himself, he ensures that they will always be with him, that they will be unable to do him harm, that they will never be there—outside. The wish to incorporate is a fusion of loving and destructive impulses, wishes to destroy and wishes to unite with,[4] as in the Keats passage.

The kinds of images in a literary work that would make you expect you are dealing with an oral situation are, naturally enough, almost anything to do with the mouth or with "taking in": biting, sucking, smoking, inhaling, talking, and the like; or their correlatives, food, liquor, tobacco, and especially words, particularly curses, threats, and vows, words which "bite," constituting a kind of action in themselves. A common defense against oral fusion and merger is putting something out of the mouth instead of taking something in; the something is usually speech, as in a great deal of Shakespeare's or Lawrence's writing, though it may be almost anything—in the Keats poem, it is the nightingale's "pouring forth thy soul abroad" that signifies the bird is "not born for death."

Still another development of the oral phase has to do with seeing—"feasting one's eyes." We "take in" through our eyes, and unconsciously, to look at is to eat, as when we "devour" books. Often this looking can became aggressive, as in various fantasies of the evil eye. Conversely, seeing secret things can bring down dread punishments, death, or castration,[5] as in so many horror or gangster movies: "He's seen too much. Get rid of him." Characteristic of oral fantasies is either-or thinking; thus, absolute words often go with oral fantasies: every, all, never, no, and the like, as in Marlowe. Such words create issues of fusion and merger as they both create and blur distinctions.

In the early oral phase, the child associates his mouth chiefly with a sense of dependency, of receiving things through the mouth. One of his principal fears is a fear of betrayal, that a source of comfort or power (his mother) will be taken away by a rival (a parent or sibling). Similarly, the child, when he is older, may imagine that the conception of children somehow takes place through eating (as in certain Melanesian myths), or that birth takes place through the child's emerging from the mouth (as in some creation myths).

In the second (sadistic) oral stage, the child thinks of mouths as a threat. He may imagine himself devouring or being devoured, being sucked dry, or getting rid of things by eating them (a great deal of science fiction seems to embody these fantasies). The child may imagine that he empties the mother's body by devouring out of it various threatening objects (maybe his forthcoming sibling rivals). The child may think of himself as incorporating threatening objects into himself by eating them. In adult life, this defensive eating could become the attempt to create a cushioning, defensive wall of fat between oneself and the rest of the world (as perhaps Falstaff does).

Of all the different levels of fantasy in literature, the oral is the most common (at least in my range of reading). Apparently, just as in life the sense of trust and of self that we obtain in this first phase underlies all our subsequent development, so literature seems to build on orality. No matter what other issues from later stages appear in a literary work, one almost always finds at the core some fantasy of oral fusion and merger. Dr. Edmund Bergler has suggested that all writers are involved in this deepest of human wishes; that writers emit words as a way of defending against the fearful desire to obliterate oneself in a total at-oneness with some primal mother.[6] It may be so—at least, fantasies of and defenses against primitive wishes for fusion appears in almost all literature.

At the age of about a year, the child enters on the second phase (which, of course, cumulates upon the first): the anal phase.[7] The child feels pleasure in its acts of excreting, but there are two conflicting sources of pleasure, elimination and retention. Further, these pleasures conflict with the child's growing wish to control and master its own impulses. Still further, at this time, the first moral (if I may call them that) demands are made upon the child. He begins to be told not to do things; he begins to be trained to obey rules and laws. At the same time, he becomes aware of what words mean and begins to make them himself, and all these things get mixed up. His first moral imperative comes in the field of toilet training: some psychoanalyst with a happy gift for phrase has called it "sphincter morality."

The question of holding onto or giving up this part of his body becomes of paramount importance, both to himself and to his parents. A good deal of his language and theirs is devoted to commands and decisions on this matter, and therefore, it is, oddly enough, as much in this anal stage as in the oral that attitudes toward language are formed. The earlier polarity, activity-passivity, now takes on the form defiance-submission, and it is in this phase that lifelong habits about rage, giving up, or giving in are formed. The child is likely to feel that he is being forced to give up a treasured part of himself, perhaps even a living being like himself. He may confuse the process of defecation with that of giving birth, both taking place in about the same covered and tabooed part of the anatomy. The child's confusion as to whether his excrement is a living thing or not may grow into a confusion between people and objects and a tendency to treat people like objects or objects like people. "My daughter! Oh, my ducats!"

In this same phase, the child learns for the first time disgust, and he learns to distinguish objects which are precious and valuable from those to which we are indifferent. He forms attitudes toward messiness or neatness and towards retaining and possessing things. One of the most important results of this phase for the adult is the gradual metamorphosis of the child's wish to keep within himself his precious productions. He learns to transfer his desire to keep and collect things onto objects less disgusting to others, although to his housecleaning mother, the dirt, insects, frogs, or other small animals or vermin that he is likely to shift his interests to, do not seem much of an improvement. Later on, by reversal, he will begin to collect such things as shells or stones, which others regard as attractive. Finally, his interest in holding onto things can develop into adult pastimes like collecting such beautiful and precious objects as postage stamps, coins, or (if he is prosperous) money, gold or jewels. "The art of our necessities is strange," Shakespeare says, "that can make vile things precious." A writer, often, will collect jargons—take them into himself, then excrete them in his works—in the manner of Ben Jonson or Thomas Wolfe.

"Anal writing" is very striking, easy to recognize once one has met the type. Images of dirt are the essential clue. The oral fantasies of being engulfed or devoured become, in anal writing, fears of being enveloped by what is foul, dirty, or sordid. Realists (such as Jonson) tend to be anal writers. Often, though, the anal writer will escape the grimy reality that threatens to engulf him into idealism, frequently seen as a foggy, misty, or impossibly pure other, as, for example, the sky or air or star Gerard Manley Hopkins so often refers to or, in Gogol's *Dead Souls*, Chichikov's wishes for the governor's daughter, pure and bland "as a small newly laid egg."

As for imagery, one finds in anal writings a preoccupation with dirt, with smells, particularly those which evoke disgust, and then with their transformations: fog, mist, sweet smells, pure air, light, even, ultimately, *logos*, the word of God. By this mechanism of "displacement upwards," the ear may come to stand for the anus —sounds are common anal images. The child-in-us may unconsciously fantasy that insemination takes place by fluids or air or words entering the ear (as in various paintings of the Annunciation analyzed by Ernest Jones). Anal fantasies tend to stress laws and rules, particularly meticulous, precise, petty behavior, which deals especially with collecting or excessive cleanliness or rituals. Control, either by oneself or by another, is an important theme.

Another theme of anality is doing things in time: thus, impatience, procrastination, or things running by fits and starts would suggest that we are dealing with an anal fantasy, as would a concern with precise timing. Often, an intricately "musical" development of themes and images, as in Mann's *Death in Venice* or Mailer's *An American Dream*, will accompany, as in those two novels, anal themes like dirt, corruption, the devil, and intercourse *a tergo*.

An important anal theme in literature is dehumanization: What is dead and what is living? More exactly, what is autonomous and what is controlled by another as a thing would be? The child or the child-in-us (the adult unconscious) tends to regard his excrement as a precious object, perhaps even a living part of himself. Thus the child may fantasy that the column of feces within him is either a phallus or a baby, and many anal fantasies are concerned with puzzles about whether things are living or not, animate or inanimate. A common anal survival involves thinking of people as things (like Dickens's mechanical types) or as possessions or in terms of the amount of money that can be gotten out of them, as in Jonson's plays. In general, a preoccupation with getting things out of other people or thinking of oneself as being forced to deliver things—these are common anal fantasies.

Closely linked to the anal phase is the so-called urethral phase.[8] Somewhat later in time, this period is nevertheless also marked by an interest in retaining or releasing, but the objects retained or released are not solids but fluids. The child will have fantasies about wetting, drowning, or their opposites, such as fire. The anal aspect of the child's development seems to relate to the ability to follow rules and laws; the urethral aspect seems to determine his ability to wait or, put in adult terms, to think conceptually in terms of consequences rather than act on whim or impulse—the psychopath or the beatnik are typical urethral types. The restless early novels of Jack Kerouac instance quite fully the urethral in literature, for example, the final image of *On the Road*: urinating off the back of a speeding truck. The urethral stage is not markedly separate from the anal, but there are some images which have specifically urethral connotations, particularly those of fire and streams, flowing and wetting of all kinds. Abstractions seem to be associated with urethral processes, as does constant movement or a sense of restlessness, urgency, or discomfort, as, for example, "burning ambition."

After the urethral stage, the child enters upon the most complex phase of infantile development, the phallic.* The child discovers that his genitals give especial pleasure and, moreover, that adults have very special attitudes towards those particular parts. The phallus with its power to stand erect becomes identified with the boy's own recently acquired power to stand up and his other skills such as talking.

> That man that hath a tongue, I say, is no man
> If with his tongue he cannot win a woman,

so Valentine in *Two Gentlemen of Verona*. Seeing, learning, or otherwise prying into things lend significance to the phallus. Conversely, to be without a phallus is to be feminized, helpless, liable to be overwhelmed. Thus, the fear of castration or other body damage represents a later form of earlier fears—of being overwhelmed and engulfed (oral) or of being robbed of part of your body (anal).[9] Now, the fear is of loss of autonomy and capability, a basis for our fantastically complicated adult attitudes toward the genitals. We cover them, surround them with secrecy and elaborate restrictions, yet often genital rituals such as circumcision or cutting off hair play a part in the most sacrificial gestures of human life.

The child's discovery of the pleasure associated with his genitals and the fact that they are somewhat taboo and secret give rise to terrible pressures in his relations with the big people around him on whom he is absolutely dependent. These parts of his body become a source of trouble and anxiety, yet at the same time they are all he has with which to compete with his father; in fact, they seem to be his only key to becoming an adult. Life itself seems bound up in these parts of him—one could call the feeling a body-

* Though many psychoanalytic writers do not draw a distinction between a phallic and an oedipal phase, for our purposes, it is useful.

phallus equation. The most terrible tortures adults dream up, amputations, mutilations, blindings, and the like, symbolize this earliest feared punishment. Similarly, because the child's interest in his genitals is involved with his sexual knowledge and discoveries, his mind itself can sometimes serve as a symbol for these parts of his body. Thus, it is a widely held but medically very naïve belief that sexual over-indulgence will be followed by insanity (another castration symbol, namely, removing "mental potency").

At this stage of development, the phallus becomes the visible and narcissistic embodiment of one's own autonomy, a precious possession, equivalent almost to the self, loss of which would be equal to or worse than, death itself, just as adults (soldiers, for example) tend to fear amputation or blinding more than death. Eyes, hands, legs, head, or mind can all symbolize the phallus in castration fantasies. In Apuleius' *The Golden Ass*, for example, hair symbolizes the phallic self and is torn out or cut off accordingly. Phallic fantasies often symbolize the phallus by the whole body; then phallic fantasies can become stories of poking or prying into things, particularly in a fearful or helpless way, as in *The Golden Ass* or *Through the Looking-Glass*; thus, almost any strongly aggressive or assertive plot is likely to be phallic. Medieval tales of quest, ordeal, or trial (as *Sir Gawain and the Green Knight* or the Wife of Bath's Tale) typically build on fantasies of the body as a phallus entering fearful places. So do their modern equivalents, Hemingway's stories endlessly measuring manhood. Stories that sharply distinguish the sexes (as most of Chaucer's or Boccaccio's do) are usually dealing with phallic issues, as, conversely, are stories that bring in homosexuality. A Restoration comedy, for example, often builds on the contrasts among an effeminate, foppish man, a ridiculous anal character who withholds money and sex, and a dashing cavalier who readily risks himself in all kinds of phallic ways. This hovering between phallic and anal levels occurs very often in literature, but, from my own experience, I would say that the single most common fantasy-structure in literature is phallic assertiveness balanced against oral engulfment:

Marlowe, Conrad, Lawrence, Shakespeare provide a few of many possible examples—as are the *Playboy* joke and the Wife of Bath's Tale.

The child's fear of castration in the phallic phase is complicated by his habit of magical thinking, which affects all the developmental phases. That is, for the child, as for the adult unconscious and all such seething brains and shaping fantasies, the thought becomes the deed, the word the thing, as though a mere word could murder or a name harm. The child therefore fears that he can be punished just as much for his thoughts as for what he does.

A large group of fantasies for literature stems from this childish or primitive habit of mind known as animism, or the omnipotence of thought. Images in such fantasies can be supernatural powers of all kinds (either benevolent or threatening, both usually associated with parent-figures): magic, the occult, transformation, verbal formulas, and rituals (though these may also be related to anal fantasies). Another group of images has to do with thinking things into being, as in fears of the dark, telepathy or telekinesis, in general, inanimate objects becoming animate. Often the root of such a fantasy is the childish substitution of a mental power to create for an adult genital power to procreate. In general, animistic fantasies seem to deal with the child's sense of helplessness in the face of some other nameless power (adult or supernatural), and a vast number of ghost stories and tales of supernatural horrors build on these fantasies. (Freud analyzed their method in "The 'Uncanny.'")

Closely linked to omnipotence-of-thought fantasies are those of repetition. In some of his later essays, Freud pointed to the tendency human beings have to get themselves into the same situations over and over; he termed this phenomenon the "repetition compulsion" and regarded it as characteristic of all basic drives. Obvious images for such a compulsion are cycles and circles of all kinds. Hitchcock's film *Vertigo*, for example, brilliantly develops this cluster of fantasies and symbols. Often, the repetition compulsion manifests itself in a sense of "I've been here before" (partic-

ularly useful in ghost stories); such a sense symbolizes a wish to return to one's warm, hungerless paradise before birth, or in the
somewhat misleading layman's phrase, "return to the womb." We
can see this fantasy in the equation of womb and tomb, the love-
deaths of *Romeo and Juliet*, for example, or *Antony and Cleopatra*. We seem to associate this cyclical sense of reality with
women in general, the mother in particular, or with the three relations a man has to woman: mother, mate, and "mother earth,"
that Ingmar Bergman so often uses. Also, this cyclical sense of doing things in time and a corresponding interest in birth and death
(the animate becoming inanimate) finds a natural form of expression in anal fantasies as well as in animistic.

A particularly rich and complex set of fantasies stems from the
child's thoughts about what adults do when they are alone, particularly what they do with the organ which has become so important
to him, and by his own curiosity about where he came from. He
has what the psychoanalysts call "primal scene fantasies," which
form the basis for a later interest in watching drama and other
performances.[10]

The child imagines that he watches or hears his parents in the
act of love. He brings to his fantasies the confused impressions he
may have from such a sight in actuality, from having watched animals, or simply from having seen his parents in their nightclothes
come in to see him after he has gone to bed or when he gets up in
the morning. He may think of sex in terms of the strange noises he
would hear at night in even the most discreet of households.

The child apparently imagines the sexual act as a struggle followed by a death-like sleep.[11] He may regard his father's phallus as
a weapon with which he wounds the mother. "He cares not what
mischief he does, if his weapon be out," Mrs. Quickly says of Falstaff, "He will spare neither man, woman nor child." The child may
regard his mother's body as a trap, a Hell or darkness or sulphurous
pit which engulfs that precious organ. Excited and frightened, the
child may imagine the scene with himself watching it, and he may
also imagine the scene with himself playing his father's role. Yet,

knowing that this downright way of creation is a matter his parents surround with the greatest secrecy and taboo, feeling that his thoughts are a kind of deed, the child fears that his father will retaliate with the most terrible mutilating punishments imaginable.

One finds several clusters of images in such fantasies: first, darkness, a sense of vagueness and the unknown, mysterious noises in night and darkness; second, vague movements, shapes shifting and changing, nakedness, things appearing and disappearing; third, images of fighting and struggling, blood, the phallus as weapon—*Macbeth* is virtually a thesaurus of primal scene imagery. Conversely, the fantasy may be defended against in images of quietness, motionlessness, or death, as with so many of Donne's pairs of lovers, enraptured, entombed, separating, or getting out of bed. Explicit images for such primal scene fantasies are those of watching, peeping, and spying, as in Hitchcock's *Rear Window*, which is a theme and variations on a primal scene fantasy. Other common symbols are watching performances such as a stage play or a movie or televison. The question, What's happening? may lead back to another set of fantasies and wonderings, Where did I come from?

A very special and important set of unconscious fantasies are those arising from the oedipus complex. According to psychoanalytic observation, even as adults we tend to respond to others as we responded in our first relations with other people, in other words, as we responded to our family. Every woman in our lives is partly a mother, every man partly a father. Almost any interpersonal relationship has oedipal elements, and, by the same token, any work of art dealing in depth with relations of love and hate between people is likely to contain some oedipal fantasies.

Thus, when we move from pregenital—oral, anal, phallic—fantasies to the oedipal level, we make an important transition both in life and letters: from solitary or one-to-one relations with others to the complicated triangles and quadrilaterals of adult relationships. "Preoedipally," notes Dr. Maxwell Gitelson, "the people around a child are either good or bad, gratifying or nongratifying, positive or negative. Only in the oedipal situation do they become clearly differentiated into male and female with positives and negatives attached to both." [12] It is safe to say, as a general rule, that a work of literature builds on an oedipal fantasy whenever it deals with relationships involving more than two persons or whenever it makes us feel fairly realistic versions of adult love or hate, not, for example, the simple primitivity of

> Come live with me and be my love,
> And we will all the pleasures prove . . .

Lyrics almost always tend to be highly stylized and the poet is usually a solitary singer. Lyrics, thus, are almost inevitably pre-oedipal, while oedipal fantasies are confined to drama, cinema, and narrative (though these may be pre-oedipal, too). *Märchen* and fairy stories are often oedipal, but oedipal fantasies mostly express themselves in fairly realistic plots and characters, accompanied by pre-oedipal versions of the core fantasy in images and symbols and episodes (as in the Wife of Bath's Tale). The typical "oedipal story" contains in it earlier forms of the later developmental issues; it has a built-in range of psychic levels. Thus, most of the greatest literature—*Oedipus Rex, Hamlet, The Brothers Karamazov,* and the like—builds from an oedipal fantasy. Nevertheless, it is a curious but, I think, accurate estimate that far more good literature builds on pre-oedipal materials than on oedipal, despite the built-in range of oedipal fantasies. Paradoxically, the great bulk of cheap fiction and drama is oedipal—nominally, therefore, more mature.

The oedipus complex itself is an outgrowth of earlier phases. Even in early infancy, the child has longed for the exclusive possession of his mother; he has wished there were no competing demands on her time, that the father and any siblings were out of the way, that he had to keep no corner in the thing he loved for others' uses. By the phallic phase, however, these oedipal wishes are complicated by his own greater powers of thought and deed and by his confused awareness of what sex is like between adults. In the lurid imagery of childhood imaginings, he wishes to kill or castrate his father and then possess his mother absolutely, that is, in the aggressive, violent struggle he understands as sex.

His fears of mutilation are suddenly augmented by the horrified realization that half the world's population have, as it were, already been castrated, that "as well a woman with a eunuch played / As with a woman." He reinterprets the earlier polarity, active-passive, in terms of his phallic concerns: to be active is to be masculine; to be passive is to be feminine, that is, castrated.[13] And he fears this will really happen, because, after all, does he not wish to do the same to his father?

Under the pressure of these intense wishes and fears, the little boy accepts a compromise solution. He gives up, to a large extent, his desire to replace his father in the father's relationship with the mother (the positive oedipus complex), and he surrenders himself to the father (the negative oedipus complex). He may even wish to become a love object to the father in much the same role as his mother. Ultimately, he decides (in normal development) that the solution to his problem is to identify, to become one with the father or as much like him as possible. He longs to know the secrets his father knows and to do the grown-up things his father does.

The little girl's development is somewhat different because she feels, as it were, that the damage has already been done. In her case, the threat of castration is no longer meaningful. She, however, may give up the mother for a different reason, namely, that the mother is contemptible in that she too has lost the precious organ. The little girl may become as we say, a tomboy, trying to be as like her father as possible. Even so, the pressure to identify with the father is less. The little boy incorporates into himself his fears of his father, and in this surrender develops his superego or conscience, the basis for his later social behavior, in which his father's commandment lives in his brain unmixed with baser matter. Freud was fond of saying that in women the conscience was less developed.

In literature, then, the basic oedipus fantasy is the boy's longing to become his father and make a child in his mother; or the girl's to take her mother's place and have a child by her father. Similar is the wish to be one's own father which tends to express itself in rescue fantasies; the child by rescuing his father proves his innocence of any wish to kill him and at the same time by paying a life back, as it were, he owns his own life free and clear of any father, as in any number of Horatio Alger stories. A related group of fantasies are those of poor or obscure birth: "My father is so insignificant he is non-existent."

Other fantasies concern the mother. The child thinks of her in the two Victorian extremes: she is either absolutely untouchable, unattainable, pure, taboo, a virgin-mother, or she is a slut, common, fickle, available to anyone (notably the father). So we see her in Dickens, Thackeray, and many other English novelists. Freud identified another group of fantasies as the "family romance": "These are not my parents, only my foster parents; my real parents are rich and powerful and famous people who wish to remain anonymous but are guiding my destiny from afar" (as in the Greek romances). The anonymity symbolizes the taboo that surrounds the parents in the child's oedipal thinking.

Similarly, the original incest fantasy can translate itself into almost any other incestuous relation: brother-sister, uncle-niece, or into racial taboos. The child may translate the taboo into a sense of secrecy, feeling that a parent or sibling has secretly betrayed or tricked him in his deadly rivalry. In general, the forbidden love objects can be symbolized by any dark, unknown, obscure, banished, or debased persons. Thoughts about visitors may project a wish that the father were not here to stay or a fear that the mother may go away. Naturally, such fantasies give rise to a good deal of guilt. This guilt may be expressed abstractly, as in such concepts as original sin or it may be imaged as, say, a money debt (which in turn can regress to anal fantasies or rescue fantasies of paying one's parents back, as Kafka's *Metamorphosis*). But behind the guilt, the

basic punishment the child fears is castration. The mutilation of
Rochester in *Jane Eyre* marks the achievement of oedipal wishes
—though of Jane's as much as his.

Once an author breaks through from pre-oedipal to oedipal
materials, his imagination seems to proliferate. Often, as in *The
Brothers Karamazov*, a variety of images of the basic triangle will
interact. Oedipal fantasies are especially various and hard to generalize about, but they are easily identified by looking at the fictional
women as mothers and the fictional men as fathers and sons.

Beyond these oedipal fantasies, though, it becomes quite difficult
to generalize about our responses to literature, they become so
varied and individual. At the risk of being personal, let me give an
instance. One day I found myself quite entranced by the following
line from a Shakespearean sonnet in which time does various
things:

And delves the parallels in beauty's brow.

If we look at the line in terms of the deep fantasies we have listed,
it is not too difficult to see that it has to do with the anatomy of
older women. But that day I realized that the line was affecting me
especially because I had been thinking about two L-shaped rooms
important to me—and associated in my mind with older women.
How could one anticipate such a response? One can easily see that
the line plays with *-el* sounds, but it is impossible to say how they
might or might not affect any particular person at any particular
time. Paradoxically, then, a psychoanalytic reading can reveal
"deep" fantasies that many people are likely to experience in a literary work, but it cannot generalize about certain very intense
sources of pleasure at a relatively conscious level. They come from
one's own highly individual experience.

It is possible to get a rough idea of the relative roles of these two
kinds of appeal by considering the most basic division that marks
off individual from individual: gender. By and large, most of what
the child reads up to and during the oedipal phase appeals to both

boys and girls: the Pooh books, *Wind in the Willows*, fairytales, adventure stories, and so on. During latency, much reading becomes sex-differentiated: *Heidi*, *The Little Mermaid*, or other heroines for girls; *Treasure Island*, *Tom Sawyer*, and the boy-heroes for boys.[14] In cheap literature for adults, these differences persist —the magazines of romance for women or adventure for men. More sophisticated readers, though, do not differ by sex: men enjoy Jane Austen, women, Hemingway. Probably, then, the "deep" appeal of serious literature stems in large part from the fantasies of the developmental phases prior to latency, before fantasies and reading choice become markedly different for boys and girls.

In general, I think it is safe to say that the closer a piece of adult literature is to raw fantasy, the later in development that fantasy will be and the more individual our response to it. Think, for example, of the James Bond or Mike Hammer novels built on violent oedipal and post-oedipal fantasies. Conversely, the more the literary work manages and disguises a fantasy, the deeper the level of the fantasy will be and the less different will be our individual responses. The typical lyric, for instance, strongly manages a pre-oedipal fantasy, and sophisticated readers, I think, tend to respond more alike than unlike to a given lyric. Pornography, least modified of literary fantasies, is written for men almost entirely, hardly at all for women, and even so there are very different kinds of pornography to appeal to each different taste.

To an adult, pornography seems at least a possible mode of realistic experience, while the deeper, childish fantasies we have considered seem far more absurd and ridiculous, if not downright disgusting. Naturally. We become adults by adopting just that attitude. Yet, if in a disinterested, scientific frame of mind we look for these fantasies in the world of human behavior around us, the evidence for them becomes quite overwhelming. In looking for the unconscious content in human behavior, such a dictionary of recurring fantasies as this (and it is by no means exhaustive) can only serve as a clue or hint. Nevertheless, we can find these and other fantasies and defenses recurring constantly in dreams, slips of the tongue, clichés, jokes, advertising, myths, folklore, proverbs, and, of course, in works of art of all kinds (even philosophies and scientific disciplines). Phrases like "filthy lucre," "making a pile," or Shakespeare's "vile gold," tying money to dirt, are typical anal survivals. Men often sow wild oats before they screw their courage to the sticking point and put all their eggs in one basket. You would hardly get married, though, to cut off your nose to spite your face —and so on.

The psychoanalytic theory of literature holds that the writer expresses and disguises childhood fantasies. The reader unconsciously elaborates the fantasy content of the literary work with his own versions of these fantasies (my L-shaped rooms, for example). And it is the management of these fantasies, both his own and the work's, that permits their partial gratification and gives literary pleasure. Psychoanalytic studies by the hundreds demonstrate the presence of these fantasies in literature.

Equally clearly, though, except for pornography, literature is not just these fantasies—something happens to them. To see what that something is, it is useful to know what happens to these fantasies in life. To put the matter very briefly, they get defended against. In life, a defense mechanism is an unconscious strategy of the ego, put into effect automatically at a signal of danger from reality, superego, or id. We learn defenses as part of growing up.

In the first months of life, we are not aware of ourselves as such; we do not conceive of a self separate from the world around us, and our drives operate in a mysterious manner, both chaotic and inchoate. Sometime around the eighth month of life, we become aware both of a self and of objects separate from the self, though for the time being our drives take the self as an object rather than something external. Gradually, the world external to the infant becomes clearer: his own body, the parts of his body, his mother, his father, their bodies; and gradually, we can see the infant begin to take the several parts of this world as the objects of his drives. But the child cannot unite his self with the object he loves, his mother.

say. Reality denies him the direct and full satisfaction of his drive. She disappoints him in this, he resents her, his love turns to hate and he wishes to destroy her. But that, too, reality denies him. Indeed, it would be a fearful thing were he to destroy the very source of his well-being or even to wish such a thing.

There are, in short, dangers from without and dangers from within, and out of them come the fears that condition the child to modify his original, raw drives. From the differentiation of self and object come defenses and adaptations. Double-edged, they are what make maturity and character and also sickness and unhappiness. Art and life, symptom and syllogism, joke and jeremiad, loves and hates, virtually all that we know as living is a compromise between the mighty opposites of drive and defense.

The most basic of defenses is repression which we can define as keeping an idea or feeling from consciousness, as, for example, you (and I) were thinking a few sentences ago, No, I never wished to destroy my mother (though which of us did not at some time hit a parent as hard as our tiny fists could). Repression defends against the danger from within; for the danger from without, we use the defense termed denial, not seeing something in reality we don't want to see. Dickens's Mr. Podsnap has it down pat: "I don't want to know about it; I don't choose to discuss it; I don't admit it!" Denial acts against perceptions of the outer world, repression against perceptions of the inner.

Repression, in effect, buries alive an impulse or fear or feeling or fantasy, buries "alive," because the drive does not lose its force, and we constantly expend energy to hold down tabooed material. We can see the energy in those jokes based (in Freud's phrase) on "inhibitions we have already established." Further, the repressed can return. Like the Lady of "The House of Usher," they rise up from the tomb to trouble the living, either in their own form, or, more typically, in some other.

The original drives to love and to hate, to unite with another or to destroy another, turn up in all the variety of life itself. They are, to use the technical term, displaced. That is, the value attributed to one thing (the cathexis of aim or object) is taken from it and put on another thing. For our limited purpose, the analysis of literature, we can somewhat oversimplify the various defenses as different kinds of displacement corresponding to different qualities in the thing displaced onto (with repression being the zero case of displacing onto nothing else). Freud showed how pervasive displacements are in jokes as in dreams. By seeing defenses as displacements, we can extend his linking of dreams and jokes into a model for literature in general.

For example, if the important attribute of the aim or object displaced onto is that it is the opposite of the thing displaced from, we would speak of reversal (if the object takes the opposite form) or reaction-formation (if the aim takes the opposite form). Consider, for example, how a censor's mind might be working. On the surface, our hypothetical censor seems a man whose greatest wish and preoccupation is to prevent others from seeing pornography; we might guess, though, that this is a reversal of a repressed wish to peer at pornography himself (and we might also note the "return of the repressed" in that his job as censor entitles him to do just that). The Player Queen in *Hamlet* avows at great length her love for her husband; the real Queen drily says, "The lady doth protest too much, methinks," the classic phrasing of the mechanism of reaction-formation. The Chorus comes to Oedipus as "the man surest in mortal ways and wisest in the ways of God," and yet he does not even know how or where he was born. In general, irony, either as figure of speech or plot, saying or doing one thing but meaning the opposite, corresponds to a defense of reversal.

The defense of undoing is akin to reversal or reaction-formation; some types of neurotic try to wipe out an event or impulse by some ritual action. For example, the childish ritual, "Don't step on the crack or you'll break your grandmother's back," wipes out the hostile impulse by a little magical trick of warding-off. Often, pointing a moral at the end of a story, as in Aesop or Ovid, is a way of wrapping it up, tying it down, and cancelling it out.

Where the essential thing about the displacement is that it runs from the self to the outside world, one would speak of projection. In projection, says Freud, "An internal perception is supressed, and, instead, its content, after undergoing a certain degree of distortion, enters consciousness in the form of an external perception." In *Oedipus Rex*, for example, the hero has no desire to kill his father and possess his mother—the gods and oracles make him do it. It is Aphrodite, not Phaedra, who makes Phaedra love Hippolytus. Our hypothetical censor is saying, "I don't want to look at dirty pictures—they do." John Donne, no voyeur he, often speaks of others watching him and his love.

The opposite of projection is introjection, where an impulse initially perceived as outside the self ("He hates me") is felt as unbearable there and brought inside where it can be better (?) handled—"I hate me." Introjection is one of the means by which we internalize, put into ourselves, the superego whose "still, small voice" reminds us of the values of our parents and society. Hamlet's inscribing his father's command "Within the book and volume of my brain" is a classic instance of introjection. Thus, introjection lies very close to the defense known as identification with the aggressor: "If you can't lick 'em, join 'em." Uriah Heep's humility masks this kind of identification which so clearly shows in his subsequent tyranny. A closely related defense is turning against the self: an impulse unacceptable if directed toward some object in the outer world is turned inward against the self, as a child in a rage at someone else will suddenly start striking himself, tearing his own hair, or throwing a tantrum. "Young Goodman Brown" punishes himself for others' sins, because he cannot tolerate the idea of their guilt. The Frankenstein story is one of impulses projected outward, then returned upon the self; so also "Dr. Jekyll and Mr. Hyde." Projection, introjection, identification with the aggressor, turning against the self—all can be viewed as displacements of aim or object from outer to inner world or vice versa.

Where the important feature of the displacement is the shifting of aim or object from a dangerous present to an earlier, safer time, one can call it regression—for example, when we speak of the "good old days" (why are they always "good"?). In a novel or movie, a flashback from a particular tense, climactic movement to the background or cause would be a kind of regression. The knight's giving up phallic drives to be mothered in the Wife of Bath's Tale is regression, as is Silas Marner's initial movement from mature heterosexual love to anal miserliness.

If the essential factor in the displacement is the breaking up of one thing into several, the term is "splitting" or "decomposing." For example, in *Through the Looking-Glass*, two different attitudes toward the mother are split into the Red Queen and the White Queen. For literary purposes, splitting is an extremely important way of expanding an unconscious fantasy, because (I suppose) nothing will quite so quickly elaborate a simple residue of childhood into a complex, multi-faceted work of art as the doubling or splitting of characters. Consider, for example, the multitude of father figures in *Hamlet* or *Henry IV, Part I*. Conrad's *The Secret Sharer* (and many other of his novels), Dostoevsky's *The Idiot* and *The Brothers Karamazov*, Shaw's *The Devil's Disciple*, Euripides' *The Bacchae*—these are only a few of the myriad works which split off different psychological positions into different characters, their common ancestry symbolized by kinship or juxtaposition.

The only form of defense which is more important to literature than splitting is symbolization, which, for the purposes of this somewhat oversimple classification, we can consider a displacement from one thing to another based on a physical or psychic similarity between the two. In this day and age, few of us have not heard of phallic and feminine symbols—they have even penetrated the nursery rhymes:

> Jack be quick, Jack be nimble,
> Jack jump over the phallic symbol.

We should note, however, that there are many other kinds of symbols besides phallic and feminine ones. An archaeological past, Freud shows in his analysis of *Gradiva*, can symbolize childhood. In *Through the Looking-Glass*, snow symbolizes the mother (the snow suggesting emotional coldness, but the context is reversal: "It covers them up snug, you know, with a white quilt"). Psycho-analytic theory suggests that anything can acquire a symbolic value to the unconscious, just as in figures of speech, anything can serve in a simile, the trope that corresponds to the psychological process of symbolization.

Symbolization lends itself to sublimation, the changing of a for-bidden impulse or idea into something socially or morally accep-table, or even more important, acceptable and pleasurable to the individual's ego. Sublimation might be called "the normal defense" in that it can be the basis for positive and healthy human adapta-tions. So Silas Marner, by accepting a golden-haired child to love in lieu of gold, progresses toward fatherhood. Closely akin to sublima-tion is rationalization, finding intellectual reasons for something patently illogical (as persons doing absurd acts under post-hypnotic suggestions will do). Raskolnikov justifies what is essentially mother-murder by a theory of Napoleonism. Such rationalizations, though, can be the basis for valid intellectual endeavors, as when a fear of being devoured drives so many of Shaw's radicals to sophis-icated political and social positions. Often, the intellectual posi-tion will symbolize its unconscious roots: the absurdism of Camus's *The Stranger* intellectualizes the failure of mother-love.

Whenever we talk about symbols, however, it is most important to remember that symbols are flexible and dynamic: they vary with the context. They do not represent a code of one-to-one corre-spondences that can be looked up in some "Freudian" dreambook. The only one who can really tell what unconscious meaning a sym-bol has is the one who is using or responding to it.

Repression, denial, reversal, reaction-formation, undoing, projec-tion, introjection, identification with the aggressor, turning against the self, regression, splitting, symbolization, sublimation, rational-ization—these are the major defenses, themselves (usually) uncon-scious against unconscious impulses. In order to extend Freud's early model for jokes to literature in general, we have treated them as different forms of displacement.[15] To be exact, a defense is an unconscious process of the ego which the ego puts into action automatically at a signal of danger from the external world, the id, or the superego. Such a thing, of course, happens in a mind rather than a literary text.

What we have found, though, is that, just as literary works embody fantasies familiar from psychoanalytic experience, so they handle these fantasies by techniques that resemble familiar defensive or adaptive strategies. Irony looks like reversal or reaction-formation; omission looks like repression or denial; improbable causality in a story resembles projection; pointing a moral seems like rationalization, and so on. While a few of these defenses (or displacements) lend themselves to purely linguistic form (irony, for example), most seem to shape plot. What, then, about the language of literature? Does it correspond to any psychic techniques?

In Freud's essay on jokes,[16] he distinguishes jokes based on displacement, that is, conceptual jokes, jokes that could be translated out of one language into another, from jokes based on condensation, that is, jokes which depend on a particular linguistic form, such as a pun or cliché.* He is, in effect, implying that condensation lies at the root of all particular linguistic effects in literature. Freud's example is a joke of Heine's, about the poor lottery agent, Hirsch-Hyacinth, who boasts of his relations with the wealthy Baron Rothschild: "And, as true as God shall grant me all good things, . . . I sat beside Solomon Rothschild, and he treated me quite as his equal —quite famillionairely." The joke involves the compression into one word of the words *familiär*, and *Millionär*; the thought behind the joke is, Rothchild treated me quite *familiär*, that is, so far as a *Millionär* can, and this Freud calls condensation: two or more lines of thought combine in a single representative.

Such a process obviously has a great deal to do with the element of brevity in wit. Less obviously, the process of making a joke this way is very like the process of working up a dream; condensation combines several hidden thoughts (the "latent content"). Thus

---

* By and large, students of translation have not followed up this extremely interesting suggestion: that which can be translated looks like displacement, that which cannot, like condensation, and both those second terms can be explicated empirically from clinical evidence.

Freud notes, a merely laconic remark does not (usually) constitute a joke—it lacks this quality of combining two or more hidden thoughts. More importantly, he notes in passing that condensation involves an economy, a point to which he will return and which will turn out to be the central point of his study of jokes. Condensation, then, would seem also to provide the basis for such purely formal economies as rhyme, alliteration, stanza-form, and the like. Further, condensation corresponds to what literary critics would call ambiguity or, if the condensation is sharp and sudden, wit. In fact, Ernst Kris and Abraham Kaplan have shown how Empson's famous "seven types of ambiguity" constitute different ways in which unconscious symbols are overdetermined.[17] Overdetermination in turn (Freud's work had shown) corresponds to condensation in jokes.

Condensation thus plays a role much more than simply linguistic. In dreams, any particular element in the manifest dream generally expresses several elements in the underlying dream thoughts; and a single element in the dream thoughts will express itself in several elements of the manifest dream. The dream thoughts undergo a process of condensation into one expressive element. And so in literature. For example, even a simple phallic symbol can be many things depending on its unconscious "context," the fantasy of which it is a part; and, moreover, it can mean all these things at the same time. One group of fantasies might be the aggressive and sadistic ones, those treating the phallus as a weapon, as, for example, in the various Renaissance jokes about "dying" as a synonym for the sexual act or the Restoration metaphors about "the wound of love." Then there are those jokes about Falstaff's "weapon" in Henry IV, Part II. The fantasy may be that the phallus emits hot, poisonous, or corrosive fluids or, alternatively, objects that give rise to children, eggs, seeds, and the like. Still another group of phallic fantasies is associated with fears of amputation, mutilation, or blinding, which symbolize castration, in general, tearing something off. The entire body may be an adventuring and risked phallus. Such fantasies, however, may also be onanistic, as in Freud's analysis of the recurring fantasy that "a child is being beaten." In the context of onanism, the hands may be thought of as dirty or stained or (by displacement) as phallic symbols themselves. Anything that keeps the hands busy, playing-cards, for example, or a camera or tools can be defensive substitutes for a phallus.

Alternatively, phallic symbols can be associated with the so-called "phallic mother," a sort of single parent-figure prior to the child's distinguishing his parents by sex, or a mother thought of as punishing like a father, or, in still another context, the phallic symbol can represent the child's horrified realization of the difference between man and woman. In such "phallic mother" fantasies, the breast can be thought of as a phallic symbol—or vice versa. The mind itself, in contexts of "mental potency," can be a phallic symbol. In short, the apparently simple notion of a phallus can be expressed in an astonishingly wide range of symbols. And sometimes, Freud is supposed to have said, "A cigar is just a cigar." (Freud was particularly fond of cigars.)

Usually, symbols do double duty, and fantasies overlap and interlock in amazingly complicated ways. In *Macbeth* alone, the single image of birds sometimes stands for a baby; sometimes it is a vehicle for omnipotent thoughts (as in an omen or augury); sometimes it is a phallic symbol (with particular reference to the bird's power to rise in the air); sometimes birds stand for parents—nest builders—sometimes as scaly, beaky, threatening things or as a wish-fulfilling reversal: parents are small and delicate. In even a short lyric poem, you may find a half-dozen fantasies and symbols. Obviously, then, to go further in any quest for a psychology of audience response, we need to look at particular works of literature, and so we shall.

What this chapter, even though general, has gained for us is a dictionary of fantasies—some guidelines as to what we are likely to find in literary works if we look at them psychoanalytically. Obviously, any such list can give no more than guidelines, for the fantasies children and adults have and re-experience in literature are legion. We have also gained a very brief dictionary of psychological defenses although they are even more numerous, variable, and idiosyncratic than the fantasies. Nevertheless, even so brief a list offers clues to their literary equivalents, those purely literary ways of handling fantasies that, if they happened in a mind instead of on a page, would look like psychological defenses—or adaptations or displacements or condensations. We shall find labels like displacement or reaction-formation are rarely specific enough to describe literary techniques. Even these two inadequate dictionaries, though, will serve to cue our expectations. Images of dirt signal anal themes, patterns of irony are likely to be defensive reversals, and so on.

Incidentally, in making up these dictionaries, our first notion—literature as transformation—has been refined somewhat. Such a model stems, ultimately, from Freud's study of jokes. He found that dreams often have a joking quality—as John Updike once put it, "Dreams are a series of ingenious puns." Freud therefore studied jokes to show how the verbal techniques of the joke match the verbal and visual processes of the dream. Our method has gone further, to match the techniques of literature in general to mental processes of a very general kind.

When we do, we find a model for the literary text that involves the reader in different ways at different levels:

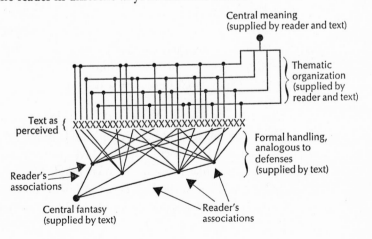

That is, a literary work presents itself as a text, written or spoken or seen. You or I use our conscious knowledge of the language, written, spoken, or visual (as, for example, our knowledge of what close-up or flashback mean) to perceive the text as things we know in life: people, events, objects, durations, and so on. Consciously, we supply intellectual or other meaning to the text by the process of successive abstraction described in Chapter 1.

Unconsciously, however, we bring quite other things to the text, for example, my association of L-shaped rooms to the *-el* sounds in a line from Shakespeare. In our associations to small details of the text, we are probably very personal and idiosyncratic. But the text also presents us with a central core of fantasy that is evidently much more universal, for we find the fantasies listed in our dictionary very generally in literature and in both men and women. Similarly, in dreams, our associations to a dream will have to do with our immediate life situation, but the "deep" wish of the dream will reach to a widely shared childhood experience. Also, as in dreams, that nucleus of fantasy may be visible in several developmental forms at once, oral, anal, phallic, and oedipal.

The text, however, does not present us with the fantasy raw but rather modified and shaped by manipulations that in literature are usually called "form" but which resemble defenses in people. Ultimately, it is the writer's act of imagining and writing that puts the fantasy and its defensive handling in the text. What fantasies he chooses and what defenses, how he manipulates them in the modes of his art, these are, of course, questions about the nature of the creative process—rather more answerable, I think, than they once seemed, but only indirectly related through the text to our concern, the reader's response.

He seems to have two different relations to the text. On the conscious level, he is actively engaged in perceiving it and thinking his perceptions into meaning. Unconsciously, the text presents him with fantasies and defenses like those in his own mind. Our next question, then, must be, What is the link between his unconscious mind and, so to speak, the unconscious mind of the literary work?

3   The "Willing Suspension of Disbelief"

Quite possibly the most puzzling part of our entire response to literature is what Coleridge called the "willing suspension of disbelief." [1] Somehow, even before the curtain rises, even before our eyes have run over the screen credits or the first line of a poem or story, we have made a special gesture of "as if." We adopt some odd mental stance or "set" in which we are willing to accept all kinds of unrealities and improbabilities—for example, that a witch can solve a young executive's problems or that he will believe she can. The joke tricked us as the witch-mother tricked the young executive—but how? How were we solid, rational, and alienated twentieth-century folk persuaded to accept the idea that a worldly young executive would believe a witch could take care of embezzlement? Somehow, what we would not believe in reality, we will believe, even in a work of sub-literature. A mere joke can make us ignore (or, in psychological terms, deny) the unreality of what we know is unreal.

"Think of yourself as a spectator in the theater, watching an engrossing drama," writes Professor Irving Singer.

> The hero dies, and you begin to weep. Now for whom are you crying? Surely not for the actor: you know that as soon as the curtain falls, he will scramble to his feet and prepare for a great ovation. Is it then the character in the play? But there is no

such person. You are fully aware that Hamlet (at least Shake-speare's Hamlet) never existed. How can his death, which is purely fictional, sadden you? Yet it does, more so perhaps than the death of real people you may have known. What happens, I think, is that you respond *as if* the actor were really Hamlet and *as if* Hamlet really existed. The "as if" signifies that although you *know* the actor is only acting and Hamlet only fictitious, your imaginative involvement causes you to express feelings appropriate to real people. At no point are you deluded. The "illusion" of the theater is not an illusion at all. It is an act of imagination.[2]

That is the key, is it not? "Imaginative involvement." But what precisely is the nature of this involvement in which we invest or bestow life upon the fictitious characters of stage, page, or screen?

It is evidently not clear, for many critics still write of our suspension of disbelief as though it were really a belief; they still speak of a theatrical "illusion" in which we fancy that we see real people walking and talking before us. But director Tyrone Guthrie is probably right when he says, "I do not believe that audiences past the mental age of eight are apt to accept this." A director, he says, should not try to create "illusion" but rather,

> to interest the members of an audience so intensely that they are rapt, taken "out" of themselves. You may say that if they are taken "out" of themselves, then they must be taken "into" something else, and, logically, that "something else" is the imaginary world of the play. Agreed. But is this absorption the same thing as illusion? I do not believe so. You can be absorbed listening to music, quite without illusion; you can be absorbed by a great painting without supposing that what it depicts is real; you can be absorbed by a novel without the illusion that you are yourself David Copperfield or Huck Finn; you can even be absorbed in a philosophical argument without any illusion that you are someone, or somewhere else. How, in the theater, is the absorption of the audience induced? What takes an audience "out" of itself and "into" the fiction? [3]

That, aptly stated by Mr. Guthrie, is precisely the problem this chapter attempts to deal with. Equally apt are the metaphors he uses to describe the state of an audience involved with a play: "taken 'out' of themselves," "taken 'into' something else," "absorbed," "rapt," with its older meaning of being seized up.

Bernard Berenson uses similar language to describe "the aesthetic moment" in the visual arts:

> In visual art the aesthetic moment is that flitting instant, so brief as to be almost timeless, when the spectator is at one with the work of art he is looking at, or with actuality of any kind that the spectator himself sees in terms of art, as form and colour. He ceases to be his ordinary self, and the picture or building, statue, landscape, or aesthetic actuality is no longer outside himself. The two become one entity; time and space are abolished and the spectator is possessed by one awareness.[4]

The phenomenologist Gaston Bachelard says of poetry, "It is as though the poet's being were our being. . . . Or, to put it more simply, . . . the poem possesses us entirely." [5] Again, the imagery is of being absorbed or rapt into the work of art.*

Nor is this experience of merger confined to professionals with the sensitivity of Guthrie, Berenson, or Bachelard. My daughter, aged eight, told me, "When I read a book, I sort of feel like I'm invisible and walking around unseen with the things or people in the book (a Hobbit is just a thing). When I read it, just word by word, then it's just like reading a book. But when I get into a stage of reading, sort of, then it feels like a dream." A movie fan told Siegfried Kracauer, "In the theater I am always I, but in the cinema I dissolve into all things and beings," [7] a curious echo of Kafka's comment on movies: "Sight does not master the pictures, it is the pictures which master one's sight. They flood the conscious-

---

* Something of the same sort seems to happen in the creative process: "Whenever I was able to break free from the urge to make a mechanical copy and a new entity had appeared on my paper," writes Marion Milner, "then something else also had happened. The process always seemed to be accompanied by a feeling that the ordinary sense of self had temporarily disappeared, there had been a kind of blanking out of ordinary consciousness; even the awareness of the blanking out had gone, so that it was only afterwards, when I returned to ordinary self-consciousness, that I remembered that there had been this phase of complete lack of self-consciousness." [6]

ness." [8] I have asked a number of subjects to describe their feelings when they are engrossed in an "entertainment," a detective story, a murder mystery, science fiction, television, or a simple old-fashioned fun movie. They speak of "escapism, a feeling of joyful unreality, lack of any worry" or "involvement—at its best a motion with the work." "I am gathered up, carried along, and unaware of being a reader, viewer, etc." "I lose track of time." "I am attentive and absorbed, unaware of surroundings except those in the book or show; for example, when I am watching good T.V., I don't see the knobs or floor or anything else."

They, of course, are describing entertainments rather than great works of art. But, to judge from the statistics for best-sellers, moviegoing, and television watching, this experience of total absorption is far more typical of entertainments than of masterpieces. And this reaction to entertainments is not confined to naïve subjects. A group of university professors of English report as their reaction: "Total anesthesia," "Absorption," "A sort of drugged or fascinated absorption in the events as they unfold." "The continuum goes from totally absorbed (cinema) to fairly distanced, self-conscious hunting for something (non-fiction). Fiction can go either way (rarely a blend though)." "Varies but usually I'm completely absorbed—even by crude stuff—in fact, apt to be more critical, aware and less absorbed by 'high art.'" Since, then, the "willing suspension of disbelief" seems to take place more with "entertainments" than with "high art," let us, for the time being, confine our attention to entertainments rather than significant literary works.

If we do, we can say that people get involved with entertainments in three closely related ways: they cease to pay attention to what is outside the work of art; they concentrate their attention wholly on it; then—and this is the special and important thing—they begin to lose track of the boundaries between themselves and the work of art. People get "gathered up, carried along," "absorbed," "taken 'out' of themselves."

We have already seen (in Chapter 1) that literature embodies fantasies; also that it manages and transforms those fantasies toward significance by devices analogous to the defenses one would find in a man's mind. In other words, the work of art acts like the embodiment of a mental process. Then, our professional and amateur aestheticians speak of being "at one with the work of art." For the engrossed viewer, "aesthetic actuality is no longer outside himself." The mental process embodied in the literary work somehow becomes a process inside its audience. What is "out there" in the literary work feels as though it is "in here," in your mind or mine.

To say that, however, is simply to describe the phenomenon without explaining it. How does this fusion or merger of self and book take place? To what degree? If it breaks down, how does it break down? Most important, why does this fusion or merger take place at all?

We can begin to answer these questions by considering the way we react to non-fiction, to something where we don't willingly suspend our disbelief, a history, for example, or biography or autobiography. Here is a passage from a somewhat whimsical history of the Middle Ages:

> The high and puissant Prince, Philip "the Good"—Duke of Burgundy, Luxemburg, and Brabant—was versatile.
> He could fight as well as any king going; and he could lie as well as any, except the King of France. He was a mighty hunter, and could read and write. His tastes were wide and ardent. He loved jewels like a woman, and gorgeous apparel. He dearly loved maids of honor, and indeed paintings generally . . . He had also a rage for giants, dwarfs, and Turks.

Now what is going on in your mind as you read that little historical sketch? I suspect that you are wondering as you read it, "Did the King of France actually lie?" "Did the Duke of Burgundy in fact carry on with his maids of honor?" "Did he really collect giants, dwarfs, and Turks?" "Is all this really so, really an accurate picture?" These, at least, are questions students have asked when they thought it was from a history book.

It is not from a history book, though, but from a novel, specifically, Charles Reade's *The Cloister and the Hearth*. My deception
was to permit an experiment. How do you feel when you read the
passage over, knowing that this is not history but fiction? Please do
reread it.

As for myself, I feel the earlier questions drop out of mind. I no
longer seem to care whether Philip the Good really was as Reade
describes him. Instead, I have an almost palpable feeling of relaxation. I can feel myself accepting the passage in a far more passive
way than when I imagine it is historical.

Usually, one cannot tell from an isolated paragraph whether a
work is fiction or non-fiction. Yet our responses to the two genres
differ sharply. Therefore, it must not be the paragraph alone that
shapes our response. Rather—or so the experiment was designed to
show—it is the expectation we bring to the paragraph that determines the degree to which we will test it against our everyday experience. If we think the paragraph speaks truth, we will check it for
truth. If we think it speaks fiction, we will not.

Experiment aside, I suspect most of us have felt in everyday life
that special relaxation into the mental set appropriate to fiction.
Sometimes one picks up a short story that is not so labeled. The
moment some incident cues us to realize it is a fiction, we relax
and accept it as such. Sometimes, it is a wildly unlikely statement
such as the old woman's "I am a witch," that cues us into acceptance. Think, for example, of an American tall tale like "The Celebrated Jumping Frog of Calaveras County." It begins as an apparently factual account of a story told to Mark Twain, but as
improbability piles on improbability, we finally realize that he—
and therefore we—are being told fiction, not fact, and we relax to
the point of laughing. The joke is on us, as it was in the tale of the
young executive. Both stories build on a paradox: it is precisely our
conscious knowledge that we are dealing with unreality that makes
it possible for us to relax, to suspend our disbelief, and in a way to
respond to the unreality as though it were real. Conversely, during
the time we think the fiction is real, we are tense, sometimes even
to the point of displeasure.

In effect, I am simply trying to state from the point of view of reader response what many critics, especially in the Renaissance, have pointed out from the writer's point of view. As Sir Philip Sidney put it, "For the poet, he nothing affirmeth, and therefore never lieth."

> What child is there that, coming to a play and seeing *Thebes* written in great letters upon an old door, doth believe that it is Thebes? If then a man can arrive to the child's age, to know that the poet's persons and doing are but pictures what should be, and not stories what have been, they will never give the lie to things not affirmatively but allegorically and figuratively written. And therefore, as in history, looking for truth, they may go away full fraught with falsehood, so in poesy, looking but for fiction, they shall use the narration but as an imaginative groundplat of a profitable invention.[9]

It is, in other words. precisely our knowledge that we are dealing with a fiction that enables us to experience it fully—in Sidney's conception, to use it as a basis for a profitable imagination; in a psychological sense, to experience within ourselves the transformation of fantasy toward meaning. Guthrie is quite right: it is not belief in an illusion that draws us into a play or story—just the opposite. It is a conscious disbelief that becomes suspension of disbelief. But why should this be?

Some critics confuse this "undisbelief" with belief (in an illusion), and we can see why by another appeal to experience. I was privileged to see one of the early performances of a play by A. R. Gurney, Jr., *The Rape of Bunny Stuntz*. Mr. Gurney gave his play the format of an occasion like a P-T.A. meeting, though part of his point was that the subject of the meeting never became explicit. It was just another meeting of the kind middle-aged suburbanites seem to get drawn into. When you walk into the theater the houselights are half on and the stage contains simply a speaker's table, a cashbox (evidently for receipts or something), a few papers, a chair. The heroine, Bunny, comes to the table and addresses the audience exactly as though it were the P-T.A. (or whatever) that had come to one of its regular business meetings.

As soon as this situation became clear, one sensed all through the audience a tightening and edginess. Gradually, this wore off, but at the outset the atmosphere of tension was almost palpable. On asking members of the audience after the play, I found that others had felt as I did: they were afraid they would be called on to do something, to speak or second a motion or vote in response to the events on the stage. And the tension relaxed only when it became clear that, because of Bunny's distractions, the meeting was not going to be a meeting, but a play. We were not going to have to do anything ourselves.

Mr. Gurney was artfully toying with perhaps the most basic of artistic conventions. Literary or artistic experience comes to us marked off from the rest of our experiences in reality. We frame the picture, house it in a museum, surround it with "Do Not Touch" signs. Poems and cartoons are printed in such a way that we immediately recognize them as different and separate. Plays happen in special places—I remember one theater where you had to cross water (a moat) to enter that half-magic world. Short stories and novels are usually labeled as such—certainly a sentence or two tells us we are dealing with fiction, not truth.*

Behind the "frame," then, there is a still more basic convention: we do not expect to act as a result of literary or artistic experience. On the contrary, the work of art, indeed the whole artistic situation, presents itself as divorced from usefulness, calling for no action on our part. The altarpiece becomes art when it hangs in a museum rather than a church. The rain dance becomes art when it no longer serves to bring rain, only tourists. Sometimes the work of art presents itself so divorced from utility; sometimes we do the di-

---

* It is a curious episode in the history of fiction that the earliest fictionists in the modern tradition (I am thinking of writers like Boccaccio, Cinthio, Belleforest, Painter, even Defoe) typically said they were telling a true story. In part, of course, they were trying to ward off Puritan or Platonic objections to untruth. But might we also understand such a device as a pervasive distrust by critics, the reading public, even writers themselves during an age unaccustomed to realistic prose fiction, of emotions not restrained and corrected by a knowledge they were directed against real things?

vorcing ourselves, as when we put aside whatever religious feelings we might have to look at an altarpiece still in its church in a secular, aesthetic way or at a teakettle as a masterpiece of design. "Thus," notes Professor Northrop Frye,

> the question of whether a thing "is" a work of art or not is one which cannot be settled by appealing to something in the nature of the thing itself. It is convention, social acceptance, and the work of criticism in the broadest sense that determines where it belongs. It may have been originally made for use rather than pleasure, and so fall outside the general Aristotelian conception of art, but if it now exists for our pleasure it is what *we* call art.[10]

In other words, it is our suspension of disbelief and the pleasure which results therefrom that makes literature, not the literariness of a given writing that makes us suspend disbelief.

Professor Morse Peckham has put forward a trenchant definition: "A work of art is any perceptual field which an individual uses as an occasion for performing the role of art perceiver." Then, "The distinguishing character or attribute of the perceiver's role is search-behavior focussed on awareness of [formal] discontinuities," that is, a purely aesthetic attention to form. Hence,

> Any object (or perceptual field) from any culture may, then, be properly categorized as having been the occasion for artistic perception if a chronologically arranged sequence of such objects [Bauhaus teakettles, for instance] shows both functional identity and non-functional stylistic dynamism.[11]

In other words, it is precisely the non-functional of art, its unrelatedness to conduct, that lets it be art. "It is a realm," writes Berenson, "where reactions of physical pleasure or pain cannot take place, as neither can cross its frontiers without leaving behind every active principle." [12] Some arts, of course, cannot be wholly divorced from a call for judgmental action—advertising, for example, or propaganda—and I suppose this is why we can experience advertising and propaganda as arts only by a radical effort of imagination or after the product or cause has passed into history.

In the literary situation, we are almost always put into an inactive position. We sit in a theater seat or an armchair. We may laugh, squirm, bite our nails, cry—but we do not act or expect to act on the world external to ourselves. And a mere expectation that we might have to act on the external world, even an innocuous action, like seconding a motion, creates a considerable amount of anxiety, as in Mr. Gurney's P-T.A. format for a play. "The ego will not stand idly by," notes Professor Simon O. Lesser, "while decisions affecting conduct are being reached. The dangerous fantasies embodied in fiction or poetry or plays are tolerated only on condition that, and only so long as, they are taken as fantasies." [13] Otherwise, the ego will respond with anxiety to the fantasies literature mobilizes; we will defend against the literary experience and "snap out of" our absorption in it.

It is, I suppose, not difficult to see that a divorce between a literary experience and our actions affecting the external world greatly facilitates the literary experience. What is harder to see, I think, is how deeply this conventional separation of action from literature reaches into our mental life. One would not expect so much from mere convention, but the inactivity involved in our willing suspension of disbelief returns us to our very earliest modes of thought. Motor inactivity permits (at least when we are engrossed in "entertainments") a sort of total immersion in fantasy. Why?

I am not sure anyone knows the answer, but we can provisionally adopt a suggestion of Freud's in the metapsychological conclusion to *The Interpretation of Dreams*. In earliest infancy, he suggests, we took the shortest path to the gratification of our wishes and needs—we simply hallucinated satisfaction. Indeed, we had to learn to imagine the gratification of needs and wishes as the first step to achieving gratification in actuality through motor actions. Thus, the second time a need arises,

> a psychical impulse will at once emerge which will seek to . . . re-establish the situation of the original satisfaction. An impulse of this kind is what we call a wish; the reappearance of the perception is the fulfillment of the wish; and the shortest path to

the fulfillment of the wish is a path leading direct from the excitation produced by the need to a complete cathexis of the perception. Nothing prevents us from assuming that there was a primitive state of the psychical apparatus in which this path was actually traversed, that is, in which wishing ended in hallucinating. Thus the aim of this first psychical activity was to produce a "perceptual identity"—a repetition of the perception which was linked with the satisfaction of the need.

The bitter experience of life must have changed this primitive thought-activity into a more expedient secondary one. The establishment of a perceptual identity along the short path of regression within the apparatus does not have the same result elsewhere in the mind as does the cathexis of the aim perception from without. Satisfaction does not follow; the need persists.[14]

In other words, we learn to resort to complicated actions in the real world in order to achieve satisfaction. We develop motor skills. We learn to use tools. We learn also to use other people to re-establish perceptual memories of satisfaction. But at night, when we sleep, we no longer act.

Dreams, which fulfil their wishes along the short path of regression, have merely preserved for us in that respect a sample of the psychical apparatus's primary method of working, a method which was abandoned as being inefficient. What once dominated waking life, while the mind was still young and incompetent, seems now to have been banished into the night . . .[15]

Or into our experiences of art, where also we do not act.

Freud's brilliant guess more than half a century ago at the intimate connection between motor inhibition and regression into fantasy has received some recent experimental confirmation. For example, experimenters have shown that muscle tone, already low during sleep, drops to a kind of absolute zero when we dream; our muscles relax more during dreaming than in the deepest phases of sleep.[16] Another line of experimentation has shown that suggestions about motor activity have far more effect on dreams than fantasy materials.* Psychologists of perception have performed dozens of experiments (I am thinking of the work of Richard Held and his associates) which tend to confirm the converse of Freud's hypothesis: that perception of reality depends heavily on checks through motor activity; that when subjects are inhibited from action, the most rudimentary perceptions through eye and ear become distorted. Observations of children by this group also show the crucial importance of motor activity in the development of perceptual skills.

In short, our ability or inability to act on the external world seems deeply involved with our ability or inability to regress into fantasy. Activity in the inner world and activity in the outer seem mutually exclusive. To be active in the inner world, we must be passive toward the outer, for action outward binds us to reality; inaction lets us lapse into our most primitive method of gratification.

Gratification—if it is motor inhibition that licenses our lapse into literary fantasies, it is the promise of gratification that lures us into it. We must approach literature as we approach just about everything else in life, with a wish for pleasure. By convention, by our own past experience, by someone's telling us—somehow we come to works of literature and art expecting them to give us pleasure. No doubt we expect other things as well: information, sophistication, status, pity and fear, satisfaction of curiosity, but, for our purposes, understanding the most primitive level of response to fairly primitive artistic experiences, "entertainments," we need posit only a wish for pleasurable experience.

We have already seen the nature of that pleasure: literature as

* The experiment was an intriguing one. Before going to sleep, subjects were given one of three stimuli: (1) a film of mild, neutral content; (2) suggestions, while extraneous sights and sounds were muffled, that the subject's right hand was heavier than his left or that he would have difficulty unclasping his hands; (3) some fairly grisly films, of the birth of a baby, a subincision rite, or a mother monkey eating her dead baby. Surprisingly, it was the suggestions relating to motor activity that had great impact on dream content, producing anxiety dreams for as many as two or three nights. The other stimuli seemed to have little effect.[17]

transformation. In effect, the literary work dreams a dream for us. It embodies and evokes in us a central fantasy; then it manages and controls that fantasy by devices that, were they in a mind, we would call defenses, but, being on a page, we call "form." And the having of the fantasy and feeling it managed give us pleasure. We bring, then, to works of art two expectations that permit a "willing suspension of disbelief": we do not expect to act on the external world; we expect pleasure. Even if the work makes us feel pain or guilt or anxiety, we expect it to manage those feelings so as to transform them into satisfying experiences.

As adults, we come to works of art having experienced a long sequence of developmental stages. We bring, therefore, to works of art memories of similar pleasures we have had. At an adult level we bring memories of recent aesthetic pleasures. At a somewhat earlier level, we bring the memory of the intense fantasies and reading of latency. Still earlier, we may recall being read to by our parents, perhaps being held on their laps and cuddled at the same time. Still earlier, at a time prior to conscious memory, we had our first experience of pleasure, being held by a nurturing mother and being fed. All these experiences make up a kind of matrix in us ready to receive a literary or artistic work.

In particular, that earliest experience of gratification has a number of properties that bear on the literary situation, that make "matrix" precisely the word for the expectation of pleasure we bring. It was an oral pleasure we first felt. Specifically, we took something into ourselves that quieted our hunger. Curiously, or perhaps not so curiously, even as adults we associate reading with eating, as when we call a man who "devours books" a "voracious" reader. We "take in" a movie. A certain novel may be a "treat." A parody may be "delicious." "Some books are to be tasted," said Bacon, "others to be swallowed, and some few to be chewed and digested." Even the Book of Common Prayer enjoins us, "Read, mark, learn, and inwardly digest."

This "hunger for knowledge" has an important adaptive side, too. Susan Isaacs has written of th infant:

> The instinctual drive towards taking things into his mind through eyes and fingers (and ears, too), towards looking and touching and exploring, satisfies some of the oral wishes frustrated by his original object. Perception and intelligence draw upon this source of libido for their life and growth. Hand and eye retain an oral significance throughout life, in unconscious phantasy and often, as [above], in conscious metaphor.[18]

With works of art, of course, looking usually takes the place of touching. In a literary situation, we are almost always looking, either at a person or a printed page or a screen. Many years ago, Otto Fenichel pointed out, "In the unconscious, to look at an object may mean various things, the most noteworthy of which are as follows: to devour the object looked at, to grow like it (be forced to imitate it), or, conversely, to force it to grow like oneself." [19] Thus, if the literary process is succeeding, we are not only devouring the object; we are making our minds like it or it like our minds.

Orality explains the open-mouthed wonder with which we "absorb" a theatrical performance through our eyes and ears. Suspense, too, has an oral quality: a writer like Dickens or Scott or Hitchcock creates a problem in us and what amounts to a hunger for its resolution so great we can scarcely wait for the next episode. Nor is it surprising we feel a peculiarly sharp frustration, even a sense of rage and betrayal, when "Network Trouble" flashes on the screen or when the movie film breaks or when we find the last pages of a novel torn out. Our sense of frustration and anger becomes particularly sharp if what disrupts our visual feast is a person; we go through a miniature and adult version of the overwhelming rage of a child whose feeding is interrupted. Thus, too, we can guess the reason virtually all cultures mix eating with drama and literature: the symbolic eating of the slain hero in Attic drama, the beer and oranges of the seventeenth-century playhouses—even the popcorn in the movie theater of today, or the chocolate-nibbling of a modern novel-reader. Literature creates a hunger in us and then gratifies us.

There are, though, still other features of that earliest oral gratification in the literary transaction. That time was long before we
had any clear sense of reality as such. Even at the age of five, children have trouble telling whether a story is really true or not or
whether their dreams really happened, and we are talking about a
much earlier period, a time prior to the eighth month of life. Life
then was simply a quest for pleasure; in the jargon, we were totally
under the domination of the pleasure principle. Nor were we in a
position to do much reality-testing through motor actions. Further,
we could find considerable satisfaction in the mere hallucination of
gratification—as we take pleasure now in the fantasies of a work of
literature.

More technically, we are speaking of the period prior to "self-
object differentiation." We have considered it before—in Chapter
2—as it bore upon fantasies of fusion and merger in literature.
Here, though, it seems to be the foundation of all literary experience, our basic relationship with the literary work. "Originally,"
writes Freud, "the ego includes everything, later it separates off an
external world from itself. Our present ego-feeling is, therefore,
only a shrunken residue of a much more inclusive—indeed, an all-
embracing—feeling which corresponded to a more intimate bond
between the ego and the world around it." Originally, we did not
distinguish ourselves from the nurturing external world. "An infant
at the breast does not as yet distinguish his ego from the external
world as the source of the sensations flowing in upon him." [20] He
learns to do so because he learns to expect satisfaction from another. He learns to wait for his mother to come and gratify his
(primarily oral) needs. Erikson has called this ability to wait "basic
trust," because it is only through this ability to trust that his
mother will come and will gratify him that the child can learn to
trust that "other," all the outer realities which are not his own fantasy. "Basic trust in mutuality is that original 'optimism,' that assumption that 'somebody is there,' without which we cannot live."
"One may well claim for that earliest meeting of a perceiving subject with a perceived object (which, in turn seems to 'recognize'

the subject) the beginning of all sense of identity." [21] That is, the child cannot conceive of himself as a separate being until he can trust, await, have faith in his mother as a separate being. Because he accepts her as separate, he can recognize he himself is also separate. Even in adult life, our very sense of identity is predicated upon this sense of "basic trust" in an environment that will support us.

In the literary setting, however, we are not expecting that other: we are in the process of being gratified by it. We are responding, therefore, from a level of our being which existed prior to the sense of another reality. We have partially returned to that original "all-embracing" feeling before the ego "separates off an external world from itself." It is because part of us has regressed so deeply that we can so easily make the concerns of a literary character our own or project our concerns onto him.

> Psychoanalysis assumes the early process of differentiation between inside and outside to be the origin of projection and introjection which remain some of our deepest and most dangerous defense mechanisms. In introjection we feel and act as if an outer goodness had become an inner certainty. In projection, we experience an inner harm as an outer one: we endow significant people with the evil which actually is in us. These two mechanisms, then, projection and introjection, are assumed to be modeled after whatever goes on in infants when they would like to externalize pain and internalize pleasure, an intent which must yield to the testimony of the maturing senses and ultimately of reason. These mechanisms can characterize irrational attitudes toward adversaries and enemies in masses of "mature" individuals.[22]

And these mechanisms arise, I take it, not just in political movements like Nazism, but in audiences collectively hating a film villain who is "really" just a shadow on a lenticular screen.

Our ego boundaries between self and not-self, inner and outer, become blurred as we approach, in part, the undifferentiated state of earliest infancy. And thus, too, this chapter returns to its earliest phase, the initial remarks of the professional aestheticians, Guthrie,

Berenson, and Bachelard, and the amateurs. An audience is taken out of itself and into the imaginary world of the play—"absorbed." The "aesthetic actuality is no longer outside" the spectator. "The poem possesses us entirely." "I am gathered up, carried along, and unaware of being a reader, viewer, etc."

The pediatrician-psychoanalyst D. W. Winnicott has said of this undifferentiated state in infancy: " 'There is no such thing as an infant,' meaning, of course, that whenever one finds an infant one finds maternal care, and without maternal care there would be no infant." [23] Could not the same thing be said of an audience? There is no such thing as an audience as an entity-in-itself, for whenever one finds an audience one finds a literary work creating it, and without a literary work there would be no audience.*

Be that as it may, we are now in a position to state how and why we willingly suspend disbelief. We come to a literary work with two conscious expectations: first, that it will give us pleasure (of an oral, "taking in" kind); second, that it will not require us to act on the external world. The literary work thus finds in us a matrix reaching back through many, many experiences of gratification in fantasy to our earliest experience of passive satisfaction. That occurred prior to our recognition of ourselves as separate beings, and literature re-creates this undifferentiated self: we absorb and become absorbed into the literary experience. Indeed, as Tyrone Guthrie's examples show, we can become absorbed in any external reality to which we come with those two expectations, to be fed pleasure and not to act: music, painting, novel, or philosophical argument. Camus's phrasing shows the link between "absorption" and orality: "Plongée dans la beauté, l'intelligence fait son repas de néant."

---

* *Infans* literally means "unable to speak." We do not (ordinarily) speak when we are engrossed in a literary work. The etymology and the analogy return us to Dr. Edmund Bergler's suggestion: that writers may acquire their predisposition to become writers because in early infancy they use words coming out of their mouths as an important defense against masochistic impulses aroused by their mothers' putting food in.[24] But, as readers, we do the opposite: we do not emit words to defend against passively being fed.

Thus, Coleridge's term, marvelous as it is, does not tell the whole story. It is true that we suspend disbelief or, more exactly, we do not reality-test as we do in everyday life. But something much more profound has happened. We do not reality-test because, in part at least, we have ceased to feel we are separate from external reality. To some extent, we fuse with the literary work. In absorbing it, we become absorbed.

A more useful phrasing, then, of the phenomenon Coleridge was describing is that what is in fact happening "out there" in the literary work feels as though it is happening "in here" in us, or, still more exactly, in some undifferentiated "either." To paraphrase, except ye become as little children, ye shall not enter the kingdom of literature. And we do—we become infants prior even to an awareness of ourselves as such, quite unable to disbelieve. Or so we do in part.

We may be somewhat childlike when we respond to movies and plays, but we are not totally infantile. Dr. Avery Weisman draws a useful distinction—between "reality-testing," a matter of intellect or concepts, and a "sense of reality" such as we have towards a dream.

> Reality sense is a function of the libidinal attachments of the personality and of the cathexes of the ideas and objects that comprise the ego image. The sense of reality is fundamentally irrational in that it requires no justification for acceptance since it is the nature of irreducible justification itself.[25]

In simpler language, Irving Singer contrasts the "appraisal" of value ("This car has a trade-in value of $436") with the "bestowal" of value ("I love this old car; I wouldn't take a million for it"). In the literary situation, our relatively passive merger or fusion with what we are seeing paves the way for something more active, "an act of the imagination" Singer calls it.

> On entering the theater, you have entered the dramatic situation. You have allowed your imagination to engage itself in one specific channel. With the assistance of the realistic props, the

surrounding darkness, the company of other people doing the same imagining, you have invested the actors and characters they represent with a capacity to affect your feelings as real persons might.[26]

Shakespeare himself asks us: "Eke out our performance with your mind."

> Piece out our imperfections with your thoughts:
> Into a thousand parts divide one man
> And make imaginary puissance.
> Think, when we talk of horses, that you see them
> Printing their proud hoofs i' th' receiving earth:
> For 'tis your thoughts that now must deck our kings.

In effect, our minds are split in two. Our ordinary testing of reality persists to some extent, but at the time we are able to give conviction, a "sense of reality" to the work we are reading. Dr. Weisman asks:

> Why do we not believe that the actor, *in reality* (that is, from every point of view), has committed murder on the stage? Although members of the audience may react to the event with conviction, by hating, crying, or fearing . . . their active reality testing is able to differentiate the *play* of murder from the *fact* of murder. . . . Reality testing is able to index the staged events and the ensuing emotions into a specific conceptual field, which states, in effect, that criminals do not run around loose in theaters to commit murder by prearrangement. Within this range of meaning, stage actions are real in the domain of artistic phantasy, but are unreal as crime.[27]

Within our fusion with the literary work and because of it, we create a "sense of reality"; yet we never entirely lose our "reality-testing."

Thus, though it is tempting to call our involvement with literature a "regression," something more is happening. That term connotes a single level of mental functioning lower than one's ordinary level. But in the literary situation, while we reach down to our earliest, most primitive state of merger with our gratifications, we still retain some of our highest levels of mental functioning. The kind of total immersion we have been describing is at best the major part of our response in "entertainments," not great writing. We do not read Shakespeare or Tolstoy as we read Ian Fleming or Conan Doyle.

Even when we are reading "entertainments," high ego functions persist. We reality-test the "as if" itself. We put letters together to form words. At a play or a movie, we are perceiving shapes and events and people. We are remembering what has gone before and anticipating what will come next. We are judging such things as plausibility and probability. We bring to different kinds of literature different expectations of rather complicated kinds: expectations about meter or rhyme, expectations about syntax, expectations about levels of lifelikeness (we tolerate things in science fiction we would not in a naturalistic novel), and so on. Simon Lesser says,

> There is a willing suspension of disbelief because we want to obtain the satisfactions which prompted us to read a given book. But our willingness to meet a book halfway must be requited: we are constantly judging and appraising, and if a work seems false or otherwise unworthy of our trust, we will become increasingly critical and less and less immersed in it.[28]

The word "trust" is crucial—it applies not only to the infant's (or the reader's) "basic trust" toward what feeds him; it applies equally to the more sophisticated expectations we bring to literature.

Rather than speak of regression, then, we can say our minds during the literary experience undergo a "deepening." It is as though a pianist had been confined to the upper three octaves because there was some danger if he played the low notes—perhaps an explosion would be triggered off, as, in everyday life, we feel it dangerous to respond to reality with much affect from the massive, primitive depths of our earliest selves. In the literary situation, though, we know no explosion will occur, for we know we are not going to act. Our minds are therefore free to range up and down the entire keyboard of our prior development. We have seen (in Chapter 2) the wishes and fears and fantasies that may be brought into play. But, in particular, we take in the literary work, all literary works, in a very primitive oral way: what is "out there" is felt as though it were neither "out there" nor "in here"—boundaries blur.

Our awareness of ourselves as such becomes markedly less. As for myself, I find that as I watch an "entertainment," I am totally engrossed much of the time, but at various moments I become restless and aware of myself again, aware, perhaps, that I am sitting in a theater, that there are people around me, that the theater is overheated, and so on. Then, if I am enjoying the play or film, I lapse back and become absorbed in it again. Bernard Berenson describes aesthetic fusion as a "flitting instant, so brief as to be almost timeless." A statistical study offers some evidence that many people have this all-or-nothing style of absorption.*

Other people tell me they do not experience aesthetic fusion as an on-off sort of thing. As Lesser puts it, "We are constantly judging and appraising." Students' phrasings suggest (quite accurately) that these higher functions serve to defend against an involvement feared as too deep: "The philosophic part . . . keeps me from going under emotionally." "I tend to identify strongly until I see faults, note trends, try to put together plots . . ." "Become involved in a book, movie, but at the same time I attempt to keep some part far enough away from that involvement to analyze the work's structure, content . . ." Conscious efforts are required to avoid fusion.

There is, of course, in all of us, a continuation of such higher

* "When involved, as during the reading of the central portions of these stories, the subjects made fewer literary judgments. This apparent inverse relationship does not conflict with the earlier finding through partial correlation technique of a high positive relationship between the total response in these categories [literary judgments and statements of self-involvement]. The two types of responses seem to reinforce one another, with readers who are emotionally involved formulating more literary judgments even though the responses occur at different times. Many of the evaluations of the story as literature occur either before the reader has become involved or after an extended period during which the subject seems considerably involved in the central experience or the character whom he is interpreting or identifying with or rejecting. Only when the reading of a story is completed do literary judgments become a major concern." [29]

ego-functions. The difference between people seems to be the degree to which we are aware of them. Does the spotlight of our conscious awareness spill over from its intense concentration on the work of art to shed a little light on the self? Or does it show up only the work? Or does it swing back and forth a little from self to work? Different people evidently have slightly different degrees of awareness, but in broad outline our experience is the same.

At a very primitive level of our being we are fused with the work of literature; we feel what is going on in it as though it were going on in us. Our experience of oral gratification in early infancy forms a matrix for our willing suspension of disbelief when we come to literature later. Perhaps we can see that primitive level of response more clearly if we compare it to other adult experiences that also build on the infant's experience of merger with his earliest gratifications.

One such adult experience is psychoanalysis itself. The analytic setting systematically encourages regression by duplicating a number of features of infancy—as literature does. The environment is made constant, and one's entrance into it becomes a ceremonial routine (like going into a theater). The patient brings magical expectations to the authority-figure of the analyst; in the same way, the literary work has a kind of authority over its expectant audience. The sense of time is reduced as is the sense of personal responsibility. The number of persons in the setting to whom the patient can relate is reduced (to one in the analytic situation, to just the characters of the work in the literary setting); also reduced are the possible ways of relating. The end result of all these quasi-infantile elements in the analytic situation is regression to a point where the patient is —at one deep level of his being—as dependent on and involved with the analyst as he once was with his mother.[30]

The patient becomes as an audience, ready, willing, and able to indulge in all kinds of displacements, projections, and introjections. He is willing to bring to the analyst as he would to a character in a play his feelings toward his father, mother, wife, or any important person in his life. He finds himself able to let his everyday perceptions be distorted by his fantasies. (A balding red-haired analyst once told me of a patient who repeatedly described him as having a full head of brown hair—like Samson's.) From our point of view, however, the most interesting feature of the transference situation is the split in the patient's ego—rather like the split in an audience's. Analysts speak of a "participant ego" and an "observing ego," meaning that while one part of the patient is giving his fantasies full rein in free association, another is, as it were, watching him do so and commenting on the significance of what he is saying. The sensation is quite vivid to anyone who has been in analysis. The tongue runs on almost of its own accord, the mind behind it relaxed, drowsy; then, suddenly, some still-alert part of oneself notices a word or a phrase or a pattern, and a significance becomes clear. The feeling is not at all unlike one's feelings as an audience or reader.

The most exact analogy to the literary situation, though, is hypnosis. (Indeed, "Analytic transference manifestations are a slow motion picture of hypnotic transference manifestations.") [31] In one of his earliest papers, Freud described the phenomenon of suggestion which had so impressed him in his work at Charcot's clinic and which led him to the conception of an unconscious:

> I should like to put forward the view that what distinguishes a suggestion from other kinds of psychical influence, such as a command or the giving of a piece of information or instruction, is that in the case of a suggestion an idea is aroused in another person's brain which is not examined in regard to its origin but is accepted just as though it had arisen spontaneously in that brain.[32]

In other words, we willingly suspend disbelief.

Hypnosis is induced, like our engrossment in a literary work, by restrictions of perception, thinking, and motility. There are still other parallels. Fenichel summarizes the early theories when he describes hypnosis as a "nostalgic reversion to that phase of life" when "passive-receptive mastery" represented the primary means of

coping with the outside world; that period when security was
achieved by participation in a "greater unit," the all-powerful parent [33] (as the student described himself, "gathered up, carried
along"). Gill and Brenman's more recent study refines this early notion: "Hypnosis is a complex dovetailing relationship between the
two participants," "a mutual identification with oral wishes to devour and be devoured playing a prominent role," a "mutual interpen-
etration of identifications." "We as well as others have emphasized
oral features in hypnosis . . . the mechanism of identification and
the underlying fantasy of oral incorporation." Gill and Brenman
found "frequent and striking evidence of some variety of oral conflict" in their "good subjects," those most easily hypnotized.[34] One
would expect the same (albeit to a lesser degree) in those who suc-
cumb easily to the blandishments of poetry, drama, and fiction—
again, we come back to Bergler's suggestion that the ability to be a
creative writer or reader stems from oral conflicts.

In hypnosis, the ego tends to lose autonomy from both the id
and the environment, and these two weakenings combine their
effect. Loss of autonomy from the id resembles dreaming, artistic
creativity, or scientific creativity in which the investigator is led by
a "hunch." Loss of autonomy from the environment resembles scientific creativity when the investigator is led by the "material,"
and, as a result, motivations are restructured by the environment
(as, when engrossed in a novel, we ourselves become committed to
the problems and needs of quite fictional people).[35]

Gill and Brenman suggest as a central proposal for a theory of
hypnosis that, once a hypnotic state has been achieved,

> a subsystem is set up within the ego. This subsystem is a re-
> gressed system which is in the service of the over-all ego; it has
> control of some or all of the apparatuses, and to the extent that
> it has control, those apparatuses which were de-automatized are
> now re-automatized. It is this subsystem alone which is under
> the control of the hypnotist, and it is by virtue of this control
> that the hypnotist can control and direct the apparatuses. The
> over-all ego also maintains a relationship with the hypnotist, the
> nonhypnotic reality-orientated relationship. The over-all ego re-

linquishes control of the subsystem to the hypnotist only temporarily and tentatively. It is the fact that this relinquishment of control is only provisional to which we pointed when we earlier described evidences of persisting control of the apparatuses by the ego during the hypnotic state; the over-all ego can yield control of the subsystem to the hypnotist but can at any time take it back.[36]

Such a view of hypnosis is very like our situation in literary involvement.

At one level of our being, a very primitive level, we feel the process of transformation the literary work embodies as a transformation in us. We have introjected the literary work; it has become a subsystem within our own egos. But we still have other ego functions: putting letters together to form words, remembering what happened before and guessing at what will happen next, judging probability, and the rest. And we are also busy (to use Simon Lesser's term) "analogizing," supplying personal associations to our literary experience (like my thoughts about L-shaped rooms to "delves the parallels in beauty's brow"). We can best think of our engrossment in poem, play, or story as our introjecting the literary work, letting it form a core (or subsystem) within us which is the literary work, but within a rind of our ordinary selves.

The subsystem formed within a man by hypnosis is the most exact analogy to our incorporation of literary works, but unfortunately not many of us have been hypnotized. A more familiar, if less exact, analogy to our engrossment in literature is dreaming.

In dreaming, as in the trances literature evokes, we wish to receive pleasure; dreams are wish-fulfillments. Motor inhibition defines our ability to dream, as it does our literary absorption. And we are not sure whether the dream is real or not. Though we tend not to be aware of them, a number of higher ego-functions persist: bladder control, some perception of the outer world (as when we work the sound of the alarm clock into our dream), some awareness of time. Higher functions reveal themselves too in the so-called "secondary elaboration" of the dream, the creative effort that works it into a semi-coherent plot. Further, says Freud, "I am driven to conclude that throughout our whole sleeping state we know just as certainly that we are dreaming as we know that we are sleeping. We must not pay too much attention to the counter-argument that our consciousness is never brought to bear on the latter piece of knowledge and that it is only brought to bear on the former on particular occasions . . ." [37] In the same way, we are aware, we know, no matter how deeply we are engrossed, that "it is only a play" or novel or whatever, even though we may not be aware of our knowledge at any given moment.

Just as higher ego-functions persist in dreaming, so dreams reach down to our most primitive selves. Freud's basic description of dreaming is: thoughts left over from the day before sink to deeper levels of unconsciousness where they draw strength from infantile wishes and are elaborated by the kinds of radical condensations and displacements that make the dream into a visual fantasy. Then the dream proceeds to consciousness through a secondary elaboration that makes it approximate coherence.

That dip into the deeper levels of the mind is deep. Bertram Lewin's researches have suggested the existence of a "dream screen," not unlike the white screen in a movie theater against which the content of the dream is projected. Such a dream screen, he rather convincingly shows, stands ultimately for the breast, and the act of dreaming builds upon a merger with that earliest gratification. Apparently, just as our oral merger with the work of literature establishes the base upon which we experience it, so the oral-level dream screen is the base upon which the dream is played.[38] It acts like the unraised curtain in a theater, the blank screen of cinema, the book about to be opened—all of which we hope will gratify us. Even television, notes Dr. Gitelson, "provides a dream screen which 'is' the breast." [39] "Though the wishes of life become progressively more complex and subtle, this [the ever-recurring wish for a primary breast experience] remains as the deepest substrate occasionally to be revealed in regressive experiences during the course of analysis or other intense psychological vicissitudes," [40] such as, presumably, our excitements over literature. Literature, in a way, is a dream dreamed for us, which we then introject. The phrasing, "we are absorbed," reverses the true state of affairs. We absorb it, making the literary work a subsystem within us.

Psychoanalysis, hypnosis, dreaming—all three show the basic split essential to our "willing suspension of disbelief" in the literary setting: the persistence of adult ego-functions along with an encapsulated regression to our earliest oral experience of a pre-self in which we are merged with the source of our gratification. In one sense, they are only analogies, but in another sense they go farther, to become—partly, anyway—confirmations. If in psychoanalysis, hypnosis, and dreaming, we have a kind of "core" in ourselves which is regressed to the most primitive level of our being and, surrounding that core, a sort of "rind" of higher ego-functions, then we might well be in the same schizoid state when we are engrossed in a literary "entertainment." Certainly the behavioral signs of that engrossment resemble our behavior in analysis, hypnosis, and dreaming.*

Given this notion of a regressed core and a persisting rind of unregressed ego, we can, I hope, clarify our relation to a literary work by a return to the diagrams of Chapters 1 and 2. There, we came to the conclusion that a literary work embodies a specific mental

---

* Incidentally, it is this dual nature of our involvement that renders inadequate the popular metaphor of "aesthetic distance." In Edward Bullough's original formulation, "distance" meant separation of the work of art from our practical, actual lives. In that sense, "distance" corresponds to "motor inhibition." But if so, it does not render the blurring of self into work. According to Bullough, "What is therefore, both in appreciation and production, most desirable is the utmost decrease of distance without its disappearance." [41] The trouble with the metaphor is that Bullough is trying to render along one axis only (closeness-distance) a phenomenon that calls for two. Along one, the artistic frame isolates—marks off—the work of art from realities toward which we act; both realities are at some relatively fixed "distance" from the self, but separated from each other. Once the work of art is thus marked off, the self tends to merge into it, and then the metaphor of the "utmost decrease of distance without its disappearance" more or less describes the limiting condition of fusion of self and art-object.

process, the transformation of a normally unconscious fantasy toward conscious, intellectual meaning. We represented that process by "stretching" the text:

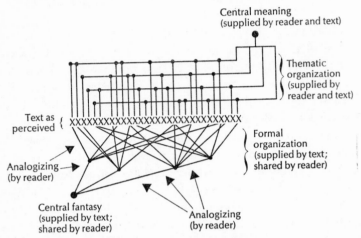

That is, there is a text of which we are half-consciously aware. We can discover in that text a nucleus of fantasy material which is disguised and elaborated by the abrupt short cuts of primary-process thought to become the text (much as the latent content of a dream coalesces into the manifest dream). By the "squarer" connections of secondary-process or problem-solving thought, we can also discover a nucleus of intellectual meaning, a "point" to which all the myriad details of the work are relevant, just as they are relevant to the nucleus of fantasy.

What this chapter has shown is that these two levels "in" the text correspond to two quite different ways we relate to the text. We supply theme and meaning by thinking about the work as a separate entity; we reality-test it. We experience the work, though, by introjecting it, taking it into ourselves, feeling the nucleus of fantasy and the formal management of that fantasy as though they were our own—hence the changes in this diagram: the central fantasy and its formal organization are not only supplied by the text but also shared by the reader.

To put the reader and his two modes of apprehending the text into the picture, it helps to abbreviate this rather complicated diagram:

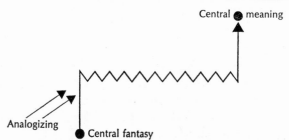

We respond to a literary work (so "stretched") in two discrete ways. In between these two ways of relating to the work, we are busy perceiving the text. If our reading is automatic, we are not conscious of it. If it requires considerable effort (as for a child or for someone trying to read a language he doesn't know very well), we will be conscious of our act of perception. We can represent these levels of reading this way:

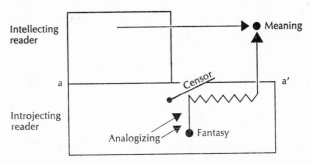

At the primitive level, the level of fantasy, we take the work into ourselves: we introject it. It is at this level that we analogize—bring to the work our own highly individual fantasies (we have been using the example of my associations to the L-sounds of "delves the parallels"). I have represented this analogizing by arrows contributing to the fantasy material the work of art must manage.

These fantasies, our own and the work's, would not be acceptable to our egos: to draw on an early concept of Freud's, a "censor" would reject them in their raw form. They become acceptable in two ways: literary form alters the fantasy content in a defensive way; the overall thrust of the work (the movement indicated by the arrowheads) transforms the fantasy content toward meaning. Once past the censor, at the "higher" level, the level of conscious, intellecting ego, we perceive the literary work as separate, we think about it, we discover its meaning. No doubt, these two discrete levels are neither two nor discrete—we are probably dealing with a continuum or a matter of degree. Given the nature of graphical representation, I can only suggest that we think of higher and lower in this picture as representing that continuum.

Even so, even if we assume that those processes are continuous, the line a-a' must remain—it represents the (admittedly) somewhat fuzzy division between consciousness and unconsciousness. If we are responding to an "entertainment" this line is high: very little of our conscious, intellecting ego is at work; we are mostly introjecting and fantasying. If we are dealing with a masterpiece, we are likely to respond more at the conscious level of meaning and significance, less at the primitive level of fusion and introjection. We could represent the two situations this way:

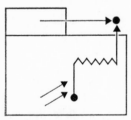
The "entertainment"

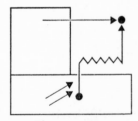
The masterpiece

Another way to represent them would be as energy spectrums. That is, we can simply indicate the two processes, conscious and unconscious, as a line of higher and lower, along which there are roughly three ranges: the deep level of fusion, the high one of conscious thought, and, in the middle somewhere, affect or emotion of which we are sometimes conscious, sometimes not. Being engrossed in an entertainment, we are involved primarily at the deeper levels; most of our psychic energy or "cathexis" is bound up there. To put it in Avery Weisman's terms, we are creating more of a "sense of reality" than a reality objectively, philosophically, considered. Conversely, confronted with "great" literature, we think and feel more and introject less (at least some of the time). We can also represent this way the curiously affectless quality of the writings of, say, Ionesco or Genet. On the one hand, we respond at the level of puzzle; on the other, we feel—at least I do—that very deep levels of unconscious material are being reached.

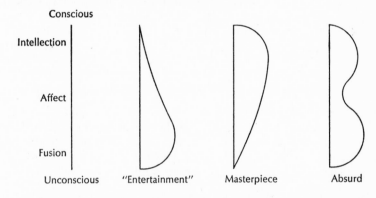

Diagrams, however, ought to repay us for their awkwardness by some extra in clarification or explanation. These, I think, do. For example, we are a step closer to explaining one of the knottier issues in our response to literature, the problem of subjective and objective. When an audience looks at a play or a movie, you might expect one of two things. You might expect everyone to react the same way—after all, they are all confronting the same stimulus. But, of course, people don't: each person has his own feelings about the play. Then, you might expect everybody to react differently, but again, people don't. If somebody giggled his way through a performance of Hamlet, you would think he was crazy, as crazy as someone who wept his way through a Marx Brothers movie. In other words, there is some sort of range of sensible responses, but within that range everybody has his own response.

The best study I know on this subject (by Drs. Gordon Globus and Roy Shulman) remains, alas, unpublished.* The authors were trying to find films guaranteed, as it were, to elicit a specific affect (to be used for other research). They selected certain films which seemed likely to produce certain particular affects (anxiety, depression, hostility). They then interviewed subjects before and after the film to see if the right affect was indeed induced. It was not.

> On the basis of a study of the literature, an initial formulation was developed that the stimulus properties of a film could be defined by the consensus of a group of investigators, and then the appropriate affect induced in the subjects. This formulation was not tenable. The conscious affect and/or the unconscious affect did not necessarily coincide with what the experimenters objectively defined as the stimulus properties of the film, and the subjects' report of affect was not necessarily congruent with the experimenters' inference of affect. . . .

> A second formulation was developed, that the affective responses are determined more by the pre-existing affective state of the subject and the status of his defensive organization than by the specific nature of the film shown, i.e., the film potentiates rather indiscriminately pre-existing affective responses. The initial analysis of the data revealed a remarkable range and

* Because, says Dr. Globus, "it will have to wait until someone establishes the *Journal of Negative Results*." From my point of view, however, the results are far from negative. Their description of the kind of regression their film-going subjects experienced sounds very like a "core" of fusion and a "rind" of unregressed ego:

> The darkness, immobility, relative lack of distractions, and isolation from objective reality-oriented interpersonal events facilitates an ego regression so that ego boundaries are diffused, affective arousal is enhanced, and more primitive defenses are brought into play. It may be conceptualized that with the loss of ego boundaries, the viewer feels as if he is there with the film characters or actually *is* one of the characters, and responds with affect appropriate to the film reality . . . In addition to the viewers' "dissolving" into the characters and affectively responding to the film as reality, unconscious mechanisms, especially identification and projective identification, are at work. In this sense, the film at times serves almost as a "day-residue" in dream formation, with the unconscious making contact with and utilizing the film for purposes of gaining affective discharge.[42]

patterning of affective experience, seemingly unrelated to the film stimulus. . . . Closer analysis, however, suggested that within this complex field of affective response certain foci were present which tended to coincide with the nature of the film stimulus.

It seems, then, that each notion is in part correct, i.e., neither can the film superimpose an affect on the subject nor can the subject remain entirely free of specific stimulus properties of the film. It is not only the film events as an affective stimulus, but, in addition, as the film events come in contact with the unique life experiences, wishes, and conflicts of the subject, whether conscious or unconscious, that the associated affective responses are elicited. In a sense, in relation to the film stimulus, the affect is in part "created" by the film, serving as if it were present reality, and is in part "recalled" from past reality as a function of unconscious processes.[43]

Globus and Shulman are, in effect, describing the interface between the audience member and the literary work he is introjecting.

Our model (perhaps even its diagrams) helps explain not only their lack of results from the initial formulation, but the difficulty of explaining the results they did get. That is, the literary (or cinematic) work embodies a mental process of transformation. Associated with that transformation one would expect certain affects, fear, hostility, and the like (the experimenters speak of "affective foci"). But these affective foci become real, felt affects only if we introject the transformational process which is the literary work. At one extreme, we may reject the work as we would a foreign body. One subject fled the film showing; a more normal reaction would be to flee it inwardly, to mobilize defenses against the film-fantasy just as one would against an ego-alien fantasy of one's own.* At the other extreme, the work may, in Keats's phrase, "strike the reader as a wording of his own highest thoughts, and appear almost a Remembrance" (or, as the experimenters say, "the affect . . . is in

---

* An obsessional patient of Dr. Weisman's "fled" a movie by withdrawing cathexis and "sense of reality" from it.[44]

part 'recalled' from past reality"). If so, then the transformation in the literary work must be one that matches a transformation familiar to the reader. Between these extremes, there can be all kinds of variations, for example, in the associations any particular reader may bring to the work (his "analogizings").

The essential thing is the introjection. If it takes place, what is actually happening "out there" feels as though it were happening "in here." The member of the audience will make the "affective foci" into his own affects. But this introjection can take place only if the transformation in the literary work is "congenial" (in Hazlitt's sense)—if it matches the reader's *genius* or spirit or basic psychological patterns. If it does not take place, his affective response will be rather independent of the "foci" in the work.

Our introjection hypothesis will also explain—and get confirmation from—cases where the artistic frame breaks down. The classic instance comes when Don Quixote attacks the puppet show. He has been watching the puppeteers work out a story, and even though he had interrupted to complain at length about various unrealities and improbabilities, even so, when a cavalcade of Moors pursues a pair of Christian lovers, "Don Quixote thought it only right to help the fugitives," and he whips out his trusty sword and massacres the paper-mâché villains.

There are many other instances. Pepys mentions that "a pretty lady, that sat by me, called out, to see Desdemona smother," and I have read of performances of *Othello* in the South where the local gentry have gathered after the play to punish the Negro who has murdered the white Desdemona in their miscegenated bed. More recently, during the first New York run of *Look Back in Anger*, a lady rushed up on stage to attack the misbehaving husband with her umbrella. These are aggressive touchings: as one would expect from Freud's account of the drives isolation protects against, when aesthetic inhibition of motor actions fails, aggression "touches" the work of art.

There are libidinal touchings, too. During the heyday of the radio soap operas, ladies by the dozens would send baby presents and wedding gifts, ask or give advice to the fictional heroes and heroines. On a simpler level, adolescent and not-so-adolescent people find a sexual rather than an aesthetic pleasure in watching a star on the screen. Indeed, the whole star system institutionalizes this sexual breakdown of isolation by imperfectly submerging the star in the part so the "real" Liz Taylor or Richard Burton peeps through the character they happen to be playing.

Someone who is reacting inappropriately to (say) a drama, tries to act out in real, motor ways his sexual or aggressive feelings toward the events depicted. In these inappropriate reactions, feelings become too strong. "I was stirred to anger," confesses Don Quixote when he is brought to his senses. The afflicted member of the audience resorts to motor action in the supposedly real world. He has not simply lost one defense; he has substituted another way of dealing with the feelings aroused in him. I can remember, in scarey movies, as the monster, robot, villain, or comedian is sneaking up on the heroine, occasionally someone would scream or shout, "Look out behind you!" And the audience laughed. And yet, if the heroine could look behind her, she could escape and be saved. When sincere, the shout does try to deal with a felt fear—though, of course, in a wonderfully inappropriate way. It is as though at that moment the shouter needed to feel that the fear could be dealt with "out there," because it was intolerable "in here." In effect, he confesses that what was objectively in front of him has become subjectively within him, and he thrusts it out again. The rest of the audience, in recognizing his error, recognizes that the events "out there" are not supposed to evoke motor responses, thus recapitulates its defense of motor inhibition, and so laughs from reassurance.

Perhaps, then, we can guess that the artistic "frame" breaks down and people try to punish or love or prevent the events and people onstage when they need very strongly to feel that what is "in here" is really "out there." Perhaps the ladies who treated soap opera families as real needed to have a world they could trust, love, ex-

pect gratification from, "out there." Perhaps the adolescent needs
to feel that the wonderful venusian sexuality of Marilyn Monroe or
Brigitte Bardot really does exist out there. Perhaps the Southern
gentleman who attacks the murderous Othello or the lady who so
sympathizes with the abused wife in *Look Back in Anger* need to
feel that those things are happening out there, not in themselves.

Artistic distance can break down in more prosaic ways, too. If
the literary work fails to give us the pleasure we expect—if we become bored or find its content discomforting—we loosen our tie to
it. Alternatively, if we become acutely aware of our separate selves
—as by physical discomfort, a loose spring in a theater seat—we
cease to fuse with the work.

Most theaters, fortunately, tend to bind us more tightly into the
drama—because of the presence of others all concentrating on the
play, we become less aware of ourselves. To be part of an audience is
to achieve anonymity; to be the subject of an audience is to be stri-
dently aware of oneself. The audience may be present, as in a theater, or implicit, as when we feel we are part of "the reading public." Reading a printed novel feels quite different from reading a
submitted typescript. The thought of others reading or seeing as
we do licenses our response. They take over some of the functions
of a superego, and, because they constitute so relaxed a superego,
my own ego need not be so self-conscious, so oriented to action as
if they were not there.

In short, our model tells us that the introjection necessary for
full experience of a work depends on two conscious expectations:
first, that the work will please us; second, that we will not have to
act on it. If either expectation is defeated, our fusion with the
work breaks down and we "snap out of it." The audience can
break the dyadic tie to the work if physical or psychic discomfort
becomes too severe. The literary work can break it, too. Our model
helps us to see how tinkering with the introjecting process can lead
to some of the more exotic effects possible in literature.

I am thinking of those novels, like *Tristram Shandy* or *Les Faux-*

Monnayeurs, which are novels about writing the novel which is the novel. In Doris Lessing's *The Golden Notebook,* for example, one of the notebooks tells about a novelist trying to write a novel. A friend asks her to give him the first sentence, and she rattles off the first sentence of *The Golden Notebook* itself. This is, of course, in the theater, the metatheatrical tradition of Pirandello and many of the absurdists. In cinema, there is the *grand guignol* scene of Bergman's *The Magician,* where we cannot tell if the magician's grisly tricks are really tricks or really real. The ending of *Dr. Caligari* raises the question whether what we have seen is real or mad. It is even possible to create such an exotic effect with criticism: a book by Charles Simmons called *Powdered Eggs* includes a supposed review of *Powdered Eggs* in which the reviewer concludes:

> There is even, in the last section of the book, a harsh mock review of the book itself, intended, I imagine, to disarm criticism. Well, it fails entirely. Many is the book reviewer, I suspect, who, like myself, will see in it his own distaste articulated. In fact, I am now quoting word for word from the same mock review.

Such effects are peculiarly unsettling. Why?

They create an uncertainty in us as to whether the supposed fiction we are reading or watching is really a fiction or a reality about a fiction. This is merely an intellectual puzzle, however. These books-within-books and plays-within-plays create a deeper, inner sense of uncertainty, an uncanny feeling such as seeing my reflection in a mirror move and act by itself would produce. Because we fuse with a work of art, to call its reality into question is to question our own. Because these effects make me uncertain as to whether I am confronting a reality or a fiction, something to be or not to be introjected in a primitive way, I find my own position in reality called into question. Have I mixed up fiction and reality as a madman would?

That is inevitably the question all literature raises. In a way, all fictions lead us into worlds as mad as Don Quixote's in which we believe—or do not disbelieve—all manner of impossible things. Yet fiction is much more than madness. We respond in special ways to what it imagines for us. Ultimately, therefore, our introjection hypothesis enables us to specify the special quality of our emotional response to literature and therefore two of its adaptive functions.

As Marion Milner has shown, illusions such as art or play serve the adaptive purpose for children and adults of letting us learn the boundaries between self and not-self.

> We know the boundaries exist but the child does not; in the primal state, it is only gradually and intermittently that he discovers them; and on the way to this he uses play. Later, he keeps his perception of the world from becoming fixed, and no longer capable of growth, by using art, either as artist or audience; and he may also use psychoanalysis. For . . . art and play both link the world of "subjective unreality" and "objective reality," harmoniously fusing the edges but not confusing them. So the developing human being becomes able deliberately to allow illusions about what he is seeing to occur; he allows himself to experience, within the enclosed space-time of the drama or the picture or the story or the analytic hour, a transcending of that common-sense perception which would see a picture as only an attempt at photography, or the analyst as only a present-day person.[45]

And again,

> If one asks, what factors play an essential part in the process of coming to recognize a world that is outside oneself, not one's own creation, there is one that I think has not been much stressed in the literature. . . . It is the capacity of the environment to foster this growth, by providing conditions in which a recurrent partial return to the feeling of being one is possible; and I suggest that the environment does this by the recurrent providing of a framed space and time and a pliable medium, so that, on occasions, it will not be necessary for self-preservation's sake to distinguish clearly between inner and outer, self and not-self.[46]

Heinz Hartmann speaks of "regressive adaptation . . . precisely because of the detour through the archaic." [47] Erik Erikson also relates artistic make-believe to the adaptations achieved by play:

The child's play is the infantile form of the human ability to deal with experience by creating model situations and to master reality by experiment and planning. It is in certain phases of his work that the adult projects past experience into dimensions which seem manageable. In the laboratory, on the stage, and on the drawing board, he relives the past and thus relieves leftover affects; in reconstructing the model situation, he redeems his failures and strengthens his hopes. He anticipates the future from the point of view of a corrected and shared past.[48]

The artist does this for himself directly; he does it for the rest of us to the extent we fuse and commit ourselves to his work.

One of literature's adaptive functions, then, is that it allows us to loosen boundaries—between self and not-self, inner and outer, past, present, and future. In this loosening process, we have emotions of a special tone and kind. If you respond as I do, your feelings as you are involved with a literary work differ somewhat from your feelings toward everyday life. For one thing they seem purer, less messy and confused. For another, feelings (mine anyway) when I am reading, seem in a curious, hard-to-describe way both stronger and weaker than feelings toward the real world.

The introjection model explains both these reactions. As for the purity and clarity of feelings in the literary situation, the sense of appropriateness and completeness, the literary work acts out a psychological process which we introject. That process is the transformation of a central fantasy toward a central meaning. In everyday life, our minds in any given minute may be toying with half a dozen fantasies, transforming none of them toward a meaningful totality. The psychological process we take over from a literary work forces words and events into a far more orderly structure than our ordinary mental processes. Moreover, it orders not only the fantasy it embodies but all the related fantasies which we bring to it when we analogize. In short, we feel the ordering and structuring powers of literature (ultimately, of the writer) as though they were our own.

As for our emotions in the literary situation, they seem weaker because we do not expect to act on them. In an older terminology, we feel, but we do not will. In psychoanalytic terms, we experience affects but, because we do not act on them, we withdraw cathexis from them. We know "it is only a play."

Yet, in another sense, our emotions in the literary situation seem stronger than in everyday life. There, we stress our conscious and intellectual responses. We judge and evaluate events with an eye to acting on them. But within the literary "as if," because consciously we know we need only fantasy in response, we sink down to deeper levels of our mind. The aesthetic stance inhibits our motor activity; it therefore engages our moral and intellectual selves, not in suppressing or judging our deeper feelings, but in accepting and transforming them. Our "rind" of higher ego-functions, our "core" of deeply regressed ego—these make up a richer, longer kind of self than our ordinary one. This is the second great adaptive function of literature: to let us respond in richer, deeper ways than we can to reality. We feel more fully, more profoundly. We bring to the events of a work of literature a much longer range of response, one that alters our very perceptions. A picture of a can of tomatoes acquires a monumental quality when someone puts a frame around it, labels it "art," and so asks us for an "as if." The events in a work of literature seem larger than life, not because they are, but because we are.

Similarly, we make literary events bigger than their apparent selves because we analogize, we bring to the literary work even feelings it did not stimulate, and we ask that it—its form, its plot, its characters—manage feelings for us which are disproportionate to the literary events themselves. In this sense, Coleridge was precisely right when he said, we "transfer from our inward nature a human interest and a semblance of truth sufficient to procure for these shadows of imagination that willing suspension of disbelief for the moment, which constitutes poetic faith."

Not just in literature, though, but in all things toward which we adopt an aesthetic attitude, this "as if," this "willing suspension of disbelief," happens. It is the *sine qua non*, the unvarying precondition for art's mass and stature, art's power to make us not just know but inwardly, richly, deeply experience moral, social, and intellectual meaning. This "as if" comes even before the curtain rises, even before we look at the first line of a poem or story. It is a beginning, and like all beginnings, like basic trust, like Janus, god of beginnings, it has two faces. One is as mad as Don Quixote's: our willingness to accept all kinds of impossible things. But the other side of the "as if" is the face of a larger, wiser self, both deeper and higher—at least for the long moment of a work of art.

4   Form as Defense

Thus far, we have taken three steps toward a psychology of literary response. In the last chapter, we considered the "as if" we bring to literature, our willing suspension of disbelief: it involves a "deepening," that is, in technical terms, a partial, selective, ego-syntonic ego regression, an extension of ego boundaries downward to the level of basic trust. The result is, at the deepest level of response, a kind of fusion or introjection based on oral wishes to incorporate, so that what goes on at a fairly primitive level in the literary work feels as though it is going on within us or, more exactly, not outside us.

Second, we have considered what things in fact might be going on at a fairly primitive level in the literary work: various fantasies, oral, anal, and phallic, that are common in our culture; also various defensive modes of handling those fantasies. Most basic to the model, we have considered literary meaning and found it a dynamic process of transformation: a literary work means by reworking those rather unsavory wishful or fearful fantasies at its heart into social, moral, or intellectual themes which are consciously satisfying to the ego and unconsciously satisfying to the deep wishes being acted out by the literary work. Further, because of our "as if," these transformations—in their early stages or deeper levels—take place not just in the literary work, but also in us who have introjected them:

transformation "out there" is felt as transformation "in here."

Obviously, our next step should be to look at the ways literary works handle the unconscious fantasies at their nucleus so as to achieve this transformation. At this point, however, our tidy, step-by-step investigation runs into a thicket, for, as we shall see in subsequent chapters, virtually all the familiar entities of literature—plot, character, and form—serve at least partly as defensive modifications of unconscious content. For example, the Wife of Bath's Tale builds on a fearful fantasy of phallic wounding leading to helplessness, impotency, in general, loss. The plot handles this fear by a regression to an earlier, oral position of mutual trust. The *Playboy* joke handles a similar fear of loss by just the opposite maneuver: an abrupt return to reality serves as reassurance by cancelling out a fearful oedipal fantasy that had replaced a trusting and dependency. What both these plots have in common, though, is that each looks very like a defense or adaptation: regression in Chaucer's story; reality-testing in *Playboy*'s.

From a psychological point of view, however, the terms "defense" or "adaptation" do not quite fit. We have already seen that this kind of transformation does not correspond exactly to a defense, for a defense is an unconscious mechanism of the ego that comes into play automatically at a signal of danger. The plot in a story does serve as a way of handling dangers; but it is not unconscious, nor is it automatic.

By contrast, an adaptation is more autonomous than automatic and goes beyond the mere resolution of conflicts toward progressive, constructive, and maturational mastery of drives. A plot resembles adaptation in being more autonomous than automatic, but there is no guarantee that a plot—or any other transformational device in literature—moves in the direction of maturation. The plot and theme of the Wife of Bath's Tale, for instance, do not resolve the phallic conflict and move toward further growth. Rather, they ask us to regress to an earlier position and give up phallic demands. To be sure, a story's act of meaning is adaptive, for meaning transforms primitive fantasies toward social, moral, and intellectual (ego-syntonic) themes. But the particular devices that intricately combine to make this transformation (symbolization, reversal, splitting, and so on) are probably in themselves not adaptive.

In short, to describe psychologically the combination of agents of transformation in a literary work, we need a generic psychological term that does not exist: for something that is not necessarily in and of itself adaptive, but can add up to a kind of adaptation; for something that looks like such well-known defenses as regression, isolation, reversal, and the like, although it is not an unconscious, automatic psychic mechanism like them but rather an explicit handling of an implicit fantasy. Possibly we could speak of "defensive mastery" or an "adaptive strategy" or a defense "maneuver" instead of a defense "mechanism." But these are clumsy. I shall continue to speak simply of "defense," and ask you to remember that I mean something that looks quite like particular well-known unconscious defenses, but which occurs explicitly in the literary work—as plot, character, or form.

Form—the word reminds us that terminology is not much better in literature than in psychology. Simon O. Lesser has defined form in the broad sense as "the whole group of devices used to structure and communicate expressive content," and that is probably as good a definition as there is. In the next chapter, I shall deal with verbal form, here, with form in a larger sense: form as the ordering and structuring of parts.

The distinction between form and content is, of course, more honored in the breach than the observance. Yet we can certainly say form includes at least the ordering of the parts of a literary work, the way one line or image follows upon another. For form in this sense, there is one particularly useful test case—a short passage that a great many people feel comprises an ordered lyric, and that at least one distinguished poet-critic finds a disordered and unformed excerpt.

In *Macbeth*, one speech stands out over all the others as a setpiece to be mouthed in the beardless lips and cracked tenors of thousands of adolescents whom teachers will make memorize it. It is the one speech in *Macbeth* which every actor must dread, for his audience will lean over collectively to its neighbor and, to show its erudition, whisper the first three lines in unison with his solo. It is, of course,

> Tomorrow, and tomorrow, and tomorrow
> Creeps in this petty pace from day to day
> To the last syllable of recorded time.
> And all our yesterdays have lighted fools
> The way to dusty death. Out, out, brief candle—
> Life's but a walking shadow, a poor player
> That struts and frets his hour upon the stage
> And then is heard no more. It is a tale
> Told by an idiot, full of sound and fury,
> Signifying nothing.

Famous and brilliant as it is, Mr. John Crowe Ransom in *The World's Body* complains of it. The speech moves illogically from metaphor to metaphor, he says, and while such catachreses may be all very well for a speech presenting the turgid state of mind of a character in a play, they will not do in a separate poem, even a metaphysical poem:

> It is a very fine speech. But instead of presenting a figure systematically it presents a procession or flight of figures. The tomorrows creep along till they have crept far enough, and bring up against—what? A syllable; remarkable barrier. After the tomorrows, in the whirling sub-logical mind of this harried speaker, the yesterdays, by the suggestion which prompts antithesis; and, at a venture, he remarks that what they did was to light fools to their death. (I do not know why dusty death; it is an odd but winning detail.) But speaking now of lights, out with this one, a mere candle! Lights also imply shadows, and suggest that life is a walking shadow. Then the lights lead to the torches of the theatre, and the walking shadow becomes a strutting player, who after an hour will be heard no more. Finally, since one thing leads to another, we may as well make life into the thing the player says, the story whose sound and fury have no meaning. . . . Dramatically, this speech may be both natural and powerful; so I am told. Metaphysically, it is nothing.[1]

In effect, Mr. Ransom is questioning the form of the speech or its structure, anyway, the ordering of its parts. He is saying that the discontinuities of the speech are all right as part of the continuous flow of a play, but the speech does not have the logic and closure that will make it stand by itself as a separate poem.

But then what about all those people (including me) who take pleasure in the "tomorrow" speech as a set-piece or separate poem? Clearly, for us, the speech has a logic and coherence that it does not have for Mr. Ransom. The trouble is, I think, that he is looking at the text alone and applying to it criteria of logic and consistency. He is looking at the speech in the problem-solving terms of secondary-process thought. But evidently, to judge from the fact that even fairly sophisticated readers can accept the "tomorrow" speech as an isolable poem, the form of the speech (the feeling of completeness it gives) comes from some "gut" sense of unconscious or preconscious logic. We need to supplement Mr. Ransom's look at the form in the text by looking at form from the other end of the literary transaction: form as what shapes our response to the words on the page rather than form as simply the objective sequence and pattern of the words by themselves.

Surely it is impossible, is it not, to look only at the words on the page without modifying them by one's own perceptual matrices? Literature is an objective text, but also a subjective experience. Form, too, is both objective and subjective; we can see it in the text, but form only comes alive as it shapes our response. To look at form in this sense, then, we need to look first at the way the poem makes us feel. But, of course, when we do, we confront our old *bête-noire:* the problem of subjective and objective. The text is fixed, but people respond to it in rather widely varying ways— just as some people will laugh at a joke and others won't. The best the critic can do, then, is consult within himself, articulate as best he can his own feelings and the reasons for them, then look for what in the poem seems to be shaping that response. If he can find form in that sense—objectively—he can then (perhaps) understand the subjective reactions of others who bring to the poem other personalities, other experiences, traits, or needs.

To me, the passage brings a tremendous feeling of reassurance and peace, admittedly a gloomy sort of peace, but peace nonetheless. The reaction is perhaps odd, for the passage is, after all, one of the great statements of disillusionment, grief, and frustration in the language. The reaction is odd, too, if the passage is an unsystematic flight of figures—for how could a jumble of images be expected to give a feeling of peace?

The images of the passage seem to ask me, in a way, that question which so many parts of *Macbeth* ask, What is a man? Many of the key words bring up such basic human skills as walking and talking: "Creeps," "walking," "struts," "syllable," being "heard," "a tale," "Signifying." Other images deal with less basic skills, extinguishing a candle, telling time, or play-acting. Like these skills, the personages of the passage hover between child and adult: an idiot, a poor player, a walking shadow, fools.

The passage has also a curious vagueness of image, the odd metonymies Mr. Ransom notes, in which tomorrow creeps, yesterdays are a candle, and life is an actor. In effect, against such big, vague words as "tomorrow," "yesterdays," or "life," the similes set clear, vivid images: the candle, the player, the idiot, his babblings full of sound and fury. But these images themselves go out, become silent, signify nothing. Both in appearance and duration, they, too, seem to be surrounded by an empty, silent space. In other words, my response moves from blankness to concreteness to blankness again. The form lets an image appear, then erases it. If we think of this form as being like a defense, we would call it "doing-and-undoing" or "denial by exaggeration." * But what is this undoing operating against? What is the "unconscious content" of the images in the poem? And are they really as incoherent as Ransom says?

Clearly, they are not a jumble once I look at them as expressing an unconscious, that is, infantile, fantasy. If I look at the images

---

* "*Denial by exaggeration:* a particular and often encountered response which exactly exaggerates, often in a caricatured way, the element which is laden with anxiety, to the point that it becomes apparently 'foolish' and unreal." "*Undoing:* balancing or canceling out an unacceptable action, affect, or thought by a subsequent action, affect, or thought in contradictory terms." [2]

from a child's point of view, they make a perfect progression. The tomorrows of the opening line and the yesterdays of the fourth place me, as it were, at night, creeping between tomorrow and yesterday. They lead me quite naturally to the next image, lighting my way to bed and putting out the candle, but "dusty death" replaces the normal event of sleep. This is, of course, a common childhood fear that sleep will equal death (as in the prayer, "Now I lay me down to sleep . . . Should I die before I wake"). It is odd, though, to find it expressed in the poem so as to give a feeling of peace and reassurance. Then suddenly, the image shifts to a walking shadow (a figure seen, so to speak, against the light from another room), then to the stage! This indeed seems a jump in imagery, from going to bed to seeing a shadow to watching and hearing a play, but the shift is not at all odd if we consider the play-acting and the tale as reminding me of dreams or other imaginings.

In effect, the unconscious content leads me to bed for the night, a kind of regression, and prepares me for imaginings. Curiously, though, that shift from going to bed to the stage-play is accompanied by a shift from visual images (the candle, the walking shadow) to aural: a strutting and fretting which is *heard* no more, a tale full of *sound* and fury which signifies nothing. There is thus also a shift from the direct experience of life—the immediacy of "Creeps" and "Out, out"—to merely being told about something. Similarly, the days of the first five lines give way to night, a night vivid but at the same time distanced as dream, stage-play, or tale, a night, in other words, of imaginings. There is still a third shift in the imagery: the day was associated with creeping or a syllable, rudimentary skills, while the night is marked by complex adult activities, telling a tale or play-acting.

The images act out a going to bed followed by frightening imaginings associated with adult activities, namely, a stage play. Psychoanalysis deals with subjective states; generalizations are therefore difficult. Nevertheless, there is a well-documented and well-nigh universal unconscious meaning to dreams and fantasies of watching

stage performances: they signify a child's fantasies of watching what
he takes to be the sadistic, bloody violence of his parents in
the struggle of love ending in a death-like sleep.[3] So the poem ends
in the blankness of "no more," "nothing." So, too, the poem distances the stage-play as sound rather than sight. Similarly, the
phrase, "Out, out, brief candle," becomes ambiguous if we consider possible phallic symbolism: it may be a command to withdraw the penis concealed in the sexual act or detumescent after.
"Walking" distances sexual activity into another kind of erect action.

In short, if we translate the poem into terms of impulse and defense, the impulse is bifold: to see but not to see that exciting but
frightening performance. The poem defends against the wish to see
by distancing the performance into sound, "a tale" to be "heard,"
and it symbolizes the watched sexual act into a more or less respectable adult activity: watching a play. The poem deals with the wish
not to see by, indeed, not seeing the performance but hearing it,
and even more, by its fundamental strategy of denial: the player
"is heard no more"; he signifies "nothing."

Even before we get the image of the stage, the poem reassures us
with that word that Mr. Ransom singled out as "an odd but winning detail"—"*dusty* death." To me, at least, "dusty" connotes
something tactile but undisturbed, silent, unmoved for a long time.
In effect, the line tells me that though I (or "fools") are lit to
bed, I will find the place unmoving, peaceful, even if I (or they)
have to be dead to render it so.

With this awareness of the basic pattern of impulse and defense,
we are now in a position to say why these nine and a half lines
should stand out as a set-piece over other, perhaps finer passages. It
is a little odd, in fact, that they should do so, for on the conscious
level the passage preaches a Housmanesque message of gloom
which, I suppose, few of us would greet with enthusiasm. But the
popularity of the passage is not at all odd when we recognize its
unconscious appeal: it hooks its message of gloom to a tremendous
and splendid reassurance.

On the conscious level, the passage says all the tensions of our yesterdays and tomorrows, our vast stretches of adult life are trivia, creeping, fools' candles, a tale told by an idiot, in short, childishness of the most tedious kind. Days just come and go. But on the unconscious level, there is a wish-fulfilling reversal: *nights* just come and go. The tense, terrible sexual imaginings of the night, the sound and fury, the strutting of the parent, these are just that, imaginings—and those who went to bed are fools, the player is poor, the tale is an idiot's, it all signifies nothing. "Out, out."

The conscious content, the days, tend to be concentrated in the first four lines and in the intellectual and abstract words. The unconscious content, the nighttime imaginings, occur in the vivid images, mostly in the second half. The two tensions are resolved in the final, flat "signifying nothing." I begin the passage with a tension on the conscious level; I dip, as it were, into another tension of unconscious fears and horrible imaginings; and I come up again with "no more," "nothing." I have made a magnificent denial—I have taken those aspects of parents, adults, most challenging and terrifying to the child-in-me, and I have said they are themselves childishness, the creations of an actor or an idiot, signifying nothing. I paved the way for this childish denial by letting the passage first reverse my patently unrealistic, unconscious wish—gloomily I say at a conscious level that adult life, the life of the parent-in-me, is like the slowest, most helpless progress of a child in creeping and syllables that an adult can imagine. The passage lets me feel in two different ways that adult life is not violent, passionate, sexual. In short, the passage appeals because its form accomplishes the doing and undoing of its content: the imagining of adults in nighttime "play."

This reading of the fantasy content and its management, farfetched as it may seem, gets confirmation from other critics' more conventional readings. Often, one can hear in a critic's words the faintest echoes of a response to the unconscious content or the defenses in the work he is talking about. Thus Lascelles Abercrombie writes:

> There is no depth below that; that is the bottom. . . . There
> is no meaning anywhere: that is the final disaster; death is noth-
> ing after that. And precisely by laying hold of this and relishing
> its fearfulness to the utmost, Macbeth's personality towers into
> its loftiest grandeur. Misfortune and personality have been until
> this a continual discord: but now each has reached its per-
> fection and they unite.[4]

I can hear faint echoes of a fantasy about a puzzling and fearful
sexual clash by night in Abercrombie's words about meaningless
bottoms with death coming after or a phrasing like, After a "con-
tinual discord," "each has reached its perfection and they unite."
Defensively, Abercrombie uses upright imagery, Macbeth's personality towering into loftiest grandeur, as an assertion of self against
the "fearfulness," just as the passage itself uses "struts" or "walking." Similarly, Hardin Craig uses primal scene imagery when he
says, "Even the death of *the wife bound to him in virtue and in
crime* moves him scarcely more than *any casual, dark event*" (italics mine).[5] Mark Van Doren concludes, "The future is a limitless
desert of tomorrows," [6] and I hear in his words the passage's use of
days as a defense against nights. Elder Olson comments:

> Macbeth's despair is so complete that he cannot imagine any
> life as different from his own; therefore life is a mere shadow,
> though it seems to be real, and all action is only the motion of
> a shadow. It is worse than that; for *we* think our actions mean-
> ingful and real (and there the horror lies) whereas we are only
> players moving briefly in a mockery of life and action, to an
> eventual silence. It is worse even than that: a play has a story
> with meaning behind it; whereas life is a tale meaningless in it-
> self, accompanied by wild and meaningless sounds and gestures.
> And it is hope and tomorrow and hereafter that have deceived
> us into thinking otherwise.[7]

Like the others, he reflects the unconscious symbolism of the
primal scene in phrasings like "wild and meaningless sounds" or
"all action is the motion of a shadow." He half-consciously recognizes the defensive use of "tomorrow and hereafter" to deceive "us
into thinking otherwise." Further, his comment shows an aware-

ness of the use of the fictitiousness of a play as a way of denying the "moving briefly in a mockery of . . . action to an eventual silence."

If the inference of a primal scene fantasy at the core of the passage is correct, then we can draw three conclusions. First, the images and metaphors of the passage are not, as Mr. Ransom claims, mixed. On the contrary, if we look in them for words that will arouse an unconscious fantasy in us, we find they are quite logical and coherent. The poem is a familiar handling of a familiar fantasy: perceiving and denying the primal scene. Second, as we would expect (from Chapter 1), the intellectual "meaning" of the passage—the acceptance of disillusionment—represents a kind of sublimation of its primitive content: recognizing but denying the importance of nighttime sights. (The word "dis*illusion*ment" was artfully chosen.) Third, we have seen, at least in a preliminary way, how form (here, the sequence or ordering of content) shapes a response by controlling what we are aware of at any given moment. In this poem, the ordering of the images acts like the defense of denial or, perhaps, doing and undoing. It permits me to glimpse the "play" at night, but then it erases what I saw, denies its significance, and undoes its effect. The syllables do become in Mr. Ransom's phrase, a "remarkable barrier."

I can then guess the reasons Mr. Ransom finds the passage jumbled: because he finds the denials and symbolizations unsatisfactory as form (or defense) and asks instead for system and logic (as in the ballad progressions of much of his own poetry). One can hypothesize that logic rather than denial suits Mr. Ransom's own patterns of defense. Alternatively, one might guess that primal scene fantasies are less available or less threatening to him. But one can only guess: to know, we would have to know unseemly things about Mr. Ransom's personality, specifically, what fantasies and defenses he favors. At least we know, though, what fantasies and defenses to look for as links between this poem and his or any other reader's personality.

At least we know, too, that the sequencing of content acts out something like a defense for the reader. But form has other functions, particularly when we use the word "structure." Then, I take it, we mean there is a pattern in the ordering of materials, as when a play regularly alternates between two plots or a poem between two kinds of speaking. Such a poem is "Dover Beach." [8]

> The sea is calm to-night.
> The tide is full, the moon lies fair
> Upon the straits;—on the French coast the light
> Gleams and is gone; the cliffs of England stand,
> Glimmering and vast, out in the tranquil bay.   5
> Come to the window, sweet is the night-air!
> Only, from the long line of spray
> Where the sea meets the moon-blanch'd land,
> Listen! you hear the grating roar
> Of pebbles which the waves draw back, and fling,   10
> At their return, up the high strand,
> Begin, and cease, and then again begin,
> With tremulous cadence slow, and bring
> The eternal note of sadness in.
>
> Sophocles long ago   15
> Heard it on the Ægæan, and it brought
> Into his mind the turbid ebb and flow
> Of human misery; we
> Find also in the sound a thought,
> Hearing it by this distant northern sea.   20
>
> The Sea of Faith
> Was once, too, at the full, and round earth's shore
> Lay like the folds of a bright girdle furl'd.
> But now I only hear
> Its melancholy, long, withdrawing roar,   25
> Retreating, to the breath
> Of the night-wind, down the vast edges drear
> And naked shingles of the world.
>
> Ah, love, let us be true
> To one another! for the world, which seems   30

To lie before us like a land of dreams,
So various, so beautiful, so new,
Hath really neither joy, nor love, nor light,
Nor certitude, nor peace, nor help for pain;
And we are here as on a darkling plain   35
Swept with confused alarms of struggle and flight,
Where ignorant armies clash by night.*

"Dover Beach," according to *The Case for Poetry*, is the most widely reprinted poem in the language; certainly, it seems to be the most widely explicated. We can abbreviate, though, by taking from the fifteen or so explications of the poem just four points which bear on its structure.[10]

First, all the explicators see the poem as profoundly dualistic, as contrasting the tranquil sea and the restless speaker; or the sea as representing nature and the land, the dry, critical mind (with pun intended); or, more simply, illusion and reality. Second, the point of misery and conflict comes right at the edge or mingling of these two contrasted areas of experience. Third, as a part of this dualism, each of the four stanzas itself divides sharply into two parts, corresponding to the dualistic theme. Fourth, for all but stanza two, these two halves—illusion and reality, if you will—appeal to different senses: the first, hopeful half comes in images of sight; the disillusioning second half comes in images of sound.

In general, the poem moves back and forth between here and there, past and present, land and sea, love and battle, but most importantly, between sweet sight and disillusioning sound, between appearance and reality. What informs the poem as a whole is an attempt to re-create in a personal relationship the sweet sight of stability and permanence which the harsh sound of the actual ebb and flow of reality negates.

* The reference to Sophocles in the second stanza, all commentators agree, is rather vague, but it seems quite clear that for the final image Arnold had in mind the episode in Book VII of Thucydides where, during the ill-fated Sicilian expedition, the Athenian troops became confused during the night battle at Epipolae. The enemy learned their password, and the Athenians went down to disastrous defeat.[9]

To look at the poem and its form psychoanalytically, however, we need to look not only at the text by itself, but also, as we did with the "tomorrow" speech, at our subjective experience of the poem. Naturally, such experiences will vary (our constant problem in this book is subjective and objective). Even so, if I can discover by analyzing my own reaction the drives and fantasies the poem stirs up in me and the defensive maneuvers the poem acts out for dealing with those drives, then I can understand the different reactions of others for whom those fantasies and defenses are less congenial or adequate—as in the "tomorrow" speech.

To me, "Dover Beach" is a tremendously peaceful, gently melancholy poem. It gives me a feeling of almost sensual satisfaction, surprisingly, since "Dover Beach" is a poem at least partly about disillusionment, loss of faith, despair. Why should such a poem seem peaceful or satisfying? Because, I think, the poem offers such a heavy, massive set of defenses.

We begin with the exquisite description of the seascape in which everything is vast, tranquil, calm—any disturbance in that calmness, such as the word "to-night" in the first line, the appearance and disappearance of the light from France, is immediately balanced and corrected. Only after this strong reassurance does Arnold give us a stronger disturbance, the eternal note of sadness—and immediately, he flees in space and time to Sophocles and the Ægæan; he turns the disturbing thought into literature and far-off, ancient literature at that. And thus defended, he can permit the disturbance to come back again: "We / Find also in the sound a thought," but even as he returns to the here and now, he defends again. He turns the feeling of disturbance into an intellectual, symbolic, metaphorical statement in a line that never fails to jar me by its severely schematic and allegorical quality, "The Sea of Faith." Defended again, he can again return to the disturbing sound, and in the most pathetic lines of the poem he lets it roll off the edge of the earth in long, slow vowels. In the last stanza, he brings in the major defense of the poem, "Ah, love, let us be true / To one another." He offers us as defense a retreat into a personal relationship of constancy with another person, and so defended he can give us the final, terrible image of the ignorant armies that clash by night. In short, the poem gives me this tranquility because I am over-protected; because Arnold has offered me strong defenses against the disturbance the poem deals with—even before he reveals the disturbance itself in the final lines.

Further, that disturbance itself is never very clearly presented. It is described obliquely, by negatives. For example, the sea is calm "to-night"—and the "to-night" acts as a qualification: there are other nights when the sea is not calm, but we do not see them. The window in line six comes as something of a surprise—it is as though the poet were reaching back for his companion even as he reaches out to take in the seascape, a special form of the dualism that pervades the poem. But the disturbance is dim and oblique. We do not see the room or the person addressed, only the window facing away from them. The "grating roar" of the pebbles is humanized and softened into music: "cadence" and "note." "The turbid ebb and flow of human misery" seems metaphorized, distanced, more than a little vague.

The world, we are told, seems like a land of dreams and is not, but what it is we are not told. Faith is gone, and while most critics seem to assume Arnold's "Faith" means religious faith, that, it seems to me, is only one of its many meanings. The word "Faith" is not explained until the last stanza, and then only explained by what is missing: the ability to clothe the world with joy and love and light, to find in the world certitude, peace, and help for pain. But the poem does not tell us what the world is like without these things, except metaphorically, in the image of the ignorant armies. In other words, the poem offers us not only massive defenses, but also a specific line of defense: we do not see the disturbance itself; we only see what it is not.

There is a second specific line of defense. This poem sees and hears intensely; it gives us pleasure through what we see and hear, but at the same time the seeing and hearing operate defensively. Often, in life, to see and hear one thing intensely may serve to avoid seeing and hearing something else. In this poem, we look and listen to the sea, the shingle, to Sophocles—what are we not looking at? What is being hidden from us that we are curious about, that we would like to see? I trust you will not think me irreverent if I remind you that this is a poem at least partly about a pair of lovers together at night. As for myself, I am curious as to what they are up to, but the poem tells me very little, for only six of its thirty-seven lines deal directly with the girl; and three of those six are so general they could refer to all mankind.

Again, then, the poem shows us something indirectly, defensively, by showing us what it is not. The particular here-and-now relationship between the poet and the girl substitutes for the always-and-everywhere condition of all mankind: let us be true to one another for the world proved false to me. The poem works by a double negative. We know of the poet's wished-for relationship with the girl only that it must be what his relationship with the world at large is not.

What, then, is this world which the girl must replace? As the explicators point out, it is a world rather sharply divided into two aspects roughly corresponding to illusion and reality or, in the terms of the poem itself, the *sight* of a bright, calm seascape representing a world without faith and the *sound* of agitated pebbles representing a world without faith. Consider, for a moment, the two senses, sight and hearing. Why do we speak of "feasting" one's eyes or "devouring" with a look? Why do we speak of "the voice" of conscience or of God as "the word"?

"Dover Beach" taps the earliest experience of our two major senses. Sight the child comes to first. As early as the third month of life, a baby can recognize a human face as such. By the fourth or fifth month he can distinguish the face of the person who feeds and fondles him from other faces. Sight becomes linked in our minds with being fed, with a nurturing mother. Fenichel suggests as a formula, "I want what I see to enter me." [11]

Thus, for example, in "Dover Beach," the strong sight images of the first five lines lead to a demand that a woman come, a taste image ("sweet"), and even, if we identify kinaesthetically with the poet, an inhaling of that sweet night air. In a crude, symbolic way, the cliffs are breasts, "glimmering and vast"; the sea and air are the nurturing fluids, "full," "fair," and "calm." * They are seen, for, in infancy, sight becomes associated with a taking in, specifically a taking in from a mother in whom we have faith, whom we expect will give us joy, love, light, certitude, peace, help for pain. Our first disillusionment in life comes as that nurturing figure fails to stand calm, full, fair, vast, tranquil, always there, but instead retreats, withdraws, ebbs and flows. And the poem makes us hear this withdrawal.

Our important experience with hearing comes later than seeing. Not until we begin to understand words does hearing begin to convey as much to us as sight, and it seems to be in the nature of things that a good deal of what the one- or two-year old child hears is—"Don't." We experience sound as a distancing from a parent, often a corrective, not something we anticipate and expect, but something we must willy-nilly put up with, since we cannot shut our ears as we can our eyes. In "Dover Beach," then, what the poet wishes for from the world, but knows will not come, is the kind of fidelity, trust, "Faith," or gratification a child associates with the sight of his mother, but the sound the poet hears routs his expectations. And the poem, by associating sight with the world as we wish and hope it would be, sound as a corrector of that wish, finds in us a responsive note, for this has been part of our experience, too.

But what, specifically, might the harsh sound of grating pebbles bring to our minds, particularly as Arnold describes it in the poem? For one thing, as the explicators show, the point of misery and conflict seems to come right at the joining or mingling of land and sea. For another, the disturbance seems to lie in its very periodicity, its rhythm. The opening seascape is very solidly there, calm, full, tranquil—"the cliffs of England *stand*" (and the internal rhyme

---

* There is some confirmation for this view in that line 10 in Arnold's first version read, "Of pebbles which the waves suck back & fling." [12]

demands heavy stress). The disturbance, however, is an ebb and flow, a withdrawing, a retreat, a being drawn back and flung up; the waves "Begin, and cease, and then again begin." The sound suggests the coming and going of something that should always be there. Slowly, though, what was simply a harsh, rhythmical sound gains other overtones. The bright girdle is withdrawn and we are left with "naked shingles." The world does not "lie before us like a land of dreams." Rather, the "Begin, and cease, and then again begin" has become a naked clash by night.

The poem is evoking in me, at least, and perhaps in many readers, primitive feelings about "things that go bump in the night," that they are disturbing, but exciting at the same time. As in the "tomorrow" speech, there is a well-nigh universal sexual symbolism in this heard-but-not-seen, naked fighting by night. This is one way Arnold's poem turns our experience of disillusionment or despair into satisfaction, namely, through the covert gratification we get from this final primal scene fantasy. Arnold is talking about hearing a sexual "clash by night," just as children fantasy sex as fight. In fact (it has been suggested to me), the "darkling plain" may evoke in us thoughts of a bed, the "struggle" a man's active role in the sexual act, and the "flight" a woman's more passive situation (perhaps even that a wish that she would be in "flight" rather than lying there). Unlike the "tomorrow" speech, the image here operates defensively. As elsewhere in the poem, the image deflects our attention from a pair of lovers in a sexual situation and sublimates it into a distant, literary, and moral experience, a darkling plain from Thucydides.

The conventional explicators have found some logic underlying that final startling image: a logical development from brightness to darkness, from the pebble beach to the darkling plain. Ordinary explication, however, offers little basis for the armies, while psychological explication offers considerable. The poem begins with a world which is very solidly there, a world which is seen, a world which is invested with a faith like a child's trust in the sight of his nurturing mother. The poem moves into sound, to the later, harsher sense and with it the sounds of withdrawal and retreat. Thus, the sound of the ocean shifts from the rhythm of waves to the more permanent, even geological, withdrawal of the "Sea of Faith." The feeling is one of permanent decay, a sense of harsh reality akin to a child's growing and inevitable knowledge that his mother does not exist for him alone. She has an adult life, wishes of her own, which cause her to go away from him and come back, retreat and withdraw.

The final image brings in a still stronger feeling of rhythmic withdrawal, a child's excited but frightened vague awareness. That other, separate adult life has a naked, nighttime, rhythmic sound. It does not lie there like a land of dreams—rather, it is violent, passionate, brutal; the bright girdle is withdrawn and bodies clash by night.

Roughly, we could say that the lovely appearances seen in the poem, the moonlight, the cliffs of England, the stillness, correspond to a faith in a mother. The harsh sounds of withdrawal then heard correspond to the disillusioning knowledge first, of her withdrawal, then of her relationship with the father, he expressed perhaps as Sophocles or, covertly, Thucydides (for Arnold's father did edit Thucydides). In the manner of a dream, the two individuals hidden in the poem, a father and mother, are disguised as two multitudes, "armies" and they, usually all-seeing, all-wise, become in the violent moment of passion, "ignorant."

M. Bonnerot offers a curious confirmation of the reading here suggested, that the sea in "Dover Beach" evokes feelings like those toward a nurturing mother. Immediately after his commentary on the poem, he quotes (free associates to?) the following from Arnold's *God and the Bible:* "Only when one is young and headstrong can one thus prefer bravado to experience, can one stand by the Sea of Time, and instead of listening to the solemn and rhythmical beat of its waves, choose to fill the air with one's own whoopings to start the echo." It is not too difficult to hear under Arnold's "whoopings" something like a child's anguished howls to prevent his mother's withdrawal or bring her back ("start the

echo") or replace the void she leaves ("fill the air"). There is further confirmation in Arnold's letter to Clough of 29 September
1848, where he describes himself as "one who looks upon water
as the Mediator between the inanimate and man."

But how does form or structure turn this disturbing fantasy of a
mother's withdrawal into a pleasurable experience? So far, we have
considered the fantasy level of the poem, and we have noted the
defenses the poem uses: the flight to Sophocles, symbolic disguise,
intellectualization, most important, division—keeping a sharp
difference between the seen appearance and the heard reality:
hence, the dual, sight-sound structure of the four stanzas. In
general, the poem defends before it presents its disturbance, and
we do not see that disturbance—we only see what it is not. Similarly, we do not see the relationship between the lovers; we see
only what it should not be. Such defenses, however, can only prevent unpleasure—how does the poem give us pleasure and create a
satisfying, rounded experience?

The pleasure lies in that aspect of the poem that the commentators almost without exception ignore (thus proving the success of
Arnold's defensive maneuvers). Let me remind you again that this
is a poem that talks about a man and a woman in love and alone
together at night. Yet how oddly and how brilliantly the poem
handles the stationing of its speaker!

For the first five lines, we have only the vaguest inkling where he
is: looking at a seascape near Dover. Then, in line six, we suddenly
learn, first, that he is indoors or near a window; second, that there
is someone with him, someone whom he wishes to take in what he
is taking in. Yet the poem does nothing more with this sudden
placing. Instead, the curiosity it arouses, the faint feeling of disturbance, is displaced onto the sound heard in the lines after line six.
The sequence makes us feel the sound as disturbing and compli-
cating the scene; it also associates the companion with the sound—
"Listen! *you* hear the grating roar . . ."

The next two stanzas do little more with stationing. Stanza two places the speaker in space—by showing us where he is not, the Ægæan; then, it places him by "a distant northern sea," where we already knew he was. The "we" of line eighteen has all the ambiguities of the editorial "we"—it could be the poet as a public speaker; the poet and his companion; the poet and all his contemporaries.

Stanza three places the poet in time, again, negatively: not "once" when the Sea of Faith was full, but "now"—again, something a bit vague and something we already knew. But stanza three splits intellectual from unconscious significance more drastically than stanzas one and two, considerably sharpening the significance of "the grating roar of pebbles" which had been rather vague up till now: "the eternal note of sadness," "the sound." Now we learn it all has to do with the Sea of Faith—on an intellectual level—and at a less conscious level, with the withdrawing of a girdle, a roar, a breath at night, and nakedness. But this sharpening and knowledge comes to the poet alone: "I only hear . . ." His companion now does not.

Abruptly, stanza four begins with something new again—that the poet is in love with his companion (who did not hear the sexual undertones of stanza three). Their relationship emerges from the rest of the poem like shadowy figures materializing, until, at last, only two lines from the close, the poem firmly stations the poet and his love: "And we are here." Even here, though, there is some blurring, for the "we" could be the editorial we of stanza two as well as the we of you-and-I. And, further, we are no sooner "here" than we are there, metaphorically flown by "as" to the darkling plain swept by ignorant armies.

In short, the stationing of the poet and his love involves a good deal of shifting and ambiguity. As always in this poem, it is telling us what things are obliquely, by telling us what they are not. The ambiguity about where the poet and his love are suggests we look to see where they are in another, more formal sense—and there, indeed, we can locate them quite precisely: they are right there in lines six, nine, eighteen, twenty-four, twenty-nine, and thirty-five.

They occur precisely at the points of division in the poem where it moves from sight to sound, from appearance to reality, or, in stanza two, from a far-off, literary Sophocles to the here and now of "we" by the northern sea.

To put this structure another way, the lovers come between the two kinds of experience the poem creates. This is the importance of the clause, "And we are here," which makes us feel the closure and completeness of the poem. Read over the last lines with variant phrasings to see the importance of that statement:

> . . . nor peace, nor help for pain;
> And the world is, as on a darkling plain
> Swept with confused alarms of struggle and flight,
> Where ignorant armies clash by night.

> . . . nor peace, nor help for pain;
> And I am here, as on a darkling plain
> Swept with confused alarms of struggle and flight,
> Where ignorant armies clash by night.

For me, the poem needs the finality both of being *here* and of being *we*, for "And we are here" is the poem's ultimate defense.

To see why, we need to recapitulate. Stanza one opened with sight, taken as reassuring, constant, full, and it closed with sound sensed as a kind of corruption penetrating the fair sight. Stanzas two and three fled this conflict both in time and space, and fled it in another way through the poet's universalizing his feelings, spreading them over all time, all space, all peoples. And yet this defense left him disillusioned, and he turned at the opening of stanza four to the girl as a way of dealing with the problem.

He begins by saying, "Ah, love, let us be true / To one another," and "true" is the key word. He wants to re-create in his relationship with her the lost sense of faith; he wants her to be "true," not to withdraw as the earlier sight (of a woman) had done. "True" also suggests that the relationship of the two, the poet and his love, will not be like the relationship of the two halves of the world as he sees them.

The last stanza then moves into a series of lists that act out the poet's feeling toward the world that has failed him, that though it seems

> To lie before us like a land of dreams,
> So various, so beautiful, so new,

it

> Hath really neither joy, nor love, nor light,
> Nor certitude, nor peace, nor help for pain.

The lists give us the first stanza's feeling of inclusiveness, of taking it all in, but the lists are negative, first "neither," then "nor," "nor," "nor"—echoing the twice-mentioned "roar." One disturbing sound in the world corrupts the land of dreams, negates all the things the poet wants to take in, and he in turn denies all the world.

Then, in the key line, "And we are here," the poet turns back to the girl. "We are here," solidly, constantly, silently, as the seascape was in stanza one, and we are quite distinctly separate from what conflicts with that solid, constant trust—the ignorant armies with their sexual undertones. They are quite distinctly not "here" for they are distanced from "we" by "as," that is, by metaphor and by literary reference. That "we are here" stands firmly between the "land of dreams" corrupted by a rhythmic, nighttime sound and that confusing, struggling sound itself, the "clash by night." "And we are here" thus does at least three things by its formal placement: it prevents the "clash by night" and the "land of dreams" from mingling; it isolates the lovers as a couple from the "confused alarms" as the "I only hear" of stanza three did; it turns away from the passive experience of hearing that nighttime sound into the active experience of being "here" (and being "true"). Paradoxically, as Theodore Morrison pointed out many years ago, the poem uses love precisely to prevent the disillusionment involved in a knowledge of sexuality.[13] "The ordinary degree of aggressiveness, the normal joy of conquest and possession, seemed to be wholly absent from him. The love he asked for was essentially a protective love, sisterly or motherly; in its unavoidable degree of passion he felt a constant danger, which repelled and unsettled him." *

We can then, understand the poem as involving three layers, to each of which any given reader may respond differently: first, a nuclear fantasy; second, defensive modifications of that fantasy; third, a resultant intellectual meaning. Put crudely, the fantasy involves a wish to take in from a nurturing "world" (ultimately, the mother). Countering that wish is a sound, associated initially with her withdrawal, then with father, finally with a naked clash by night—a primal scene fantasy. The poem counters the despair involved in these sounds by conjuring up the image of lovers asexual and therefore "true to one another."

At the level of intellectual meaning, I have suggested, "What informs the poem as a whole is an attempt to re-create in a personal relationship the sweet sight of stability and permanence which the harsh sound of the actual ebb and flow of reality negates." This intellectual theme is a transformation of the fantasy content: an attempt to counter sounds associated with a mother's sexualized withdrawal from sight by creating the image of asexual lovers. As with the "tomorrow" speech, one would expect to hear faint echoes of the unconscious theme in the commentators' analyses of the conscious content. And we do.[15] Professor Wendell S. Johnson suggests "Dover Beach" resembles a dialogue within the mind between the natural, spontaneous, self-sufficient existence of the sea and the dry, critical mind represented as the land—we can recog-

---

* Anthony Hecht, in his parody written from the girl's point of view, "The Dover Bitch: A Criticism of Life," catches this antisexual quality:

> She told me later on
> That after a while she got to looking out
> At the lights across the channel, and really felt sad,
> Thinking of all the wine and enormous beds
> And blandishments in French and the perfumes,
> And then she got really angry. To have been brought
> All the way down from London, and then be addressed
> As a sort of mournful cosmic last resort.[14]

nize in his intellectual terms, transforms of the nurturing mother and the interfering father. Professor Krieger speaks of the poem as "the repetitive inclusiveness of the human situation." Again, we recognize a transformation of the child's trust that he will be nurtured, that he will be able to take in and be taken into some comforting environment. Where we have seen the lovers in the poem as an attempt to re-create the world as it once was, in childhood, Professor Krieger speaks of repetitiveness and "the tragic sense of *eternal recurrence*." We heard the disturbing sound of ebb and flow as that which cuts down a child's faith that his nurturing world will always be there. M. Bonnerot speaks of "the sea-rhythm of the world in general and also of the poet's soul which finds itself mysteriously in accord with that cosmic pulse," while Professor Delesanta speaks of "terrible incompatibility." They say just the opposite, but both are responding to the same stimulus if we understand it psychologically. "Mysteriously in accord," "terrible incompatibility"—the phrases simply describe one or the other side of the child's ambivalent trust and anger as he regrets or awaits his withdrawn nurturer.

Intellectual meaning is a transformation of unconscious fantasy. What intervenes between the two are defensive maneuvers. "Dover Beach" defends so strongly against the disturbance it describes that we are more aware of what it is not than what it is. We never see it directly: we hear it (until the last stanza) as the absence of something.

Partly, Arnold's choice of words and images works out these defensive and transforming maneuvers, but the form of the poem also acts them out. Notice how the sequence of images lets us experience for ourselves the experience the poem describes. It gives us, first, the somewhat vague seascape, evoking in us both a wish to take in more, and a feeling of trust and security. Then the poem surprises us with the presence of another. We feel a disturbing influence, which the poem tells us is a sound. So it is, the sudden speaking voice of "Come to the window," and we want to know more, to take in more. Instead, the second and third stanzas try to intellectualize and distance the disturbing influence, but these defensive tactics fail and it comes back, building up tension in us.

The fourth stanza abandons these earlier attempts to deal with the problem. First, it suddenly retreats from the external world to the smaller world of the lovers; second, it shifts in metaphor from the Dover seascape to the ignorant armies. The fourth stanza gives us the vague hope, "let us be true," and, as at the beginning of the poem, we feel trust, security, and also a desire to take in more. But now we learn that the danger, the moving back and forth, is elsewhere; we take a metaphorical flight in time and space to the plain of Epipolae. The efforts at flight that failed in stanzas two and three succeed in stanza four because "we are here." The phrase is almost parental, and thus, by the very acceptance of disillusionment, the poem gratifies us, because it does, ultimately, let us take in what we ambivalently wished to take in in the first place: it lets us see two "true" lovers together with a glimpse of a "clash by night"—but elsewhere.

Similarly, the dualism of the poem carries out these defensive techniques. First, the poem contrasts the speaker and his companion with their environment. The poem thus avoids looking directly at the lovers by intensely looking at and listening to something else, the sea, the shingle, Sophocles, and so on. Second, the poem places its "you" and "I" between illusion and reality so as to keep up a division, to prevent certain things from mingling or penetrating. The feeling is that if the negative sound touches the positive sight, one must reject them both. One must either accept the world wholly or reject it wholly. Both these defenses the psychoanalyst would call forms of denial: denying the existence of forbidden things by seeing only what they are not; denying compromise or imperfection.

Then, third, the poem tries to re-create in the relationship with the lover a simplified, more childish, but more satisfying version of an adult, sexual love for another person or the world as a whole, set off as the "clash by night" or the "land of dreams" of the last stanza.

The lovers are, therefore, pivotal. On the one hand, they are what we wish to see and thus a potential source of pleasure. On the other hand, they are a defensive barrier positioned to prevent the sounds corrupting the fair sight. The lovers take part both in the poem's content and its form.

Form is our theme, however, not content. Yet "Dover Beach" and the "tomorrow" speech show all too clearly the truth of that old critical maxim: form and content are inseparable. One cannot separate them even in a very simple model: content as the intellectual statement; form as the abstract patterns of meter, rhyme, or stanza. Even so, for as formal a couplet as Pope's, the sense cannot be separated from the divisions for rhyme and caesura, for they will align themselves with syntactic breaks essential to the sense.

Further, our model is much more complicated than that. We have not one "content," but two. An unconscious content—a wishful or anxious fantasy—becomes transformed into intellectual content—an idea that the literary work is "about." By and large, we would tend to associate the act of transformation with defensive maneuvers resulting from formal devices—verbal strategies, stanzaic divisions, the sequencing of images, and so on. Yet, we have already seen that, as in a dream, some of the transformation of unconscious content takes place in the very act of representing it. When Shakespeare chooses a stage and Arnold the Sicilian expedition to represent a primal scene fantasy, they have already partially transformed unconscious material into intellectual content. Similarly, when the two poets choose to shift from visual to aural imagery, they are performing an act which deals both with content and with form; merely by representing the nuclear fantasy as sound, they are pushing it toward a central intellectual statement, because sound accents later stages in development than sight.

We can, however, isolate "purely" formal devices: in "Dover Beach," the positioning of the lovers at the centers of the stanzas, the division of the stanzas, and, in both poems, the sequencing of images. When looked at that way, we can see that these "purely"

formal devices serve to modify defensively the unconscious content
of the poem.

Very loosely, then, we can say that form in a literary work corresponds to defense; content, to fantasy or impulse. More generally, though, just as in life impulse and defense interact and shape
each other, so, in literature, form and content are inseparable. Certain impulses seem to call forth certain defenses, and I suspect that
it is no coincidence that these two poems of "disillusionment"
draw on primal scene fantasies to cancel them by denial and so
give us pleasure.

We should remember, too, that, just as the lovers in "Dover
Beach" serve both as a source of pleasure and as a defensive mastering of the initial conflict, so, in every poem, any given element
may serve as a representation of content or as part of a formal and
defensive maneuver. Freud, for example, showed how verbal play
in jokes served as a source of pleasure in itself and, because it did,
it licensed expression and therefore the larger pleasures possible
from the drives mobilized by the joke.

Perhaps it is also true of form in the larger sense of structure
that it gives pleasure even as it defends. For example, in the "tomorrow" speech, the abstract words at the opening and the final
phrases erase or obliterate the concrete images between them. In
fact, each of the sense-units ends with a reduction or destruction:
"To the last syllable," "dusty death," "Out, out," "no more,"
"nothing." The very form of the poem, in acting out a denial, may
gratify an aggressive wish to annihilate those guilty of the offending
sight. Perhaps denial or undoing always does this, but certainly the
denials of this miniature poem obliterate the adult world, not inappropriately in a play that kills parents and children as if to root out
the very fact of parenthood, to make "nature's germens tumble all
together / Even till destruction sicken." Perhaps other forms, that
is, other defenses, such as sexualization, identification, or affectual-
ization might gratify libidinal rather than aggressive wishes, as does
the placing of the lovers at the end of "Dover Beach." In either
case, though, the key to the most successful literary works (in my

experience, anyway) is that their very defenses give me pleasure.

The reason seems to be that pleasure from defenses has a peculiarly powerful effect. Freud (in "Creative Writers and Day-Dreaming" as in *Jokes*) suggested for the fore-pleasure of artistic form or sexual foreplay the model of a bribe or "incentive bonus." In more modern psychoanalytic terms, we can think of pleasure in form as a pleasure *achieved as part of* a defensive maneuver (as the denials and undoings of the "tomorrow" speech gratify aggressive wishes). In life, defenses stand off and modify drives and so cut down the amount of pleasure we get even if the drives are gratified. If, however, the defense itself gives pleasure, there is a net increase in pleasure, and that increase in pleasure (according to Freud) buys a permit for "a still greater pleasure arising from deeper psychical sources," the gratification from the drive (or, in literature, unconscious content). Thus, even the pleasure from satisfying the drive becomes greater. It is as though a kind of multiplier came into play like those in economics, so that a little pleasure in form releases a far greater pleasure in content. If so, then we have found in form the locus of that peculiarly powerful pleasure in literature that sustains our "willing suspension of disbelief."

Perhaps, though, there is a truth here for life as well as literature: that where a defensive maneuver in and of itself satisfies drives, it very greatly increases the potential gratification from other drives defended against. If this is so, the individual must become "locked in" to an activity that (like a regenerative feedback) reinforces defensive actions with multiplied bonuses of pleasure. One thinks of sexuality with its defensive (delaying, tension-heightening) but also gratifying foreplay. Jokes and literature might well work in this double way as would any occupation which represents a successful sublimation, that is, a defense pleasurable in itself. If such defenses lead to a kind of passionate commitment, this may be the key not only to the reader's pleasure, but the writer's. Is the formal or defensive aspect essential to creativity? Once again, we are led to the surmise that the poet's secret, the novelist's, the film-maker's, perhaps the mere literary critic's, lies in his being able to take pleasure not only from the drives but also from the very defenses inherent in what he does. Possibly, but certainly this is an empyrean speculation that goes far beyond "form as defense."

5　The Displacement to Language

Form, in the larger sense of sequence or structure, acts out for its audience something in the nature of a defense: splitting or denial or regression or projection. But "form" for literary critics often means something rather more special than sequence or structure: linguistic form, the particular choice and ordering of particular words. Form in this sense acts in a smaller, more intricate way, quite unlike form in the larger sense. That is, "literary" writing displaces its psychological issues to the level of language *qua* language. There, our own muscular responses, the logic of the language itself, the gratification and violation of our formal expectations—these and perhaps other devices of language seem to master the original psychological issues.

To discover this special effect, one has only oneself for a sensing instrument. I can respond and by a kind of self-analysis get at the things in the literary work that shape the less conscious aspects of my response. I can then guess the same or similar things are shaping the response of others. Not without reason, to judge from a distinguished linguist's account of people's responses to sentences like those of poetry or proverb. Professor Noam Chomsky writes:

> Given a grammatically deviant utterance, we attempt to impose an interpretation on it, exploiting whatever features of grammatical structure it preserves and whatever analogies we can

construct with perfectly well-formed utterances. We do not, in this way, impose an interpretation on a perfectly grammatical utterance (it is precisely for this reason that a well chosen deviant utterance may be richer and more effective).[1]

Consider, for example, "Golf plays John." Because it is, on the face of it, ungrammatical, the sentence alerts us in a way that "John plays golf a lot" does not. To interpret the sentence, we analogize "Golf plays John" to "John plays golf," "Golf is played by John," "John plays a fish," "Irma plays on John," and so forth. In doing so, we discover something about the nature of golf and about the way John is driven or clubbed by his particular *daimon*.* In a more poetic vein, there is Marvell's lovely phrase, "a green thought in a green shade." From a grammatical point of view, a thought can no more be green than golf can play or John be played. But the semi-grammaticality of the utterance asks us to imagine a green thought, to form whatever analogies we can with well-formed utterances.

Such sentences introduce a notion of "degrees of grammaticalness." For example, "John plays and" leads to no such whimsy as the previous ungrammatical sentence. Contrast "Scientists truth the universe" with "A scientist truth universe." Somehow a little too much grammatical distortion pushes a sentence across some line that marks off poetry from gibberish. Precisely what that line is, linguists will be able to describe, if not now, then at least soon.

Linguistics aside, what Chomsky is describing looks like what a psychoanalyst would call displacement. That is, our conscious attention shifts (to some degree, at least) from the content of the utterance to its form. Attention, concern, if you will, psychic energy, are taken away from substance and given to language. In terms of our model, such a displacement weakens our involvement with the deeper, fantasy levels, fraught with fear and desire; instead, we concentrate our involvement on the verbal level. The words-as-words may themselves introduce deep fantasies, but usually they will be "higher" and more neutral in the transformational process from unconscious fantasy to conscious meaning.

* Compare the Japanese proverb, "At the third cup, wine drinks the man."

One would expect this displacement to language, then, to attenuate or thin out our emotional response. So it does, in the extreme
displacements toward language one sees in the work of a comic
poet like Ogden Nash who can take acutely painful social or sexual
thoughts and make them laughable by turning the issue entirely
into a verbal one—will he make his rhyme? In something like
W. S. Gilbert's "Lord Chancellor's Song," we lose track of the fact
that we are dealing with the terrors of nightmare; we enjoy it as
verbal gymnastics.

We can surmise that such a displacement is a matter of degree.
In theory, any atypical phrasing, any that differs from the way we
would ourselves phrase the matter, shifts our attention to that
extent from substance and onto form. At the other extreme, there
is the line the linguists will draw for us, the degree of ungram-
maticality at which an utterance passes from sense to nonsense.
Within these limits some degree of psychological displacement toward a purely verbal level will take place.

The concept of displacement provides us only with a framework
for our response to literary language. Within that framework, other
subtler and more particular things are happening. Consider, for
example, what has always seemed to me one of the loveliest sentences in English, Shakespeare's half-line, "Our revels now are
ended." There is scarcely any deviance from grammaticality in
Chomsky's sense; whatever displacement from fantasy to verbalism
we experience comes from the poetic context rather than the
sentence itself. Within that displacement, however, the sound of
the sentence operates in a special, particular way. The two *e* sounds
of "*revels*" repeat in "*ended*," but the consonants have changed.
The continuing sounds of *r*, *v*, and *l* have been replaced by a
double dental, *d*, *d*. In effect, when I read the lines, I act out in a
muscular way the stopping the line describes: I press my tongue
against my teeth to end the "*revels*" of the first half of the sentence. To generalize, we can say that, in poetic language, within
the general displacement toward language, particular sounds in
volve muscular actions that somehow match the sense.

I realize that that lame and impotent conclusion puts me peril-
ously close to the massy lucubrations of Dr. Johnson's prototypical
critic, Dick Minim:

> He is the great investigator of hidden beauties, and is partic-
> ularly delighted when he finds *the sound an echo to the sense*.
> He has read all our poets with particular attention to this del-
> icacy of versification, and wonders . . . that the wonderful
> lines upon honour and a bubble have hitherto passed without
> notice:
>
> > Honour is like the glassy bubble,
> > Which cost philosophers such trouble;
> > Where, one part crack'd, the whole doth fly,
> > And wits are crack'd to find out why.
>
> In these verses, says Minim, we have two striking accommo-
> dations of the sound to the sense. It is impossible to utter the
> two lines emphatically without an act like that which they de-
> scribe; *bubble* and *trouble* causing a momentary inflation of the
> cheeks by the retention of the breath, which is afterwards forci-
> bly emitted, as in the practice of *blowing bubbles*. But the
> greatest excellence is in the third line, which is *crack'd* in the
> middle to express a crack, and then shivers into monosyllables.[2]

"This notion of representative metre," Johnson continues elsewhere, "and the desire of discovering frequent adaptations of the
sound to the sense, have produced, in my opinion, many wild con-
ceits and imaginary beauties. . . . It may be suspected that in such
resemblances the mind often governs the ear, and the sounds are
estimated by their meaning."

He instances his point with Pope's translation from the *Odyssey*
of the lines describing the labors of Sisyphus (as, centuries before,
Aristotle had used Homer's original lines to instance the same
sound effect).

> With many a weary step, and many a groan,
> Up the high hill he heaves a huge round stone;
> The huge round stone, resulting with a bound,
> Thunders impetuous down, and smokes along the ground.
>
> Who does not perceive the stone to move slowly upward, and
> roll violently back? But set the same numbers to another sense:

> While many a merry tale, and many a song,
> Cheer'd the rough road, we wish'd the rough road long;
> The rough road then, returning in a round,
> Mock'd our impatient steps, for all was fairy ground.
>
> We have now surely lost much of the delay, and much of the
> rapidity.[3]

So we have, though I think Johnson does not give enough weight to Dick Minim's kind of analysis in explaining the loss.

That is, Johnson is surely correct when he says it is not the "numbers," the rhythm alone, that creates Pope's effect. Johnson retained Pope's rhythms, but in changing the words set to those rhythms he changed more than just the sense. The *h*'s in Pope's second line, which create much of the effect of effort, become in Johnson's second line *r*'s, a much more relaxed muscular gesture for his reader. Similarly, Johnson loses the assonance of the rhyme pattern, *groan, stone, bound, ground,* a sound effect that asks its reader to work (like Sisyphus) to adjust his expectations. The bounce we feel in Pope's "bound" comes not just from the sense of the word, but from its rhyme with "round" earlier in the line; Johnson's third line drops out this effect. The point is simply that, in discussing the sound effects of poetry, it makes little sense to isolate a single set of relations like rhythm; one must take into account all the sound, particularly as we experience it in our kinesthetic muscular identifications. In that sense, Johnson's test proves, if anything, the foolishness of treating rhythms as though they were entities apart from the sounds they embody.

Johnson, however, issues a much more important dictum in his refutation of the "notion of representative metre." "The mind," he notes, "often governs the ear, and the sounds are estimated by their meaning." That is, when Johnson changed the words set to Pope's rhythms, he changed more than he perhaps realized; he changed not only the explicit but also the fantasy content. Pope's lines deal with bodily effort, directed up and down, exerted against "high hill" and "huge round stone," objects bigger than the solitary "he" who confronts them. At some level of our being we are experiencing Sisyphus' own feeling of helplessness and impotency, and we are experiencing it in an immediate bodily sense, possibly even sexual, if we are willing to play at dream symbols. Johnson, however, has replaced the solitary "he" by an evidently companionable "we." What in Pope's lines was bodily becomes in Johnson's much more mental: "merry," "cheer'd," "wish'd," "impatient." Johnson deals, as Pope does, with a situation of helplessness where the ground overcomes the person on it, but he treats it in mental rather than physical terms; an intellectual puzzle rather than a bodily frustration.

Literature, we have seen, transforms unconscious fantasies toward significance; sound must be one of the agents of that transformation. Johnson's lines deal with a fantasy of impotence, but his choice of words presents it in mental rather than physical terms. The sense of the lines already embodies some transformation of the unconscious fears they evoke; there is that much less transformation for the sound of the lines to do. We expect less from the sound of Johnson's lines—and we get less. Pope strikes much closer to the bone. His words are physical, his subject solitary. With Johnson. "we wish'd"; with Pope, "he heaves." Whatever fears of a physical helplessness Pope's lines evoke, they are closer to our awareness.

We do not come vacantly to the sounds of poetry. Rather, "The mind . . . governs the ear." We ask that the sounds act out for us some management of the fantasy the sense embodies, and the poet's art consists of giving us not too little and not too much management through the sounds—muscular acts—he chooses. The sound of Johnson's lines we scarcely notice because there is no work for it to do. In Pope's lines, the sounds are so striking because we come to them needing more in the way of control and management; his choice of sounds gives it to us. If anything, Pope overmanages our response, for we become more concerned with the sound effects than with Sisyphus.

In short, sound effects in poetic language invite us to act out (as we consciously or unconsciously mouth the lines) muscular ways of dealing with the fantasy content. As Northrop Frye has said, there is in all poetry something of the college yell. Dr. Johnson, then, is quite right to doubt "adaptations" or "accommodations" of sound to sense—conscious sense. Rather, the sound deals with unconscious sense. The old critical formula, "Sound echoes sense," should give way to the more accurate, "Sound manages sense."

We can see this process of managing going on at length in a passage we have already analyzed for its fantasy content, the "tomorrow" speech:

> Tomorrow, and tomorrow, and tomorrow
> Creeps in this petty pace from day to day
> To the last syllable of recorded time.
> And all our yesterdays have lighted fools
> The way to dusty death. Out, out, brief candle—
> Life's but a walking shadow, a poor player
> That struts and frets his hour upon the stage
> And then is heard no more. It is a tale
> Told by an idiot, full of sound and fury,
> Signifying nothing.

In considering the passage's structure (or "form" in the larger sense), we saw that it begins with days, dips, as it were, into nights of unconscious terrors and fearful imaginings, and then erases them into "no more," "nothing." The form was acting to manage the fantasy content of the lines—it let us glimpse, then deny a primal scene.

Now, if I consider the passage simply as sound, I find it affects me most immediately by repetition: most obviously by the three *tomorrow*'s of the first line, but also by "*day* to *day*" and "Out, out." The word "and" occurs (in a passage of only nine and a half lines) six times on its own and once buried in "*cand*le." Particular consonants are also repeated (rather bluntly for Shakespeare's middle style) in such phrases as "*petty pace*," "*dusty death*," "a *poor player*," "a *tale* / *Told*." Clusters of consonants are repeated, for example, the *s*'s, *t*'s, *st*'s, and *ts*'s referring to the poor player, "Tha*t struts* and fre*ts* his hour upon the *stage*." Similarly, "du*sty*

death" puts a quietus to "*yesterdays*": both show the same conson-
ant-vowel arrangement, CV*st*V*d*VC. The *b, f,* and *l* of "*brief* can-
dle," are followed by the *l, f,* and *b* of "*Life's but.*" The hard *c* of
"*candle*" crops out in the next stressed word, "*walking.*" In the
same way, the *f, s,* and *n* of "*full of sound and fury*" are summed
and canceled in the next phrase, "*Signifying nothing.*"

In this particular passage, while the consonants repeat, the vowels (to a modern ear) tend not to. The passage, for one thing, is
not rhymed, though "long" *a* occurs in a rhyming position four
times in the nine line-endings: "day," "player," "stage," and
"tale." There are a few repetitions—we have seen that "and" is repeated and so, naturally, is front or "short" *a*: it occurs twelve
times. The most frequent vowel repetition occurs in the last three
lines where high, front or "short" *i* occurs nine times, four times in
the last half line alone.

As one would expect, however, from this general tenseness in the
vowels in the middles of the lines, the passage has a rather irregular
rhythm. A single line like "Creeps in this petty pace from day to
day" moves from an initial long vowel and stressed cluster of consonants ("Creeps") to a series of less stressed short vowels with
more consonants ("petty pace") and closes with open, long vowels
("day to day"). The lines themselves as units move in the same
way. First, there is the irregularity of "Life's but a walking shadow,
a poor player"; then the constricted consonants, tense vowels, and
tight rhythm of "That struts and frets his hour upon the stage";
finally, the thought closes with the absolute regularity and long
vowels of "And then is heard no more."

This pattern runs through all six of the sense units of the passage, which fall into three more or less symmetrical pairs. In the
opening half of each of these pairs each phrase becomes an isolated
rhythmic unit, and the rhythm seems irregular, dictated by the
phrasing rather than the iambic meter. I feel tension and a wish
for regularity at such phrases as "and tomorrow," "Out, out, brief
candle," or the long phrase, "It is a tale / Told by an idiot." In the
second half of each sense unit, the iambic meter reasserts itself so

strongly as to create another kind of tension, a wish for variation, as in "And all our yesterdays have lighted fools," "that struts and frets his hour upon the stage." Finally, at the end of each unit, the verse comes to a dead stop (both in rhythm and sense) with such words as "time," "dusty death," or "no more." The last such stop, "signifying nothing," with its final four-fold repetition of short *i* signifies the end of this miniature poem. In short, the "poem" plays off two kinds of rhythm, the first based on tightly defined phrases as the rhythmic unit, the second based on a strong iambic or trochaic meter overriding the natural rhythmic phrasing. Then, the tension between these two rhythms is resolved in the final phrases in which the two kinds of rhythm coalesce.

There is, then, in the consonant repetitions a pattern of tentative, half-hearted repetition, followed by a blatant and constricting repetition which then leads to a kind of open blankness, the "nothing" which ends the passage. The rhythm also moves from one tension to another kind of tension and finally to a resolution. The sound patterns, in short, make me feel the same partial blankness, followed by a tense, constricted concreteness followed by total blankness, that the sequencing of the imagery does.

Thus, form in the narrower sense of rhythm and rhyme and sound matches form in the larger sense of structure. Both serve to manage the fantasy content of the lines. Form in the larger sense does it by sequencing different aspects of the fantasy so that they reinforce or counterbalance one another; essentially, form in the larger sense dictates what we are aware of at any given moment. Form in the narrower sense of sound works differently, enabling us to imagine, even feel, movements of the mouth that simulate muscular ways of dealing with the fantasy content. But these two kinds of form necessarily co-act, and part of the poet's art is to see that they co-operate and do not cancel each other out.

Form manages content—the statement seems straightforward, perhaps obvious. But its application to even a poem of nine and a half lines involves considerable complexity. One can see this managerial action of form, though, in so short a "poem" as the single sentence, "Our revels now are ended." The line's basic defense is to stop its content with the double *d* at the end. But this sound effect cannot be separated from content. If we change just one letter of the line, so that it becomes, "Our rebels now are ended," the line becomes sing-song—a clue that form is over-managing content. The sound effect works only with the word "revels," which suggests that we need to understand the unconscious content of that word before we can understand what the double *d* is acting against.

Our responses to a single word must needs be highly subjective; even so, the word itself is a given. "Revels" connotes noisy, boisterous amusement, but also (to any reader of Elizabethan drama) plays. The unconscious significance of plays we have already seen in the "tomorrow" speech; they symbolize, almost invariably, a primal scene fantasy, here a noisy, boisterous one. In its context in *The Tempest*, the word's symbolic value is clear: the "revels" are a wedding-dance and masque which are to negate any pre-nuptial sex between Ferdinand and Miranda. The "revels" quite explicitly substitute for a primal scene and they are cut off in a moment of the father's anger. Prospero reassures Ferdinand:

> You do look, my son, in a moved sort,
> As if you were dismayed: be cheerful, sir.
> Our revels now are ended. These our actors,
> As I foretold you, were all spirits and
> Are melted into air, into thin air . . .

The double *d* that stops these revels acts out the psychological denial that Prospero's whole dismissal of the masque does. "Ended" serves to quiet any boisterous activity, and its *-ded* acts much the way the "dusty death" of the "tomorrow" speech did.

Thus, form and content are also inseparable in the sense that one cannot understand the function of form unless one understands what the form is defending against. "Our rebels now are ended"—some readers, at least, are not nearly so interested in making rebellion "ded" as in seeing and then not seeing primal scenes.

From this point of view, we can understand the paradox that changes in sound are not so destructive of sound effects as changes in sense are. "Our revels now are finished" or "Our drama now is ended" retain (to my ear, anyway) more of the "poetic" effect of the original line than "Our rebels now are ended." They do because the fantasy content and the denial embodied in words like "ended" or "finished" persist; even though the pure sound effect is lost, the total experience of fantasy-and-defense is closer to the original than it is when one changes "revels" to "rebels."

But perhaps you do not hear these differences the same way I do—certainly one would expect responses to such changes to be highly subjective and variable. We can agree, though, that all change is destructive; the slightest tinkering with the wording of a joke or a lyric radically changes its effect. As Mark Twain was fond of remarking, "The difference between the right word and the almost right word is like the difference between lightning and the lightning bug." Now we are in a position to see why small changes in wording can produce such big changes in effect—any given word in a poem is not just a word, a change in which would matter little, but the embodiment of conflict. Our response even to single words is a complex interaction of wish, fear, and defense, not only those explicit in the language, but those we bring to it (my response to *el*-sounds no doubt enters into "revels," too). Poetic language balances the pressure from a great deal of fantasy, and just as in any other situation of balanced forces—a mechanical toggle, a trigger, a Wheatstone bridge—the slightest imbalance produces an immediate and decisive effect. The fantasy may become too raw so that we perceive the sound as inadequate to manage it. More typically, strong sound will seem to over-manage weakened content. Either way, the change in effect will be very much larger than the actual change in wording.

Sound, of course, is not the only resource poetic language has for managing fantasy content. The basic displacement toward language permits other purely verbal devices to manage our unconscious fantasies. One in particular seems to have a powerful—and somewhat inexplicable—effect. To alter a term from Freud, we could call this verbal device *economy*. We can see it in the way the first and second halves of Shakespeare's sentence echo each other (again, to a modern ear). That is, in "Our revels now are ended," the sound sequence *our re-* occurs again in the second half as the sequence, *ow (a)re e-*. Pronounce the line muting the bracketed letters: Our re[vels n]ow are e[nded]. One could call the effect an internal rhyme, but it seems more accurate to say a sequence of phonemes is repeated so that the total number of new sequences of phonemes we hear is sharply reduced.

Such an effect is, of course, related to rhyme, as in the couplet of Marvell's we have referred to before:

> Annihilating all that's made
> To a green thought in a green shade.

The lines, rhyming, repeat *-ade, -ade* and somehow give us a feeling of completeness. But the long *ā* of *-āde* appears first in *annihilāting* and that word as a whole seems a stretched-out version of *all*. The second line not only completes the rhyme but repeats *green*, indeed whole syntactic patterns, "To a green [noun] in a green [noun]," so that the line becomes two tight, closely paralleled phrases.

Such economies are particularly common in "touchstones" like Marvell's couplet or Macbeth's "tomorrow" speech. Some poets, Keats, for example, or Edith Sitwell, make many more such phonemic repetitions than others, but they appear in all language we think of as "poetic," and they are markedly fewer in language we would call "prosy." Freud, in analyzing jokes, concluded that this kind of repetition of vowels or consonants was a source of pleasure in itself—he related it to the babblings of children, drunks, or schizophrenics.

No doubt he is correct, but it seems to me the total poetic effect probably draws on deeper sources of pleasure as well. There is an economy in phonemes, true, but, particularly with rhyme, there is a

kind of pseudo-logic in the sounds themselves. When *made* and
shade rhyme, they give us a feeling that something has somehow
been accomplished, quite apart from the sense of the words. Childhood chants like "Eeny, meeny, miney, mo" or "Hickory-dickory-
dock," have this same pseudo-logical style, not unlike Hopkins:

> How to kéep—is there ány any, is there none such, nowhere
> known some, bow or brooch or braid or brace, láce,
> latch or catch or key to keep
> Back beauty, keep it, beauty, beauty, beauty, . . . from
> vanishing away?

Or at a still farther remove, the sibilants and long *i*'s of Keats's

> Thou still unravish'd bride of quietness,
> Thou foster-child of silence and slow time . . .

Such repetitions create an effect of logical inevitability, completeness, mastery, derived not from the sense of the words, but from
their sound. There is probably something here of the sense of
power that children and primitives feel in the act of naming
things.

Thus, poetry, having displaced our deepest concern from the
fantasy content of the words to their syntactic and phonic surface,
offers us a pseudo-solution at this surface level to the conflicts that
inhere in the deeper content. Within the total displacement toward language, the particular words themselves act out for us (or
induce us to act out) a logic of their own, based not on sense, but
on klang associations. Again, form manages content. We have already seen how some sound patterns induce in us muscular movements of the mouth that seem to handle the fantasy content. Now,
we are seeing how rhyme external and internal, assonance—in general, phonemic repetitions—create in ear and brain a feeling that
some kind of order or logic is being imposed on content.

Rhyme and rhythm, however, play still other roles, two, to be
specific: they satisfy expectancies—and violate them. Many critics
have commented on the first. For example, "What metre in itself

gives," says Northrop Frye, "is . . . the pleasure of seeing a relatively predictable pattern filling up with the inevitably felicitous words." [4] Professor Morse Peckham characterizes the feeling we get as a sense of "openness to demands," "adequacy," or "smoothness of behavior." [5] I would suggest (as above) a feeling of mastery or control or ordering. Though our phrasings of the sensation might vary, I have no doubt most of us feel much the same way when a poem fulfills its rhythmic pattern or rhyme-scheme.

Arnold, for example, uses the highly irregular rhyme-scheme and metrical pattern of "Dover Beach" to work out the poem's basic problem for us, the rejection of one part of reality in order to accept another.* Notice for example, the strong broken and then rebuilt rhythm of line twelve, "Begin, and cease, and then again begin"; the long withdrawal of the last four lines of stanza three; finally the clotted consonants that accompany the image of the ignorant armies. These points where the sound becomes particularly strong are all points where the theme of disillusionment predominates in the poem. In general, strong rhyme seems linked to passages of expectation or trust or acceptance; strong rhythm seems linked to a sense of reality and solidity. Rhythm is strong at the opening of the poem with its great feeling of regularity, solidity, thereness. The rhymes become strong in stanza two, the intellectual acceptance of disillusionment, and in stanza four, the emotional acceptance.

In the first three stanzas of this poem of division and dualism, rhyme and rhythm tend to be divorced from each other. At points where we are strongly aware of the rhythm, the rhyme tends to disappear from consciousness or even from the poem. Conversely, at points of very regular rhyme, as in stanza two, the rhythm becomes irregular and tends to disintegrate. This sound pattern seems to be a part of the general defensive strategy of the poem—to divide the world and deal with it in parts, to show us things by showing us what they are not. Similarly, Arnold divides every one of the lines from two to six halfway—again, part of this general strategy of di-

* The poem is reprinted on pp. 115–16.

vision in the poem. But also, throughout, Arnold deals with the world of the poem as he deals with the world described by the poem: he divides it in two to deal with it in parts. Finally, at the close of the poem, not only rhythm, but also rhyme becomes strong, a strengthening of defensive form as the poem comes to its moment of greatest stress and distress in content. Rhyme, rhythm, and sense all come together at the close to make us experience in ourselves the poem's final rhymed acceptance of a disturbing reality expressed as strongly rhythmic sound. Unconsciously, we have seen, that rhythmic sound itself has a disillusioning sexual significance; pairing it with strong rhyme at the end makes it possible for us to handle it.

A poem's fulfillment of patterns of rhythm and rhyme gives us a feeling of something like security—many critics have noted this. But many critics have also noted that we seek not only satisfaction of pattern but variation from it. We would not think twice of Milton if all twelve books of *Paradise Lost* thumped along line after line, di-*dum*, di-*dum*, di-*dum*, di-*dum*, di-*dum*. Indeed, the old notion of the normal English meter as five iambic feet seems to be quite wide of the mark. As Professor Frye says, "A four-stress line seems to be inherent in the structure of the English language," and, more recently, linguists have become able to develop a transformational model for iambic pentameter that suggests certain variations of blank verse are built into our expectations about blank verse.[6]

The poet, then, in varying his verse must be meeting our expectations more than he realizes. Even so, it would be a dull world, artistically speaking, if works of art simply complied totally with our expectations, and they don't. No worthwhile work of art is totally predictable in its formal aspects. Rather, as Professor Peckham's study amply demonstrates, works of art disorient us; they violate our predictions and expectations:

> The distinguishing attribute of the artist's role is to create occasions for disorientation, and of the perceiver's role to experience it. The distinguishing mark of the perceiver's transaction with

> the work of art is discontinuity of experience, not continuity; disorder, not order . . .[7]

The situation is particularly clear in music where virtually a history of music can be written in terms of the way successive composers have varied traditional forms or "permitted" new chords and intervals. But the situation is clear too in poetry, where Wordsworth does things with the sonnet Milton could not have dreamed of, though he, in his age, wrote sonnets unthinkable to a Shakespeare. In even so "tight" a form as Pope's couplets, it is the minute variations, not the regularities, that catch our prosodic ear. The situation is even more obvious in French poetry where a slight change in the stress pattern or the caesura of an alexandrine signals a major innovation.

It is easy enough to see that satisfying a pattern ought to—and does—give us a pleasurable feeling of satisfaction, acceptance, completion, mastery, or something like them. But why should the violation of expectation please us? The answer is, it doesn't. Professor Peckham describes his reaction to an unfamiliar musical style:

> My own experience with Schoenberg's twelve-tone music moved from total disorientation, to the perception of individual notes, to the perception of melody and the acceptance of the harmonies, to the realization, which came after the event, that the appropriate form was the chromatic scale. My judgement moved correspondingly from irritation to boredom to toleration to emotion to, now, the experience of finding this twelve-tone music ravishingly beautiful . . .[8]

In other words, if I read Professor Peckham right, violating expectations does not produce pleasure but "irritation" or "boredom," and it is only when one can perceive the work of art as partly fulfilling (and partly violating) its "appropriate form" that one finds pleasure in it.

What, then, is the role of this residual violation of "appropriate form"? Peckham himself supplies the answer: "The distinguishing character or attribute of the perceiver's role is search-behavior focussed on awareness of discontinuities." [9] When we confronted

Marvell's semantic impossibility, "a green thought," we found our attention distracted from the fantasy level of the poem (the poet's merger with his environment) to the semantic problem. In the same way, when, to take an extreme example, Ogden Nash steadily and strongly violates our expectations as to rhythm and rhyme, he concentrates our attention on the verbal texture of his work and away from the fantasy content. In other words, violating patterns of rhyme and meter reinforces and sustains the original displacement of our involvement from the fantasy level to the level of purely verbal phenomena.

Thus, the fulfillment and violation of fixed patterns complement each other in our response. The violation of fixed patterns elicits, in Peckham's phrase, "search-behavior"; in our psychoanalytic terms, a displacement of cathexis from fantasy content to purely verbal devices. This displacement, in turn, makes it possible for the fulfillment of fixed patterns to give a feeling of adequacy and mastery. We take the pseudo-logic of rhythm, rhyme, and all klang associations as masteries of the underlying conflict at the fantasy level.

This displacement to language applies to other languages besides the one we speak: "languages" like music, dance, or the visual arts. Some of these "languages" express semantic content directly, those of cinema or theater or the iconic visual arts, for example. Then, these "languages" defensively manage the content they have expressed, just as the language of poetry does. In film, for example, when we introject a given shot, we absorb conscious and unconscious content. Then, the formal devices of cinema act out for us ways of dealing with the unconscious content. Cutting acts like displacement, flashback like regression, superimposition or a dissolve like condensation, and so on.

As Professor Peckham suggests, formal devices give us a feeling of mastery when they gratify our expectations. When they violate them, they reinforce the displacement of our involvement from content onto form. We say that particularly "arty" techniques "call attention to themselves." More accurately, they displace our attention from content to the logic of the techniques themselves, which thus become doubly strong ways of managing content. The more drastic techniques in languages such as cinema, theater, portrait or landscape painting deal with our response just as the more drastic techniques of poetic language do. In a film like Fellini's *Juliet of the Spirits*, for example, the heavy use of superimposition overmanages a fantasy content which does not stir us very much (what will Juliet do about sex?). The result is the film seems dull to all but the most resolute connoisseurs of film technique. By contrast, in Antonioni's *Red Desert*, the techniques (defocusing, delayed framing) are not so drastic as Fellini's and the unconscious fantasy content is much more disturbing—schizophrenic fantasies of being engulfed. The perilous balance of fantasy and defense worked out in cinematic language is far more exciting.

The situation is somewhat less clear in the so-called arts of "pure form": the non-iconic languages of music, architecture, or nonobjective painting and sculpture. Our formula, "Form manages content," seems to break down because such arts apparently have no content. True, as Peckham points out, a piece of music is a sequence of signs, and these signs probably have some semantic content for us: upward pitch motion might signify demand; downward pitch motion, acceptance; major keys, adequacy; minor keys, inadequacy, and so on.[10] But these significations cannot tell the whole story, for there is a huge discrepancy between such vague terms as "demand" or "adequacy" and the subtle, intricate details of particular pieces of music.

Simon O. Lesser states the problem—and its solution: "Little, if any, music has objective expressive content, and it is inconceivable that music could move us as it does and yet be devoid of such content. The solution which suggests itself is that we *supply* the expressive content, following the patterns of rising and falling excitement, conflict and resolution, laid down for us." [11] In other words, a semantic art, like literature, will ordinarily express a fantasy for us, which we enrich by bringing our own associations to it. A non-semantic art, like music, expresses fantasy, if at all, only in very general terms—it is we who bring the particular fantasies. Then, the music manages the fantasies we bring by its patterns of rigidity or flexibility, energy release or energy conservation, demand or acceptance, and the rest. Thus, it is precisely a measure of sophistication in music to be able *not* to daydream, but rather to "lose oneself" in the autonomous logic of the music itself. Within that logic, as in poetic language, gratification of our expectations will give us a sense of mastery and control; violation will further draw our attention away from fantasy and toward the "pure form" of the music itself.

Sound, then, does manage sense, in music no less than poetry. The difference is that the poet provides the (unconscious) content; the composer asks us to provide it. But in both, our minds undergo a "displacement to language." Such a theory explains the many experiments with music in which different people react in such different ways to the same musical piece: one will find it gloomy, another cheerful, a third mysterious, and so on. The variable is not the music but rather what we bring to it: our fantasies and the different values each of us finds in such fixed entities as minor key, rising pitch, slow speed, and the rest. The "language" of music differs from the language we speak in that it has no unconscious meaning, but, once we have supplied the unconscious fantasy content, music handles our feelings as the sound of poetry does.

In general, form manages content, with the arts of "pure form" at one end of the spectrum. At the other are those arts—I am thinking of non-fiction prose—where content is all and form seems almost missing. Yet, even with them, an artist has his resources: "purple" prose, artful transitions, the use and abuse of logic. Even mere syntax can become the formal device by which he creates and sustains a "displacement to language" within which his syntactic choices manage the fantasies we experience from the material. Consider this passage in which Arnold prescribes for literary critics:

It is of the last importance that English criticism should clearly discern what rule for its course, in order to avail itself of the field now opening to it, and to produce fruit for the future, it ought to take. The rule may be summed up in one word,— *disinterestedness*. And how is criticism to show disinterestedness? By keeping aloof from what is called "the practical view of things"; by resolutely following the law of its own nature, which is to be a free play of the mind on all subjects which it touches; by steadily refusing to lend itself to any of those ulterior political, practical considerations about ideas, which plenty of people will be sure to attach to them, which perhaps ought often to be attached to them, which in this country at any rate are certain to be attached to them quite sufficiently, but which criticism has really nothing to do with.[12]

Arnold sustains for page after page this voice, urbane, balanced, sensible. Even at his most indignant, he seems somehow reassuring. It is possible to account for at least my reaction psychologically, by understanding the sample as the interaction of a fantasy and a defense, just as we would a poem. Obviously, though, in non-fiction prose, whatever fantasies the passage expresses have already been pushed pretty far along the path of transformation toward meaning. Even so, the phrasing,

The rule may be summed up in one word, *disinterestedness*,

seems more tense and vital than,

One word, *disinterestedness*, may sum up the rule,

or,

Disinterestedness may sum up the rule in one word.

Arnold's choices, both of vocabulary and syntax, are somehow managing the admittedly attenuated fantasy-content of the line.

Professor Richard Ohmann points to Arnold's way of converting actions into nouns or nominatives.[13] In this passage, the first of these nominalizations comes at the outset, the long subordinate clause, "that English criticism should . . ." But there are a number of others: "keeping aloof" from the kernel 'criticism keeps aloof'; "following resolutely" from 'criticism resolutely follows'; "a free play of the mind" from 'the mind freely plays'—a whole series of linguistic transformations that turn clauses with active verbs into modifiers. Arnold takes a condition or action and treats it as a fixed, manipulable entity, to be named and understood through its name.

Once Arnold arrives at a name that satisfies him, he not only repeats it, he uses it in multiple ways. One word in the surface structure will play several grammatical roles in the underlying structure. "Criticism," for example, is the subject or object of about twenty underlying structures in less than a page. Related to this tendency is Arnold's repeated use of "it" and "which." Having established in the second clause that "it" stands for "criticism," he uses "it" three times in the first sentence and three more times in the last. Similarly, in the last, having established "which" as "practical considerations about ideas" (a nominalization of an action, as, indeed, "criticism" itself is), he repeats the "which" four times. Again, once "them" is set to stand for "ideas," Arnold repeats that pronoun three times.,

Partly as a result of this labeling tendency, Arnold has a propensity for forms of "to be." All three of the thought-units in this passage (sentences 1, 2, and 3–4) have the structure: noun plus a form of "to be" plus a predicate noun. Thus, "It is of the last importance that . . ." "The rule may be summed up . . ." "And how is criticism to show . . ." Forms of "to be" sometimes come in by way of passive verb forms, but others Arnold seems to introduce almost for their own sake: for example, "will be sure to attach" instead of, simply, "will attach"; or, "which is to be a free play" instead of "which is a free play." The effect is to attenuate the activity even of the active verbs Arnold uses.

Related, I suspect, to the extra "be's" are Arnold's variations upon ordinary sentence order. The last thought-unit, sentences 3–4, substitutes a rhetorical question-and-answer form for the ordinary word order: "Criticism is to show disinterestedness by keeping aloof . . ." Similarly, the second sentence transposes ordinary,

"One word, disinterestedness, may sum up this rule," into a passive, "The rule may be summed up in one word,—*disinterestedness*." The first sentence follows ordinary NP + VP word order, but only for the first clause. The second, subordinate clause interrupts the natural relation of object and verb with two longish purposive phrases. Most stylists, I think, would have written, ". . . English criticism should clearly discern what rule for its course it ought to take in order to avail itself of the field now opening to it and to produce fruit for the future." Typically, the effect of Arnold's word orderings is to put the strong assertion at the end: "it ought to take"; "one word,—*disinterestedness*"; "but which criticism has really nothing to do with." Arnold prepares us in the first part of a sentence for the assertion at the end. He buffers his strongest medicine.

We can isolate, then, three characteristics of Arnold's prose. He tends to turn actions or conditions into nouns or pronouns which he then manipulates as fixed entities. Partly as a result of this naming, partly for the word's own sake, he tends to introduce "be's" even when not necessary. His word orderings present strong assertions only after considerable cultivating of the ground. Ohmann sees the naming as Arnold's "trying to fix conceptually an unstable world or one that threatens to become unstable"; the buffering as his "shying away from contact, direct expression of the physical." Certainly this is the tenor of Arnold's writing here as in many other passages. His metaphors, however, suggest deeper roots for this intellectual attitude.

This passage has few metaphors, as such, and those are mostly idioms. Even so, I think it is possible to discern the unconscious fantasy that leads to Arnold's labeling and buffering. English criticism "ought to take" a "rule for its course." The rule may be "summed up." Criticism should be "following the law." I would call these metaphors (or idioms) of rule-following, perhaps even of navigating.

The second half of the passage has a number of expressions about spatial relations: "keeping aloof," "free play," "which it touches," "refusing to lend itself to," the three references to attaching, then, finally, having "nothing to do with." All these relate to touching and keeping distance, and the idioms of navigation state as a purpose, keeping criticism from touching practicality. The only conspicuous metaphors occur in the first sentence and they concern that tabooed practicality: criticism is to keep its distance "in order to avail itself of the field now opening to it, and to produce fruit for the future." I take it they are (roughly) agricultural.

In short, the metaphors of the passage seem to say, criticism should navigate so as to keep clear of things and bear fruit that way. If I listen to such metaphors with the third ear, I hear as their very deeply buried fantasy content a wish for procreation without touching. Farfetched as this may seem, I think the fantasy becomes quite clear later in this paragraph, in a sentence whose unconscious content is revealed by a single deletion. Arnold is complaining of the present state of English criticism: "Our organs of criticism are organs of men . . . having practical ends to serve, and with them those practical ends are the first thing and the play of mind the second." Though they are very deeply buried, words like "organs," "ends," and "serve" have sexual connotations. I am perfectly sure Arnold did not consciously intend these connotations—but he did choose the words he did.

If I am correct, Arnold's quite reasonable intellectual position, that criticism should eschew practicality, has unconscious roots in a wish to avoid sexual touchings. His prose mannerisms of labeling and buffering serve to put off or avoid some final active meshing in the sentence. From a psychoanalytic point of view, I would characterize Arnold's naming and looking and question-and-answering as defenses against or intellectual substitutes for words of action, action being felt as sexualized.* And it is this constant intervention

---

* "Dover Beach" builds on the same or a very similar fantasy. We should recognize that this kind of analysis of syntactic pattern, like an analysis of fantasy content, enables us to understand a man's prose style as part of his total personality.[14]

of Arnold's that gives me, at least, the feeling "someone is there," someone who fends off whatever might disrupt balance, urbanity, or sense.

Thus, our formula "form manages content" seems to hold at both ends of the spectrum, the arts of "pure form" and the arts of almost "pure content." In one, form is almost everything; in the other, form is almost nothing. But in both, form acts to manage fantasy content. In the arts of pure form, we bring the fantasies, and we bring them in a form sufficiently raw so that (if we are paying proper attention to the music as music) they never even become conscious. In the arts of pure content, the fantasies have already been heavily sublimated by intellectual concerns, and there is little for form to do. We do not pay much attention to it, but it does nevertheless play a limited role in handling the quite heavily disguised fantasy content.

To summarize, form can only be understood as managing fantasy content. Form in the larger sense of structure or sequence manages content by controlling what we are aware of at any given moment. Devices like point of view, juxtaposition, omission, cross-cutting, splitting—these all handle fantasy content in large units. Form in the smaller sense of particular rhythms, rhymes, and sounds manages content in more detailed ways.

Form in this smaller sense operates within a framework: a displacement of our psychic concern (cathexis) from the "deep" fantasy level toward a "higher" level of verbal activity. We respond less from the level of unconscious ego, more from the level of conscious ego. Such a displacement of cathexis (or, loosely, attention) becomes possible whenever the expression of fantasy comes in language other than that we ourselves would have used. But this displacement is a matter of degree. It is almost total in very special languages like those of Ogden Nash or music. The displacement is minimal in ordinary language like the prose of this book.

Within this displacement, language manages fantasy in at least three ways. First, we introject the sounds of poetry or music kinesthetically. We take in crashes and codas, dentals and sibilants, as muscular ways of dealing with content: spitting out, hissing at, biting off, striking, stopping, and so on. Second, on a more mental level, we find in the sounds of poetry or music a sort of pseudo-logic that offers mastery of the fantasy material. Particularly effective are economies—repetitions of sound sequences that reduce the net number of sound patterns we have to deal with. Third, particular details both gratify and violate our expectations as to form. If they gratify, they give a pleasurable sense of mastery (up to a point—then boredom). If they violate expectancies, they affect us like "syntactically deviant utterances"—they confirm our original displacement toward language.

There may be more than these three modes, but even these three offer considerable explanatory power. For one thing, by recognizing that form manages content, we can understand why form and content are so touchy. The slightest change in either makes a big change in effect—because we are dealing with a balance of forces. This balancing goes on in each word of a literary text; that is, each word both expresses fantasy and fits into a formal pattern that manages fantasy.

Further, and more important, we are beginning to see in fairly detailed terms how literature arouses our emotional response. Our affect comes from massive fantasies massively managed by formal devices which are analogous to defenses. The sources of affect show most clearly in the contrast between music and non-fiction prose. Form plays a minimal role in prose. What fantasy content there is, the writer has already reworked rather far in the direction of meaning. Form plays a maximal role in music, and we respond far more emotionally to music. It seems a fair inference that our emotional response to works of art comes much more from form than from the act of meaning. But, as anyone knows who has ever abstracted a form (say, the rhyme-scheme of a sonnet), form alone does not excite. Now we can see it is only form as manager of fantasy that arouses.

If so, then we can understand the truism that we respond more

directly and immediately and emotionally to music than to literature. Music is entirely the management of fantasy—and, moreover,
those fantasies that inevitably excite us most, our own. Literature,
by contrast, constrains us to the writer's fantasies. But this is probably not the crucial factor, for people are pretty catholic in their
literary tastes. We find we can respond richly to many fantasies
that are not our own favorites.

The crucial difference is that literature works with language. I do
not mean to imply that the "language" of music is any less a matter for the conscious ego than the language of literature—on the
contrary, we learn music much later in development than words.
Rather, because literature works with words, inevitably, it must, in
expressing fantasy, transform fantasy at least somewhat toward
conscious social, moral, intellectual, or religious meaning. Inevitably, then, there is less managing of fantasy for form to do. In
music, the sounds do not express the fantasy—we bring it, raw,
unmediated, half-unconscious. Form must do all the defensive
managing, and, since this managing seems to make the biggest
part of our emotional response, our response is greater.

Similarly, through the notion of form managing fantasy, we can
understand the special place of poetry among the literary genres. I
think most critics today (like their neo-classic predecessors) think
of poetry as "higher" than prose, with epic, dramatic, or narrative
poetry "outranking" the lyric. Yet, even the most sophisticated
readers, I think, can "lose themselves" more easily in Ian Fleming
or Conan Doyle than in *Paradise Lost*. Most people respond to
prose fiction, good, bad, or indifferent, more directly than to
poetry. For example, pornography (by which I mean simply literature which arouses sexual desire); there is no such thing as verse
pornography. Bawdiness, yes. Pornography, no.

In other words, part of our emotional response comes from the
presentation of fantasy directly (not transformed toward meaning). Music draws on this source of response, though it is we who
present the fantasy. In fiction, the writer presents it. In narrative
poetry, too, the writer presents a fantasy, but he presents it dis-

placed upward into language that concerns us with language as such. We feel poetry is "higher" because it does indeed appeal to higher ego levels, stages later in development than the visual fantasies of theater or drama or cinema or the more easily visualized fantasies of fiction. Some people make this displacement of fantasy to language readily. For most, it is an ability not easily acquired, and, for that reason, poetry itself is a not easily acquired taste. The narrative poet inevitably provides more defensive management of fantasy than the prose storyteller. Prose tends to transform fantasy toward meaning; poetry does that but also displaces cathexis to the verbal level. Inevitably, then, a narrative in prose will make a stronger, more direct appeal as fantasy than the same story in verse.

Given these two sources of emotional appeal—the response to the fantasy; the management of fantasy by form—we can understand Auden's statements about the comic poet: *

> In the process of composition, as every poet knows, the relation between experience and language is always dialectical, but in the finished product it must always appear to the reader to be a one-way relationship. In serious poetry thought, emotion, event must always appear to dictate the diction, metre, and rhyme in which they are embodied; vice versa, in comic poetry it is the words, metre, rhyme which must appear to create the thoughts, emotions, events they require . . . Again, while in serious poetry detectable padding of lines is fatal, the comic poet should appear openly and unashamedly to pad.[15]

In our terms, the serious poet tries not to over-manage fantasy content, not to force too strict a displacement to language, so as to preserve our responses to the fantasy material itself. He prefers to see fantasy managed by sequence or structure rather than by displacement to language. The comic poet, however, by displacing more and more of our concern to a purely verbal level, over-manages the fantasy content, leaves us with little emotional re-

* Quoted in the Preface as an example of critical insight with hidden psychological assumptions.

sponse to it, and we achieve "comic detachment." He wants us to feel the fantasy content as quite weak compared to the overpowering logic of the verse form.

But, more important than these comparisons among artistic genres, understanding that form manages fantasy enables us to see art in relation to life itself. How can it be that something as artifically and arbitrarily structured as a symphony or a sonnet can make us have an experience like our experiences in real life? We seem to encounter in art heightened, purified versions of life, because when we experience art, we fantasy and we work with the work of art to manage our fantasies defensively. But virtually every moment of our lives we manage fantasies defensively. The artificial structures of the sonnet or the couplet or even the limerick simply do for, or really, with us, what we must ordinarily do by ourselves. In a way, we seek literary forms because we wish we could manage life itself as adroitly as a sonnet does. In the human mind, then, art re-creates its own paradoxical dual nature, the compounding of sound and sense, artificial form and lifelike content. And it is precisely the artificiality, the unlifelikeness of artistic forms that lets us find in art one great and continuous harmony with life.

6 Meaning as Defense

Meaning, we have seen, is not static but dynamic: a transformation of the fantasy at the core of a literary work into terms satisfactory to an adult ego. But meaning is more, as we can see when meaning is—or seems at first to be—absent, a situation nowhere so visible as in contemporary cinema. Late in 1958, Janus Films released on a largely unsuspecting American public Bergman's *The Seventh Seal* and so started a flood in the art theaters of what seems to be a new genre in film, "the puzzling movie": *Hiroshima, Mon Amour, Les Amants, Les Cousins, The Magician, L'Avventura, Juliet of the Spirits, Red Desert, Blow-Up*—to name but a few of these films, most of which almost dazzle with their richness, their sheer filmic excellence. As a genre, they represent perhaps the only sustained group of films after the advent of sound to be truly and overwhelmingly visual: these films look good like a cinema should.

Arthur Schlesinger, Jr., has suggested they are creating a new "Movie Generation" to replace those of us who grew up, cinematically, on the popcorn and cheesecake Hollywood classics of the 'thirties.[1] Another reviewer calls these the "undergraduate movies," and there is much truth in the adjective, if we extend it to include not only the four-year kind, but also the perpetual undergraduates on the other side of the lectern. These are indeed films that make their chief appeal to the academic and the intellectual.

But why do they appeal to anybody? If you stand outside an art theater as the audience comes out from a "puzzling movie," you will hear over and over again in a variety of phrasings and degrees of profanity, "What was *that* all about?" As an academic joke has it, one sophomore to another, "Have you seen *Last Year at Marienbad?*" The other slowly, thoughtfully, "I—don't know." The feeling these films almost invariably leave us with is, "It means something, but just what I don't know," and the theorist of meaning must ask, Why should that feeling of puzzlement give pleasure to us?

It doesn't, of course, to everyone. Popular as these films may be among intellectuals and academics, there are plenty of people who find them simply boring. At a somewhat more sophisticated level (I am thinking of the usual reviewer for the daily paper), we hear two kinds of complaint. First, these films make just one more statement of the moral and social confusion of the century. Second, we are likely to find a sexual indignation, for these films are rather strikingly casual about such matters. There were, for example, the two proper Bostonian ladies who went to see *The Virgin Spring*. During that appalling rape scene, one leaned over to the other and whispered, "You know, in Sweden, things are like that." And, in fact, sex in these films does tend to be either rape or mere amusement, a kind of bedroom Olympics in which neither the Russians nor the Americans stand a chance—only Common Market countries.

Sex and *mal de siècle*—these films have them in abundance, but the quality that still stands out is the puzzlement they create. Contrast a film-maker like Eisenstein. He uses montage, symbolism, and the rest not very differently from the way the makers of the puzzling movies do, but Eisenstein aims to communicate his socialist and Marxist message, and his symbols serve that end. The maker of the puzzling movie, on the other hand, as much as hangs out a sign that says, "Figure it out—if you can." His symbols serve not so much to communicate as to suggest or even to mystify. (Think, for example, of the devilfish at the end of *La*

Dolce Vita and all the different interpretations of it.) Yet, despite the intentional mystification, we take pleasure in them just the same—these films are puzzling in more than one sense.

In particular, there are two ways they puzzle us. They puzzle us as to their meaning in a total sense. They puzzle us scene-by-scene simply as to what is going on in a narrative or dramatic way. Let me consider, first, our puzzlement as to meaning—Why should these films, that seem almost to hide their own meaning, please us?

To answer that question, it helps (as usual) to take a detour by way of the joke, for jokes often have the same riddling quality as, say, a film by Antonioni. Often, we have to solve some little problem before we "get" the joke—for example, the old saw cited by Freud, "A wife is like an umbrella—sooner or later one has to take a taxi." The riddling form draws and holds our attention to the joke. In a puzzling movie, it draws and holds our attention to the film. As Marshall McLuhan puts it:

> Fellini and Bergman pull the story line off the film and the result is that you become much more profoundly involved in the film process. When you put a story line on a novel or a film, you're much less involved. Edgar Allan Poe discovered that if you take the story line off the detective story, the audience has to participate and make the story as it goes. And so, paradoxically, pull the story line off any situation and you get a much higher level of creative participation on the part of the reader, or the audience. Fellini's "8½" is a world where the audience has to work very hard. The same as abstract art.[2]

More specifically, as the mention of Poe's detective stories suggests, the riddling form engages our processes of intellection; in technical terms, the ego's secondary-process or problem-solving thinking. The riddling form busies us with solving the riddle and incidentally enables less relevant, less presentable thoughts prompted by the joke to sneak up on us, to take us unawares, as it were. So with the puzzling film: its enigmatic promise of "meaning" not only draws and holds our attention to the film; it also distracts us from the real source of our pleasure in the film, the thoughts and desires it evokes.

That is, if we think of meaning simply in terms of Freud's early model, a joke's promise that there will be an intellectual meaning, a "point," enables us to relax and enjoy a playing with words and ideas that we would ordinarily dismiss as childish or insane: intellectual content justifies form. At the same time, the play with words and ideas acts as an additional and preliminary source of pleasure. The pleasure in this play unbalances the usual equilibrium between our tabooed impulses and our censoring defenses, and it provides the extra to topple those defenses—we laugh. In other words, the promise of "point" (or intellectual content) in the joke justifies the form; then the pleasure we take in form allows another kind of content to break through, and we gratify through the "point" a disguised version of some sexual or aggressive impulse we would ordinarily hold in check.

The same process seems to operate with the puzzling movie. The feeling we have is: "This means something, but I don't know what." "This means something," the first part of our reaction, acts like intellectual content in the joke—it justifies form; it bribes our reason to accept the incoherent stream of images or the incoherent narrative of the puzzling movie. Then, our pleasure in those images, the sheer visual beauty of the films in this genre, acts like form: it allows us to enjoy the forbidden content of the film.

But what is this forbidden content? In the joke-situation, we can usually identify the hidden impulse of hostility or obscenity that the joke works with. The content of the puzzling movie is not so easy to get at.

We can get a clue, though, from the adverse reactions to the films. Those reviewers and audiences for whom the puzzling quality doesn't work complain of two things: the casual attitude toward sex and the feeling that the films express in a peculiarly negative way the moral confusions of the age. For the disappointed critics

of these films, the form didn't work, and the fantasies prompted by
the film came through raw and repulsive: sexual promiscuity and a
fear of moral confusion.

The sexual angle is the easier (and more pleasurable) to see.
These films are extraordinarily free about such matters—I am
thinking of such scenes as Jeanne Moreau's taking a bath in *Les
Amants* and *La Notte*; the striptease in *La Dolce Vita*; the scenes
of lovemaking in *Hiroshima*; rape in *The Virgin Spring, Through
a Glass Darkly*, or *Marienbad*. In effect, the puzzling quality
of the films gives us an intellectual justification for gratifying the
simplest of visual desires, looking at sexy things. This, I hasten
to add, is a crude, first-order effect, but nevertheless a very important part of the appeal of even these very sophisticated and intellectual films. Or, for that matter, their lack of appeal—read Bosley
Crowther.

The puzzling movies are an intellectual's version of the old De
Mille Bible epic, where we gratify our sexual desires by watching
the wicked Assyrians, Philistines, Romans, or whomever carry on
their grand pagan orgies, but we are justified by the ponderously
moral content of the film. The biblical frame allows us to gratify
almost shamelessly the seventh and least of the sinful impulses. I
say, "us," but no doubt I do you an injustice: no proper intellectual would be fooled by the crudity of the moral sop in the De
Mille versions of the Bible, and this is not the kind of justification
the puzzling movie gives us. The puzzling movie presents itself as
an intellectual and aesthetic problem rather than a moral one, and
then perhaps it does fool the intellectual in the same amiable way
that jokes and works of art do: the puzzling movie engages his intellectual attention and lets the dark underside of the self (which
even intellectuals have) gratify its chthonic wishes.

We can see the process *in statu nascendi*, as it were, in Leslie
Fiedler's remarkable review of a "nudie" movie, *The Immoral
Mr. Teas*.[3] He looks at this film and finds in it "ambiguity," "ir-
reality," "a world of noncontact and noncommunication." He
treats this jolly and ribald movie as an index to the American na-

tional character, illustrates from it American attitudes toward the body, and (most strikingly) contrasts the nudity in *The Immoral Mr. Teas* with the more humane nudity in *Room at the Top* and *Hiroshima, Mon Amour*. In other words, Mr. Fiedler's astute analysis has erected such an intellectual "meaning" for this film (though it is scarcely above the level of a stag movie) that any self-respecting intellectual could go see it with a clear conscience and a blithe spirit—of analysis. Mr. Fiedler does it with criticism; the puzzling film-maker does it with his camera; but, in either case, the intellectual promise of "meaning" justifies the simpler and more primitive pleasure.

Leslie Fiedler treats *The Immoral Mr. Teas* in intellectual and aesthetic terms, whereas the "meaning" that justified the content of the biblical epic was its religious and moral "message." This displacement from moral message to intellectual meaning is itself a source of pleasure in the puzzling movie, particularly for the intellectuals to whom the puzzling movie makes its chief appeal. After all, moral and religious issues have a strong and perhaps frightening emotional overtone. Aesthetic and intellectual "meaning" seems much more manageable. The notion that the moral confusions of this the most trying of centuries can be shifted over to the very kind of aesthetic and intellectual puzzle at which highbrows are adept is itself a very comforting hope indeed. And again, confirmation of this source of pleasure comes from those in the audience who find no pleasure in this displacement: the films clearly deal with moral problems, but for those in the audience who cannot accept the films' translation of moral issues into intellectual ones, the puzzling movies seem merely to express moral problems without answering them, and these critics say the films just prove the sickness of the century.

So far, then, we have found three sources of pleasure in the way these films puzzle us as to meaning. First, we feel that somehow this film "means something," and that promise of content or "point" enables us to take a straightforward sensuous pleasure in the seemingly incoherent and puzzling visual form of the film. That preliminary visual pleasure in form combines with a less acceptable source of visual pleasure in content: peeping at some very erotic scenes. The combination of these pleasures from form and from content unbalance and override our usual inhibitions. At the same time, these films displace moral and social inhibition into aesthetic and intellectual demands for "meaning," something that intellectuals (at least) find much easier to resolve, and the puzzling quality so provides yet a third source of pleasure.

This kind of economic analysis, however, seems highly abstract. Somehow, we are missing some of the essential quality of these films. We can get closer by looking at the second source of puzzlement: not total "meaning," but the scene-by-scene, simple narrative riddle of, What's going on?

I have suggested that one of the brute, root sources of pleasure in these films is simply that of looking at sexual scenes. Yet sex in these films has a peculiar and special quality. Jeanne Moreau's bath scenes in *Les Amants* and *La Notte*—the first occurs in the context of a casual affair; in the second her husband is simply bored by the sight. Similarly, the husband is bored by Romy Schneider's long and lovely bath scene in the Visconti episode of *Boccaccio 70*, a visual feast but an emotional fast. The striptease in *La Dolce Vita* and virtually all the sex in that film is without any emotion but simple desire. Again, there is simply lust or hate in the rape scenes of *The Virgin Spring* or *Rocco and His Brothers*. The same quality shows in those seductions tantamount to rapes by the heroine of *Through a Glass Darkly*, by the nymphomaniac at the hospital in *La Notte*, or the lover of *Red Desert*. The opening love scenes of *Hiroshima, Mon Amour* set out another casual love affair; the woman's voice drones on the sound track throughout the sequence much as the narrator's voice drones on in *Marienbad* debating with himself whether he took the woman by force or not. *The Seventh Seal*, perhaps the finest film in the genre, seems to vary this emotionless pattern, but not really: Bergman isolates sex *cum* love in the juggler and his wife, those who escape Death; while the knight and his wife, the squire and his girl rescued from rape, the black-smith's wife seduced by the actor, all show the same dogged love-lessness which seems to be the distinctive feature of human rela-tionships in the puzzling movie.

This emotionlessness does not confine itself to sexuality, either. Think, for example, of the cryptic face of Max von Sydow in *The Seventh Seal* or Monica Vitti's classical mask in the Antonioni tril-ogy. These films are cryptic on the simple level of, What's he thinking? What's he feeling? The suicide of Steiner in *La Dolce Vita* reveals some underlying emotional reality his aesthetic and in-tellectual life had screened, but what? The disappearance of Anna in *L'Avventura*, her earlier cry of "Sharks!" in the swimming se-quence—these tell us something about her inner life, but what? The long, circling walk of the lovers in the last third of *Hiroshima, Mon Amour*, the fashion-plate style of *Marienbad*, the disguises in *The Magician*, all show us cryptic outward actions as a substitute for inner emotions not revealed.

All through the puzzling movies, in other words, we are seeing events without understanding their meaning, particularly their emotional meaning. We are simply not permitted to become fully aware of what is going on emotionally. This sensation, though, is not by any means a new one, special to the puzzling movies. In fact, these films duplicate an experience we have all had, which was at one time irritating, even frightening, a constant reminder of our own helplessness in the face of forces much bigger than we. I am thinking of the child's situation, surrounded by a whole range of adult emotions and experiences he cannot understand. "What's that man doing, Mommy?" is a not inappropriate comment on the whole genre of "puzzling movies."

Typically, the child does not even have the words with which to grasp these adult emotions and experiences, a circumstance these films duplicate by happenstance. That is, they are foreign-language films which put us again in a position where the big people, the ones we see on the screen, have all kinds of complex experiences which they speak about in a language we cannnot understand.

Even for those of us who spent some time with the tongues, these films make us regress, grow backward into children, a second way by their intentionally visual and filmic quality. They take us back to the picture language of the comic strip, of children, and of dreams.

There is still a third way these films take us back to the child's frame of mind: in sexuality. The child's dim awareness of adult sexuality very much resembles the sexuality of the puzzling movies. He can see or, more usually, imagine the physical act, but he cannot feel the whole range of complex emotions and experiences the adult knows as love. Rather, the child understands the act of sex as something associated with violence and danger,[4] as we see it, for example, in *The Virgin Spring, Rocco and His Brothers, La Dolce Vita, Hiroshima, Mon Amour, Last Year at Marienbad, Les Cousins, Red Desert,* and the rest. The child is aroused at his sexual fantasies and a bit afraid of his own arousal, as indeed we ourselves tend to be at a puzzling movie. Further, the child's general uncertainty about the adult world finds a focus for itself in his uncertainty, arousal, and fear at this particular area of adult life—sexuality. It serves as a nucleus for his total puzzlement at adult emotions and actions, just as the sexuality in the puzzling movies serves as the nucleus of the total atmosphere of mysterious, baffling emotions and motivations.

In various ways, then, the puzzling quality at the story level of these films takes us back to a childhood situation of puzzlement, but presents it now as an intellectual and aesthetic puzzle rather than an emotional one in real life. "This event obviously says something about the emotional life of these people, but I don't know what, and it's only a film anyway." The film puzzles, disturbs, presents us with an emotional riddle, but puts it in an intellectual and aesthetic context.

Further, it transforms the emotional puzzle into precisely the kind of puzzle that an "undergraduate" audience might feel it could solve, an intellectual and aesthetic puzzle instead of an emotional one. In other words, not only do these films take us back to child-

hood disturbances; they seem to say we can master those disturbances by the strategies of our adult selves, our ability to solve aesthetic and intellectual puzzles. And we dutifully try to puzzle them
out.

One way, then, the puzzling movies appeal to their intellectual
audiences is by offering the possibility of mastering childish puzzlement by the defenses of the adult intellectual. For example, most
intellectuals have a good deal of curiosity. The reason psychologists
give is that their early attempts to solve the puzzles of childhood
became a way of life. In technical jargon, infantile curiosity became
sublimated into the intellectual and aesthetic curiosity of the adult.
Now the puzzling movie comes along and enables us to do, or
think we can do, just what our life style has been wanting to do all
along: solve the riddle of emotions and sexuality by purely intellectual means. Would that we could!

The puzzling movies play into the intellectual's life style in another way. Academics and intellectuals often present the appearance to other people of "cold fish," the reason being that it is typical of the highly intellectualized person that he puts up a barrier
between sensuous emotional experience and the intellectual problems with which he concerns himself. The puzzling movie enables
him to do this again—to put aside the emotional mysteries of the
film and see it coldly, using intellection as a defense. In short, the
puzzling movies take us, as any great work of art does, along the
whole spectrum of our development from infancy to adulthood; or,
at least, they do for most of their "undergraduate" audience.

There is, though, one special reaction that deserves notice: some
critics feel no uncertainty at all—at least on the narrative level.
The usual review of an Antonioni film for example, in a film magazine or a literary quarterly, will tell you scene by scene and scowl
by scowl what each of the characters is thinking at every given
moment.[5] For this kind of person, there is no mystery in the
puzzling movie, or, more properly, his careful observation of the
film enables him to say that he has seen everything there is to be
seen. There is no mystery—he understands the emotional riddle.

This response offers a variant but no less pleasurable way of over-coming that residue of childish bafflement in us—instead of shift-ing it to an adult intellectual problem, the critic simply says it doesn't exist at all: there is no puzzle. And this procedure is no less satisfying than the other ways the puzzling movie works.

To bring all these ways together, the puzzling movie turns its puzzling quality into pleasure in two large areas. First, it presents itself as an aesthetic mystery: What does it "mean"? As in a joke, the oblique promise of a "point" enables us to relax our demand for coherence and take sensuous pleasure in the incoherent visual form of the film. Then, that visual form lets us take pleasure in the sexual content and, at the same time, shifts any moral qualms we might have to intellectual and aesthetic qualms. Second, the puz-zling movie presents us with a mystery on a simple narrative or dramatic level: What's going on? This second kind of mystery displaces a child's feeling of bafflement into an aesthetic mystery that a sophisticated, intellectual audience, no longer children, can feel confident about solving.

There is a lesson here about movies in general, for all movies take us back to childhood. They give us a child's pleasure in look-ing at things, which film critics respond to in their demand that the film be true to its medium, that it be visual. Similarly, the film takes us back to a pre-verbal stage of development; and, again, crit-ics demand that the picture make its point, not through words on the soundtrack, but through pictures. Most important, however, there is that certain feeling people have, that looking at a film is somehow "passive." In fact, of course, the film involves no more passivity than reading a novel or watching a play, and yet there is something akin to passivity in the cinematic transaction.

Wolfenstein and Leites, in their classic study of the psychology of the movie audience, find part of that sensation of passivity in the audience's "peering with impunity" at the big people on the screen:

> What novels could tell, movies can show. Walls drop away be-fore the advancing camera. No character need disappear by go-

ing off-stage. The face of the heroine and the kiss of lovers are magnified for close inspection. The primal situation of excited and terrified looking, that of the child trying to see what happens at night, is re-created in the theater; the related wish to see everything is more nearly granted by the movies than by the stage. The movie audience is moreover insured against reaction or reproof from those whom they watch because the actors are incapable of seeing them. The onlooker becomes invisible.[6]

The actors, in short, can't fight back, and that is one way the film seems a "passive" medium.

The other side of the coin is that we can't provoke the actor. Unlike the stage situation where the length of our laughter or the solemnity of our listening will affect the actor's performance; unlike the television situation where we can turn the box off, get up for a beer or whatnot, we have no such effect on the film which grinds away its twenty-four pictures a second as relentlessly as Niagara Falls. We are powerless, as we were when we were children, to change the doings of the "big people." Now, though, we are immune, the giants on the screen cannot affect us, either. Our regression is safe, secure, and highly pleasurable.

This regression to the safe but powerless child, it seems to me, is the reason people feel watching a film is somehow "passive": the big people cannot act on us; we cannot act on them. This regression, of course, is a key source of pleasure not only in the puzzling movies, but in all films, and especially those which, like the puzzling movies, make their appeal visually, that is, those in which the pre-verbal element of the film is especially strong.

In fact, we could define cinematic achievement in terms of what it does with this visual, pre-verbal element in the situation of safe helplessness induced by the motion picture. In the case of silent comedy, the action on the screen says to us, in effect, "This mysterious pre-verbal world of violence and disaster is really harmless— it's all right." Eisenstein's films and others of the montage school say, "This mysterious pre-verbal world you see is meaningful. You understand it, and you respond to it emotionally and morally." The puzzling movie says to us, "This mysterious pre-verbal world you see, though you don't understand it, still it can be solved."

The puzzling film pleases us because it is, as in the last analysis all art is, a comfort.

What is special about the puzzling movies is that they use their very obscurity to achieve the comforting transformations of drive that other works from friendlier ages achieved through meaning. In effect, they invite us to view them as aesthetic and intellectual puzzles—and we do, because we need to feel that our watching has a "point" and, many intellectuals of the 'sixties would prefer, a purely intellectual rather than an emotional or moral "point."

The puzzling movies tell us why we supply meaning, and they hint what a literary work's not supplying meaning does to our response. But what does the more conventional literary work do to our response when it does supply meaning? To put the issue more concretely, how does Brecht affect us compared to Ionesco? [7]

Both playwrights decry the use of the theater to provide moral, intellectual, or emotional exercise. Both continually analogize to boxing or tennis or acrobatics. Brecht, in particular, seems obsessed with the idea that audiences should be able to smoke so they will achieve "an attitude of smoking-and-watching."

Yet one should not take this professed anti-intellectuality or meaninglessness too seriously. I know of no more intelligent explication of the meaning of The Bald Soprano than Ionesco's own simple phrase, "the tragedy of language" or of The Chairs than his flat statement: "The theme of The Chairs is the ontological void, or absence." Then there is Brecht's elegant comment on Galileo: "He thinks out of self-indulgence."

The insistence on meaninglessness rather means, I think, that Ionesco, at least, is asking his audience to respond to the world as he—and many of us—perceive it in the 'sixties. The beliefs and actions of the 'thirties seem out of date, as does its improvable world. Our cosmos seems rather to be polarized into a self of private, internal states confronting a vast, incomprehensible world to be managed, if at all, by experts. No wonder the puzzling movies came into being, duplicating in their audiences a child's situation surrounded by big and unmanageable forces. This polarization shows, too, in the so-called "theater of the absurd" or, better, "metatheater" (plays which call into question their own standing as plays). Martin Esslin has made abundantly clear the intellectual basis of "absurd" theater in an external world felt as sensuous, incomprehensible, and uncontrollable—it seems to me equally clear that the opposite or emotional side of the coin is a retreat into the self. Thus, Ionesco writes:

> To discover the fundamental problem common to all mankind, I must ask myself what *my* fundamental problem is, what *my* most ineradicable fear is. I am certain, then, to find the problems and fears of literally everyone.

> An avant-garde dramatist . . . is making a real attempt to return to the source. But what source? That of the theatre. A return to an inner ideal of the theatre, for it is in oneself that one discovers the deep and permanent foundations of theatre.

Against such a self, Ionesco poises an unchangeable world ("It is the 'historical' which is moribund, and the non-historical which remains alive") or a world with no pretensions toward truth:

> A world we invent cannot be false. It can only be false if I want to fabricate a truth and imitate truth, for in so doing I fabricate a false truth . . . to me it is the world that seems irrational.

One way to achieve such an invented world, he says, is to find the source of a play in

> a mood and not an ideology, an impulse not a program; the cohesive unity that grants formal structure to emotions in their primitive state satisfies an inner need and does not answer the logic of some structural order imposed from without; not submission to some predetermined action, but the exteriorization of one's psychic dynamism.

Another way to achieve such an invented world is to translate subjective states into metaphor and then act out the metaphor literally: "The unseen presence of our inner fears can also be materialized. So the author is not only allowed, but recommended to make actors of his props, to bring objects to life, to animate the scenery and give symbols concrete form."

The method is that of madness and Ionesco often sounds schizophrenic. He interviews himself as "ego" and "alter ego" or writes:

> At certain moments the world appears to me emptied of meaning, reality seems unreal. It is this feeling of unreality, the search for some essential reality, nameless and forgotten—and outside it I do not feel I exist—that I have tried to express . . .

> I have never quite succeeded in getting used to existence, whether it be the existence of the world or of other people, or above all of myself. Sometimes it seems to me that the forms of life are suddenly emptied of their contents, reality is unreal, words are nothing but sounds bereft of sense, these houses and this sky are no longer anything but facades concealing nothing, people appear to be moving about automatically and without reason; everything seems to melt into thin air, everything is threatened—myself included—by a silent and imminent collapse into I know not what abyss . . .

Ionesco is describing a crisis of self-object differentiation, an inability to distinguish between subjective states and objective reality, a schizophrenic crisis. While I feel fairly sure he is not literally mad, he does tempt his audiences into his own *furor poeticus.*

As an "absurd" playwright, Ionesco presents us with a seemingly nonsensical action onstage. As we have seen, every work of art, every play, as it involves us in itself, blurs the line between the self and the work of art the self confronts. We internalize the impulses acted out objectively by the work; we make them subjectively our own. Then the form and action and meaning of the play all serve as ways for us to deal with the conflicts aroused in us by those impulses. But the "absurd" playwright gives us no action, no relations between the characters, no readily available meaning, just a seemingly nonsensical set of actions. We try to make sense out of them; thus the absurdist, like the maker of puzzling movies, makes us take problem-solving intellection as our way of dealing with the conflicts created in us by his work.

At the same time, Ionesco is a metatheatrist; he calls into question our relationship to the work in the manner of Pirandello. He makes us aware that we have blurred ourselves into it. The metaplay creates, as *Don Quixote* does, a sense in us of personal uncertainty, uncertainty about our very selves and therefore a doubly radical quest for certainty again—we again strive to solve the riddle of the play.

In short, the absurd or metatheatrical playwright creates in us a state approximating schizophrenia: affectlessness, concretized metaphors, klang associations, depersonalization, an unclear relation of self to object; then he offers intellection as a self-defeating way of dealing with this miniature psychosis. This schizophrenic quality of absurdism and metatheater comes out most explicitly in Adamov's relation in *L'Aveu* of his own breakdown into schizophrenia and metatheater and his subsequent return simultaneously to health and a Brechtian social concern in his plays.

Brecht is metatheatrical in his use of "alienation," his calling into question the relation between the audience and the work or, in psychological terms, between self and object. He demands an acting style which is "a barrier to empathy." "Ceremonious. Ritual. Spectator and actor ought not to approach one another but to move apart." There must be "no illusions that the player is identical with the character and the performance with the actual event." "The audience must not be able to think that it has been transported to the scene of the story." "The actor has to discard whatever means he has learnt of getting the audience to identify itself with the characters which he plays."

Brecht is an absurdist in his quest for affectlessness, for being "cool": "The right attitude to any really important phenomenon is a casual (contemptuous) one, because it is the only one which permits complete concentration and real alertness." He calls for "coldness" in his audience, "an attitude of inquiry and criticism," a "verdict," and "understanding." He calls his plays "parables" and demands acting that will "enable and encourage the audience to draw abstract conclusions."

But Brecht, to the extent he is a Marxist, takes us back to "meaning as transformation." His plays have both a social concern and a placing of events in historical space and time that provides meaning: "True, profound, active application of alienation effects takes it for granted that society considers its condition to be historic and capable of improvement."

Brecht's plays thus differ from those of the absurdists much as Eisenstein's films differ from the "puzzling movies." Brecht's plays involve a belief, and thus Brecht, though he confuses his audiences in an absurdist way, offers something more than a riddle as a way of dealing with the confusion. Because a Brecht play offers belief as a solution to the conflicts of the play, we take this belief in with all the passion those conflicts arouse in us. Brecht can quite honestly say, "the 'attitude of criticism' which epic theater tries to arouse in its audience cannot be passionate enough for it." Thus, though Brecht decries interest in the self, though Ionesco proclaims it, it is Brecht who accepts the passionate self and Ionesco who calls it into question, who writes plays as affectless as schizophrenia.

Ionesco's plays are less moving than Brecht's, for Brecht has taken the best of both worlds. As a metatheatrist, Brecht gives us the special *frisson* we feel when our "willing suspension of disbelief" comes into question. And as absurdist, he denies us a realistic representation of people and events to act out for us fantasies and defenses for handling them ("The motions of the individual psyche are utterly uninteresting"). But as Marxist he does act out a defensive maneuver for us: he gives us belief in an ideology as a way of handling the unconscious conflicts his plays arouse. Rather than thrust us back on our own intellections, he does that work for us, and, as a result, we can respond more emotionally.

In effect, then, "meaning as transformation" does some of our responding—intellection—for us, so that we can respond in deeper ways. As Ernst Kris puts it (in another context): "The full investment by the ego, the syntonicity of the event with superego and id strivings may then lead to the feeling of certainty, to the change from 'I know of' to 'I believe.' " [8] And with belief, we have come round full circle to the "willing suspension of disbelief."

At a Brecht play, alienation there may be between actors and audience so that we disbelieve the fiction we see, but Brecht cannot totally avoid the laws that govern our response. We introject his play just as we do any other, and it stirs unconscious fantasies and conflicts in us. Then, when he gives us an ideology or "meaning as transformation" as a way of handling those unconscious issues, we commit ourselves to it; we "believe" for the length of the experience. We do so because we need the various strategies built into a work of art to handle for us the competing demands of id, ego, and superego.

Brecht's *Verfremdungseffekt* may correct our tendency to suspend our disbelief in his fictions, but he cannot turn us off entirely. We require strategies. If nothing is there to believe, as with Ionesco, we feel the need of it and we try to supply it by our own problem-solving faculties. We thus split off our "high" intellectual responses from our "low" sensuous ones; in doing so, we lose the emotional responses that in conventional literary works would join the high and the low.

In short, we seem to *need* meaning. We have already considered meaning as the transformation or sublimation of the unconscious fantasy embodied in the work. Presumably, meaning in that sense gratifies us as any sublimation would, with pleasure from the disguised satisfaction of drives. But, evidently, since we seem to need meaning, it must serve defensive as well as pleasurable functions. To see what they are, we must recapitulate.

In these first six chapters, we have been building a model of literary response. We began with a text which is, ultimately, a discrete collection of words to which we, the audience, give meaning and life to the extent we are "absorbed" by it. The metaphor of "absorption," however, reverses the true state of affairs. The reader, or member of the audience, at a rather primitive level, introjects the literary work so that what happens "in" it feels as though it were happening "in" him, more properly, in some undifferentiated "either." When the reader takes the work in, it brings to him its potentialities for fantasy, for defensive transformations, and for meaning. The reader in turn brings to it his capacity to fantasy and his own defensive structures (which I have loosely labeled, from Freud's earlier terminology, the "censor"). He also brings—and this is a vital element in his response—his own associations, fantasies, and fears related to the conscious and unconscious content of the literary work. For this, we have been using Simon O. Lesser's term, "analogizing": [9] when we perceive things in life, we bring to them our pre-existing psychic structure and experience; we do the same when we perceive literature. What we bring may be pleasurable fantasies or guilty or anxious ones, defensive structures like form, or intellectual ideas of meaning. And, of course, we bring our "higher" capacity to recognize the literary work as separate from us and to think rationally about it, specifically to explore its meaning. We have spoken of the introjecting and the intellecting reader.

For the purposes of our model, we have "stretched" the text to represent these two different kinds of reading as though these responses were "in" the text itself.* Consciously, as described in Chapter 1, we give or find in the text "meaning" by a process of successive abstraction and classification from the words and events of the text. Unconsciously, we introject the text and feel its nuclear fantasy as though it were our own unconscious fantasy—yet we are not aware of it as such.

In consciously analyzing the text for its core of fantasy, though, we arrive at it by a process of abstraction similar to that for intellectual "meaning." However, instead of using the social, moral, or intellectual categories appropriate to theme and meaning in their customary sense, we use a "dictionary" of likely fantasies (Ch. 2); and we make connections, not by the logical processes of secondary thought, but by the peculiar shortcuts and associations of the primary process. Both the "meaning" and the fantasy act as "central" ideas that inform the text: if we have analyzed them correctly, they will bring every element in the text to a central focus. Further, "meaning" and fantasy are related: intellectual meaning is an ego-

---

* See the diagram on p. 61.

syntonic transformation of the unacceptable fantasy content (Ch.
1). We have called what does this transforming, "form," that is,
what shapes our response and makes it different from our response
to the raw fantasy.

That response itself has conscious, unconscious, and preconscious
components. Meaning represents our conscious intellection about
the text as a separate entity. Form, we are not normally aware of,
but we can become aware of it if we concentrate on it—hence it is,
roughly, preconscious. The nuclear fantasy we find in a literary
work we normally cannot recover without considerable effort, and
perhaps not even then—hence, it is unconscious. We are arriving at
it here, first, by decoding symbols (a questionable shortcut); second,
by my finding through self-analysis the nuclear fantasy which I am
experiencing and which I assume you share. As for the text itself,
each word is, of course, conscious as we perceive it, though a word
several hundred pages back may be only preconscious. In that
sense, the text as a whole shades off into preconsciousness or even
unconsciousness. For the purposes of our model, we have been
considering these relations between the reader and the work picto-
rially:

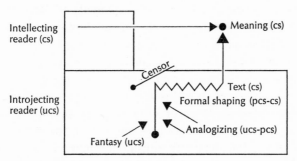

The model describes the potentialities. When we actually become engaged in literary response, when we are "with it," the actuality is the process of transformation, in which each of the levels
(fantasy, form, meaning) offers pleasure in itself and modifies the
possibilities of pleasure from other levels. We take in the fantasy
which is an "hallucinatory gratification." In literature as in life,

such a fantasy will typically both give pleasure and provoke anxiety. To the extent it gives pleasure, we simply get pleasure from it. To the extent it provokes anxiety, it must be modified to reduce the anxiety. Form and meaning are the two agents that control and manage the fantasy, and they in turn may be sources of pleasure in themselves.

The devices in the text that we have lumped together as "form" may give pleasure in at least three different ways. First, to the extent the unconscious fantasy evokes guilt or anxiety, form gives pleasure (or, more properly, removes pain) as it defensively manages that part of the fantasy (Ch. 4). The defenses built into the literary work enable its unconscious content to get around the reader's censor and achieve imaginary gratification. Not only that, these defenses can manage the fantasies the reader analogizes to the work, and conversely, his own pre-existing defenses may manage the work's fantasy. Second, form as displacement to a verbal level and as verbal play may be pleasurable in itself (Ch. 5), and so may, as Freud suggested, overbalance the "censor" (I have shown him tipped). Third, form may in and of itself gratify libidinal or aggressive drives (as, in Chapter 4, I suggested, denial or splitting might satisfy aggressive drives). If so, form represents an extremely powerful multiplier of pleasure to "bribe" the inhibiting censor.

The act of meaning may offer pleasure simply as a disguised version or sublimation of the original fantasied gratification (Ch. 1). This chapter, however, somewhat complicates our notion of meaning by finding additional sources of gratification from it, gratifications analogous to those of form. That is, people typically respond to works like the "puzzling movies" or Ionesco's plays by trying to supply the apparently missing meaning: we try to "solve" them. Since we do, meaning must do something for us in the literary experience more complicated than the more or less direct gratifications shown in our preliminary model (drawn above and in Chapter 3), for we would not "need" the pleasure of our own intellections. Rather, since we do feel a positive need for meaning, meanings must do something for us analogous to what a defense does—if it is missing, we try to supply it.

This is another sense in which form and content are inseparable: form acts like a defense to permit the partial gratification of fantasy; so does meaning. We could represent this more complicated, final model this way:

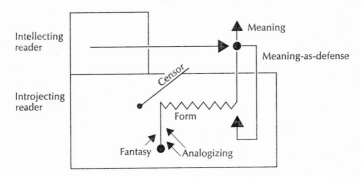

We supply meaning in order to permit expression of and pleasure from the core fantasy. This final model * shows meaning's dual role: a sublimation "in" the work itself of its own fantasy content; something analogous to a defense which we supply and without

---

* The metapsychologically inclined may be curious about the relation of this, the completed model, to the five criteria of psychoanalytic explanation. Basically, the model is a dynamic one, treating the "unconscious content" of the literary work as a fantasy in its audience pressing toward gratification, eluding the barriers of repression ("the censor") by defenses in the reader and defenses built into the literary work. I have no doubt the model could be stated economically as cathexes and countercathexes in the manner of Freud's fourth chapter in *Jokes*, but I think such an extension had best be left to someone who finds the notion of "psychic energy" more congenial to work with than I do.

As for the structural hypothesis, it would not be difficult to assign fantasy, form, meaning, intellection, introjection, and censorship to id, ego, and superego. Lesser, for example, has already analyzed the contributions of the various structures to literary response. Primarily, though, our response to literature takes place within the ego, a drama played out among id-representatives, superego-representatives, and functions of the ego. The nuclear fantasy is properly an id-representative in the unconscious ego, as are the reader's analogizings. The text is read with autonomous ego-functions and analyzed by conscious ego. Introjection stems from drives to incorporate and takes place within the unconscious ego. The "censor" is simply the defensive ego, stemming from pressures of the superego on the ego; it, too, is unconscious. Since, however, I am working with texts as much as with minds and since the reader's response is primarily an

which our egos cannot accept the unintelligible but highly charged work of art. The most explicit and simple works will not ask us to provide meaning-as-defense; the most obscure and difficult will themselves provide little or no sublimatory meaning; but most art will stand between these two extremes. In most art, there will be both kinds of meaning.

The act of meaning—either type—offers three sources of pleasure analogous to the three sources of pleasure in form. First, we have seen in this chapter that (in literature as well as in life) a feeling we are engaged in a socially, morally, or intellectually responsible enterprise assuages guilt and anxiety. In the puzzling movies (or *Mr. Teas*), we can enjoy looking at the sex or nudity, free of guilt or anxiety, provided we feel we are also engaged in making statements about our world. In this sense, meaning or even the mere promise of meaning is a sop thrown to the superego. Second, though I have not tried to demonstrate it in this chapter, it should be fairly obvious that meaning also serves as an economizer. Like rhyme and other formal devices, it makes a condensation. We recognize recurring patterning of theme just as we recognize recurring patterns of sound; they create expectation and trust and gratify them. Like any perceived pattern, meaning also serves to economize the handling of incoming perceptual data. As a result, there would be gratifications associated with the ego. Finally, meaning offers drive gratification to the extent it handles the fan-

---

ego response, the older topographical entities work out somewhat more neatly than id, ego, and superego do.

Because we are considering only the adult reader, I am not really offering a genetic or developmental model except to the extent I locate the "unconscious content" in infantile fantasies. It is not difficult, though, to relate this model to developmental models such as Elizabeth R. Zetzel's: [10] the "rind" of unregressed ego represents autonomous ego functions; the "core" of regressed ego has stretched back along the developmental curves she sketches to the point of self-object differentiation or the "dream screen."

We have considered adaptive issues only with respect to sublimatory meaning (as the ego-syntonic transformation of fantasy). For a fuller discussion of the adaptive function of literature, I refer the metapsychologically inclined to the conclusion of the book.

tasy materials. Meaning offers mastery, as play does, and, like play, it satisfies whatever libidinal and aggressive drives are involved in turning passive experiences of fantasy into active ones—so, at any rate, Brecht's remarks on passionate commitment would seem to suggest, or Erikson's remarks on play.[11]

That is all, really, that meaning-as-defense need do: offer a mastery of the fantasy content—"make sense" of the text. A reader does not, therefore, need to settle for himself the exact, stringent kind of sublimatory meaning described in Chapter 1. Nor, in this context, need there be only one central meaning. Almost any kind of coherent thought about the work will open up the paths of gratification, so long as it "makes sense" of the text. Historical generalizations about period or genre or style; the resonant pronouncements that American Studies critics are likely to make about the American character; psychological comments about characters, author, or theme; phenomenological statements bringing out the essence of the writer's subjectivity; statements of moral, philosophical, or political import—all are ways different readers may "make sense" of a text, that is, make it acceptable to the conscious ego and so permit the fantasy content a disguised and sublimated gratification.

In one sense, then, it does not matter whether the meaning is "in" the text or whether the reader supplies it—either way, meaning opens up a kind of sublimatory path for fantasy gratification. Nevertheless, there is a difference: if the reader (in McLuhan's phrase) "has to participate and make the story as it goes," he must necessarily be less "absorbed" and more a separate, working person. His basic relationship of introjection and fusion with the work will be weakened. In their extreme form, the demands meaninglessness makes on an audience can lead to the special, emotionless kind of response we associate with "absurd" plays like Ionesco's. That is, imagine our model with the line associated with the text's act of meaning cut:

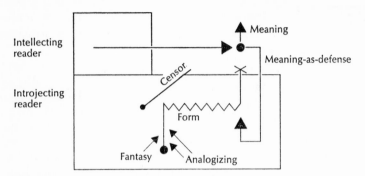

In order to get the defensive functions of meaning to which it is accustomed, the audience must step up its own intellection. We become more aware of ourselves as thinking beings, separate from the play. We are also more separated from our more primitive selves, for the "absurd" play does not make that connection for us. Not unsurprisingly, we often laugh at absurd plays, for they typically involve the same kind of radical dissociation of the intellect from the drive-gratifying self that a joke does. We split off our "high" and "low" responses, whereas more conventional literature tends to fuse them.

We are, in effect, dealing with a new kind of dissociated sensibility, on which T. S. Eliot's statement remains definitive. Contrasting the metaphysical poets as "intellectual" and the Romantics and Victorians as "reflective," he notes that the reflective poets

> do not feel their thought as immediately as the odour of a rose. A thought to Donne was an experience; it modified his sensibility. When a poet's mind is perfectly equipped for its work, it is constantly amalgamating disparate experience; the ordinary man's experience is chaotic, irregular, fragmentary. The latter falls in love or reads Spinoza, and these two experiences have nothing to do with each other, or with the noise of the typewriter or the smell of cooking; in the mind of the poet these experiences are always forming new wholes.[12]

In the mind of the modern poets of 1921–50, that is. But the "absurd" movement represents a new kind of romanticism, not one that stresses feeling and leaves intellect out, but one that stresses intellection and fails to make the emotional connections from the sensuous level of our response to the intellectual. As so often in literary works, Ionesco's artistic strategy makes us act out for ourselves his world-view: an incomprehensible world of sensuous experience which man madly tries—and usually fails—to make meaningful.

That is, of course, a maneuver in the work of art itself, but readers, too, maneuver. Our model or any analysis of a work based on it defines an experience in terms of different sources of pleasure—from fantasy, form, meaning, and their interactions. Our theory begins with an objective text and moves to an objective mechanism of response—to describe fantasy, form, and meaning and their interactions in the terms of an objective psychology. But, obviously, our subjective experience of literature varies widely. As introjecting readers we bring to literary works all kinds of different fantasies, associations, defenses, and drives.

Consequently, for different people, these different psychological elements in the text—fantasy, form, and meaning—will give different kinds and degrees of pleasure. For some, the assuaging of guilt or anxiety through form and meaning will be more gratifying than the fantasy-gratifications; for others the reverse. A man who readily accepts displacements of theme or fantasy to purely verbal forms will like poetry more than one who doesn't. To some people, the recreation of a world in "Dover Beach" will be inadequate as a defense, and they will feel the poem as utter despair. To others, the denial and divisions will over-manage the anxiety and to them, the poem will seem flat and trite. For still others, the nuclear fantasy and the poem's ways of managing it will match and add up to a rich, satisfying experience.

Our model cannot—and probably should not—try to define such subjective experiences. It can, however, explain them, and it does tell us how to look for the reasons. If someone tells us he prefers Brecht to Ionesco, he tells us not only something about them but also something about his own personality. If a man tells us he tremendously likes the Wife of Bath's Tale, we might guess that he finds the notion of submission to womanly power attractive or, alternatively, that he enjoys an experience of regressing from the phallic position. What in his psyche might cause such preferences are far too variable for a literary theory to generalize about—I simply wish to show that our model points us toward the implications for any given individual's psyche of things in the text. Therefore, to the extent people's differing responses bear on the value they attribute to literary works—and they certainly do—the model inevitably leads to evaluation.

Before turning to evaluation, though, it might be useful to contrast this model to others. If we represent Freud's statements about response by the same graphic conventions, they would look like this:

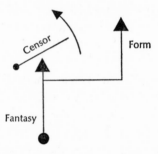

Both in *Jokes* and "Creative Writers and Daydreaming," he spoke simply of a fantasy or drive evading the usual restrictions of censorship. Form serves as a "bribe," "incentive-bonus," or "fore-pleasure," which overbalances the usual defenses:

> The writer softens the egotistical character of the day-dream by changes and disguises [an early statement of "meaning as transformation" or sublimation], and he bribes us by the offer of a purely formal, that is, aesthetic, pleasure in the presentation of his phantasies . . . which is offered us in order to release yet greater pleasure arising from deeper sources in the mind . . .[13]

Freud complained of "the present state of our knowledge" (he was, after all, writing in 1907, long before the great expansion of the concept of defense in the mid-'twenties). He admitted that the "great pleasure" of literature "probably arises from the confluence of many sources" of which he was only mentioning two.

Subsequent writers have suggested some of these other sources. Ernst Kris, for example, while following Freud's basic model fairly closely, notes an implication in it: "the shifts in cathexis of mental energy which the work of art elicits or facilitates are, we believe, pleasurable in themselves." [14] That is, the movement of psychic energy to and from different levels of the mind is itself pleasurable. In Freud's model and ours, this movement is expressed simply in the arrows which connote both shifts in psychic level and a general, overall press toward conscious, pleasurable gratification. Others, notably Simon O. Lesser, have related the various sources of literary appeal to Freud's post-1923 structural concepts of id, ego, and superego. The model I am here suggesting differs from theirs in that it proceeds more from the literary text than the psyche and it stresses the role of defense more than these others do. [15]

Defense, in a literary work, takes one of two general modes: meaning or form. Typically, the unconscious fantasy at the core of a work will combine elements that could, if provided full expression, give us pleasure, but also create anxiety. It is the task of the literary "work" to control the anxiety and permit at least partial gratification of the pleasurable possibilities in the fantasy. The literary work, through what we have loosely termed "form," acts out defensive maneuvers for us: splitting, isolating, undoing, displacing from, omitting (repressing or denying) elements of the fantasy. Meaning, whether we find it or supply it, acts more like a sublimation: giving the fantasy material a disguised expression which is acceptable to the ego, which "makes sense."

Many meanings are possible; many forms are not. To use Twain's phrase again, "The difference between the right word and the almost right word is like the difference between lightning and the lightning bug." The reason is that form operates defensively, against the press of the fantasy toward expression. Form must balance that force, and, like any balance, the balance of form and unconscious content must be delicately set. Meaning is far more flexible, since it does not work so much against the pressure of the fantasy material as with it. Any statement that "makes sense" of the text allows the unconscious content ego-acceptable expression (as we have seen in the unconscious content of comments by various critics on "Dover Beach" and the "tomorrow" speech).

As I have described them, though, literature's two broad devices for managing the fantasy content are broad indeed. Even so, even in this very general state, the outline of our model is complete. We are now in a position to use it to understand more specific and traditional literary entities such as character, style, or effect. But before doing that, we would do well to pause and follow out the implications of this model of people's responses for their evaluation of literature.

II The Model Applied

7 Evaluation

People often say that the ultimate aim of any theory about literature (and that would include our model) must be evaluation. Frankly, I find it rather puzzling that anyone in this last third of the twentieth century should hold such a view. After all, it was in the 1910's that G. E. Moore exposed the uncertainties inherent in evaluation by pointing to the "naturalistic fallacy." [1]

Moore showed that it is impossible to move logically from a series of descriptive statements to an evaluative one. That is, if we say, "*Moby-Dick* has properties X, Y, and Z. Therefore, it is good," then all we mean when we say, "*Moby-Dick* is good," is "*Moby-Dick* has properties X, Y, and Z." In effect, the word "good" has simply dropped out of our critical vocabulary and, therefore, out of all future statements about "good." For if we now say, "*The Bank Dick* is good," we are really only saying, "*The Bank Dick* has properties X, Y, and Z."

As Edmund Wilson puts the issue, "Different schools have at different times demanded different things of literature: *unity, symmetry, universality, originality, vision, inspiration, strangeness, suggestiveness, improving morality, socialist realism,* etc. But you could have any set of these qualities that any school of writing has called for and still not have a good play, a good novel, a good poem, a good history." [2] For example (to take a common substitution for

X, Y, and Z), would it make sense to say, "*Maud* has unity, complexity, and intensity, but it is nevertheless an awful poem"? Certainly, people do make such statements. Would it make sense to say, "*Howl* lacks unity, complexity, and intensity; nevertheless it is a great poem"? Again, people certainly do make such statements; they evidently convey something. Would we have better luck with some list other than "unity, complexity, and intensity"? In all history, no one has ever devised such a list, and it is hard to imagine a list of necessary and sufficient conditions for aesthetic "good" such that contradictory statements like those above would not convey something to a hearer.

Moore's argument states, in essence, that there is something extra in a word like "good," that goes beyond any set of descriptive statements you could use to define it. As for what that something is, one could write a history of twentieth-century philosophy in terms of the various answers to the question. An extreme positivist would have answered that there is nothing extra—the statement, "*Howl* is good," to the extent it is non-verifiable, is gibberish. The emotive theory held that such statements simply expressed the speaker's emotional state. In Freud's words, "One thing only do I know for certain and that is that man's judgements of value follow directly his wishes for happiness—that, accordingly, they are an attempt to support his illusions with arguments." [3]

These are fairly primitive answers. Other theorists, such as Margaret Macdonald, hold that value statements are performative, like giving a medal or reaching a verdict: "To affirm that a work of art is good or bad is to command or condemn, but not describe." [4] Professor Irving Singer suggests a notion of "bestowal" is appropriate to evaluations of works of art as well as loved persons: a statement like "*Howl* is good" represents our response to values we have bestowed upon the poem, as when, attracted to a pretty girl, we say, "She's beautiful" or simply whistle. [5]

One could go on, but whatever that something beyond description is in "good," this much is clear: it is vague, elusive, and rather

persistently so. Since it is so vague, why make it the aim of criticism? What purpose is served when some critic pronounces the
latest Broadway play good, bad, or indifferent? Such a statement
has a limited use as a guide to what to see or read. If I happen to
know I tend to respond as John Simon does, then when he says a
play is good, I know I should buy tickets and find a babysitter. But
there are a great many if's in such an arrangement—and even John
Simon is fallible. Further, such a functional view of criticism leaves
no room for judgments of *Tom Jones* or *Hamlet* or any classic, except that they mean, "You ought to read it," which is as true of
bad classics as good ones.

Most of today's working critics use value judgments as a way of
displaying ingenuity, verbal and otherwise, at the best, a gleaming
talent for invective, so that reading criticism becomes listening to
literary chatter, a not very satisfactory substitute for reading real
literature. Many critics use aesthetic judgments as an excuse for lay
sermons—Yvor Winters and his followers explicitly; F. R. Leavis
and his implicitly. The result is an intolerable degree of smugness.
If moralism is the aim, let us have moralism frankly and leave
poems and novels out of it.

There is, of course, a prescriptive use for evaluations. Early in
this century the Imagists decided poetry ought to be in images.
That is, "good" meant "written in images." As a result, many poets
started writing in images, and many readers began reading for
images. As long as the fashion was new, I think better reading and
better writing resulted (though some fine poets, Shelley, for example, were left by the wayside). This kind of valuation, however,
comes before one reads and helps one to read. When people say
the ultimate aim of criticism is evaluation, I think they rather
mean a judgment pronounced after reading like a verdict to inspire
(or, more often, inhibit) other readers.

Frankly, such a judgment, far from being the ultimate aim of
criticism, seems to me a quite unnecessary and useless by-product,
often positively harmful in that it puts people off from things they

might otherwise enjoy. Eliot, in many ways the founder of "New Criticism," seems to me precisely right when he says (in an early essay): "The critic must not coerce, and he must not make judgments of worse or better. He must simply elucidate: the reader will form the correct judgment for himself." [6] And again, near the end of his life, "The critic to whom I am most grateful is the one who can make me look at something I have never looked at before, or looked at only with eyes clouded by prejudice, set me face to face with it and then leave me alone with it. From that point, I must rely upon my own sensibility, intelligence, and capacity for wisdom." [7]

For a generation now of readers, students, and critics, the New Criticism has made the analytic side of reading far firmer and more skillful. By contrast, as of, say, 1920, literary criticism was what we would call today, "impressionistic." Anatole France put it, "The good critic is he who narrates the adventures of his soul among masterpieces." The old, impressionistic criticism gave us emotional effusions in response to the Romantic poetry of Keats or Shelley or their attenuation in Tennyson. The New Criticism was designed for twentieth-century poetry; for emotional response it substituted explication or explaining because, in twentieth-century poetry, there was obviously a good deal of explaining to do. For the old impressionistic criticism, poetry was appreciated, according to Housman, in "the pit of the stomach"; for the New Criticism, poetry demanded intelligence. "Precision," "tension," "hardness," "irony," "paradox"—these became the plus-words. Where the old criticism tended to maunder about in literary history or anecdote, biography or impressionistic evaluation, the New Critic insisted on the close verbal analysis of particular works, an analysis that often became as objective as two other manifestations of this century's credos: behaviorist psychology or analytic philosophy.

Now, "There is, I think, a general consensus," notes Robert E. Lane, "that the tendency of the critics of the modern day has been to devote less attention to the judgmental function of the critic and rather more to the analytical." [8] Northrop Frye, in a standard handbook for graduate students, distinguishes "academic" criticism from "judicial" criticism:

> There is a traditional metaphor which makes the critic the "judge" of literature. Such a metaphor may imply that Shakespeare and Milton and other impressive people are, relatively to the critic, in the role of prisoners or petitioners, a prospect so exhilarating that many critics wish to leap into a judicial role at once, on the Alice-in-Wonderland principle of sentence first, verdict afterward. I am aware of the weight and influence of critics today who insist that criticism is primarily evaluative, and my next sentence, whether right or wrong, has been carefully considered. The metaphor of the judge, and in fact the whole practice of judicial criticism, is entirely confined to reviewing, or surveying current literature or scholarship: all the metaphors transferred from it to academic criticism are misleading and all the practices derived from it are mistaken. The reviewer of a current book, whatever its content, is expected to lead up to a value-judgment, to give a clear indication of whether or not he thinks the book worth reading. But an academic critic, concerned with the scholarly organization of literature, is never in this judicial position. He is dealing with a body of literature which has all, whatever its merits, been accepted as a valid subject of scholarly study. . . .
>
> It is worth insisting on this point, because the whole conception of academic criticism, as something which grows out of and completes the work of scholarship, is a relatively new one. One feels that criticism has played a rather minor role in the literature of the past; that, especially in English literature, it has not had enough authority to affect the main body of literary creation, and that it is extremely fortunate for literature that it has not had such authority. The reason for this is that most criticism in the past, as well as much of it in the present, is judicial criticism, which is very apt to go wrong when it assumes an academic function.[9]

Again, as with Eliot, I simply agree.

Consider, for example, the following critical analysis, and notice how very little (if any) of it depends upon or demands aesthetic value judgment.

THE SCRUTINIE

I.

Why should you sweare I am forsworn
          Since thine I vow'd to be?
Lady it is already Morn,
          And 'twas last night I swore to thee
That fond impossibility.

II.

Have I not lov'd thee much and long,
          A tedious twelve houres space?
I must all other Beauties wrong,
          And rob thee of a new imbrace;
Could I still dote upon thy Face.

III .

Not, but all joy in thy browne haire,
          By others may be found;
But I must search the black and faire
          Like skilfull Minerallist's that sound
For Treasure in un-plow'd-up ground.

IV.

Then, if when I have lov'd my round,
          Thou prove the pleasant'st she [10]
With spoyles of meaner Beauties crown'd,
          I laden will returne to thee,
Ev'n sated with Varietie.

                              Richard Lovelace (1649)

Essentially, the poem builds on a paradox, a just injustice, which
leads to a variety of ambiguities and witty reversals. The most obvious one is the title, "The Scrutinie," which in 1649 meant not a
careful looking-at something so much as an investigation, a critical
or judicial inquiry. The poem, in effect, uses this meaning two
ways; the first two stanzas are a "scrutinie" or judicial inquiry into
the rights and wrongs of jilting the "Lady"; the second two stanzas
suggest a judicial inquiry, a scrutiny, into the merits of other
women.

The paradox of a just injustice gives rise to the style of the poem: the tension between the conventional euphemisms ("Beauties," "imbrace," "joy") and the physical fact of promiscuity; the tension between the rigid form of the poem and its conversational, argumentative, even flippant, quality. Still another tension arises from the progression of images. In the first stanzas, they are, in essence, judicial. The poet is saying he cannot be held liable for promising an impossibility or, alternatively, he has lived up to his contract to love the lady much and long. The cruelest line in the poem—the casual indifference with which he contemplates his love taking a new lover and "a new Imbrace"—masquerades as an argument of fairness and equity. By the third stanza, the images change—he becomes the insatiable, amoral scientist. In the fourth, he becomes the conquering warrior.

Balancing this increasing violence or cruelty is the tight form of the poem and the smooth, artful way the images link the stanzas. Morning and night in the first stanza lead to the twelve hours of loving in the second. The face at the end of the second becomes the "brown hair" at the beginning of the third. The "ground" at the end of the third rhymes with "round" that begins the fourth. That rhyme itself is part of the poem's slickness and polish: Lovelace is using a very strict rhyme-scheme, only six rhyme-sounds in twenty lines. Furthermore, the rhymes work out his idea at the end of stanza four that he will return to the lady by picking up the -ee rhyme which he used in the first stanza: "sated with Varietie," "thine I vow'd to be," "I swore to thee," "that fond impossibility."

The poem, then, moves away and comes back. It comes round again to the lady with whom the poem started. The last line, "Ev'n sated with Varietie," I take it, means "sated with variety—even as I am this morning," bringing the poet not only back to the lady, but back to her in the same condition that he is in after this somewhat exhausting night. Or, perhaps, "sated with variety—and longing for one love." In either case, the going away and coming back completes the paradoxes of the poem, that to break his vow is reasonable and right, that a short affair is a "long" and "tedious" one, that to wrong the "Lady" is to do right by all other beauties.

The most striking feature of the poem, of course, is the third stanza with its grandly Freudian images of searching in her hair and probing for treasure in unplowed ground. No one who has read much seventeenth-century poetry would assume that this symbolism was unconscious. What may be unconscious are the implications of Lovelace's phrasing. In effect, Lovelace is comparing the finding of joy in a woman to the finding of treasure in earth—dirt. The image is hardly a very complimentary one to the fair sex, and indeed he refers in the fourth stanza to the ladies he contemplates seducing as "meaner Beauties." His images treat love as possession, and in the fourth stanza the word "spoyles," a military term, introduces the idea of triumphing over the woman. In effect, Lovelace sees love as taking or possessing—and this where he began in the first stanza:

> Why should you swear I am forsworn,
> Since *thine* I vowed to be?

The poem is saying that Lovelace will not be possessed by the lady of the poem—rather he will seek to possess, briefly, "all other Beauties." The first and last stanzas describe a man free to choose, unpossessed by any woman; the middle stanzas describe a man psychologically driven.

In a second sense, then, the poem goes away and comes back, just as the poet promises to do with the lady of the poem: he proclaims his freedom at the outset; he admits his captivity to "all other Beauties" in the middle; he announces his freedom again at the end. We could sum all this up by saying that the poem is, in essence, about detachment and involvement, freedom and captivity: a man free from any one woman, but held captive by the idea of woman.

This analysis or explication is, I think, a fair instance of how much a New Critic can say about a poem without ever touching on aesthetic "good" or "bad." The basic limitation, the ground rule we set ourselves, was to look first and foremost at the words on the page. We did not refer to Lovelace's biography, to the historical setting of Cavalier poetry (except for a little dictionary information about "scrutiny" and love-symbolism); we did not compare this poem with other poems. Such a procedure leads inevitably to a series of statements descriptive of the poem which are cumulative and verifiable in the limited sense that anyone who looks at the poem can confirm or deny from the text the correctness of what I have said. Evaluation gets left out because, as Moore showed, one cannot from a system of quasi-scientific descriptive propositions "deduce" evaluative statements.

It would seem there is no sensible way of getting from the text to an evaluation. But surely this cannot be so—and it isn't. "Nothing," wrote Henry James, "will ever take the place of the good old fashion of 'liking' a work of art or not liking it: the most improved criticism will not abolish that primitive, that ultimate test." James is right, and his dictum provides a toehold for a psychoanalytic approach to the problem of evaluation. The route from text to evaluation proceeds through someone's mind, someone who likes or dislikes what he has read. The classics, the masterpieces, are those that have pleased the best readers for a long time. We come, inevitably, to the "test of time."

Like any other theory of evaluation, it has its weaknesses. One trouble with the test of time is that it takes so long, usually a century or two. How can it help the critic confronted with today's book or tomorrow's movie, which he must pronounce on the spot good, bad, or indifferent? What does it mean when a critic says such-and-such a book or poem of today is "good" when it has not had time to take the test of time? We can solve that problem by saying the critic is making a *prediction* that the work will pass the test of time. He is saying, in Dr. Johnson's phrase, that this is a work that "can please many and please long." Similarly, what does it mean when a critic overrules the test of time? For example, he might say such-and-such a masterpiece is "overrated." Or he might dig up a "neglected classic," that is, a work that has flunked the test of time. Here, too, I think, we can say the critic is making a prediction, namely, that after his verdict has been heard, the work in question will be viewed differently.[11]

This "predictive theory of value" (as philosophers call it) has, of course, no more power to escape the "naturalistic fallacy" than any other theory. It does, however, provide a convenient formula to bridge the gap between text and evaluation. We can now phrase the question this way: What in the text leads someone to make the prediction it "can please many and please long"? Behind that question is another: What does it mean to say something will please people in an aesthetic way? How does the aesthetic pleasure of a poem differ from the simple sensuous pleasure of a well-mixed martini?

From the point of view of our model, literature is a species of play. That is, to play is "to hallucinate ego mastery." [12] Both play and literature can be understood in this sense as first, letting a disturbing influence happen to us, then, second, mastering that disturbance. The classic example is the "doctor game." Little Eyolf is frightened by his visit to the doctor. His parents, having read their Spock, buy him a toy doctor's kit, and (typically) within a few days the little lad is enthusiastically acting out the part of the doctor. The "doctor game" satisfies him because he re-creates the disturbing influence but, instead of being overwhelmed by it, masters it by identifying with the aggressor. The "doctor game," for many children in our culture, is a satisfying form of play—it "pleases." When literature "pleases," it, too, lets us experience a disturbance, then master it, but the disturbance is a fantasy rather than an event or activity. This pattern of disturbance and mastery distinguishes our pleasure in play and literature from simple sensuous pleasures.

Saying a literary work is "good," then, from the point of view of our model, is predicting that it will pass the test of time; that it "can please many and please long"; that it is a widely satisfying form of play; or, more formally, that it embodies a fantasy with the power to disturb many readers over a long period of time and, built in, a defensive maneuver that will enable those readers to master the poem's disturbance. Given this frame of reference, we should be able to look at the text of "The Scrutinie" and make psychological predictions as to whether or not it will elicit some primitive, ultimate act of "liking" it.

For me, it won't. My own visceral reaction to the poem, and I know many readers share it, is that it is rather a nasty poem, cruel, clever, somehow lacking in real emotion, ultimately not in the highest rank of poetry. Can I discover what in the text is causing my not "liking" it? I think so.

The poem is working out a well-known set of attitudes, those of the Don Juan. The poem shows quite explicitly two of the four elements that Freud suggests as defining this kind of behavior: the tendency to run through an endless series of women; the tendency to think of these women as low or debased.[13] Freud suggests that the quest for an endless series represents a quest for something we fear to have directly; the series is "endless for the reason that every surrogate . . . fails to provide the desired satisfaction." For the Don Juan, the woman he really desires is the mother, and it is, as the poem says, a "fond impossibility" to be the "thine" of that first love.

Notice, in this context, the primitive terms in which the poem's courtship is carried on: swearing and forswearing, "doting upon thy face," and then, finally, "sated." These are oral terms from the first and most primitive love. The poet runs away from the lady as from a devouring mouth that wishes to make him forever hers, to incorporate him, to hang onto his phallus. He presents his running away, not as a fear of being possessed by someone it is dangerous to be possessed by, but under the guise of logic and fairness; having loved the lady, the poet would be unfair to her and to all other beauties not to love as many other ladies as possible. And, of course, in a psychological sense, he *is* being logical: since the lady gave in, she cannot be that ultimate love he is looking for, a quite explicit working-out of the Don Juan idea that the woman who has given in is low and unsatisfactory. Also, though the poem does not say so, we can guess that the masculine logic and justice the poet invokes conceal another threatening figure, the father, fear of whom drives him away.

At the same time, however, the poem shows a second Don Juan-trait; it treats women rather harshly. We have already noted that women are described as "un-plow'd-up ground"; later he speaks of the women he will sleep with as "meaner beauties." The title itself contains a hidden pun: Lovelace wrote enough Latin poetry to know that "scrutiny" comes from Latin *scruta* meaning trash or garbage, and this scrutiny, whether we consider it an investigation of the rights and wrongs of his leaving this lady or his scrutiny of other ladies, is ultimately a picking over of trash. Love in this poem is aggression and debasement; emotions are turned into things. Embraces are something you can be robbed of, like an object; joy is something you can "find"; sexual satisfaction is treasure to be dug up out of the dirt. The lover triumphs over the lady he conquers, bringing home the "spoyles" of victory. In short, the poem presents us with the basic conflict in the Don Juan: the failure to bring together the affectionate and sensual currents in love.

But there is a still deeper conflict beneath this ambivalence at the phallic level. Were the poet really to love the "Lady," he would be "thine." In effect, he would lose his self which he "must" assert by playing the Don Juan and treating emotional relations as things. It is as though Lovelace saw only two alternatives: proving his separate existence by phallicly degrading women; accepting loss of identity by falling, "sated," back to his first love and being "thine." Not unpredictably in this poem which treats genital love in terms of vowing, tasting, forswearing, and verbal argument, we are finding an oral conflict: the problem of establishing a self separate from an all-supplying Lady. To love in a real sense is to be engulfed; to achieve a separate self, one "must search the black and faire," totally and dispassionately in control "Like skilfull Mineral-list's" probing dirt. In effect, or so the poem seems to say, it is *only* by separating the affectionate and sensual currents in love that the speaker can retain an identity.

Freud suggests that the failure to bring together the affectionate current in love and the sensual is universal among civilized and educated people, at least in some degree. And certainly, we have all gone through the very early oral crisis of discovering our selves as separate from our mothers. From the point of view of psychoanalytic evaluation, then, we can say that Lovelace's "Scrutinie" introduces two universal disturbing influences to which, I think, we can all respond.

But how does the poem master these disturbances? In the phrase "new imbrace" and in the image of "others" finding "all joy in thy browne haire," especially in the genital symbolism of the third stanza, the poem conjures up a vivid image of other men having sexual intercourse with the woman the poet has just had. I suspect that for many men, as certainly for me, the visual image of another man having one's woman, though it may be titillating, is also repugnant in the extreme, involved with a variety of oedipal, homosexual, and primal scene fears. Similarly, the second half of the third stanza images Lovelace plowing a variety of female fields. Again, I suspect one man's pleasure at another man's amatory successes must be a rather mixed one.

The fourth stanza seems aesthetically somewhat stronger than the third, except for its last line which strikes me as the weakest in the poem. I think my initial pleasure comes from Lovelace's erasing the details of his sexual adventures in the more abstract language of "lov'd my round," "the pleasant'st she." Further, the last stanza does resolve the conflict between the affectionate and the sensual in favor of a more or less affectionate return to the lady. The poet having "lov'd [his] round," the lyric, too, comes round to its conclusion, closes itself off with the rhymes with which it began. The lover, conditionally, at least, returns to his lady, even sated as he was at the beginning of the poem.

The final stanza has achieved its sense of coming round again to the beginning by the fourth line: "I laden will returne to thee." But the line following, the last line of the poem, "Ev'n sated with Varietie," is totally anticlimactic as well as ambiguous. There is a

sense of superfluity in the final couplet, as though the poet did not
choose as a developed personality to return, but (perhaps driven by
his rhyme-scheme) simply lapsed back, sated sensually, but still in
an emotional sense unsatisfied. It is late in the day for me to set up
as a seventeenth-century poet, but, though presumptuous, it is not
too difficult to see how to improve the final stanza:

> Then, if when I have lov'd my round
>   Thou prove the pleasant'st she
> With spoyles of meaner Beauties crown'd
>   I laden will returne to thee,
> And be thine, as thine I vowed to be.

Such a last line suggests, as Lovelace's does, coming round to the
beginning, but the reference to the "vow" also suggests rational
and responsible choice instead of a child's oral satiety. Such an
ending would suggest a real resolution of the underlying fear of engulfment by asserting the poet's responsible self, at the same time
reconciling the sensual and the affectionate.

In short, the poem presents us with two well-nigh universal disturbances: the fear of engulfment, the separation of the sensual in
love from the affectionate. But it does not handle those disturbances in a way that pleases. Instead, it heightens the fearful or
repugnant elements in the fantasy. The last line leaves the basic
oral conflict in the poem restated but unresolved. A critic reading
"The Scrutinie" for the first time would be justified in predicting
this poem is not of the quality that "can please many and please
long." Certainly, few—if, indeed, any—anthologies print it; few, if
any, critics discuss it.

By way of contrast, consider another poem by Lovelace, which
though psychologically very similar, is endlessly anthologized and
explicated:

TO LUCASTA, GOING TO THE WARRES

I.
Tell me not (Sweet) I am unkinde,
    That from the Nunnerie

Of thy chaste breast, and quiet minde,
To Warre and Armes I flie.

II.

True; a new Mistresse now I chase,
The first Foe in the Field;
And with a stronger Faith imbrace
A Sword, a Horse, a Shield.

III.

Yet this Inconstancy is such,
As you too shall adore;
I could not love thee (Deare) so much,
Lov'd I not Honour more.

This poem, like the other, talks one girl into letting the poet leave for others (at least metaphorically), but the whole thing has been pitched to a higher plane. In the first stanza, Lovelace stresses Lucasta's chastity, the fact that the world she creates is a "Nunnerie." As in the other poem, he visualizes himself as possessed, almost held a passive captive by Lucasta in that nunnery. He must escape, "flie," and in the second stanza, he no longer addresses Lucasta; he is in the world of the active lover, chasing, embracing. Where in the other poem he used images of aggression for love, in this poem, Lovelace uses images of love to describe aggression. He is unpossessed by the new mistress; he is the one doing the chasing and embracing. He is outside the new mistress, where in the first stanza he had to fly from within the nunnery. As in "The Scrutinie," Lovelace sees being in love (the first stanza) as a dangerous passivity, while phallic aggression (second stanza) establishes a man's identity. The second stanza thus provides a basis for the poet's shift from, in the first stanza, rather passively restating Lucasta's complaint to actively asserting his own point of view in the third.

In a psychological sense, then, this poem, like the other, separates the current of affection in love (the first and third stanzas) from the sensual current (the second stanza). The first stanza, with its series of long *i*'s ("I," "thy," "unkind," "quiet mind," and so on), its slow phrases like "thy chaste breast," calls for muscular acts that are tranquil and respectful. The words treat Lucasta in terms of affection. The second stanza with its *s*'s, *t*'s, *th*'s, and *f*'s (the "*f*irst *f*oe in the *f*ield") makes the mouth spit out a hurly-burly of sensual aggression and love. It indulges in the same kind of hostile justification as "The Scrutinie"—the intellectual cleverness only pretends to balance the vivid, sensual act of embracing a horse or a shield. Had this poem ended with the second stanza, we would find it no more satisfactory as play than the other poem.

The third stanza, though it goes beyond the merely witty resolution of the second, still does not resolve the real conflict. Instead, the current of affection or esteem takes over entirely from the sensual qualities of love. The third stanza emphasizes again the chastity of Lucasta, the adoration of honor, the love of an abstraction. As one critic has it, the tension of the first two stanzas is resolved in the third "not basically as a separation of divisible bodies, but as one of indivisible spirit." [14] In the tension between sacred and profane love, the poem settles for sacred alone.

The third stanza achieves this pseudo-resolution the way "The Scrutinie" did—by verbal paradox; but here, I think, we feel the paradox is supremely successful. Both Lucasta and the poet shall "adore" (a religious term that matches the "Nunnerie" of stanza one) his inconstancy because it is in the name of "Honour," something higher, bigger, better than both of them. The word "Honour" is the key: for him, it is the soldier's honor, his good name and reputation for courage. But honor for Lucasta means something quite different: it means her chastity, a chastity that contrasts with the chasing and embracing of the second stanza and turns us back to the nunnery of the first. This poem, like "The Scrutinie," goes away and comes back. In effect, the last lines are saying that he loves Lucasta precisely because he—and she—love honor more, love more the fact that he cannot possess her, that she must remain "chaste breast" and "quiet minde."

We can guess, then, that (as in "The Scrutinie") there is an element of fear in the poet's flying the two-person world of love and the "Nunnerie" for the many-personed world connoted by

"Honour." In this context, the poem as a whole becomes a reversal in which the social world of fearless, masculine honor serves as, if not itself a nunnery, at least a monastic retreat from the love of the first stanza, felt as dangerous and engulfing. This element of fear, perhaps not so strangely, shows most clearly in the celebrated last lines: we can read them, I could not love thee (Deare) so much, Had I not the defense of loving Honour more. We can also think of these lines as a reversal (in the manner of dreams) of the real thought underneath: I could not love Honour so much, Loved I not thee, Deare, more—or, perhaps, feared I not thee, Deare, more.

The second stanza also reveals in its phrasing this unconscious flight. The lines alternate or hover between the conventional terms of heterosexual love, "Mistresse," "Faith," "imbrace" (lines 1 and 3), and the terms of all-male combat, "Foe," "Sword," "Shield" (lines 2 and 4). In effect, there is a strong homosexual component to the poet's renunciation: he turns away from heterosexual love to "chase" and "imbrace" a masculine "foe." The abrupt bumping back and forth, line by line from love to fighting, itself suggests the to-and-fro not only of battle but also of the sexual act. Thus, stanza two merges in form as well as content male aggression and love between a man and a woman. This defensive maneuver, translating heterosexual love into homosexual competition or aggression represents, strange as it may seem, a sublimation widely accepted and even encouraged in our culture as well as Lovelace's—think, for example, of the usual schoolroom reading of *Antony and Cleopatra*: that Antony ought to leave off effeminate loving so he can engage in the cruel, coldblooded conquests that represent the masculine "high Roman fashion." *

This poem does not resolve the psychological conflict underlying it any more healthily than does "The Scrutinie." It works out a sublimation of the poet's Don Juan impulse into the homosexual

---

* It seems likely that for many people the "moral function of poetry" consists of such compliances with socially approved defensive patterns or those the moralist-critic wishes were socially approved. See p. 195.

world of war. The poet enjoys and accepts an honor which includes Lucasta's chastity, the very thing that demands the sublimation he embraces. "Where natural resistances to satisfaction have not been sufficient," says Freud, "men have at all times erected conventional ones so as to be able to enjoy love. The very incapacity of the sexual instinct to yield complete satisfaction as soon as it submits to the first demands of civilization becomes the source . . . of the noblest cultural achievements which are brought into being by ever more extensive sublimation of its instinctual components." As one critic points out, the word "Deare" in the next-to-the-last line connotes a far higher level of value and respect than the first stanza does; it would be a flaw had the poet used the first line's oral, primitive "sweet," suggesting mere enjoyment, in place of "dear," suggesting esteem: I could not love thee, sweet, so much, Loved I not Honor more.[15]

We have, then, two poems very similar in intellectual and psychological content and style, but one of which *feels* very much the better poem. In terms of play, the two poems embody the same disturbing fantasy, but defensively they manage the fantasy quite differently. Against real, emotional, hexterosexual love, felt as confining and restricting, the first poem offers male promiscuity as a defense; the second poem offers as a defense homosexual aggression. Both defenses are deeply charged but the second poem offers a second line of defense—sublimation into "honor"—while the first only heightens the fear and repugnance by its sexual imagery. The second poem thus provides a more complex and satisfying mastery. It would be sensible to guess that, for most readers, the second poem will offer more satisfaction as "play" than the first.

"For most readers." Our culture favors aggressive homosexual competition in business and in sports. "To Lucasta" may well appeal more to somewhat straitlaced, perhaps even prudish and old-fashioned people. Certainly, it is a great favorite with anthologists for the schools. Conversely, someone who does not share traditional notions of male honor or traditional attitudes toward promiscuity might well prefer "The Scrutinie." Thus, I can offer a scintilla of evidence for the so-called "sexual revolution": over the past five years, I have noticed an increasing proportion of students prefer "The Scrutinie" to "To Lucasta."

The point, however, is that a psychoanalytic reading of the poem in terms of fantasy-and-defense enables me to explain my own liking and disliking. I can find what in the text of the poem causes my reaction. Knowing something about my own society, I can extrapolate and estimate whether a given poem "can please many and please long."

The two Lovelace poems differ in the defensive handling of essentially similar underlying fantasies. In many ways, I feel my response to the two different modes of defense was culturally conditioned. But neither defensive modes nor cultural acceptability are the only factors for evaluation indicated by a psychoanalytic reading. To see others, we can contrast two films of Federico Fellini.

Three-hour, three-million gross, triple-goddessed, Church-banned, myth-packed, and Totalscoped, La Dolce Vita [16] amazes indeed the very faculty of eyes and ears. Eyes and ears are not just the targets, though, but recurring symbols for what the author-director has on his mind. His protagonist, Marcello, is a reporter and would-be novelist, a man questing (admittedly, rather ineffectively) after truth in the form of sounds and language. Indeed, at one point, Marcello rather shamefacedly mumbles something of the sort. As against this basic stance for sound and language, Fellini shows his people preoccupied with seeing, most obviously in the form of the ubiquitous *papparazzi*, the photographers who contrast with the verbal reporter Marcello—they swarm about virtually everyone and everything in the film as though Sartre's flies had been outfitted with flash cameras. Images of seeing and being seen run all through the film, as, for example, the sunglasses everybody wears. Sights in La Dolce Vita are mostly Ziegfeldian sights of women, culminating in Nadia Gray's striptease in the final party, but represented earlier, for example, by the pictures of female ancestors in the "haunted castle" sequence, the sight of the magnificently pneumatic Anita Ekberg, or the non-miraculous non-sight of the Virgin Mary in the televised "fake miracle."

Against these images of seeing and being seen, Fellini poises many fewer, but far more striking images of hearing. At the home of Steiner, Marcello's intellectual friend, we hear folk songs and poetry and a tape recording of the sounds of nature; conversation reigns supreme. Steiner himself had earlier gone into a church to practise the Toccata and Fugue in D Minor. At one point, Marcello retires to the seashore to renew his work on the Great Italian Novel; he cannot write for the loudness of the song from a jukebox played by a virginal young blond waitress he calls an "Umbrian angel." It was, of all people, Robinson Crusoe (though he was surely not the first) who pointed out that sound and language are the means by which human beings can achieve more than an animal relation with each other. Sound and language in *La Dolce Vita*, however, seem always to fail to create such a relationship. In the "haunted castle" sequence, Maddalena, one of Marcello's light o'loves, seats him in a room and goes outside to talk to him through a speaking-tube arrangement (a kind of "ear of Dionysius"). In the only serious moment of their relationship, we hear her propose marriage to him; we see her giving herself to another man.

The opening and closing bits (they are scarcely episodes) frame this recurring contrast of sight and sound. The opening shows a gilt image of Christ helicopter-borne over the Eternal City (which Fellini renders as a vast flux of running children and rising buildings); a second helicopter follows, carrying reporter Marcello and his photographer sidekick, apparently fishing for a story. Beneath them, they see a far more gripping sight than the Second, airborne Coming: four girls in bikinis sunbathing on a roof. As the helicopter hovers overhead, Marcello tries to speak to them, but they cannot hear one another over the noise of the chopper. The pattern is: the sight of a symbol; the sight of woman; the failure of sound. So in the finale: Marcello and assorted sodomites, usurers, grifters, and fornicators from the striptease party drift down to the sea (in shots reminiscent of Botticelli). At the sea's edge, some fishermen pull up a huge devilfish, and the camera closes in on its still-staring evil eye. As Marcello turns to go, the "Umbrian angel" appears on the shore nearby, but there is water between them, and though he sees her and she him, they cannot hear each other for the sound of the waves. He shrugs indifferently and leaves; she turns to watch him go. In a brilliant cinematic touch, Fellini pans the camera as she turns so that the final shot is an extreme close-up of the Umbrian angel staring out at the audience—or us staring at her—the audience has become image, and the image is the audience.

It is an evocative moment and not the only one, for *La Dolce Vita* has that same strange hankering after myth as Fellini's other films. His script for *The Miracle* reached essentially toward the traditional mating in the fields of sun-god and mortal woman. *The White Sheik* with its horseplay on different kinds of hats balanced the impotent male of church and marriage against the absurdly sexual male of the *fumetti* (visual images again). *I Vitelloni* constitutes a parody of the whole male pantheon, while, in *Le Notti di Cabiria*, a tawdry and pathetic image of Venus renews herself in water after venal Adonises have chosen and abused her. *La Strada* is the clearest of them all, a classic agon between *eiron* and *alazon* over a (more or less) mute woman that could have come straight out of Cornford's *Origins of Attic Comedy*. *La Dolce Vita* has the same theme and mythic dimension as the others, men overpowered physically, morally, or psychologically by the gorgon-like image of woman. As Steiner says, "I am only this tall," and he holds up his finger. In the "fake miracle" (an earlier form of which appeared in *Cabiria*), an old woman gives us the tip-off. As the television cameras and photographers close in on two children who have been gulled into saying they saw the Virgin, the crone says, "What does it matter whether it was the Virgin or not? Italy is full of strange cults." And indeed Fellini's Italy is.

The first one we see, the first full episode in the film, is a kind of temple prostitution. The gilt Christ of the opening shots dissolves into the mute sinuosities of a gilt Siamese dancer in a night club where Marcello picks up a rich nymphomaniac, Maddalena (and the name, I take it, is not without significance). They ride off in her white Caddy convertible, boredly pick up a prostitute, and drive her home. Fellini goes out of his way to make them go out of theirs, go underground to the prostitute's basement apartment, cross the waters of her flooded basement, and there, in this doubtful chthonic sanctum, make love.

The second is the advent through the air from another land of an Aphrodite Pandemos, Anita Ekberg, cast as a Hollywood love-goddess, Sylvia (again, the name is not without significance). Ritually, she is offered the fruits of the Roman fields (in the form of a giant pizza); then, in an hilarious press conference, she is consulted as an oracle. During the day, she bounds up the endless stairs to the top of St. Peter's, dressed in a parody of a priest's gown. The true aphroditic rituals, however, took place on the tops of mountains or in caves, and that night, bobbling out of her evening gown, Sylvia leads a revel through the baths of Caracalla, complete with rock 'n roll Orpheus and faun in the form of a goatish American actor on whose shoulders she rides. "Why, Federico," Miss Ekberg is said to have remarked during the filming of these sequences, "you are making a fool of me." Despite this insight, Miss Ekberg can take comfort in the fact that Fellini was also making her a goddess. In some rituals, her celestial prototype did indeed ride a goat, and Marcello tells her she is mother, mistress, wife, home, "everything." They ride off in his Triumph, where he makes the old college try, but cannot find a place to go. (Throughout the film, blonds are unattainable—or at least unattained by Marcello—unlike the brunets, for example, Maddalena.) Our pandemotic love-goddess, however, seems (again like Aphrodite) concerned as much with mothering animals as with mothering Marcello; anyway, she howls like a dog on a mountaintop, and in an exquisite sequence she picks up a stray white kitten and, holding it before her like a monstrance, glides through the narrow corridors of midnight streets. She strides into the Trevi fountain;

Marcello follows: "You're right—I'm on the wrong track—we all are." She puts water on his hair in a mock baptism, and to cap the parody, just then the fountain is turned off. They return to her hotel, where her opposite number, Lex Barker as a dipsoid American actor, awaits them, another mythic figure: "To think he once played Tarzan," sighs a *papparazzo*.

There are other "goddesses"—the missing Virgin Mary in the fake miracle; at Steiner's house, an old artist cries the praises of Oriental women, notably Mother Eve. In the "haunted castle" sequence, Maddalena standing before a row of matrilinear portraits puts a veil over her face; Marcello seduces a mysterious other-worldly "Lady Jane" with streaks in her hair like antennae: the ghosts, nighttime, the cemetery, the surrounding plutocracy give the whole episode a persephonic aura. Finally, of course there is the "Umbrian angel," the virgin by the sea, image of a renewal and innocence, a kind of Aphrodite Urania, whom Marcello cannot accept.

In this matriarchal world, men become mere consorts, lover-kings, ridiculous, impotent. The clearest case is Marcello's father who turns up just before the necrotic "haunted castle" sequence. An aging lecher, he gets his son to take him to an old-fashioned nightclub, where the walls glitter like a temple's and everywhere there are statues of women. During the conversation, we find he was usually away from home, rather a philanderer and a wine merchant, indeed, "sold wine all up and down Italy." Playing vanishing parlor-tricks with one of the chorines, he is compared to a donkey. Meanwhile, the acts of the nightclub entertainers parody still other aspects of ass-headed Dionysus. The first routine shows a triad of mock-ferocious cat-women ridiculing their quite ineffectual male tamer; the second shows us girls in a Charleston routine out of the father's youth; finally, in an exquisite act, the clown Polidor appears as a doddering Pied Piper, awed by the images of women about him. A few pathetic notes of his almost limp trumpet and he shuffles out, trailing clouds of—empty balloons. Marcello's father goes to the chorus girl's apartment ("to eat spaghetti"), but suffers a stroke of some kind as they are making love. Pathetic, aging, his face always turned away, he wants only to return to Marcello's mother. In one of the most beautiful moments in the film, sick and exhausted as he is, he stoops and silently smooths out the bed, removing his last trace; it is as though he had never been. So much for fatherhood.

Throughout the film from the vulgarized Christ at the opening to the transvestite dance of the homosexuals at the end, man seems weak and helpless. Throughout, women lead men—Maddalena leads Marcello to the prostitute's apartment; l'Ekberg bounds up the steps of St. Peter's leaving behind clusters of exhausted Romans, and the "haunted castle" sequence ends with the old principessa-matriarch leading the shamefaced "men" of the tribe off to Mass. Throughout, men seem awed, overcome by women, often trying to make themselves into women, sinking down into women. The men seem unable to get places; they have to clamber, grope, break into places women seem to sink into effortlessly. When men do achieve heights, "rise above it all," they flag and gasp, revealing their impotency—Marcello climbing St. Peter's; Marcello's father up in the chorine's apartment; the cameramen's lights on high platforms shattering and popping in the fake miracle; the insignificance of the helicoptered Christ; the insignificance of our modern Mars—Marcello Rubino.

The exception (for a time, anyway) to all this is Steiner, Marcello's intellectual friend whose short unhappy life forms the most puzzling episode of the film. Unlike the other characters whose lives are dominated by sights and shows, Steiner lives in a world of sound and language. When we first see him, he is returning a Sanskrit text. He offers Marcello jobs in publishing, encourages him in his writing. Steiner, moreover, is a father with a lovely wife and charming children. Homespun, sturdy (Fellini originally wanted Henry Fonda for the part), he alone seems master of his fate. In fact, the whole situation is so goody-goody, it cloys. Then, inexplicably, Steiner commits suicide, destroying not only himself but his children, destroying, in effect, his own fatherhood, his limited claim to be part of the flow of life, a total suicide. The film gives no particular reason for Steiner's suicide. It seems just one more in the long series of improvisations that make up *La Dolce Vita*. Impulse and improvisation are the ways the other characters work, however—not Steiner. In the first scene in which he appears, he tries to improvise jazz on the church organ, but at a gentle rebuke from the priest obediently shifts to the Toccata and Fugue, a frozen, "perfected" improvisation, as it were. At his house, he says, "In a work of art, everything is planned and perfect. We need to be a work of art, detached, perfect, in suspended animation," and yet, he also said his own life was too much so (the goody-goody quality of everything associated with Steiner). There seems to be no room in his life for the new, the unexpected. His suicide is at once the only improvisation left him and, at the same time, the closing or framing of his perfected life. It leaves his wife to be photographed by the *papparazzi*, she, now, image of the *mater dolorosa*. Quite the opposite is the only other sustained human relationship Marcello has in the course of the film, that with his mistress Emma. Squabbles, flirtations, attempted suicides, reconciliations, their relation is one long series of improvisations as she tries to "catch" him, fix him into matrimony and fatherhood, a Fury valiantly striving to be a hearth-goddess.

The film, then, uses its two central images, sight and sound, to set off men against women. The women are goddesses, mythical, unreal *belles dames sans merci*, the sight of whom bewitches men into a kingdom of improvisation and illusion. Man is impotent, helpless, Marcello's dying father or Steiner, with his sounds and language, frozen, turned into stone by the fixity of his life. Marcello—Everyman—is caught between these two alternatives, male and female, his mistress vainly seeking to play the role of goddess and petrify him into matrimony.

These themes all come together in the final dreary episode, the despairingly hedonistic party that follows Marcello's appearance at the scene of Steiner's suicide. The subjugation of men culminates in the dance of the homosexuals and gigolos, and the image of woman culminates in the striptease (to the same song the Umbrian angel had played on the jukebox). Marcello presides over the dispirited merrymaking (the only case where a man is the "leader"), and as the party whimpers to its close he baptizes the departing revellers with feathers, a grim parody of the earlier, Ekbergian baptism, just as his white suit is now the negative of the tuxedo he wore in the earlier episode. The effect is rather like snow, perhaps the snow of the ninth circle, perhaps also that "snow falling faintly through the universe and faintly falling, like the descent of their last end, upon all the living and the dead." This, the last party, gives way to the film's final image of man, a devilfish gasping in air, an eye caught in a net, and the final image of woman, the Umbrian-Uranian angel.

As with any important work, *La Dolce Vita* defines its own art. Fellini's concern about turning people into images finds its expression in what might be called the rotogravure style of the film. Fellini had both sets and costumes of *La Dolce Vita* designed to photograph in exaggerated blacks and whites, so that everything in the film would have the hard, contrasty look of a flash photo. The film itself seems almost to be composed as a series of stills rather than a moving picture. Fellini's sense of the new, the unexpected, his theme of improvisation, finds its expression in the episodic structure (here, as in *I Vitelloni*, this episodic quality seems a weakness of the film; only in *La Strada*, it seems to me, did Fellini overcome this his besetting vice). Fellini's brilliant use of dissolves also suggests a kind of impulse or improvisation (the best example being the opening dissolve where the gilt image of Christ suddenly, startlingly becomes a gilt Siamese dancer). But, pervading and informing the whole, is Fellini's view of man: a helpless and abject improvisor confronting the gorgon-like, all-powerful image of woman.

8½, Fellini's next major film, marked a shift in his work toward autobiography, a path extended in *Juliet of the Spirits*. Between *La Dolce Vita* and 8½ Fellini made only the brief, whimsical fantasy he contributed to *Boccaccio 70*. The "all-powerful image of woman" became forty feet of Anita Ekberg stepping down from a billboard to offer permission, forgiveness, sex, and milk but also torment to the puritanical Dr. Antonio, a one-man vice squad, waving his puny umbrella against those mighty breasts. In both *La Dolce Vita* and *The Temptation of Dr. Antonio*, Fellini used his fantasies about woman to condemn morally those who cannot accept *Mutterrecht* and the matriarchal stance.

8½,[17] however, is about Fellini's troubles making 8½. The title says so: it means Fellini had previously made six feature-length films and three shorts (each counted at a half); this film was therefore 8½. It weaves three strands together—all of them autobiographical: Fellini's professional life while making 8½; his personal life with wife, mistress, and friends; then, binding the other two together, his inner life of dreams and fantasies. In *La Dolce Vita*, Fellini turned his characters into the contrasty stills one would see in a photo mag. In *Boccaccio 70*, his chief character became a caricature and a forty-foot billboard. In 8½, his characters become merely versions of his own interior life. The men are all derivatives of his father, associated with his own efforts to "rise" professionally and monetarily and his fears that he will be pulled down to earth by moral or intellectual criticism and so suffocated or drowned in a sea of talk or buried in the blackness of a dark screen. Women are white, associated with maternal love, healing, and forgiveness; they are also to be looked and lusted at.

Fellini's theme, again, in 8½ is man against woman. Man, he senses as essentially passive, impotent, and dying, but in spite of it concerned with "rising" to the top in terms of money, profession, religion, words. Man is concerned with words at the expense of the really important thing: the image of woman's face and body offering the white drink of life (contrast the two *cardinali*, Claudia Cardinale and the old, puritanical cardinal with his prohibitions). Fellini degrades sound in his films, turning it either into raucous music or meaningless jabber: it is not too difficult to guess that he is working out an unconscious wish to return to a pre-verbal life consisting mostly of looking at mother, taking her in, so to speak. Fellini seems to be saying that to use words (a script, for example) is to grow old and die—hence his improvisatory style of filming. At the same time, to improvise means (in 8½) to experience directly the sources of inspiration, to be passive and femininely receptive to the old world within. There are risks involved in such passivity—or so we can guess from his pictures of men, dying and impotent, or the way he portrays his mother (in 8½). She seems seductive in the extreme, a woman who would have been quite overpowering to a small boy, and perhaps this is why he represents danger in the nightmare sequence that opens the film as being suffocated, over-whelmed, or drowned: one could be trapped in that old world within and without.

Thus, he approaches this feminine world gingerly, by being casual and improvisatory. In 8½, for example, Guido-Fellini asks his mistress to pretend he is a stranger into whose room she has accidentally blundered. One keeps one's distance. Woman may be the source of sustenance and life, but she is better approached when she is a little dehumanized—into an image, something a man can master and control, even multiply, if need be. Further, looking at something presupposes a certain distance: if you can see a thing, you know you haven't been engulfed by it; but if you see only blackness, you may have been. So don't eat—just look. And even then, don't look all the time. You must look away to be sure you still can tear yourself away, and perhaps this "need to look away" is the key to the curiously episodic structure of Fellini's films, which skip along from one episode to the next with gaps and blanks be-tween. As for the images themselves, black things (like the hat) seem to suggest imageless, masculine thought, also darkness as clothing and obliterating the self; while a white, high-key screen suggests a body—even a world—made clean and orderly, as pure as milk.

These three (2½) films of Fellini's build on the same images, all draw on the same infantile material, and the two feature-length films, at least, show a striking similarity in style and pace. Yet, if I may hypostatize my judgment, both *The Temptation of Dr. Antonio* and *La Dolce Vita* clearly outshine 8½. Why? We could say that it is the weakest of the three because it is so autobiographical. To use Freud's phrasing, Fellini has failed to soften the egotistic character of his fantasies so as to overcome "the feeling of repulsion in us which is undoubtedly connected with the barriers that rise between each single ego and the others." But after all, autobiography can be fun, and the most exquisite moments in 8½ are the most intensely autobiographical, those like the screen-tests sequence, in which making a film and living adult life and remembering childhood all flow into a single image on the screen. The trouble seems to be more complicated.

Autobiography can be fun, yes. But it can also be somewhat precarious from the writer's point of view. That is, if an autobiography is relatively factual (like, say, Mill's or Gibbon's), the reader responds much as he does to other kinds of historical writing. If, however, the writer chooses to air his fantasies, he is likely to arouse the reader's defenses against them—we will feel this as disgust, anxiety, boredom, or any one of a number of negative reactions. He can counterbalance this tendency though, by providing either defensive structuring (so that the reader need not defend) or by providing a good deal of transformation into objective meaning or (as we have seen in Chapter 6) opportunities for the audience to do the transforming into meaning.

In *La Dolce Vita*, the basic fantasy is the helplessness of man before all-powerful woman. This is handled by a structure built around the contrast of sight and sound. There are a variety of meanings—mythic, religious, social. There are parallels to Christ and Dante. There is, in short, meaning embodied in the film and opportunities like that devilfish for the audience to project meaning into it. *The Temptation of Doctor Antonio* builds on the same fantasy of the mighty and seductive woman, but distances it as joke and social satire.

In 8½, the theme of the fantasy is the same. The fantasies,

though, are not presented either as comedy or as realistic happenings distanced from Guido, but as his dreams and life, raw, naked, blunt. Then, the episodic form is about the same as *La Dolce Vita*'s. The structural contrast of words and pictures is very like the earlier film's contrast of sight and sound. The general, objective intellectual meaning embodied in 8½ or the opportunities for finding it there seem rather less to me than in *La Dolce Vita*. In short, Fellini has disguised the fantasy material less; and he has thereby given me more to manage. But he has given me the same or less by way of defense to manage that less disguised fantasy with. As a result, I defend within myself instead of using the defenses of the work of art. I feel boredom, and evidently others do, too. As another critic put it at the time, "However fond we may be of the director of *I Vitelloni* we are not really deeply concerned about his intellectual and sexual fetishes."

Mr. Dwight Macdonald, commenting on my and other critics' negative evaluations of 8½, said: "Mr. Holland . . . dares to express openly a Puritan nervousness when confronted by useless beauty that his colleagues express more discreetly." [18] He is righter that he has any right to be. I am indeed something of a Puritan, and, as any reader of this book must have seen by now, I get much of my enjoyment of literature from actively intellectualizing about it. I am happiest when an artist gives me something to dig my explicatory teeth into. It is much harder for me to experience literature passively. And evidently, I am not the only one, for Mr. Macdonald goes on to analyze the reason for the general critical disapproval of the film. "There is plenty of symbolism here, indeed every shot is a metaphor, but they are all . . . obvious. . . . This is perhaps the difficulty; nothing for the interpretative tooth to mumble."

If I may translate, I find the fantasy content in the film insufficiently managed, either by the film itself or by its providing me with enough grist for my own intellectualizing activities. I reject the film as a whole though I enjoy isolated scenes. Macdonald's reaction to the film (and his different wording of the tooth image) suggest he can respond passively more easily than I can. Better able to tolerate unmanaged fantasy or "useless beauty," he likes the film. We have come back, in short, to Freud's statement, "Man's judgments of value follow directly his wishes for happiness." Or Henry James's, "Nothing will ever take the place of the good old fashion of 'liking' a work of art or not liking it." But we have come back with a difference: we are now in a position to understand "liking" as a result of an interaction between psychic traits in the reader and a psychic process embodied in the work.

In short, we have redefined (accepting the philosophical losses involved) aesthetic "good" as "that which can please many and please long." Looking psychoanalytically at a work as a transformation of fantasy by various quasi-defensive devices can then tell us whether a given work is likely to please many and please long. Of the different levels, fantasy seems relatively unimportant. We have already noticed how the greatest literature—but also the cheapest —builds on the relatively advanced oedipal fantasies. But much great literature is pre-oedipal, more limited and primitive in psychic range. The level of fantasy, in sum, seems to have little to do with our act of evaluation. Though some fantasies will make some people reject a given work outright, most men and women can tolerate a wide variety of infantile fantasies—a tribute to the polymorphous perversity of our early years.

What is much more important than fantasy alone in determining our likes and dislikes is the balance between the fantasy and the defensive level—meaning, structure, phrasing. The Lovelace poems differ in the psychological nature of the defenses embodied in their structure. The "better" poem offers a defense which is more complex, reaching to higher levels of moral and intellectual life, and more likely to be culturally accepted. The "less good" poem offers a less complex defense and one more likely to be associated with guilt. The "better" Fellini film presents its fantasies less nakedly than 8½. It also offers more possibilities of meaning, either in the film or projected into it by its audience. Meaning and defensive structure are, of course, only two elements in the total transformational process. Other comparisons might focus on other elements or combinations of them.

Even so, this psychoanalytic approach to evaluation is not open to the kind of objection Edmund Wilson made to checklists like "unity, symmetry, universality" and so on. "You could have any set of these qualities . . . and still not have a good play, a good novel, a good poem, a good history." Wilson is turning the act of evaluation round about—a writer could dutifully and consciously put in lots of unity or symmetry and still not write well. The psychoanalytic model cannot be turned round this way: a writer cannot consciously change his individual patterns of fantasy and defense. Further, there are no "good" or "bad" fantasies or defenses—only transformations that please or do not please readers.

In pleasing, the crucial elements lie more at the defensive than the fantasy level—meaning, structure, phrasing, form, the things critics have always held to be central. What is new in a psychoanalytic approach is that the goodness or badness, success or failure of any one of these elements can only be understood as it manages an unstated something else, the deeper fantasy. Efforts to judge a phrase or an episode without recognizing it as part of a dynamic, balanced process of transformation must end in gibberish—or, more exactly, in an opinion which merely expresses the critic's own biases as they stem from his personality. Inevitably, of course, a reader's likes and dislikes come from his inner self. But if critical dialogue is ever to be more than an "I like it" confronting an "I don't," we need to recognize the interaction of the psychic traits inherent in the response and the psychic process embodied in the work. When we do, though we may not agree, we can at least share an understanding of why we disagree. Critical evaluation can cease to be the smug assertion of one's own superiority in taste or vision or morality and become an exploration and acceptance of our common, fallible humanity.

8 Style and the Man

Comparing two or more works by one person, be he seventeenth-century lyricist or twentieth-century film-maker, inevitably raises the question of style. "The style," critics say, "is the man," and though we would be hard put to define either the subject or the predicate, the two do seem to have a natural affinity. We speak of works as Miltonic or Flaubertian or Kafkaesque or Kingsley Amish. From the opposite end of the sentence, the psychoanalyst, speaking of a man, will often talk of his "life style." That usage suggests that the literary critic might find a useful model for his concept of style in the psychoanalyst's concept of character, particularly when he is puzzled about a writer's style, as when a novel like *The Secret Agent* seems sharply marked off from the rest of Conrad's work, and yet, in some half-understood way, deeply Conradian.

In "style," the literary critic seems to include three things. First, and most obviously, he means a writer's way with words: Shavian wit or Joycean puns or Shakespearean quibbles. Second, he seems to include a writer's choice of material and his characteristic form for handling it: it would be hard, for example, to think of anything but social comedy that could be said to be "in the style of Congreve," and it is hard to think of Conrad's political novels as from the same pen as his sea stories. Third, critics seem to include in the notion of style a writer's way of dealing with his audience: the

snigger of a Sterne, the stage-managering of a Thackeray, the alle-
gorizing of a Melville.

A psychoanalyst defines "character" (the classic statement is
Fenichel's) as "the habitual mode of bringing into harmony the
tasks presented by internal demands and by the external world." [1]
There is a certain rough correspondence between the elements the
literary critic includes in style and the three terms the psychoanalyst includes in character. That is, the "internal demands" are the
Triebe, the drives, that might lead a writer to a certain kind of material. The "habitual mode of bringing into harmony" refers to a
man's defenses; they in turn correspond to a writer's ways of dealing with his material—form and structure on the large scale, sentence or verse manner on the small. Finally, the "external world"
for a writer is his reader. Naturally, in a man, as in a work of literature, these three things interact and modify one another, but we
can, I think, set up a kind of rough comparison: content is to drive
as form is to defense as style is to character (defined as the habitual interactions of drive, defense, and external reality).

By these criteria, *The Secret Agent* does not seem particularly
Conradian. In terms of form, we miss the usual Conradian narrator. At the sentence level, instead of the allegorical and symbolic
overtones spelled out in the language of, say, *Heart of Darkness*,
we have a heavily ironic and dry verbal style.[2] As for content, we
do not have man pitting his own flawed self against nature, but
rather a political story: anarchists, Verloc as *agent provocateur*, the
Professor with his bombs; also the story of a marriage, Verloc
and Winnie who married him to provide for Stevie, the idiot boy.
Yet some of the incidents show Conrad's preoccupations, though
deviously, in the manner of parody: the fatally significant lapse,
here, Verloc's using Stevie to try to blow up the Greenwich Observatory and Stevie's consequent fragmentation; the secret, both
the motive and identity of the bombers and Verloc's hoard of pay-
ments from the ministry he serves; the self-sacrificing woman—
Winnie and her mother. In some sense, then, the novel is "Con-

radian," but in what sense? Only a psychological concept of style, I think, can tell us.

Anarchic in form as well as content, *The Secret Agent* leaves us with the persistent question of the Professor, "unsuspected and deadly," just as the opening line has posed us Mr. Verloc, also unsuspected, also (in the event) deadly. Those first and last lines offer a clue to the informing principle about which the novel finds its shape and inner logic: the unsuspected—a sense throughout the book that each character has a doubleness or tripleness, a secret self. Verloc, for example—one side is the anarchist, another the bourgeois family man dealing in pornography, a third, the protector of property and servant of embassies. The late Baron Stott-Wartenheim was clever indeed to designate him $\triangle$. The three anarchists are fat or impotent or helplessly and grossly dependent on some woman. The Professor is "frail, insignificant, shabby, miserable"—but explosive.

The police, too, share this many-sidedness, for "The terrorist and the policeman both come from the same basket" (68).[3] Chief Inspector Heat must mediate between the anarchists under his jurisdiction ("our lot") and the Assistant Commissioner, who in turn feels "himself dependent on too many subordinates and too many masters." He must deal on one side with Heat and on another with his wife's friend, Michaelis's patroness, and on still a third, Sir Ethelred, himself torn between the Assistant Commissioner's discoveries and the Fisheries Bill.

Stevie has the same dualistic quality: immoderate compassion matched by pitiless rage. Stevie's mother mediates between the idiot boy and his enraged father, just as Winnie herself adopts a mother's role between Stevie and Verloc: " 'Might be father and son,' she said to herself," as, unknown to her, Verloc leads Stevie to his doom. And at the moment she kills, just as she has torn Heat's pink racing form in two, "Her personality seemed to have been torn into two pieces, whose mental operations did not adjust themselves very well to each other" (209).

The characters bisect and trisect one another, each touching only a part of the others in a chaos and maze of human relations. We begin to sense in the world of the novel the significance of Stevie's "circles, circles, circles; innumerable circles, concentric, eccentric; a coruscating whirl of circles that by their tangled multitude of repeated curves, uniformity of form, and confusion of intersecting lines suggested a rendering of cosmic chaos, the symbolism of a mad art attempting the inconceivable" (49). Not unlike Stevie, Conrad himself seems to be drawing endless circles in his novel: coins, spectacles, wheels, clock faces, haloed street lights, bowler hats, orange peel, billiard ball, the Professor's india-rubber ball, even the great dome of the observatory. And not just circles, but T-bars (the gas lights), triangles (not only Stott-Wartenheim's, also the triangular well of streets in front of Verloc's shop)—the novel fairly bristles with geometric images, as though Conrad were trying to squeeze some sort of order out of the chaos; as though he himself were trying to act out the embassy's injunction: "What is required at present is not writing, but the bringing to light of a distinct, significant fact—I would almost say of an alarming fact" (28).

The critical essay that tells us most about *The Secret Agent* is, of course, Conrad's own Preface, written in 1920 for a collected edition long after the novel's original publication early in 1907. Repeatedly, in the Preface, Conrad uses Wurmt's image of "bringing to light" as he speaks of "illuminating facts," their "illuminating quality," an "illuminating impression." He speaks of the idea precipitating like a geometry of bizarre and unexpected crystals in a colorless solution: "Strange forms, sharp in outline, but imperfectly apprehended, appeared and claimed attention" (11). As against the usual setting for Conrad's novels, the sea, "reflector of the world's light," he now saw London as the "background" for the story, "a cruel devourer of the world's light." "Slowly the dawning conviction of Mrs. Verloc's maternal passion grew up to a flame between me and that background." "At last the story of Winnie Verloc stood out complete . . . it had to be disengaged from its obscurity in that immense town," brought "out in front of the London background" (11).

As one would expect from the Preface, light and dark are the key images in *The Secret Agent*, notably in that dark London with its "sinister, noisy, hopeless, and rowdy night," "sullen, brooding, and sinister," broken by "soiled blood-red light." London becomes inner madness rendered as outer setting, and the city threatens throughout the novel to stifle, suffocate, submerge, overwhelm—Winnie is quite correct to fear in it hanging or drowning. London in the deepest sense is the engulfing sea or maze of irrationality—the very street numbers are as irrational as Stevie's circles. It is a "slimy dampness," a "slimy aquarium," "an immensity of greasy slime" "like a wet, muddy ditch." Miss Claire Rosenfield has very astutely pointed out that balanced against these images of water are fish: the Assistant Commissioner is busy catching a "sprat," Verloc, in order to get at the whale, dogfish, or witty fish, Vladimir.[4] At the moment he plunges into the murky depths of London, the Assistant Commissioner himself looks like a "queer foreign fish," and, of course, Sir Ethelred is concerned throughout with his Fisheries Bill. At the end, Winnie is, as it were, thrown back into the sea.

Fishing provides the perfect symbol for the "bringing to light of a distinct, significant fact," something all the men of the novel play at. Vladimir, Verloc, Heat, even Ossipon are all investigating—but lazily, fitfully. The novel concerns Greenwich Observatory, a place dedicated to bringing facts to light, but the novel uses the observatory only in a plot to destroy it. Ossipon invokes Lombroso as an Italian peasant would his saint. Heat's wisdom is not "true wisdom"; rather, "His wisdom was of an official kind" (79), and he is lazily willing to pin the crime on Michaelis. Two men stand out as exceptions to this general indolence. The Assistant Commissioner really tries to find the truth—and, for that, he is twice described as Don Quixote. The other truth-seeker is, of course, the mad Professor. Confronted with "this world of contradictions," "the inexplicable mysteries of conscious existence," the rest of the men in the novel want simply to relax into such facile faiths as Heat's in his favorite racing form, the easy dogmas of the revolutionaries (which Conrad describes in religious images), or Verloc's belief that he could trust any woman who had given herself to him. "Man," says Conrad, curiously echoing another melodramatic detective thriller, *Hamlet*, "Man may smile and smile, but he is not an investigating animal. He loves the obvious" (8).

Verloc's trust in his wife suggests the key to this cheerful oblivion: "Mr. Verloc loved his wife as a wife should be loved—that is, maritally, with the regard one has for one's chief possession." "She was mysterious, with the mysteriouness of living beings. The far-famed secret agent △. . . was not the man to break into such mysteries" (152). Possession substitutes for knowledge: thus Heat can rest secure on "private friendship, private information, private use of it," and Verloc, with his air of having wallowed in bed all day, can glow in his belief that he has protected "the town's opulence and luxury." Ossipon can even speak of "the even tenor of his revolutionary life." He is fat, Verloc is fat, so also Heat and Michaelis. Winnie's mother has triple chins and her legs are so swollen she can scarcely move. For Yundt laziness is the *motif*: "The famous terrorist had never in his life raised personally as much as his little finger against the social edifice" (51). Appetite and eating image Verloc's grisly complacency at his murder, eating being another way in *The Secret Agent* of achieving the security of possession. For all the men in the story (save the Commissioner and the Professor), Silenus is the emblem. Lustful, lazy, fat, they rest and feed complacently on the obvious. *The Secret Agent* is, among other things, a study in sloth.

By contrast, the women are paragons of self-sacrifice. Winnie's mother commits herself (though the failure of the male trustees to investigate her) to a death-like charitable home, all for the sake of the son, Stevie. And Winnie herself gave up her butcher-boy lover for the slothful eater Verloc so as to provide for Stevie. As for investigation—"She felt profoundly that things do not stand much looking into" (150-151), a note that Conrad sounds again and again as her leitmotif. The women of the story (one could take Michaelis's patron as the prototype) do not probe the mysteries of the world; instead, they offer to a world trusted and uninvestigated a bottomless compassion to the point where the only remedy for pain Stevie can even imagine is to be taken into his sister-mother's bed.

And yet, as the bed-wallowing Verloc finds out, it can be dangerous to relax into the sea of feminine compassion represented by Winnie. "The protection she had extended over her brother had been in its origin of a fierce and indignant complexion" (203), an "ardour of protecting compassion exalted morbidly in her childhood" (59). "Mrs. Verloc's temperament . . . when stripped of its philosophical reserve, was maternal and violent"—a curious pairing of adjectives (199). Ossipon sees her "twined round him like a snake, not to be shaken off. She was not deadly. She was death itself—the companion of life" (237). Significantly, Winnie stabs Verloc as he is lolling on the sofa issuing his mating call.

In the moment of stabbing, Mrs. Verloc literally becomes Stevie's avenging soul, that child who seems to bring to a focus the moral world of the novel. Stevie seems always to have alternated between being seduced and being beaten. His circles suggest the "chaos and eternity" he found in human relations, a confusion of intersections and hidden sides. His response to deprivation is simple, primitive, and violent: "Somebody, he felt, ought to be punished for it—punished with great severity" (146), and this reaction pinpoints the pattern of anarchism (at least in Conrad's highly personal view of it): a morass of vague sentiments from which springs a mad retaliation. "In the face of anything which affected directly or indirectly his morbid dread of pain, Stevie ended by turning vicious. . . . The tenderness of his universal charity had two phases as indissolubly joined and connected as the reverse and obverse sides of a medal. The anguish of immoderate compassion was succeeded by the pain of an innocent but pitiless rage" (144). He alternates between lazy, mindless compassion and sudden, violent action; Vladimir, Verloc, his sister-mother, and all the anarchists do the same.

Balanced against this moral and emotional anarchy are the police and the other forces of government, "the House which is *the*

House, *par excellence*," but very distinctly not a compassionate home. Government tries to impose on this violence-in-violence some sort of control and order, a constant watch, "rules of the game." And it is the aim of Vladimir, Verloc, and the rest to provoke the very forces of control into anarchy. As the Professor puts it: "To break up the superstition and worship of legality should be our aim. Nothing would please me more than to see Inspector Heat and his likes take to shooting us down in broad daylight with the approval of the public. Half our battle would be won then; the disintegration of the old morality would have set in its very temple" (71). This theme of control brings us to Conrad himself. The idea that informs the novel is anarchy masked over by control or indolence. The "secret agent" in human affairs, the "unsuspected," is the potential for violence in each of us—and, presumably, in Conrad himself (who once sprang at Ford Madox Ford's throat when Ford interrupted his proofreading).

The Secret Agent seems to stand apart from the main line of Conrad's writing. It is set in the city, not the sea; government, not navigation, is his subject. Yet this novel is perhaps more deeply Conradian than any of the others. Albert Guerard has shown that Conrad's basic theme is the conflict between the mariner and the outlaw; between the man who seeks to establish control by finding his place among the hard, infallible objects of external reality and that other, darker figure who immerses himself in the destructive, chaotic jungle within and without. Although it is clearest, perhaps, in "The Secret Sharer," between the anonymous captain and his outlaw double, we see the contrast all through Conrad's works: the twinned figures of Marlow and Kurtz, one returning from, one sinking into the "Heart of Darkness"; MacWhirr battling the "Typhoon" without and the passengers' riot within his ship; the skillful young captain threatened by the anarchic spirit of the dead one in "The Shadow-Line"; Haldin and Razumov, the outlaw rejected and his betrayer in *Under Western Eyes*; the captain and crew of *The Nigger of the "Narcissus"* striving to exorcise by seamanship the deadly thing within their ship; Lingard and Almayer in *Almayer's Folly;* Heyst and Jones in *Victory;* and we sometimes see the same dualism of control and anarchy, fidelity and betrayal, in single figures such as Lord Jim (notably) or Karain. Given such a preoccupation with the dualism of controller and controlled, how, in a sense, could Conrad have failed to write a novel about anarchy? And he wrote two, *The Secret Agent* and *Under Western Eyes.*

In *The Secret Agent,* the earlier of the two, we find Conrad's usual dualism doubled. There is controller and controlled, but then a doubleness to what is controlled: the police try to keep under surveillance and rule a violent, masculine rage which itself punctuates a feminine, complacent compassion. Thus, the atmosphere of the novel consists of indolence, obesity, dependence on women, bureaucracy, compassion, Stevie's circles, and all this in the foggy, dark, damp, grimy maze of London. In the night journey of Winnie's self-sacrificing mother, Conrad brings all these elements together and at the same moment sinks his novel to its deepest, most obscure point in the maze. The action of the novel (as contrasted to its atmosphere) is best described in the diplomat's phrase, "the bringing to light of a distinct, significant fact . . . an alarming fact": the explosion itself, the sacrifice of the scapegoat Stevie, the emergence of his name-tape, the Professor's detonator, the Commissioner's quest for Vladimir, or even Verloc's bank account (the prosaic equivalent of the buried treasure in *Nostromo* and other Conrad tales). But nothing is brought to light. Instead, at key points in the novel, the lights are turned off. All this fishing in the slimy dampness of London produces no catch: Winnie sinks into the ocean, the buried treasure slips into Ossipon's pocket, and we are left with the Professor, "unsuspected and deadly." "An impenetrable mystery seems destined to hang forever over this act of madness or despair" (249).

Psychologically, it would be difficult and unnecessary to say what that swamp or sea might have stood for in Conrad's mind—it undoubtedly stood for many things. Death; passivity; sexuality;

human relations and communication; woman or the feminine side
of Conrad's own nature; betrayal or loss of fidelity, particularly the
expatriate's failure to carry on his forefathers' fight for Polish inde-
pendence; the writer landlocked at his farmhouse desk as against
the onetime heroic seaman; perhaps the irrational in the largest
sense, particularly irrational or self-destructive aggression (there is
evidence that Conrad himself once attempted suicide)—all these
and many others may be represented in that "immensity of greasy
slime" the novelist fought to keep his head above. One thing,
however, is clear: Conrad was deeply tempted to let go his hold,
lose control, and sink into it (as so many of his heroes do). Not
only *The Secret Agent*, but all his novels deal with the control or
punishment of such an impulse.

This problem of control creates not only the events and characters of the Conradian novel, but also its form, for psychologically,
form is to content as defense is to impulse. It is surely no accident
that a novelist so preoccupied with action as a defense should
choose a style which Henry James saw was "the way to do a thing
that shall make it undergo most doing." As though Conrad felt the
very writing of his stories as a tempting but threatening anarchy,
he interposed in most of them a dispassionate narrator, ironically
commenting on and distancing us (and Conrad) from the fictive
world. He thus defended against communicating not only with his
material but also with his readers. A number of his stories (but
most notably "Amy Foster") deal with problems of communication; we hear from Ford Madox Ford about his Flaubertian search
for *le mot juste* and his composing his richest sentences in French
(for English was his third, not his second, language). Critics galore
have noted (and some complained of) the fog of adjectives Conrad puts between his material and his reader.

In *The Secret Agent*, Conrad put aside the margin of safety the
narrator represented (and his wife has written how depressed he
became during the writing of this particular novel). He relied instead entirely on the adjectives. He created a comic, ironic style
that swings between an involved periphrasis, almost neo-classic in

manner, and sudden, grimy, realistic details. The result can be such delicious ironies as our last view of Ossipon: "Already he bowed his broad shoulders, his head of ambrosial locks, as if ready to receive the leather yoke of the sandwich board" (252). In sentence after sentence and scene after scene, a "distinct, significant fact" comes to light against the prevailing murk: the fly on the window of Vladimir's office, for example, or the little cracked bell in the Verlocs' shop that marks each passing from the outer world to the inner. His artistic aim, Conrad said, was "before all, to make you see."

In structure no less than sentence style, we see him try either to flee the "immensity of greasy slime" or to bring out from it some distinct fact that can then be seen and controlled. In *The Secret Agent*, Conrad (who was the first great writer to tackle the screenplay) constantly uses flashback, as though he were retreating from the immediate material into some safer matter elsewhere. *The Secret Agent* is a detective thriller—indeed, Alfred Hitchcock has made a film of it—but it does not grow as the usual thriller does from an initial problem to a mass of revelations at the end. Instead, Conrad gives us little secrets, as though he could not stand a sustained build-up of uncertainty and mystery; rather, there must be a constant "bringing to light."

Further, the novel, in its ending, pirouettes away from the complexities of politics and policing developed in its first three-quarters; at the end we are left with two characters so peripheral they become symbolic of the two poles of the novel: the morally complacent Ossipon and the madly violent Professor. Throughout the book, Conrad seems almost to be running away from his characters as his focus shifts successively from Verloc to Vladimir to the other anarchists to Heat to the Assistant Commissioner to Winnie Verloc's mother to Winnie to Ossipon and finally and ultimately to the Professor. We sense in the structure—or lack of it—another version of Stevie's circles, Conrad's flight from and return to his material: "I had to fight to keep at arm's length the memories of my solitary and nocturnal walks all over London in my early days,

lest they should rush in and overwhelm each page of the story"
(12).

By the structure of individual sentences and of the whole, Conrad enlists us in his defensive action of "bringing to light a distinct,
significant fact," but does he make us feel the need for the defense? In most of Conrad's works in which the characters sink into
the moral swamp, he represents the morass as tempting or alluring,
justified by compassion or sheer self-defense. *The Secret Agent*
provides no such temptation for the fat, slimy, repellent world of
the anarchists—except for one thing. Conrad plays on our curiosity;
on just the first page, for example, we hear "nominally," "ostensi-
ble," "discreetly but suspiciously," "hinting at impropriety." He
tempts us to probe the secrets of the controllers and the controlled—but warns us they are both rather dreary. At only one
point does he draw us into the novel unequivocally: the chapter of
the murder where both the danger of being overwhelmed and the
vengeful justification for overwhelming reach a peak. We come in
on the side of Winnie and feel, as she does, the power of the terrible absurd urge to destroy and be destroyed into utter, total blackness. It is no wonder that all the many critics of this novel, though
they differ as to its merits, find the murder its high point.

The critics, I think, are saying Conrad's special style (or character) succeeds in that chapter, much less so in the rest of the novel.
But the novel as a whole is no less Conradian for that. In content,
the novel lets us over the side, as it were, into the London sea of
anarchy. Psychologically, such a content is a drive: Conrad describes as "a fascinating temptation" the Assistant Commissioner's
"descent into the street . . . like the descent into a slimy aquarium" (127). The defense becomes all Conrad's devices for extricat-
ing and distancing us from that tempting sea: the dry, ironic style,
the shifting of focus from one character to another, flashback.
Then, drive and defense, content and form come together as the
style and theme of the whole, pervading and informing its individual sentences: "the bringing to light of a distinct, significant fact
. . . an alarming fact." The style is indeed Conradian, for, as he

defined his own aim in the "Preface to *The Nigger of the 'Narcis-sus'* ": "The artist descends within himself, and in that lonely re-gion of stress and strife," if he succeeds, he can "hold up unques-tioningly, without choice and without fear the rescued fragment before all eyes . . ." "And when it is accomplished—behold!—all the truth of life is there: a moment of vision, a sigh, a smile—and the return to an eternal rest." The aim is a noble one, truly and stoically Conradian, and because we can understand his style psy-chologically, we can feel what he felt as something of the moral function of literature: to bring back to light, almost in the manner of a detective, a character and style of life buried in our own dark, anarchic past.

The issue, though, is not Conrad, but style, especially style and a somewhat hypothetical man. That is, we can analogize between style, understood as the habitual interaction of fantasy and defense in literary works, and character, understood as the habitual interac-tion of drive and defense in life. When we do, we can see relation-ships between particular works and a writer's total *œuvre*. We can, for example, see a continuity in Fellini's work as he moves from his relatively realistic early films like *Il Bidone* to the later, quite sur-realistic ones like *Juliet of the Spirits:* all deal with the fear and desire of woman, particularly the sight of woman.

We can also see somewhat unexpected relations among different writers—for example, that Conrad, Fellini, and Lovelace all deal with the same core fantasy, the fear of woman as engulfing. I said earlier that this is the most common fantasy in literature, but it is by no means the only one. Dickens and Gogol, for example, seem roughly similar writers. Both have a strong satirical bent. Both use highly structured language. Both tend to treat humans as objects, or inanimate things as though they had a life of their own. Both are interested in the theme of getting something out of people. Both use many images of mud, fog, dirt, smells—in short, anal images. They are, then, related albeit distantly, to other anal writ-ers, for example, Gerard Manley Hopkins. He, too, uses a highly structured language, though verse. He, too, is interested in dirt, that is, leafmeal or ooze of oil or ruck and wrinkle, tombs and worms and tumbling to decay. But he reacts against dirt by transcending it, seeing it as beautiful or shifting his attention heavenward. And Hopkins introduces a pattern of writing quite different from Dickens's or Gogol's though built on the same level of fantasy: images and themes of strain and release.

Thinking of style in terms of fantasy alone lets us see similarities between writers, but their individuality shows rather at the level of defense, in the ways different writers deal with the same or similar fantasies. Hopkins uses religious ideas to transcend his anal images. Dickens and Gogol use the reaction-formations of satire or sentimentality. Lovelace flees an engulfing other by sexually or aggressively touching many others. Conrad flees by clinging to a distinct, significant fact or act. Fellini defends by a pattern of counterphobic and phobic seeings and not-seeings, leading to the curiously episodic style of his films. Just as fantasy tells us little for evaluation, the defensive levels being more significant, so, in defining a writer's individuality or "voice," the "higher" levels of defense and particular verbal form tell us more. And yet, it is impossible to understand the "higher" levels unless we first recognize the deeper fantasy they are designed to deal with.

When we define a writer's individuality from his works this way, we are obviously coming close to the source of his creativity. Strictly speaking, the problem of the writer's creativity falls outside the scope of this book which has to do rather with the reader's. Even so, our fantasy-defense model has led us to two observations that may be of help. First, we have found that words in poetry as well as in the particular fantasies of many writers serve to defend against the wish and fear to be engulfed by a nurturing other. Actively putting words out of one's mouth defends against passively and dependently having food put in. It seems likely (to me, at any rate) that the emergence of some such preferred pattern of defense in quite early infancy is the basis for later verbal creativity. The particular form that creativity takes, though, will depend on "higher" levels of defense. As suggested above,[5] a writer probably gets a greatly multiplied pleasure from expressing his fantasies and drives when he uses a form (that is, something like a defense) which itself gratifies. This pleasure at the defensive level probably acts like an economic multiplier to reinforce that particular formal, defensive pattern, giving the writer his distinctive "style" and also a drive toward creativity and productivity in that style.

This hypothesis is borne out, to some extent, by the sequence of images in Wordworth's celebrated sonnet on the sonnet, "Nuns Fret Not at Their Convent's Narrow Room." The poem begins with a series of restraining, obsessional, or repetitive images, as in the title, or the hermit and student then mentioned, or "Maids at the wheel, the weaver at his loom." The images suddenly shift to a great sense of release in space, followed by a kind of total oral fusion:

> bees that soar for bloom,
> High as the highest Peak of Furness-fells,
> Will murmur by the hour in foxglove bells.

Then Wordsworth makes his point, that the sonnet-form, a "prison," a "scanty plot of ground," can give "brief solace" to those "Who have felt the weight of too much liberty." Put rather baldly, what he is saying is: something that would ordinarily be felt as an unpleasant, anally toned restraint can become a source of oral pleasure and merger, like the blossom round a bee.

It is striking that the same pattern occurs in Keats's less well known "Sonnet on the Sonnet." At first, the sonnet form is negative: the chains on Andromeda, associated with pain and constraint. Next, it becomes neutral: "Sandals." Then, Keats's images become anal and obsessive (very rarely does this happen in his poetry):

> Let us inspect the Lyre, and weigh the stress
> Of every chord, and see what may be gain'd
> By ear industrious, and attention meet;
> Misers of sound and syllable, no less
> Than Midas of his coinage, let us be . . .

Finally, the restraints become "garlands," and there is the same kind of fusion as that of the bees in the blossoms: the Muse "will be bound with garlands of her own."

Mrs. Milner suggests a theoretical basis for this anal, obsessive element in form:

> It is part of psycho-analytic theory that, when the infant has reached the stage of recognizing the loved mother as not created by the infant but as a person in her own right, from whom love is received and to whom love is to be given, then arises the problem of how the love is to be given, how it is to be communicated. And this stage leads eventually to the need to accept a different medium for the expression of feelings from the child's own body products; and also to the need to accept the necessity for work with that medium, since the beautiful mess does not make a picture or a poem all by itself. . . . It certainly seems that the analysis of this primary identification of the living feeling experience of the body with the non-living material produced by the body would be likely to be critical for any artist (in the wide sense), since an artist's work is essentially concerned with the giving of life to the bit of "dead" matter of the external world which is the chosen medium. For, in a sense, what the artist idealises primarily, is his medium. He is in love with it.[6]

She describes, in effect, a transformation of drive any child must make to develop normally; from the primal, undifferentiated mother-child unit to the communication of feelings through body products. What is essential to the artist is two further transformations: first, from body products to an artistic medium; second, to idealizing and loving that medium as the mother was once idealized and loved.

Thus, Keats's and Wordsworth's anal images for form show these two later transformations: the essence of artistry is the ability to get a bonus of love and pleasure from defensive or restraining modes (originally of an anal or obsessional kind) that would not ordinarily give pleasure—the ability to see them as "solace" or "garlands." If so, then in theory a writer's biographer ought to be able to read back from his subject's preferred formal devices to the defenses they represent to the circumstances in life that charged those defensive modes with pleasurable possibilities. In practice, though, it seems highly unlikely that he will find the relevant data from so early in childhood. His efforts to find the nub of a writer's creative impulse will probably have to remain inference.

It is, however, possible to read back from literary style to life style. True, one cannot know (without external evidence) whether a writer did or did not act out the fantasies of his fiction in his life.[7] One cannot, therefore, read from literary work to actual event. Our fantasy-defense model, however, does enable us to infer, first, a preferred level of fantasy (oral, anal, phallic, or oedipal) and second, preferred modes of defense. These the writer can no more shed than his thumbprint, and they enable us not only to relate his separate writings into a coherent stylistic whole but also his life and his writings as related styles. "I have often had the fancy," Yeats wrote, "that there is some one myth for every man, which, if we but knew it, would make us understand all he did and thought."

A psychoanalytic understanding of life style and literary style as a man's habitual patterns of fantasy and defense provides the kind of myth Yeats sought. Recognizing Hopkins's anality from his poems enables us to see parallels in his painting (his "minute pre-Raphaelite draughtsmanship"), his priestly renouncing of poetry until his rector remarked, "I wish someone would write a poem about that *Deutschland* wreck," or his obsessional doubts about learning Welsh. On the defensive level, his tendency in the poems to transcend dirty realities matches his religious conversion. One can understand Fellini's looking at thousands of photographs to get an actor or actress with just the right look; his films, too, deal with fears and wishes associated with charged sights. Defensively, he prefers to work in a very improvisatory way on a highly chaotic set, insisting a script can be no more than an outline. In the same way, his films skip along from one episode to the next with gaps and blanks in between—there is a kind of need "to look away," to keep free of the material as though it could take its maker over.

As for Conrad, a close look at *The Secret Agent*'s fantasy content and its defensive management lets us infer Conrad's myth: the wish to bring to light a "distinct, significant fact" and hang onto it lest one sink into engulfing depths. Though we have arrived at the myth for Conrad from just one novel, countless examples from Dr. Bernard C. Meyer's fine biographical study [8] confirm it. After examining Conrad's total *œuvre*, Dr. Meyer concludes: "Conrad's heroes are motherless wanderers, postponing through momentary bursts of action their long-awaited return to a mother, whose untimely death has sown the seeds of longing and remorse, and whose voice, whispered from beyond the grave, utters her insistent claim upon her son's return." As for his life, "Throughout . . . Conrad displayed an incorrigible restlessness, an inability to tolerate the same ship, the same house, or even the same mode of life for any sustained length of time." Conrad himself described his leaving Poland this way: "He desired naïvely to escape with his very body from the intolerable reality of things." He invented adventures in the Congo—"his claim to have been saved by a native African woman who brought him water every day and his account of being rescued at the last minute after blowing three times on a whistle as he sank helplessly in a bog." And, perhaps most revealing of all, he answered a friend who tried to interest him in Freud, "I have no wish to probe the depths. I like to regard reality as a rough and rugged thing over which I can run my fingers—nothing more."

Yeats is right—there is "some one myth for every man." And one can discover it from just a small segment of his total work. Our model, too, is right. Though the concept of literary works as fantasies modified by defenses was designed to explore the reader's mind, it can be turned around. We can go from the text not only to the audience's mind but also to the writer's and from thence to his life to confirm a pattern of fantasy and defense. Indeed, how could it be otherwise? For we have seen the essence of our response is that a Fellini or a Hopkins or a Conrad takes over, for the long moment of a literary work, a portion of our minds, ordering it according to, not our, but their creative gifts.

9   Myth

Myth criticism—the finding of myths or rituals embedded in literary works—seems to have become a major sport among students and critics. As sport, one can hardly object, but the myth critic goes further: he says that these things he finds are what create our emotional response to the work. Northrop Frye or a host of followers tell us that *Tom Sawyer* acts out again the journey to the underworld of the matriarchal cave; that within *Great Expectations* lies the tale of the wicked witch and the enchanted princess; or that behind Richard III lurks the boar that slew Adonis. And when they tell us these things, the work of art seems suddenly to drop from the immediate world into the timeless and cosmic. I, at least, get a peculiar feeling of satisfaction, richness, and depth, a sense of the prehistoric, the echoing corridors of time, the great continuities of human experience experienced again in and through myself. But why? The myth critics seem content to say this feeling of resonance comes about because myth taps some sort of collective unconscious, the deepest memories and fantasies of the race. But these are airy nothings psychologists proper have long hooted at.

Even so, a myth critic could answer, all writers, no matter when or where, seem to turn out variations on one or the other of two basic myths: first, the dying god favored by mythographers such as Frazer or Joseph Campbell or literary critics like Frye and his followers; second, the triple goddess evoked by mythographers such as Freud or Erich Neumann and applied in literary criticism mostly by Robert Graves. Certainly, once you begin to look, you can find under every literary bush a vegetation god or great earth mother, coupled or separate. From Sumer to Saul Bellow, Melanesia to Malamud, vast masses of legend and literature, pagan, Christian, Arthurian, Homeric, red Indian or brown, fit the pattern of one or both of these two basic myths. Virtually any episode in a work of literature: feast, marriage, journey, struggle, quest for Grail or whale, will match one episode in Campbell's monomyth or Cornford's. Virtually any hero—Faust or Don Juan, the picaro, the rogue-artist, the various lords of misrule—can be felt as gods dying with or without rebirth. Virtually any heroine can find her place in the Jungian pantheon of Virgin, Mother, and Crone. Even genres become the hardened crusts of myths. Comedy and tragedy (as the death or triumph of a hero) are where the theory started. Elegy, too, is obvious enough, as is epic: all self-respecting epics must have their journey to the underworld or, in mythic terms, a death-and-rebirth. Even pastoral has its link through the *bonus pastor*, the good shepherd, to Christ, dying and reborn; through *otium*, the leisurely pastoral life, to the mythic theme of the quest refused.

Clearly, one simple way of explaining the fact that these patterns turn up in all times, all genres, and all cultures is to say that we inherit these patterns as some kind of collective or archetypal or imprinted unconscious. But that is not the only possible explanation, and others do not require the troublesome assumption that our RNA and DNA, already so fraught with information, must carry Grimm's fairy tales as well.

The most obvious alternative is to say not that literature comes from myth, but that myth and literature alike stem from common psychological drives, universal because they are intrinsic to all human development. Thus, Freud in *Totem and Taboo* showed that tragedy and, in general, the myth of the slain, eaten, and reborn god act out a son's wishes toward a father (and, of course, one would now have to add the qualification from Malinowski, the father-substitute in a matriarchy, typically the mother's brother). Similarly, in "The Theme of the Three Caskets," Freud showed (if we eke him out a bit) that the myths and cults of the triple goddess act out a son's attitudes toward a mother: as fruitful, bountiful, and nurturing; as sexually desirable but unattainable; as threatening and punishing, even killing. Unlike the collective unconscious used to explain the ubiquity of myth, such recurring fantasies about parents can be documented independently of myth by thousands of case histories from couch or clinic.

The myth critic, however, when he makes his assumptions explicit, feels that he is explaining something besides the ubiquity of myth, namely, that special feeling of resonance. The great myths and legends, he claims, because they express the deepest unconscious feelings of the race, have the power to evoke in literature our deepest responses. The dynamics or economics of this process myth critics, at least, do not make very clear—perhaps the simple notion of "resonance" will have to stand, though obviously there is more to it than that.

For one thing, although all works of literature embody myths, not all give that deep, rich feeling of resonance: not *Iolanthe*, for example (based on the Great Mother), nor *Other Voices, Other Rooms* (the Grail quest), to mention two such critical *trouvailles*. Another problem: merely pointing to the myth does not tell us what the work of art does with it. "The drama," C.L. Barber aptly insists, "controls magic by reunderstanding it as imagination." [1] But, unfortunately, very little myth criticism follows Professor Barber's warning. Very little tells us what has happened to the myth or ritual as it became art or how the effect of the work of art on us therefore differs from the effect of the myth.

There are, too, strong resistances to explaining the resonance myth evokes. One, I think, is something in the nature of apologetics going on underneath much myth criticism. That is, because the two fundamental myths seem to occur everywhere and always, the myth critic claims a kind of validity or authority for the one he prefers and therefore for the particular kind of religion associated with that myth: the death and rebirth of Christ favored by Frye or the cult of the Great Mother espoused by Graves. Yet, clearly, as Freud's and Frazer's use of myths and rituals show, the ubiquity of myth cuts two ways: one can justify atheism by showing that modern religions are essentially the same as primitive ones long lacking in worshippers (except for Mr. Graves). Essentially, the ubiquity of myth simply puts all religions on an equal footing. All gain the same authority—or lack of it—and the choice of religion or none remains one's own.

Yet here the apologetics implicit in myth criticism can call upon the other datum: resonance. Myths seem to have the power to evoke or resonate our deepest selves. The religions implicit in these myths or rituals must also somehow be in tune with our deepest selves. Myth-in-literature, then, "proves" the existence of the kind of religious emotion proclaimed by Tillich and other neo-orthodox theologians. In this sense, myth criticism becomes just one more phase in Arnold's strategy of claiming for religion a poetic validity or for literature a religious sanction. Myth criticism thus paves a way for the rather vague theism so much in vogue now—on the basis of our subjective experience of resonance.

There is another block to understanding the resonance of myth —where does it come from, the work itself, the myth, or the work plus our knowledge of the myth in the work? Most myth critics, I think, believe that myths in literature make us resonate without our being consciously aware of them. I can only say I have had the contrary experience. For one thing, I find the myth critic's vocabularly itself peculiarly sonorous and rich, with its sons and seasons, winter lords and summer kings, crone goddesses and great mothers. Such phrases as "the joy of that strong generative power which impels the endless succession of seeds and sexes" stir me almost as a work of art does. Then a myth critic comes on the scene, in this case Mr. Sherman Hawkins (in the phrase above), and, by making me aware of the myths in *The Shepheardes Calender*, enables me to respond with an emotion I could not feel before. To me, it is very clear that in such a situation, I am resonating, not simply because there is myth in the work, but because there is myth and I know there is myth. My conscious knowledge seems to be a *sine qua non* for that special feeling of resonance and sonority. But perhaps instances can do more than theory can to make the matter clear.

Man and Superman makes a particularly useful instance, for the play exists, as it were, both with and without myth—or, perhaps more accurately, legend, which seems capable of the same effect. Most of us have seen the play without the Hell scene. As such, it seems to me a bright comedy, a sexual duel with some philosophical preoccupations, but not too far removed from Pinero and Jones or, for that matter, Terence Rattigan. But, with the Hell scene, Mozart's majestic chords signal a sudden drop into the timeless. The legendary dialogue casts long shadows into what preceded and what follows, and what had been simply a witty-lovers comedy becomes something else: richer, deeper, more resonant—at least for me. It is, then, my conscious knowledge of the legend that colors my response; but why?

Somehow, because I can see Jack Tanner both as his individual self and as the timeless, legendary Juan Tenorio playing a foreordained role, I get a feeling of resonance. It is something like "a feeling of an indissoluble bond, of being one with the external world as a whole." That phrase describes the "oceanic feeling" which Romain Rolland offered Freud as the "true source of religious sentiments." I, too, would associate the resonance mythic parallels make me feel with religious feelings and also with political commitments—as Erikson suggests, they, too, give one the feeling of being submerged and nurtured by a larger entity. Marvell described the feeling in "The Garden":

> the mind from pleasure less
> Withdraws into its happiness.
>
> . . .
>
> Annihilating all that's made
> To a green thought in a green shade.

Freud set out to explain this "oceanic feeling" and arrived at an hypothesis later observers have confirmed and which we have used many times—the crisis of self-object differentiation.[3] Originally, the child does not perceive himself as separate from his nurturing mother. In time, he learns she—and he—are separate beings, but even in adult life certain experiences will bring back that "oceanic feeling" of "limitlessness and of a bond with the universe," which had once been mother. Freud suggested that religious feelings brought the sensation back; Erikson has shown that ideological commitments also can. Now, it appears that mythic parallels in literature do, too. It is no coincidence that Marvell's "The Garden" builds on the myth of the primal garden of at-oneness with God; we were thrust forth from it by knowledge, knowledge, in a way, of our own separateness from God, our own identity as man.

> And the Lord God said, Behold, the man is become as one of us to know good and evil: and now, lest he put forth his hand, and take also of the tree of life, and eat, and live for ever:
> Therefore the Lord God sent him forth from the garden . . .

Thus, I am suggesting, the resonance we feel at myth represents a re-experiencing of that earlier sense of being merged into a larger matrix, a living forever in a role laid down from time immemorial.

"And eat." This sense of merging or resonance takes us back to a time when our life was primarily a life of the mouth, when our fantasies revolved around the two poles of "taking in": devouring and being devoured, as in "The Garden":

> Ripe apples drop about my head;
> The luscious clusters of the vine
> Upon my mouth do crush their wine;
> The nectarine and curious peach
> Into my hands themselves do reach;
> Stumbling on melons as I pass,
> Ensnared with flowers, I fall on grass.
>
> Meanwhile the mind from pleasure less . . .

Marvell images being fed as followed by the oceanic fusion; he thus suggests a check on our hypothesis. If the resonance of myth comes from our re-imagining our original fusion in and separation from the primal matrix, then we should expect to find oral elements: motifs of being engulfed, of devouring and being devoured, in literary works where myth plays a role and where the feeling of resonance is strong.

Certainly, we find them aplenty in *Man and Superman*. Listen, for example, to this Don Juan on love: "While I was in the act of framing my excuse to the lady, Life seized me and threw me into her arms as a sailor throws a scrap of fish into the mouth of a sea-bird." [4] By contrast, the true artist, "half vivisector, half vampire," "steals the mother's milk and blackens it to make printer's ink to scoff at her." While he still thinks Ann is in love with Tavy, Tanner tells him, "There is no love sincerer than the love of food. I think Ann loves you that way: she patted your cheek as if it were a nicely underdone chop." "Why, man, your head is in the lioness's mouth: you are half swallowed already . . . she breaks everybody's back with the stroke of her paw; but the question is, which of us will she eat? My own opinion is that she means to eat you." To Ann herself (after she has pretended to be a boa constrictor), he explains why he lost interest in her as an adolescent:

> TANNER. It happened just then that I got something that I wanted to keep all to myself instead of sharing it with you.
> ANN. I am sure I shouldn't have asked for any of it if you had grudged it.
> TANNER. It wasn't a box of sweets, Ann. It was something you'd never have let me call my own.
> ANN. (incredulously) What?
> TANNER. My soul.
> ANN. Oh, do be sensible, Jack.

Tanner's ambiguities make it seem as though Ann could eat up his masculinity like chocolate. Thus, on learning that Ann is in love with him: "Then I—I am the bee, the spider, the marked down victim, the destined prey," and he flees. At the end of the play, Tanner's engagement to Ann acts out an acceptance of his role as "the destined prey," and he capitulates. "I have no heart's desires," as though he were sated. His last tirade evokes only "Universal laughter"—an image, among other things, of millions of bared but unhostile teeth. In short, the play as a whole gives us a character talking or running himself loose from the matrix, but finally accepting his role, and we are suitably reassured: it is funny.*

That is to look at the play from Tanner's point of view—how do we in the audience recapitulate his experience of being swallowed into a role demanded by the life force, his flight from it, his ultimate surrender and trust? Shaw establishes the appropriate tension in the very first moments of the play through the highly conventional figures of Ramsden and Tavy, creatures of role, their separate identities lost in conventionality, here, submerged in the hushed tones of death. To the extent we contemn and reject them, we try to defend against such loss of identity. We are ready, then, when within a hundred lines Shaw poises against them the figure of Tanner, furiously asserting his unconventionality through pamphlets, rhetoric, in general, words pouring out of his mouth. We take his way in as our way of escaping the anonymity of Ramsden and Tavy. Then, the next character to enter is the passively masterful Ann

---

* Viewing Shaw through the lens of transformational linguistics, Richard Ohmann notes his passion for tight categories and exaggerated opposites, cliché-juggling, paradox, discontinuity, the use of imperatives and interrogatives, and persons as representing attitudes. Ohmann concludes that Shaw makes

> an affirmation of human mind and order, as against the destructive forces of mechanism and chance. The quest for likenesses is a struggle to overcome through the organizing energies of mind, the threatening randomness of experience. In embracing discontinuity, on the other hand, Shaw rejects the mechanical tyranny of past over present and asserts man's right to control himself and his world, rather than doing (or thinking, or writing) what was done (or thought, or written) last time. Similarly, his affection for the everlasting "nay" represents an unalterable opposition to the blockhead, the man who impoverishes human life by his slavery to "ideals" and deceptions.[5]

In short, Ohmann, traveling by the route of linguistics comes to virtually the same point I reach by psychoanalysis: that Shaw's basic theme is the (oral) one of talking oneself loose from an enslaving matrix (such as woman or the past) felt as demeaning or threatening the very separateness of his identity.

who will ultimately (as in this opening scene) prove the mediator and Hegelian synthesis between the two modes of character already there and conflicted. The play will introduce one other mode of defense, an ambivalent flight in space and into the timelessness of myth and Lamarckian philosophy. Our allegiance to conflicting modes of character, though, has already established the basic tension: between being swallowed into a role or asserting onself through words, with Ann offering an attractive compromise: "Never mind her, dear. Go on talking."

One of the richest embeddings of myth in literature is the rejection of Falstaff. As J. I. M. Stewart and Philip Williams have shown [6] he is compared in *II Henry IV* to the Martlemas beef and the Bartholomew boar-pig, scapegoat animals ritually slaughtered to commemorate spring and harvest. Falstaff, the myth critics tell us, is a "dethroned and sacrificed king," "the scapegoat sacrificed to cleanse a Waste Land." More reasonably, he is, in C. L. Barber's fine analysis, the Lord of Misrule from a variety of Elizabethan festivals who must be banished for the hero-king, Henry V, to come into being. Though we feel sorry for the old reprobate, we also feel his banishment as "inevitable and just," as Williams says, though for explanation he calls on "Carl Jung's concept of the collective unconscious of the race": "Archetypal images of king-fathers and sacrificial rites are our inescapable heritage." Maybe so, but how many of us, really, have inherited any Martlemas beef archetypes? There is, again, the simpler explanation: that the banishing of Falstaff recapitulates in each of us the separation of ourselves from the matrix of our mouthy infancy. Though it seems redundant even to mention it, the oral element is very strong in this play about the world's archetypal fat man. There are, though, other people in the play besides Falstaff. The entire play involves a change of identity from the madcap prince to the hero-king, and these changes are often stated in imagery of the food and mouth. The very first thing we see is Rumor, the prologue, "painted full of tongues." The whole commonwealth is a "beastly feeder," now

vomiting up Henry IV, for "Their over-greedy love hath sur-
feited." Hal himself must put aside "the feeder of my riots" to become the hero-king; he must accept the crown that "hath fed upon
the body of my father," that "hast eat thy bearer up." And when
he rejects the "surfeit-swelled" Falstaff, he does so in terms of food
and being devoured:

> Leave gormandizing. Know the grave doth gape
> For thee thrice wider than for other men.

Though, at the moment of the crowning, Falstaff called Hal, "My
Jove!" thus identifying himself with Saturn who devoured his
sons, he now must learn to accept a new identity, based on a new
relationship between him and Hal. Where formerly Hal and
Falstaff had been a unit ("Banish plump Jack and banish all the
world!"), now Hal tells him:

> When thou dost hear that I am as I have been,
> Approach me, and thou shalt be as thou wast

(the converse of the way a new "I" grows out of the separation of
two people). Hal has rejected this man he was taking in like a
"strange tongue," and now he immerses himself in another matrix:
God's, nature's, his father's. He tells Falstaff's enemy, the Lord
Chief Justice, who was "the person of [his] father," "the image of
his power,"

> You shall be as a father to my youth.
> My voice shall sound as you do prompt mine ear.

The image is the very one that Shakespeare used to harness our
hunger and merge us into the play with its first words:

> Open your ears, for which of you will stop
> The vent of hearing when loud Rumor speaks?

In *II Henry* IV, myth serves, not to dredge up some hypothetical
racial unconscious, but to make us experience for ourselves the
characters' choices. They either find identities by merging into a
primal, nurturing matrix, or they fail to fit the larger order because

of their own selfish appetites for food, drink, words, or power. For Hal, we feel this merging as triumphant, a kind of apotheosis. For Falstaff, we feel a wry and melancholy necessity. But for both (unlike the defeated rebels) we feel a reassuring return to a foreordained role.

Close chronologically and psychologically to *II Henry IV*, comes *As You Like It*.[7] There, too, the oral theme is strong. The older brother makes the younger "feed with his hinds," and the younger flees to join the banished Duke in a forest. He fights him for food first, but then learns that the forest nurtures like a mother, gives a "sweet" life ("Sweet are the uses of adversity") and the Duke and his men "fleet the time carelessly as they did in the golden world." The action is for the brothers and the Dukes to find their proper social roles again. The bad brother improbably reforms as he is about to become "Food to [a] sucked and hungry lioness" "with udders all drawn dry." As for the good brother, Orlando, Rosalind's catechism of Orlando taught him love: "Men have died from time to time, and worms have eaten them, but not for love." In the stately finale, Rosalind ritually pairs off the appropriate lovers, and again we get the sensation of a comfortable merging into a foreordained role. In the play as a whole, though, the role is not mythic but pastoral. Just as *Man and Superman* shows how legend can carry out the function of myth, *As You Like It* shows how the traditional trappings of a genre, perhaps even a simple phrase like "Once upon a time," can give the same resonant feeling of lapsing into a matrix, though to a lesser degree.

Bergman's *Smiles of a Summer Night*[8] shows that even the mere awareness of myth without certain knowledge of it is enough to permit the feeling of mythic resonance. The film divides roughtly into halves. The first presents (in a realistic setting) a series of mismatched couples: aging husband and young, virginal wife; theological son and sluttish serving-girl; motherly actress and murderous Count. This half of the film hints at a Phaedra plot, but does not act it out, and there is no particular feeling of resonance.

The second half of the film is richly mythic—and resonant: a feast at the castle of the actress, Desirée's, crone-like mother. The old woman is carried to the feast like the image of death on Walpurgisnacht, and she invokes the spell with a magic wine:

> A story is told that . . . to every cask filled with this wine a drop of milk from the swelling breasts of a woman who has just given birth to her first child and a drop of seed from a young stallion are added. This gives the wine a mysterious stimulating power, and whoever drinks of it does so at his own risk.

In the magical moment of the toast and the wishing, Bergman's camera moves from face to face with catchlights from the candles and soft-focus to suggest each character's sinking into an inner self.

The rest of the night works itself out to a ritual refrain spoken magically and quite unrealistically by the servant couple:

> The summer night has three smiles, and this is the first—between midnight and daybreak—when young lovers open their hearts and bodies.

> Now the summer night smiles its second smile: for the clowns, the fools, the unredeemable.

> And then the summer night smiled for the third time. For the sad, the depressed, the sleepless, the confused, the frightened, the lonely.

The night comforts, and perhaps the smile suggests a nurturing person (for nights do not, after all, smile).

In another exquisite image, we see the roles of man as figures that rotate on the town clock, and as the time passes, the young lovers elope; the servants couple in a haystack; Fredrik and the Count fight a duel with blanks which leaves Fredrik with a sooty face. The Count and his wife, both mechanical and sadistic, accept each other. Fredrik ends up nestling by Desirée like a tired child, as she tells her mother she is "studying [her] new role." And the servants pronounce the final words: "The clowns will have a cup of coffee in the kitchen."

In short, the action is a reassuring charm to let each find his proper role, even (wryly) to accept aging and death. The resonance is rich, even though the mythic parallel is more general than particular. There are elements of midsummer-night rituals: fires, copulation in the fields, the image of death, the wine and wishes. The ladies constitute a triple goddess: the young wife is the Virgin; Desirée is the Mother; and her mother is the Crone; with the sadistic Charlotte focusing in herself Persephone the Destroyer. At one point, Frid the porter leaps about like a satyr, and Fredrik with the soot on his face is the *melanthos* of Attic drama, having recently suffered a death-and-rebirth into the mothering arms of Desirée.

The myths and rituals are vague, though Bergman calls attention to their presence. With them, we find the oral elements of much wine, coffee, kissing, magical speech, feasting, blowing trumpets, smiling—even more important, mothering. Throughout, the men's aggressive efforts to break out of their roles are foiled by the women's managerial, motherly talents, and it is this sense of being engulfed in a matriarchy that lets our knowledge of the myths, however inchoate, generate the true feeling of resonance.

Myth by itself is ubiquitous, let alone legend (Don Juan), the traditions of genre (*As You Like It*), or the dim awareness of mythic elements without any specific parallel (*Smiles of a Summer Night*). Obviously, if myth be ubiquitous, one cannot demonstrate in a finite space that it always gives us a resonant feeling when associated with a fantasy of being absorbed into a matrix. I can, however, further the argument by instances that the opposite proposition is true. That is, where myth is embedded in a literary work and we know it is there, but where our feeling of resonance is not strong, the fantasy of return to the original mother-child unit is flawed or defeated or absent. We would expect, too, that the symbols of orality would be weak or gone.

One instance that confirms this opposite proposition is "The Rocking-Horse Winner." [9] Like so many of D. H. Lawrence's stories, it has a mythic matrix. Paul's father hints at it by his role—or lack of it. We scarcely hear of him except to learn, at the opening, that his wife does not love him, that he goes "to town to some office," that he "never *would* be able to do anything worth doing," that he is "very unlucky." At the crucial discovery scene, when Paul's mother finds the boy collapsing on his rocking-horse, the father is downstairs "mixing a whisky-and-soda." The man who takes the father's place, who has money, leisure, luck, the boy's companionship, is his uncle—the mother's brother, that is, the man who would take the father's place in a matriarchal culture, particularly if the secret of fatherhood is not known.* His first name is Oscar, derived ultimately from Osiris; his last name is Cresswell, with overtones of growth and prosperity. Correspondingly, the mother's name is Esther, derived ultimately from Ishtar. In short, we seem to be dealing on the mythic level with some kind of cult of the Great Mother—though, in the actual story, of course, Esther-Ishtar is a cold, stunted, unloving mother.

The story has elements of a later religion, too. Paul, like his saintly namesake, has both pagan and Christian roles to play. He, too, falls from his horse because of a vision, ultimately blinding, that makes his eyes "like blue stones." Bassett, his gamekeeper-mentor, tells us, "It's as if he had it from heaven." Bassett himself, lowly, lamed, and priestly, talks of winning money "as if he were speaking of religious matters," "serious as a church." In effect, Lawrence sets off a slavish, money-grubbing religion of children and slaves against an ampler, matriarchal paganism.

Knowing this mythic side, however, gives no feeling of resonance to me—or to anyone to whom I have mentioned it—though the evidence is as ample as evidence usually is for mythic readings. Perhaps we can see why the resonance doesn't happen.

---

* It is some further confirmation of the reading to note that the same mother's brother role occurs in Strindberg's *The Father* where precisely the matters at issue are matriarchal rule as against patriarchal, the question hinging on knowledge of fatherhood. It would be possible to see Paul's need to know about riding-leading-to-multiplication as a symbol of sexual knowledge—but, if so, the Lawrence story disguises the theme much more than the Strindberg play.

Lawrence's "Rocking-Horse Winner," W. D. Snodgrass suggests,[10] attacks masturbation (the boy's furious rocking on his wooden horse) as an inadequate substitute for union with another human being. We could look at the story in another, but related, way: as a tragedy of sublimation, of accepting more and more complex and devious substitutes for one's real desires. As Uncle Oscar concludes, "He's best gone out of a life where he rides his rocking horse to find a winner." We can also think of it in still a third, but again related way: as the boy's trying to achieve a real relationship or union with the Great Mother by a devious Christian money-grubbing and money-charity.

But, of course, such union as he gets with his mother comes too little and too late—though it does come, towards the end of the story:

> The Derby was drawing near, and the boy grew more and more tense. . . . His mother had sudden strange seizures of uneasiness about him. Sometimes, for half-an-hour, she would feel a sudden anxiety about him that was almost anguish. She wanted to rush to him at once, and know he was safe.
>
> Two nights before the Derby, she was at a big party in town, when one of her rushes of anxiety about her boy, her first-born, gripped her heart till she could hardly speak. She fought with the feeling, might and main, for she believed in commonsense. But it was too strong.
>
> His eyes blazed at her for one strange and senseless second, as he ceased urging his wooden horse. Then he fell with a crash to the ground, and she, all her tormented motherhood flooding upon her, rushed to gather him up.
>
> But he was unconscious, and unconscious he remained . . .

In many ways, that horrible "But" carries the whole tragedy. "The Rocking-Horse Winner" is a story of desperate hunger, seemingly for money or luck, but actually for love, and there is no satisfaction of the hunger (unless we can see Paul's death as some kind of union with an ultimate mother). This lack of satisfaction shows another way: by the few references to the mouth. What few there are speak not of feeding, taking in, through the mouth, but instead of facial expressions: "smirking," "a roar of laughter," "He pursed his mouth tight." "A cold, determined look came on her mouth." "He saw, by the lines of her mouth that she was only trying to hide something from him." This is a story about very definitely *not* being fed, *not* (except by dying) achieving union with a mother. And knowing the myth in the story does not give us the kind of resonance, the sense of an antediluvian self prior to our historical individuality, that knowing myths in other works so often does.

Miss Claire Rosenfield has found a mythic parallel in a novel we have already considered, Conrad's *The Secret Agent*.[11] She points out that Conrad's London is something on the order of a classical labyrinth with its dirty brick walls, jumbled street signs, an "immensity of greasy slime," a "slimy aquarium," a "slimy dampness." It is the hell-mouth or the bowels of the monster (in the terms of Joseph Campbell). As we have seen above, contrasted to these images of water, the action of the novel is to fish. The Assistant Commissioner tries to catch a "sprat" (Verloc) to get the whale (Vladimir). The Assistant Commissioner looks like a "queer foreign fish" when he plunges into the murky depths of London. His patron in Parliament is preoccupied with his Fisheries Bill. But, again, the myth, far from giving us a feeling of resonance, seems to parody the fishing motif, described by Frye as "bringing life out of the waters." Instead, the detectives' discovery issues not in life, but in Winnie's murder of Verloc, and she herself drops off a Channel boat into the sea.

Winnie herself is the snake-goddess (like Persephone, the destroyer) who is to her lover, Ossipon, "twined around him like a snake, not to be shaken off. She was not deadly. She was death itself—the companion of life." Indeed, Ossipon is a grotesque parody of the sun-god. Stevie, the idiot brother Winnie loved, whose death in Verloc's attempt to blow up Greenwich Observatory sets off Winnie's vengeance, is fraught with myth. Professor Guérard notes that he is both visionary and victim. Miss Rosenfield sees in him the child-man of double parentage (his real parents and his adopted: Winnie and Verloc), whose birth is described as being borne in a roomy "barque" down the "lazy stream" of Mr. Verloc's life (something in the manner of Moses). He suffers the traditional *sparagmos* of the scapegoat, being torn to pieces (by the bomb), though instead of the ritual eating of the slain god, alas, the police inspector only loses his appetite—and very nearly his breakfast—at the sight of Stevie's remains, the "raw material for a cannibal feast." The parallels are striking, but the effect, so far from being the resonance and deepening we associate with the presence of myth, is rather one of grotesquerie or parody.

Nevertheless, as we have seen, many elements in the novel have to do with the primal unit of nurturing mother and suckling child. Each of the anarchists depends upon some woman. All the men relax into easy faiths. Verloc looks as though he has wallowed in bed all day. Sinking into the moral swamp signifies, at the deepest level, relaxing into a passive position toward a nurturing woman. Thus, the very knife the "maternal and violent" Winnie uses to stab Verloc, he has just used to cut himself thick slabs of beef. The nurtured Stevie becomes "the raw material for a cannibal feast." Winnie's first lover was a butcher-boy.

The novel, though it builds on a wish to lapse into an engulfing, nurturing environment, builds against the wish. It presents that environment as dangerous and dirty: "slimy," "greasy," "muddy." Verloc is murdered for his moral indolence, his complacent willingness to take what comes. Winnie's submerging kills her. The feeding and obesity are repulsive. In the words of the ambassadorial injunction that starts the action, "What is required at present is . . . the bringing to light of a distinct, significant fact—I would almost say of an alarming fact." This is the fishing motif, but also the explosion itself, the sacrifice of the scapegoat Stevie, the emergence of his identifying name-tape (*anagnorisis*), the Professor's detonator, the Commissioner's quest for Vladimir, or even the withdrawal of Verloc's bank account. But all this fishing for things fails: Winnie sinks into the ocean and the buried treasure into Ossipon's pocket.

Though Conrad tempts us a little toward the "immensity of greasy slime" by the promise of secrets (even pornographic secrets), the style and structure and action of the novel as a whole move against it. The book persuades us that to let oneself over the side into the dark, engulfing labyrinth of secrets would be dangerous or disgusting. The right action is to fight free of it. And we feel the myth as parody.

In short, where the literary work as a whole makes us feel that lapsing into a protective, nurturing, maternal environment is pleasurable (*Man and Superman*) or necessary (*II Henry IV*) or to be wryly accepted (*Smiles of a Summer Night*), we feel the resonance of myth, joyous in one case, melancholy in another, but in all, deepening and enriching. When, however, the work of art makes us feel that such a lapsing into a succored passivity is dangerous or disgusting (*The Secret Agent*) or impossible ("The Rocking-Horse Winner"), the work of art blocks whatever feeling of resonance we might get from our knowledge of a mythic substratum.

In effect, myths in literature either work with or work against our original merger with the text. Analyzing the "as if" or "willing suspension of disbelief," we found that we approach a literary work with two conscious expectations: the work will give us pleasure; it will not ask that we act on the external world. These two conscious expectations find a matrix in us, a memory of the primal at-oneness with a nurturing other. In "taking in" a poem, story, or drama, we partly regress to that state where we did not differentiate what happened "in here" from what went on "out there." Our conscious knowledge of a timeless, mythic substructure furthers this original "as if." It, too, offers us the chance to merge the plot, characters, and ourselves into a larger sustaining matrix—the myth. Really, then, myth works in our response to deepen and strengthen our existing introjection of the work—if the tenor of the whole permits it to.

The ubiquity of myth in literature and the feeling of resonance it gives—these have led most myth critics to lean on the hypothesis of a collective memory or racial unconscious. But surely this is a difficult idea to maintain, that we inherit brain-traces of such complicated and exotic matters as the Tibetan King of the Years.

Surely it is easier to believe that it is not some impersonal racial memory, but we ourselves who make the emotional experience of art out of our own drives released through our own conscious knowledge of meaning and myth.

Our study of resonance and particularly the sometime lack of it suggest a much simpler explanation of the role of myth. The mere presence of a mythic parallel in itself enables us to re-experience a total unity of self and nurturing environment, if we passively accept the parallel. The particular content of the myth will express for us fantasies derived from our experience of our own bodies and our parents', just as any plot or symbolism does. Then, in some literary works, the tenor of the whole may resist the passive acceptance of the myth, and we will feel it as parody or irony.

What is perhaps difficult to accept is that it is not the myth *per se* that makes the feeling of resonance possible, but the myth plus our conscious knowledge of it. This seems something of a paradox: that part of the effect of a work comes from something outside it —our knowledge of its mythic underside. But we have already seen (in Ch. 6) how we need a sense of meaningfulness in order to release and transform the fantasy a literary work embodies. Indeed, how could any plot or word release our unconscious drives unless we consciously understood it?

With myth, our conscious awareness (dim or exact) of the myth can provide (if the context permits it) a rationale that lets us gratify an unconscious wish to return to an ancient, timeless, and universal at-oneness with the world. The work of art itself allows us to submerge a complex and perhaps painful sense of personal identity. Then our knowledge of a mythic parallel offers us a still greater sense of some nurturing and sustaining role into which we can relax. At the same time, that conscious knowledge of the myth provides an Ariadne thread, a way out of that engulfing labyrinth and back to a sense of self. To put aside the notion of collective memory or racial unconscious, though, to accept the more rational explanation—this is, in an even larger sense, to escape into and from the labyrinth of myth.

10 Character and Identification

Instead of the weather, Mark Twain might have talked about "identification." Politicians, pollsters, polymaths, moguls, moralists, sociologists, historians, journalists—everybody talks about identification, but nobody knows what to do about it. Especially in literature. The novelist, the playwright, the director, the actor, even the literary critic, would like to evoke identification, and we often talk very learnedly about whether an arena stage will increase involvement, what style of acting will produce an alienation effect, and so on, but I suspect we are mostly talking off the tops of our respective heads.

The plain fact of the matter is that identification, in or out of literature, is a very complicated affair that even psychologists know little about. As one of Dr. Gitelson's maxims has it, "Identification is a basket word—made to carry too much." [1] Probably, that particular word should not even be used in literary contexts, for it means, literally, "making oneself the same as." When we identify with another person, we make ourselves like them, adopting at least some of their values, ideas, attitudes, sometimes even physical traits, a distinctive gait or stance or gesture.[2] Is this what we do with literary characters? Is there no distinction between identifying with a real father or mother and a fictional character?

Closely related to identification is realism of character, another complicated problem. As Brecht's plays so clearly show, realism somehow leads to identification, lack of realism to a kind of alienation—but how? Shakespeare provides a convenient example to look at both matters, not only because his characters seem to hover between realistic and non-realistic, almost folkloric themes, but also because we can hear sharply different attitudes toward the literary character as we listen to three centuries worth of critics talking about the Shakespearean character. Over the three centuries, there have been, roughly, three attitudes.

During the neo-classic period, most critics held that Shakespeare's characters were like real people in the special sense that the audience felt that they would behave as the characters did if they faced the situations the characters faced. A minor but the earliest example is Margaret Cavendish describing in 1664 how Shakespeare "presents Passions so Naturally, and Misfortunes so Probably, as he Peirces the Souls of his Readers with Such a True Sense and Feeling thereof, that it forces Tears through their Eyes, and almost Perswades them, they are really Actors, or at least Present at those Tragedies." [3] Dennis and Rymer and Voltaire took the contrary view, but the main line of English critics came out resoundingly for the realism of Shakespeare's characters: Dryden, Pope, Lord Kames, and that most devious of critics, Dr. Johnson— "Shakespeare has no heroes," he wrote. "His scenes are occupied only by men, who act and speak as the reader thinks that he should himself have spoken or acted on the same occasion." [4]

When, however, we turn from Johnson in 1765 to Maurice Morgann, a dozen years later, we turn the corner into truly Romantic criticism of Shakespeare. Neo-classic critics like Johnson stressed our identification with the fictive character, but Morgann sees the Shakespearean character as an historical being outside ourselves. Shakespeare, says Morgann,

> boldly makes a character act and speak from those parts of the composition which are inferred only, and not distinctly shewn. This produces a wonderful effect; it seems to carry us beyond the poet to nature itself. . . .

> It may be fit [therefore] to consider them [the characters]
> rather as Historical than Dramatic beings; and, when occasion
> requires, to account for their conduct from the whole of char-
> acter, from general principles, from latent motives, and from
> policies not avowed.[5]

This historical externalization, looking at the events described by
the text rather than the text itself, forms the Romantic approach
to Shakespeare. We see it in Goethe's remarks on Hamlet in 1795
and in Schlegel's highly influential lectures. In England, though
Coleridge may theorize about the sympathetic imagination, when
he comes to talk about any particular character, he talks about him
as though he were an historical rather than a dramatic being, and so
on through the nineteenth century in the effusions of Mrs. Jameson,
Victor Hugo, Pushkin, or Swinburne. The culminating figure is, of
course, A. C. Bradley. In our own time, this approach to Shakespeare has fallen into disuse. Mostly, it survives only in high-school
teaching, in the *New York Times Book Review*, and the writings
of Miss Mary McCarthy who, in this context, keeps strange company indeed.

With one exception—the psychoanalytic critics—the twentieth
century has turned its back on Bradley and all his works. Oddly
enough, it was the arch-Romantic, Poe, who was the first to rebel
against this nineteenth-century view and insist that Shakespeare's
characters should not be treated as real people.

> In all commentating upon Shakespeare [he wrote in 1845], there
> has been a radical error, never yet mentioned. It is the error of
> attempting to expound his characters—to account for their ac-
> tions—to reconcile his inconsistencies—not as if they were the
> coinage of a human brain, but as if they had been actual exis-
> tences on earth. We talk of Hamlet the man, instead of Hamlet
> the *dramatis persona*. . . . If Hamlet had really lived, and if
> the tragedy were an accurate record of his deeds, from this
> record (with some trouble) we might, it is true, reconcile his
> inconsistencies and settle to our satisfaction his true character.
> But the task becomes the purest absurdity when we deal only
> with a phantom.

And, Poe concluded, "It seems to us little less than a miracle, that this obvious point should have been overlooked." [6]

Miracle it may be, but no one made much of Poe's 1845 point until 1933, when L. C. Knights wrote a famous essay called, "How Many Children had Lady Macbeth." Knights argued that such questions or, in general, talking about the characters as real people makes no sense in terms of the basic assumptions of "new criticism." "We start," Knights wrote, "with so many lines of verse on a printed page which we read as we should read any other poem." " 'Character,' . . . is merely an abstraction from the total response in the mind of the reader or spectator, brought into being by written or spoken words." [7] And most twentieth-century critics would agree.

The most explicit is G. Wilson Knight who says right out loud: "The persons, ultimately, are not human at all, but purely symbols of a poetic vision." [8] "Shakespeare's characters," writes Kenneth Muir, "are not real people: they are characters in a play, called forth by the role they have to act, and determined by the plot." [9] "Shakespeare," says Kenneth Burke, "is making a play, not people." "Whereas it has become customary to speak of Shakespeare's figures as of living people, the stupidest and crudest person who ever lived is richer in motivation than all of Shakespeare's characters put together." [10] And Edmund Wilson states: "It does not occur to us today to try, as was at one time a critical fashion, to examine the creations of Shakespeare as if they were actual persons about whom it would be possible to assemble complete and consistent biographies." [11] Further, in a rare instance of critical and scholarly congeniality, the critics have received aid and comfort from those theatrical scholars of the persuasion of Elmer Edgar Stoll who have shown how unrealistic Shakespeare's theater and conventions were —as a matter of historical fact.

Essentially, these new and neo-new critics are simply insisting on the formal nature of a work of art, and they deny realism of character not just in Shakespeare's plays, but in all kinds of fictions, even the naturalistic novel. "A novel, like a poem," writes Dr.

Leavis, "is made of words; there is nothing else one can point to. We talk of a novelist as 'creating characters,' but the process of 'creation' is one of putting words together," [12] and one could quote, to the same effect, Mark Schorer, Harry Levin, Virginia Woolf, E. M. Forster, T. S. Eliot. And not new critics only—from the quite alien point of view of Marxist criticism, one could cite Georg Lukács, or, in the visual arts, E. H. Gombrich. Even Freud, in his introduction to the "Dora" case, distinguishes between fictional editings of psychological reality and psychological reality as the psychiatrist really sees it (though later psychoanalytic critics by and large have not followed Freud's caution).

We have come, then, to an impasse. The old critics say we must think of dramatic characters as real people; the new critics say we must not. Logically, we cannot have it both ways, and logic comes down squarely against treating the characters as real.

Literary characters, after all, exist in the contrived, shaped world of everyday reality. It makes little sense to apply psychological concepts like Morgann's "general principles" of human nature taken from the disorderly everyday world to a quite different world shaped by theme and form and meaning. In fact, literary characters are so shaped by the world in which they exist that they cannot even be moved from book to book or play to play. One could not, for a crude example, move the characters from *Peanuts* to *Pogo*, nor would an Homeric hero fit in a tragedy of Euripides, nor one of Dostoevsky's possessed into the saner world of Tolstoy—the effect would be parody.

Even similar characters created by the same author face trouble moving from one work to another. Falstaff would bulk too large in the romantic and pastoral world of *The Winter's Tale*, and Autolycus with his ribbons and laces could hardly parade on the field at Shrewsbury or masquerade as Mother Prat of Brainford. If even such adaptable con-men as Falstaff and Autolycus cannot move from one type of Shakespearean play to another, it seems to make still less sense to apply to them both concepts of human nature from still a third world in which neither of them could exist, namely, the real world. "Our literary understanding of a character does not begin until we associate him with other *literary* characters"—so Northrop Frye (though the italics are mine). "In this process, literature as a whole is independent of real experience and something distinct from the passing of belief into action." [13]

Logically, it simply does not make sense to treat literary characters as real people. But does logic govern here? Or experience? We can use H. L. Mencken's answer. Because he was famous as an atheist, people liked to badger him on the subject, and one day a reporter asked him if he believed in infant baptism. Replied Mencken, "Believe in it? Hell, I've *seen* it!" And much the same thing is true of character-analysis. Logically, it is unsupportable, but I have seen by the dozens psychoanalytic studies which diagnose Shakespeare's characters as though they were real people on couch or in clinic; and these critics give ample, more than ample, evidence from the plays themselves. Psychoanalytic critics regularly apply psychological concepts from the world of everyday reality to characters who exist in a wholly different kind of world—it should not work but it does.

In fact, we can even do it ourselves. Mercutio makes a particularly handy example because so many critics have found him real and appealing, and yet he occurs in one of the most stylized and artificial of Shakespeare's plays; truly, *Romeo and Juliet* is Marianne Moore's imaginary garden with a real toad in it.

At first glance, Mercutio seems outrageously unrealistic. I have known a lot of witty and literary people, but never have I known anyone who was so fluent in blank verse as Mercutio or who could while away the hours of an adolescent evening by coming up *ad lib* with something like the Queen Mab speech. Yet I have known many people like Mercutio in other ways. He is the classic joker: he pours out a perfect flood of puns, rhymes, and cheerful obscenities. I have known people like that, and so, I suspect, have we all —and so has Romeo, for he recognizes Mercutio as a type: "He jests at scars that never felt a wound." [14] But what type?

We can tell from the kind of joke Mercutio makes. He aims his wit at Tybalt's Italianate duello—a "new form," he calls it, like the pose of courtly love, Romeo's initial "groaning" toward Rosaline, which also draws Mercutio's fire. He can speak of "my gossip Venus" and "young Abraham Cupid"; he can accuse Romeo of thinking Laura a kitchen-wench, "Dido a dowdy, Cleopatra a gypsy, Helen and Hero hildings and harlots, Thisbe a grey eye or so." Mercutio, in short, attacks idolatries, particularly verbal idolatries. It is no coincidence (if we can believe the current chronology of the plays) that it is this one character who cut down the whole tradition of English fairy-lore from the Celtic fays of medieval romance, adult- or child-sized, to Queen Mab. No glamorous Titania she, but oh so prosaically, "No bigger than an agate stone on the forefinger of an alderman." And so fairies and elves have been, ever since Mercutio.

And yet, even as he tears down the verbal gods and goddesses of others, Mercutio himself wishes to soar. In the very first words we hear him speak, he urges Romeo, who says he is feeling heavy, "Nay, gentle Romeo, we must have you dance," and he urges him to "borrow Cupid's wings and soar with them above a common bound," to "beat love down," as he himself does. The epitaph Benvolio gives him is all too fitting:

> That gallant spirit hath aspired the clouds
> Which too untimely here did scorn the earth.

And it is fitting, too, that Romeo should attack Mercutio's killer shouting,

> Mercutio's soul
> Is but a little way above our heads,
> Staying for thine to keep him company.

As a character, then, Mercutio works in two directions, up and down. First, he pulls down the formalisms and verbalisms of others, but, second, he sets up in their high place his own artificial gestures, puns, rhymes, jokes, set speeches, and other masks. For example, though he is invited to the Capulets' ball, he chooses instead to crash. Yet, even as he puts aside the formal invitation, he puts on a mask to disguise himself, another kind of formality.

In short, Mercutio attacks in others his own chief trait—as we all do—and we can guess his reason: a sense of his own insufficiency. He calls his mask,

> A visor for a visor! What care I
> What curious eye shall quote deformities?
> Here are the beetle brows shall blush for me.

Mercutio's wit follows the school of Hobbes: "sudden glory arising from some sudden conception of some eminency in ourselves, by comparison with the infirmity of others or with our own formerly" or Kenneth Burke's reversal of Hobbes: "not so much a glorifying of the self as a minimizing of the distresses menacing the self." Laughter, Hobbes goes on, "is incident most to them that are conscious of the fewest abilities in themselves; who are forced to keep themselves in their own favour by observing the imperfections of other men."

As for Mercutio's sense of his own insufficiency, if we look at him as a nineteenth-century critic would, we can guess where it came from, its roots in his non-existent childhood. They show in the speech just before the balcony scene where Mercutio conjures up the spirit of the absent Romeo, in the process making some grandly obscene remarks about Rosaline. The peaceful Benvolio remonstrates—"Thou wilt anger him." Not so, says Mercutio, in a barrage of sexual symbols:

> This cannot anger him. 'Twould anger him
> To raise a spirit in his mistress's circle
> Of some strange nature, letting it there stand
> Till she had laid it and conjured it down.
> That were some spite; my invocation
> Is fair and honest: in his mistress's name,
> I conjure only but to raise up him.

Raising up seems to represent, for Mercutio, a phallic child's ithyphallic notion of virility; being laid down—its opposite. It was Romeo's "calm, dishonourable, vile submission," literally, his "putting himself under" Tybalt that so infuriated Mercutio; and there is a grim irony in Mercutio's being killed "under" Romeo's arm. Mercutio has developed a life style of pushing other things down, himself up. As he tells Romeo:

> If love be rough with you, be rough with love.
> Prick love for pricking, and you beat love down.

Mercutio works on the principle that the best defense is a good offense—he is constantly on the attack against emotions that might attack him. As Romeo says, "He jests at scars that never felt a wound." But we can with a more sophisticated psychology paraphrase him: He jests at scars that fears to feel a wound—a certain kind of wound, the kind that comes from real love that would lay him low, make him undergo a submission like Romeo's.

To be a man in Mercutio's terms, you must not let someone else put you down; you have to put something of your own up, and to do that, as he sees it, you must pull someone else's something down. His jokes thus satisfy both sexual and aggressive impulses, and at the same time they serve as a defense against emotions. Mercutio's bawdry lets him put up his own verbal smokescreen; it lets him pull down to earth (or earthiness) the emotions that others put up as ideal or important. As he says of his own jokes, "Why, is not this better now than groaning for love?" that is, being pressed down by it.

Not for Mercutio is that entrance into the womb or tomb or maw which is Romeo's dark, sexual fate—Mercutio is the perpetual outsider, except for one crucial moment that has greatly puzzled critics: the moment when he chooses to intervene in the quarrel between Tybalt and Romeo. Why does he do it? We have seen that Mercutio's life style involves asserting himself in two ways: by pulling down to earth the formalisms of others; by setting up his own formalisms: jokes, riddles, rhymes, or fantasies of Queen Mab. Tybalt is another formalist: one who fights by the book of arithmetic. He makes a formal attack on Romeo, but Romeo has just married Juliet. Instead of asserting himself, he accepts Tybalt's formal insult and even the name Capulet, "which name," he says, "I tender as dearly as mine own."

One can scarcely imagine anything more threatening for Mercutio to witness. Were Tybalt to succeed in setting up his formal challenge, his pretensions, forcing Romeo down with them, he would be calling into question Mercutio's whole life style, which is built on doing that kind of thing himself, not in having others do it to him.* Thus, Mercutio, has to fight off the threat—otherwise, as he says, "*Alla stoccata* carries it away," Tybalt's formalism would win the day. Mercutio has to intervene, and when he does so, he intervenes in a specifically Mercutian way: he pushes aside both Tybalt's formal challenge and Romeo's formal submission, and he asserts his own verbalistic challenge, joking on Tybalt's nine lives.

To pull down the formalism of others and put up his own—this pattern is the very essence of Mercutio's character, and he defends it with his life. Notice, by using psychoanalysis to talk about motivation and character, we can out-Bradley Bradley. And so the psychoanalytic critics have done, they being virtually the only people today who treat Shakespeare's characters as real. It *can* be done— we *can* arrive at a realistic account of Mercutio. But should we? Somehow, it is all not very convincing.

For one thing, we are violating the basic procedures of modern criticism—we have gone beyond the sacrosanct words-on-the-page to infer in the discredited manner of Morgann all kinds of things about Mercutio, even his non-existent childhood. And we have gained nothing in return. We are no wiser than we were before as to why we "identify" ourselves with Mercutio.

Let us turn and look in another direction, namely, toward Smith College where in 1944 two psychologists performed a quite fasci-

---

* The unconscious significance of Tybalt's formalism as a pressing down peeps through Granville-Barker's phrasing of reasons for Mercutio's intervention: "Mercutio fights Tybalt because he feels he must, because he cannot *stand* the fellow's airs a moment longer." "When the moment comes, it is not his own honor that is *at stake*; but such calm, dishonorable, vile submission is more than *flesh and blood can bear*." [15] (Italics mine.)

nating experiment.[16] To a group of undergraduates, they showed an animated cartoon detailing the adventures of a large black triangle, a small black triangle, and a circle, the three of them moving in various ways in and out of a rectangle. After the short came the main feature: the psychologists asked for comments, and the Smith girls "with great uniformity" described the big triangle as "aggressive," "pugnacious," "mean," "temperamental," "irritable," "power-loving," "possessive," "quick to take offense," and "taking advantage of his size" (it was, after all, the larger triangle). Eight per cent of the girls even went so far as to conclude that this triangle had a lower I.Q. than the other. Now if Smith girls can see that much in a triangle, how much more they—or we—are likely to see in Mercutio.

What the experiment shows is that realism, like beauty, is in the eye of the beholder. From the lines we are hearing, we recreate the characters, the words on the page controlling and shaping the characters we create. Then, as in that writers' cliché, the characters "take on a life of their own," and they in turn shape and inform the words on the page. In short, we are not quasi-scientific observers of a phenomenon outside ourselves, historical as the Romantic critics would have it, or the words-on-the-page as the new critic would have it. Rather, we are involved with the text and it with us in a process as mutual as a witch's bargain. The psychologists were simply proving something Proust had said with consummate insight some years before:

> In reality, each reader reads only what is already within himself. The book is only a sort of optical instrument which the writer offers the reader to enable him to discover in himself what he would not have found but for the aid of the book. It is this reading within himself what is also in the book which constitutes proof of the accuracy of the latter. . . .[17]

And long before Proust, there was Dr. Johnson:

> The reflection that strikes the heart is not, that the evils before us are real evils, but that they are evils to which we ourselves may be exposed. If there be any fallacy, it is not that we fancy

> the players, but that we fancy ourselves unhappy for a moment;
> but we rather lament the possibility than suppose the presence
> of misery, as a mother weeps over her babe when she remembers
> that death may take it from her. . . . Imitations produce pain
> or pleasure, not because they are mistaken for realities, but be-
> cause they bring realities to mind.[18]

In the somewhat different style of the Romantic critic: "Hamlet
is a name; his speeches and sayings but the idle coinage of the
poet's brain. What then, are they not real?" asks Hazlitt, and answers, "They are as real as our own thoughts. Their reality is in the
reader's mind. It is we who are Hamlet." [19]

Whether we take it from experimental psychology or critical intuition, the point is the same: I can feel Mercutio as real because I
have known, or imagined, or even been, Mercutio. I, too, have
warded off the dangers of emotion with a smokescreen of words—
and not just as a literary critic. Once upon a time, I attended par-
ties where the girls lined up on one wall and the boys on the other,
giggling and making Mercutian jokes in their newly deep voices.
And, no doubt, from the point of view of the adolescent I once
was (or, maybe, still am), my present world of monogamy, off-
spring, and the P.-T.A. must indeed seem a "calm, dishonourable,
vile submission." But at this confessional point, let me retreat and
try to summarize.

First, we can describe Mercutio realistically, as the Romantic or
psychoanalytic critic would do. But that is not why he *feels* real.
He feels real because I can find the psychology of Mercutio in myself or my psychology in him. But this insight only leads us to another question—Why? I can recreate Mercutio, I can bring myself
to him, and I can find out what of myself I am bringing to him—
but why do I bring it to him in the first place? In short, what
makes us re-create a dramatic character? What makes me imagine
myself into a figment of another man's imagination?

The Heider-Simmel experiment holds the answer. The Smith
girls did not just look at a black triangle and say, "Ah, yes. It has a
low I.Q." Rather, they saw a film in which certain things hap-

pened. There was a rectangle with a segment in it that could be opened and closed like a door; and into and out of this rectangle came a large triangle, a small triangle, and a circle (added, one guesses, for love interest). The little triangle and the circle start out, both together. Then the big triangle comes out of the house and brings the circle in. After a while, the little triangle opens the door and escapes with the circle—and so on. In short, the Smith girls saw first and foremost a plot, and it was from the plot that they created the characters. The experimenters tell us: "The movements (or, more generally, any changes in the field) are organized in terms of acts of persons," and this is a quite traditional literary idea, Aristotle's, in fact: that we recreate consistency of character out of the incidents of the plot. But today, with a more sophisticated psychology, we are in a position to explain exactly how we make this recreation and, perhaps more important, why.

The plot or incidents cause me to have certain feelings or wishes or tensions. I feel these tensions from the play as tensions in myself, but, both intellectually and emotionally, I attribute these tensions to the characters as motives: I project or bestow my feelings on the characters. Now, if I am dealing with black triangles that is about all that happens, but if I am confronting the work of a great writer, he will have paved a way for my act of bestowal. Each of Shakespeare's characters will act out or embody in concrete form some of the same wishes or defenses that I feel, and this is the crux of a modern concept of character. A literary character exists, as it were, in two ways: first, objectively, as the nineteenth-century critics saw him; second, he exists inside my mind as I take the play in. And in this second sense, I take the character in because he offers me a way of dealing with the events and incidents Shakespeare has created and which are creating tensions in me as I take the whole play in. The more clearly a given character embodies my tensions, the more the work of art stimulates those tensions in me; the more I have those tensions in myself anyway—why, then, the more real a given character will seem. He will, ultimately, seem as real to me as

I myself, for out of my own drives and needs for defense, I have created him.

Then, what are these tensions? Professor Harry Levin has shown how a notion of "formality" pervades and shapes *Romeo and Juliet*: the artificial language, the sharp pairings of characters, and the various ceremonies, the Capulets' ball, the Prince's formal decrees, or the wedding which becomes a funeral.[20] The play abounds in images of books, reading and writing, letters of the alphabet, words and names ("A rose by any other name would smell as sweet"), and the tragedy as a whole makes me feel constantly and strongly a tension between these formalisms and the raw emotions of love and hate beneath them. This tension, however, is only one in a long series of formalized opposites in which the language and incidents of the play occur: Montague-Capulet, old-young, love-hate, male-female, water-fire, night-day, wedding-funeral, long-short, sweet-sour, vice-virtue, and even North-South and dog-cat.

As we watch *Romeo and Juliet*, we feel, I think, first a sense of these conflicting opposites (especially love and hate) that threaten to engulf and so destroy each other. Second, we are aware of verbal and other formalities that come between those conflicting opposites. For example, the opening scene begins with a mingling of sex and hate which we feel as vaguely threatening, when the two Capulet servants talk about thrusting Montague's maids to the wall, taking the maids' heads or maidenheads. A fight quickly results. Then Prince Escalus appears, stops it, and issues a formal decree against any more fighting. Things having quieted down, Romeo now enters and in painstakingly formal rhyme tells Benvolio of his formal, courtly love for Rosaline.

Now, how do we feel at this point? I think we feel that the mingling of sex and hate, as in the opening lines, is dangerous, and that formal barriers like the Prince's decree make things safe again. We are vaguely aware that the scene has two halves, the first dealing with hate, the second with love, and that the Prince serves an especially reassuring function, because he stands between these two halves, keeping them separate. We are aware, too, I think, of two competing formalisms—we notice how symmetrically the patterns of hate build up in the first half, and how formal and posy and courtly Romeo's love is in the second half. Partly these formalisms express love or hate; partly they act as barriers against the mingling of love and hate.

Something similar goes on in the second scene. In the first or Capulet half, Paris renews his suit to marry Juliet, and Old Capulet invites him to the feast that night, leaving other invitations for a servant to deliver. But the servant is illiterate and asks Romeo to read the list for him (one of the clearest instances of the play's concern with words and reading and writing). Then, in the last lines of the scene, Romeo resolves to crash the party to see Rosaline. Again, we feel safety in the formalism, Paris's stately suit for Juliet, Capulet's invitations, and we feel slightly threatened when that formalism begins to break down, when the servant cannot read, when Romeo plans to crash. This scene, like the first, has two halves (a Capulet half and a Montague half), but this time the barrier is a frail one: no Prince, only an illiterate servant.

The barrier comes down still further as, in the third scene, the Nurse rambles on and on until Lady Capulet bids her be silent and proceeds to urge Juliet to love Paris, a Paris described as a "volume," "this precious book of love," as though he were the living embodiment of the verbal formalities of the tragedy that protect love from hate. Again, we sense that words, be they the Nurse's reminiscences or what is written in the "margin" of Paris's eyes, words will somehow make things safe. But the Nurse talks clownishly, and Paris is as square as the man in the Arrow shirt.

Then, in the fourth scene, we feel the formal barriers breaking down completely as the group of Montagues prepares to put all formality aside and crash the Capulets' ball. And it is precisely at this point that Shakespeare gives us Mercutio, that one character who above all others will set up a great cloud of verbiage and formalism: words, jokes, puns, poses, and ribaldry. They are all things we can enjoy (unlike Paris's kind of formalism), and they all serve to split love and so keep love manageable, either as down-to-earth bawdry or light and frivolous fancy, as in this scene, where Mercutio seeks to have Romeo dance, soar above love, not sink in love —"We'll draw thee from the mire," he says. This is the significance of the Queen Mab speech. In it, Mercutio does three things. He cuts everything down in size; he makes small the big concerns of others—court life into curtsies, the law into fees, religion into tithes, war and all into dreams. Second, he creates his own imaginary world that completely takes over the real world of Montagues and Capulets; indeed, the speech takes over the play entirely for a good three minutes. Last, the speech seems an independent excursion, as indeed Mercutio himself must always seem to us—the perpetual outsider, the magnificent irrelevancy.

In short, we take Mercutio into ourselves because he helps us deal with our fears for the tragic victims by dismissing one half of that dangerous mixing of hate and love. So he begins, and later, with Tybalt, he will try to cut down hate, too. But, by then, he has failed to keep Romeo from Juliet (the balcony does that), and thus, he has heightened our fears, creating a sense of irony. As soon as Mercutio is killed, as soon as his formalistic line of defense runs out, the lovers do indeed touch—unite—sexually, and the tragedy proceeds to its medicinal catastrophe.

To return to the general point, the question of "identification," my argument has three steps. First, the critics left us with a dilemma. Shakespeare's eighteenth- and nineteenth-century critics said we should think of his characters as realistic; his twentieth-century critics say we should not. Step two: the Heider-Simmel experiment shows that both groups were looking the wrong way— the critics have been looking at the characters when we should look instead into ourselves, for it is we who re-create the characters and give them a sense of reality. In Shakespeare's phrase, we give "to airy nothing a local habitation and a name," or, if not to airy nothing, to little black triangles or to Mercutio. Step three: why do we do this? Because the character satisfies a need for us. The language and action of the play build up certain needs and feelings in us, and the characters act out objectively certain ways of managing those needs and feelings.

Thus, our so-called "identification" with a literary character is actually a complicated mixture of projection and introjection, of taking in from the character certain drives and defenses that are really objectively "out there" and of putting into him feelings that are really our own, "in here." And, needless to say, we do not just incorporate a character's drives and defenses—we incorporate the whole character, clothes, features, manners, physique, and the rest (as when we see adolescents live for a time as though they were Hamlet or Raskolnikov or Henry Aldrich). Our "identification" with literary characters, then, continues and specializes our oral introjection of the entire work in the "as if" or "willing suspension of disbelief."

Whether to call our relation to a literary character incorporation, introjection, or identification, I am not entirely sure. It does correspond to the third type of identification Freud describes in *Group Psychology and the Analysis of the Ego* (1921), namely, identification unconnected to any object-relation, but rather "based upon the possibility or desire of putting oneself in the same situation." "One ego has perceived a significant analogy with another upon one point . . . an identification is thereupon constructed on this point." This type of identification "may arise with any new perception of a common quality shared with some other person." [21] In Freud's instance, one girl imitates another's fit of hysterics, as Dora imitated her father's cough. Elsewhere Freud notes, "Identification has been not unsuitably compared with the oral, cannibalistic incorporation of the other person," [22] just as, in our model, the audience "takes in" the play as a whole.

The earliest psychoanalytic statements on art said we satisfy our drives vicariously through dramatic and literary characters. What I am now suggesting is that we satisfy those drives only in the economy or subsystem created by the work as a whole. We can see such a subsystem clinically in Dr. Edith Buxbaum's classic case of a boy who compulsively read detective stories and felt afraid for himself as he did so.[23] Consciously, he identified with the victim—this was the fear he spoke of. Less consciously, he identified with the criminal and thereby expressed aggressive wishes toward his parents. But his fear enabled him to say, "I am not the aggressor; I am the victim." Then, he also identified with the detective, combatting his own aggressive drives. Dr. Buxbaum makes the general point that neurotic symptoms typically serve as both drive gratification and defense. Here, the book itself and its characters took on the shape of a neurotic symptom: the detective defended against and the victim and criminal expressed aggressive wishes.

This is true, not just of detective stories and a little boy whose life is being eaten up by them, but of all literary works that embody characters with whom their audience identifies. We take in not only the drives the characters satisfy in the course of the plot, but also the defenses they act out. For example, a character like Romeo appeals mostly on the level of drive—he is the romantic lover, and we satisfy our wishes to love and be loved through him. The Nurse offers a distinctive pattern of drive gratification and defense. In many of her speeches she refers to something missing and offers a substitute, thus defending against or getting rid of the drive by gratifying it, rather an appropriate pattern for a wetnurse and a bawd.

Other characters we incorporate primarily as defenses: the Friar, the Prince, but notably our friend Mercutio. We do, it is true, get some vicarious gratification from the way he satisfies his narcissism, but mostly we take him into ourselves as a way of keeping the love and hate from mingling. He acts out for us a defense against the drives the play has stirred up. He cuts down the love and hate so important to others; he reduces them both in order to assert his own self in the form of words at the expense of emotions. In effect, he says, "Don't love, don't hate—just admire me instead." And, of course, he fails. The killing of Mercutio operates in us as the failure of a defense operates in real life—we feel a sense of inner danger and loss, and in this way we make Mercutio's and the play's tragic endings our own.

And not just the tragedy in the play—we use the drives and defenses of a Mercutio to manage tensions within ourselves, not only the tensions the tragedy creates, but also the tensions from our own lives that we bring to the play because they are close to the emotional themes of the play. We put onto Mercutio not only the love and hate aroused by Shakespeare's tragedy, but also the love and hate we ourselves feel toward parents, toward girls like Rosaline who will not give us a tumble, toward girls like Juliet who will give us a tumble, and so on. We put onto Mercutio our preexisting feelings and this much more massive second order of feelings increases our response to the play, because projecting onto the character our own feelings gives him and the play just that much more tension to manage for us. Thus, our need for the character to help manage those feelings becomes still stronger.

In essence, I am suggesting that there is no critical dilemma about the characters' being real. The characters are real or not real only as we endow the character with our wishes and defenses. We are, in effect, partners with the artist. In a way, what I am suggesting is something about Shakespeare's medium: that his medium is not words, as the new critic would have it, or imagined history as the Romantic thought, but, as Shakespeare himself put it, "To work mine end upon *their senses* that this airy charm is for." His real medium is surely the most difficult, intractable of all—our minds—and therefore all the greater an artist is he—or any writer —because he creates us into creators.

11 Affect

As you must have realized by now, there is a great gap in this attempt to set up a model of literary response. I have said virtually nothing about what is in many ways the most cherished core of our response—affect. One reason for this silence is that psychoanalysis has as yet offered no fully satisfactory theory of affect. The whole matter lies in one of the most puzzling areas of psychological study, psychosomatics, in Felix Deutsch's phrase, "the mysterious leap from the mind to the body." On the one hand, affect is psychic: we are aware of a certain feeling of rage, say, or joy or sadness or anxiety. At the same time, this feeling is accompanied by somatic changes: we laugh or cry or shudder. Pulse rate rises or falls. Breathing slows or quickens. Hands sweat. Thus, there can be "unconscious affect," where the physical symptoms show, but we are unaware of any feeling.*

Even conscious affect is hard to talk about, if for no other reason than that our language is poor in terms for emotions. My *Roget's*

* I have heard of experiments in which the fine art of literary criticism is reduced to urine testing. Subjects were shown films; urine samples were taken before and after. The samples were analyzed for changes in steroid and alkoid content that would indicate unconscious affect. Other experimenters have worked with galvanic skin reaction.[1] But surely these physiological variables are too crude, too limited in dimension and number, to correspond to something as subtle and variable as affect.

Thesaurus, for example, yields only thirty-three categories which describe emotion or affect, as against seventy-five for different kinds of sensation or forty-nine for "means of communication," matters, presumably, less vital in our psychic lives. "It is not easy to deal scientifically with feelings," said Freud, a bit glumly. "One can attempt to describe their physiological signs. Where this is not possible . . . nothing remains but to fall back on the ideational content which is most readily associated with the feeling." [2]

My own expereince has been the same. Students feel baffled if I ask them to say how they "feel" at a certain point in a story, partly, I suppose, because this is such an unorthodox question to come from an English teacher, but more, I think, because it is so difficult to say how one feels in any precise way. Most often, the response to such a question becomes a series of more or less free associations from which one can infer fantasy content or defensive management. " 'Little Black Sambo,' " says a young lady, "makes me think of other stories I read when I was six, like the story of Procrustes." One can infer that she is responding to the issue of bodily integrity, Little Black Sambo's trying to keep the clothes and the umbrella that make him "grand" as against hostile figures that want to take them—it—away. But this is an inference about the transformation embodied in the story, not about affect itself.

Perhaps our language for affective states fails us because statements about one's feelings bring us right up against the basic issue of objective and subjective elements in response and all the difficulties involved in trying to feel the feelings of another. We have already seen the troubles Drs. Globus and Shulman encountered in trying to fix an affective response for certain films.[3] They concluded the films could only be said to have "affective foci" which any given viewer might turn on or turn off according to his own defensive needs. "Neither can the film superimpose an affect on the subject nor can the subject remain entirely free of specific stimulus properties of the film." Rather, the film "potentiates rather indiscriminately pre-existing affective responses." That is, we bring to a film—or any literary work—our own life experiences, among them our affective patterns; then the film tends to accent some of our responses by presenting us with fantasies that come close to our own experiences, wishes, or conflicts. Whether or not we will respond with the affects the film offers us depends on the degree to which we introject it.

The concept of introjection enabled us to explain why there are limits to the affect associated with a given work of literature, even though much subjective variation takes place within those limits. That is, if we like a joke at all, we feel it as funny—we do not feel sadness or fear or anger. Similarly, if we like "Dover Beach" at all, we feel it as tranquilizing or, perhaps, as some other critics have done, as evoking despair or pain—but we do not feel joy or hate. There are limits, because if we introject a literary work at all, we introject a ready-made psychological process to which only certain responses are possible. Another obstacle to the study of affects is plural sources: not only can different people feel different affects (within limits) from the same stimulus, but different stimuli can also evoke the same affect. We laugh at a joke and we laugh at the comic, though the two proceed from quite different mechanisms.

In addition to this troublesome question of subjective and objective, we discussed earlier in a rather general way the quality of the affects we derive from literature. Emotions seem neater somehow, less messy, when we are responding to literature instead of everyday life, because literature involves a structuring process which we introject. The transformation of a central fantasy toward meaning creates a far more orderly mental process in us than we usually experience. There is also a kind of weakening of affect in the literary situation because we do not expect to act upon it. Yet, at the same time, our affects when we respond to literature seem deeper and larger—because we bring to a work of literature a longer, deeper range of response. When we introject a literary work, we open up within a "rind" of higher ego functions a deeply regressed "core" of self from which stronger, more profound emotions spring. But these are very general, necessarily vague accounts of affect. It would be helpful if we could see some specific literary affects.

Freud discussed affects in literature for one particularly interesting case, "The 'Uncanny,' " as he termed it—stories of terror and the supernatural as anthologists usually call them. In life, Freud said, we get the feeling something "uncanny" is happening in one of two ways. Some event makes us feel that reality is taking the form of either some material from infantile complexes (repressed because of the anxiety they engendered) or some infantile mode of thought we have not so much repressed as "surmounted" (animistic beliefs, say, or the omnipotence of thoughts). Some event makes us think these psychic phenomena are really happening in the outer world. Suppose, for example, that on a certain Friday I get a hat check, a parking lot check, and a royalty check all numbered 284.

In literature, the uncanny effect proceeds from the same two sources, but "the storyteller has a *peculiarly* directive power over us." We get the uncanny feeling only when "the writer pretends to move in the world of common reality." Then, "We react to his inventions as we would have reacted to real experiences." Thus, the uncanny feeling from fiction comes from the same kinds of events that would create it in real life—provided the writer handles his materials in such a way that when we reality-test them, they do not seem unreal (that is, so we willingly suspend disbelief, as that process is described in Chapter 3).[4]

Freud was also, in effect, discussing literary affect when he analyzed jokes.[5] Laughter, more analysts should recognize, is just as much a psychosomatic phenomenon as asthma or peptic ulcer— and a good deal easier to analyze. Freud distinguished three sources: the joke, the comic, and humor. The joke involves three people: the teller, the hearer, and someone whom the joke is "on." It achieves its effect by some joke technique which evades the hearer's ordinary inhibitions, allowing a sexual or aggressive impulse sudden expression (though why this particular psychic stimulus should result in sudden contractions of the diaphragm and zygomatic muscles, nobody knows). The comic involves two persons: one who laughs and one who is laughed at. The effect proceeds from a sudden perception (at an ego-level) of a disproportion in mental or physical effort—as when a child, toddling, crosses only with great effort a distance an adult would traverse in an instant. Humor, which "has something of grandeur and elevation," comes about when we expect to suffer or to see someone suffer at the hands of reality but instead we adopt toward reality the attitude of a parent toward a child, that its doings are of no great importance. Humor is akin to mania.

Freud puts all three together into a single phenomenon—a sudden economy. In jokes, it is an economy in inhibition; in the comic, an economy of effort; in humor, an economy in affect. These economies and their suddenness lead to amusement or, ultimately, laughter—a second instance of literary affect analyzed by Freud.

This book, too, has talked about some literary affects. The one discussed most closely is the feeling people get when they are aware of a mythic matrix within a literary work: a feeling of resonance, largeness, depths of time, a sense of being part of some larger entity. The opposite feeling—where the work parodies or denies its mythic content—is a sense of resistance, distance, perhaps even of frustration, the opposite of the oral merger and relaxation of myth positively used. Another, related literary affect is the kind of stoic fortitude Conrad makes us feel. It stems from the assertion of various phallic attitudes against an underlying wish to relax and merge at the oral level.

"Making" a rhyme leads to a literary affect, something like the satisfaction of a hunger. Similarly, a skillful resolution of plot leads to something of the same quality, and conversely, a difficult or delayed rhyme, like a failure to tie up the ends of a plot, leads to a feeling of hunger and dissatisfaction. If one can say there is a feeling, "It is good," we have considered it in discussing the question of evaluation: a proper balance of fantasy and defense leads to a satisfying sense of mastery. "Dover Beach" and the "tomorrow" speech lead to a feeling, not so much of mastery, as of tranquility or reassurance—at least to me. The affect derives from the denying or erasing of a primal scene fantasy, reassurance through disillusionment.

Intellectual puzzlement leads to a kind of blocking of affect, as in "the puzzling movies." In effect, by asking its reader to ferret meaning out for himself, a literary work to a greater or lesser extent removes the possibility of passive gratification from which affect seems to come. Playing games with the "frame," the motor inhibition associated by convention with literary works, produces a peculiar *frisson* which I can only describe as a kind of intellectual dizziness. A still greater sense of inner confusion or loss comes with the breakdown of a defense, as when a Mercutio or Nurse who had acted as a buffer against the tragic ambivalence in *Romeo and Juliet* disappears. Some characters act mostly as defenses. Others enable us to satisfy drives vicariously, as Romeo acts out for us narcissistic gratifications.

In short, though it has not been systematic about it, this book has touched on a number of literary affects. Further, even if we have not talked about them at all, there are some other affects associated with literature that one can recognize fairly easily. I am thinking of the "evocative" as we see it in Japanese *haiku*.

> On a withered branch
> a crow has settled—
> autumn nightfall.

The poem asks me to supply associations and connections to the ending of autumn, the ending of a day, the disappearance of the leaves, or the loss of life in general. Then the poem asks me to develop in my own mind the comparison of all these various endings to a black bird coming to rest. *Haiku*, notes Harold G. Henderson in a standard introduction, "usually gain their effect not only by suggesting a mood, but also by giving a clear-cut picture which serves as a starting point for trains of thought and emotion." [6] A *haiku* works only by images; it never states a feeling. Rather, it allows its reader to infer a season, a time of day, and two general ideas to be compared. But "Only the outlines or important parts are drawn, and the rest the reader must fill in for himself." And yet, at the same time that he stresses our projection into the poem, he speaks of the poem's "power of suggestion," a classic instance of the way the reader's activity and the poem's merge to create the total experience.

The Western style that corresponds to this oriental "evocative," at least, the style that evokes the same kind of feeling in me (even more than the Imagists' imitations of *haiku*), is "negative capability," best known in Keats's poems. He can say, for example, that his own mournful mood of mortality

> tells me I must die
> Like a sick Eagle looking at the sky.

The poem asks us to project into the mind of "a sick Eagle," to find in ourselves the same feelings of longing, despair, and impotence the bird would feel as he looks upward to his former heights. We must create these feelings for ourselves and bring them to the poem which, in itself, does not describe them. Similarly, Keats goes on in this, the Elgin Marbles sonnet, to say that these "wonders" bring a kind of feud or pain

> That mingles Grecian grandeur with the rude
> Wasting of old Time—with a billowy main—
> A sun—a shadow of a magnitude.

We must supply our own associations to "a billowy main—a sun," creating our own Grecian landscape. We must ourselves find feeling and meaning for "a shadow of a magnitude." The affect seems to me much the same as that I get from *haiku*. Psychologically, both types of poem ask their readers to do a good deal of projecting.

The opposite is *senryu*, the comic equivalent or parody of *haiku*.

> Shitting in the fields,
> seeing evening fires
> far off.

> Overtaken!
> She's not much
> to look at.

Senryu, no less than *haiku*, ask us to project, to imagine for our-selves the warm feeling on the bottom, the rest of the body cold, the longing to be by the fire that one's own body needs had forced one's body away from. The second calls for imagining the whole incident of seeing a girl's shapely back, hurrying a little, perhaps a little ashamed, to glimpse her face, then finding she's not pretty af-ter all. *Senryu*, like *haiku*, ask us to project, but the results are dis-appointment, and instead of the feeling of reverie, the effect is one of abruptness or wry laughter, somewhat the way mythic stories that disappoint the wish for fusion achieve parody or distance.

Senryu seem to follow fairly closely Freud's description of hu-mor.[7] They give the same kind of dry amusement as the gallows jokes Freud used as illustrations of his thesis. The superego, instead of suppressing the ego, liberates it, even reassures it. The mecha-nism is akin to mania, and Dr. Bertram Lewin has carried Freud's view further to describe the psychology of "elation." Freud de-scribes the "process in the listener before whom someone else pro-duces humor":

> He sees this other person in a situation which leads the listener to expect that the other will produce the signs of an affect—that he will get angry, complain, express pain, be frightened or hor-rified or perhaps even in despair; and the onlooker or listener is prepared to follow his lead and to call up the same emotional impulses in himself. But this emotional expectancy is disap-pointed; the other person expresses no affect, but makes a jest. The expenditure on feeling that is economized turns into hu-morous pleasure in the listener.

This description of the process of humor resembles what we have seen of *senryu*: we prepare to project massively into the poem as *haiku* ask us to do, but then we find that "expenditure of affect" is unnecessary and inappropriate. And, for me at least, the emotions I feel are very similar, though by no means exactly the same (and, as so often when discussing affect, it would be very difficult to de-scribe the difference accurately).

There are other literary situations where one can make quick surmises about affect: pornography, for example, or biaiography (writings about violence). It is hard to imagine someone's responding to pure pornography by anything but either direct sexual arousal or a defensive reaction of disgust. Similarly, highly aggressive films seem to stimulate a matching rage in their viewers. Yet, even in these direct expressions of drive, the writer's defensive maneuvers can take over and reduce their effect. Edward Young complained long ago of the muse's "degen'rate sons,"

> Retain'd by sense to plead her filthy cause;
> To raise the low, to magnify the mean,
> And subtilize the gross into refin'd:
> As if to magic numbers' powerful charm
> 'Twas given, to make a civet of their song
> Obscene, and sweeten ordure to perfume.

And he asked, "Can pow'rs of genius . . . consecrate enormities with song?" [8] Fortunately or unfortunately, the answer is, Yes, provided we do not ask too much of "consecrate." There are plenty of bawdy poems (the old *fabliaux*, for example), but there are, so far as I know, no sexually arousing poems: the displacement toward language as an end in itself takes a reader's concern away from drive satisfaction. Similarly, experiments with highly aggressive films seem to show that the aggression induced in the viewer is reduced if the film says the aggression is morally justified, that is, if there is some defensive managing of the aggressive fantasy.[9]

Now, let us consider just those literary affects discussed by Freud or earlier in this book and those easy to intuit. In these instances, we can see two elements interacting to produce affect: the fantasy content and the defensive or other management of the fantasy. Literary affect seems to derive from either or both, as in the following table on the following pages of the instances we have considered:

INSTANCE	FANTASY	MANAGEMENT OF FANTASY	AFFECT
1. Following mythic pattern	Oral merger	Gratification	"Resonance"
2. Resisting mythic pattern	Oral merger	Denial	Distancing, parody, affect block
3. "Negative capability"	Oral merger	Projection	"Evocative" feeling
4. *Haiku*	Variable, but including oral merger	Projection	"Evocative" feeling
5. *Senryu*	Variable, but including oral merger	Projection stopped short	Amusement
6. Conradian stoicism	Oral merger	Defended by phallic assertiveness	Stoical fortitude
7. Pornography	Wishes for sexual gratification	Very little	Sexual arousal
8. "Verse pornog-raphy"	Wishes for sexual gratification	Displacement to language	Muted arousal
9. Violence in films	Sadistic	Very little	Aggressive arousal
10. Justified violence in films	Sadistic	Moral justification	Less aggressive arousal
11. Successful rhyme	Hungry expectance	Gratification	Satisfaction
12. Flawed rhyme	Hungry expectance	Frustration	Mild anger
13. Solution of plot	Hungry expectance	Gratification	Satisfaction
14. Failure to resolve plot	Hungry expectance	Frustration	Anger
15. The "puzzling movies"	Sexual looking	Displacement to intellectual issues	Affect block

INSTANCE	FANTASY	MANAGEMENT OF FANTASY	AFFECT
16. Varying the "frame"	Between oral merger and reality-testing	Reality-testing yields conflicting results	Intellectual dizziness
17. Death of Mercutio	Dangerous touching of love and hate	Loss of defensive displacement	Sense of inner danger
18. Romeo	Wish for narcissistic gratification	Gratification	Satisfaction
19. The "uncanny"	Anxiety laden complex or mode of thought	Reality-testing confirms it	Anxiety
20. The "tomorrow" speech	Primal scene	Denial	Reassurance-through-disillusion
21. "Dover Beach"	Primal scene	Denial	Reassurance-through-disillusion
22. Evaluation	Variable, but disturbing	Balance and mastery	"It is good"
23. Jokes	Sexual or aggressive impulse	Sudden gratification	Amusement
24. The comic	Exertion of effort	Denial of effort	Amusement
25. Humor	Suffering from reality	Denial of suffering	Amusement

The number of instances we have considered is quite large, and several groupings suggest themselves. We could try to group these various instances by the affects they represent: for example, the resistance to a mythic pattern, *senryu*, jokes, the comic, and humor all lead, more or less, to a feeling of amusement. But affects are highly variable and subjective, and, besides, affect is what we want to find out about—the end, not the starting point for any hypothesis we can derive.

Pairings like the use of or resistance to mythic patterns (1,2), *haiku* and *senryu* (4,5), pornography and "verse pornography" (7,8), or violence in films justified and unjustified (9,10), suggest a more informative grouping. The fantasies involved are the same, but a radical change in the management of the fantasy produces a radical change in affect. Further, one can see that there are two broad types of fantasy in our various instances: fantasies of gratification (as in our expectancies toward rhyme and plot, 11–14) and fantasies associated with anxiety (as the primal scene fantasies of "Dover Beach" and the "tomorrow" speech or the anxiety-laden fantasies of the "uncanny").

These broad groupings suggest a more meaningful kind of table:

MANAGEMENT
OF
FANTASY

FANTASY	Weakly Defended		Strongly Defended	
	Instance	Affect	Instance	Affect
DRIVE-GRATIFYING				
a. toward oral merger	Following mythic pattern	"Resonance"	Resisting mythic pattern	Distancing, parody, affect block
	Haiku	"Evocative"	*Senryu*	Amusement
	"Negative capability"	"Evocative"	Conradian stoicism	Stoical fortitude
b. between oral merger and reality-testing			Varying the "frame"	Intellectual dizziness
c. toward narcissistic gratification	Romeo	Satisfaction		
d. hungry expectance	Successful rhyme	Satisfaction	Flawed rhyme	Mild anger
	Solution of plot	Satisfaction	Failure to resolve plot	Anger
e. sadistic	Violence in films	Aggressive arousal	Justified violence in films	Muted aggressive arousal

f. sexual gratification	Pornography	Sexual arousal	"Verse pornography"	Muted sexual arousal
g. sexual looking			The "puzzling movies"	Affect block
h. sexual or aggressive impulse	Jokes	Amusement		
ANXIETY-AROUSING				
i. Anxiety-laden complex or mode of thought	The "uncanny"	Anxiety		
j. primal scene			"Dover Beach"	Reassurance-through-disillusion
			The "tomorrow" speech	Reassurance-through-disillusion
k. Exertion of effort			The comic	Amusement
l. Suffering from reality			Humor	Amusement
m. Dangerous touching of love and hate	Death of Mercutio	Sense of inner danger		

As one looks at this table, a certain pattern in the affects begins to emerge. That is, for those instances where the fantasy is one of drive gratification and the fantasy is weakly defended or not much managed, the affect seems appropriate to drive gratification: satisfaction, sexual or aggressive arousal, "resonance," the "evocative," and amusement. Not a surprising result. Where the fantasy is anxiety-provoking and is not much managed, one experiences anxiety or a "sense of inner danger." Again, this seems sensible enough.

When the fantasy is drive-gratifying but strongly defended against, affects are blocked, arousals are muted, or the whole experience becomes one of intellectual distance and parody; in a couple of instances, I sense the anger of frustration. We could conclude, then, that where the fantasy is drive-gratifying but where the gratification is denied, the resulting affect ranges from zero to anger—in other words, the fantasy ceases to be the cause of the affect and the defensive or formal level takes over. The same thing happens with the anxiety-arousing fantasies. Weakly managed, we respond to the anxiety implicit in the fantasy. Strongly managed, the fantasy has less impact, and the defense becomes the more important cause of affect: one experiences "reassurance-through-disillusion" or amusement. We could say the affects are variable, but range from zero to the kind of feelings one associates with the first quadrant, positive affects associated with drive gratifying fantasies that are not defended against. This is indeed a curious result, that defenses evoke the same emotions as drives.

Before attempting to explain it, though, we would do well to recall that there is a third source of literary affects, besides fantasies or defenses, namely, the audience itself. We have already considered the experiment of Drs. Globus and Shulman * in which they found that one could not predict the affective response to a given film because any particular audience member would bring to bear on it his own characteristic patterns of defense. Thus, at one extreme, he might flee it, either by literally leaving the theater or inwardly, by blocking affects, denying parts of the film, and the like. At another extreme, he might introject the film wholly, feeling its psychological process as his own; in that case, then, one could predict that he would experience the affect "built in" to the literary transformation. Between these extremes, any particular member of the audience may modify the literary process to any degree by bringing to bear on part or all of it his characteristic patterns of defense.

Further, he may associate different affects with a fantasy than one would predict. For example, I have assumed that the primal scene fantasies embodied in "Dover Beach" or the "tomorrow"

* See pp. 94–96.

speech are primarily anxiety-arousing. But for someone else, they might be drive-satisfying, and the affect he experiences at the denial of the fantasy would be more the kind of affect one associates with frustration of a drive than with the allaying of anxiety. Evidently, some affective responses to "Dover Beach" do indeed follow this pattern, as when critics speak of "frustration" or "despair." These differences are inevitable, for it is an old psychoanalytic maxim that what one wishes, one also fears; what one fears, one also wishes. The balance, though, may vary widely. Other critics will speak of "the full strangeness and horror of the concluding analogy," suggesting that the poem's defenses against anxiety, which seem so strong to me, seem weak to them.[10] To speak of any affect as "built in" to a literary work much oversimplifies the relation between that work and its audience: an audience member may refuse to take the process in, may take it in wholly, or may perceive the balance between fantasy and defense or satisfaction and anxiety in a quite personal way.

There are, then, three variables in our affective response: fantasy, defensive management of fantasy, and the characterological defenses of the person responding .We can abbreviate our long, involved table as follows:

CHARACTEROLOGICAL ALTERATIONS VS.

AESTHETIC INTROJECTION

FANTASY	MANAGEMENT OF FANTASY	
	Weakly Defended	Strongly Defended
Drive-gratifying	I. Positive satisfaction appropriate to the drive	II. a. Muted affect of type I b. Frustration, anger
Anxiety-arousing	III. Anxiety	IV. Varying from zero toward drive-satisfaction (affect of type I)

Our table of affects, then, lists only the "probable" reactions. On the left side of the table, matters seem straightforward enough. The formal, defensive level does not modify the fantasy greatly, and we tend to experience the affects appropriate to the fantasy. On the right side of the table, though, the management of fantasy seems to take over. Where the fantasy should lead to satisfaction, the affect is either muted or a mild anger resulting from frustration. Still more puzzling is the fourth quadrant, where the formal handling of an anxiety-laden fantasy seems to replace that affect with some other. In "Dover Beach" or the "tomorrow" speech, denial replaces separation or primal scene anxiety with a feeling of reassurance. Mercutio, so long as he is present, displaces our attention from the anxiety-laden issue of ambivalence onto himself, and we feel admiration rather than anxiety.

This is a somewhat novel source for affect—defenses. Few psychoanalytic theorists would suggest that affects can derive as a kind of by-product from defensive activities. Rather, affects accompany drives. So far as the arts are concerned, Franz Alexander sums up the classic psychoanalytic view. The fact literary critics cannot tell us the appeal of literature and art cues us to look for unconscious sources, he says.

> The question is what unconscious psychological processes the aesthetic response consists of. Many emotions in various combinations produce aesthetic enjoyment. In view of the great variety of tragic, humorous, comic, or purely beautiful effects, the hope of finding a single common denominator appears remote.
>
> Obviously it is not the emotion itself, expressed through art or literature, but rather the form of its expression which produces an aesthetic experience.
>
> The fusion of form and content is the essence of art. Form makes possible the gratification of a repressed wish because the emotional discharge is attributed to something acceptable— namely, to pleasure afforded by the form. This pleasure veils the release of repressed tendencies. When form is weak, art loses its appeal. When its content appears in all its nakedness, drama

> becomes melodrama and comedy an unsavory burlesque, paint-
> ing becomes mere photography or pornography, the dance an
> imitation of sexual license, and wit a brutal derision or an un-
> disguised sexual attack.[11]

Although this is the classic psychoanalytic explanation of literary
pleasure, Alexander's formulation seems really to apply only to one
quadrant of the four in our table: the transmittal of drive gratification with relatively little modification from form. He does not
seem to allow for the quite extensive changes that form can work
againt unconscious content. Nor does he cover content which is
more likely to evoke anxiety than to lead to pleasure. Also, I doubt
that something so abstract as, say, the sonnet-form can be much of
a source of pleasure in itself.

Freud, in "The 'Uncanny,'" deals with literary fantasies which
one would expect to arouse anxiety. They do, he says, if the writer
makes us believe they are really happening. If, however, he transposes the fearful fantasy to a world we perceive as unreal, the
world of fairy stories, for example, or Dante's *Inferno* or Shakespeare's *Midsummer-Night's Dream*, we no longer feel anxiety.

> The story-teller has a *peculiarly* directive power over us; by
> means of the moods he can put us into, he is able to guide the
> current of our emotions, to dam it up in one direction and
> make it flow in another, and he often obtains a great variety of
> effects from the same material.[12]

that is, material having both conscious and unconscious content.
Freud's phrasing allows for the existence of the fourth quadrant
situation—the anxiety-arousing fantasy which is managed so as to
produce pleasurable affects. But he describes the phenomenon
without explaining it.

This omission is unfortunate, for, in my experience at least, a
great deal of literature falls into this fourth category where the
affective content seems to depend very much on the formal management of an anxiety-laden fantasy. Many more literary works
work this way than in any of the other three possibilities represented in our table. Further, the situation of an unpleasant content

managed to give a pleasurable affect corresponds to one of the classic problems of aesthetics: How is it that things which would cause displeasure in life can cause pleasure when they are framed in works of art? Aristotle suggests as the answer man's pleasure in that most difficult of aesthetic concepts, *mimesis* or imitation.

> Imitation is natural to man from childhood, one of his advantages over the lower animals being this, that he is the most imitative creature in the world, and learns at first by imitation. And it is also natural for all to delight in works of imitation. The truth of this second point is shown by experience: though the objects themselves may be painful to see, we delight to view the most realistic representations of them in art . . . The explanation is to be found in a further fact: to be learning something is the greatest of pleasures not only to the philosopher but also to the rest of mankind, however small their capacity for it; the reason of the delight in seeing the picture is that one is at the same time learning—gathering the meaning of things. . . .[13]

Arnold asked the same question, but arrived at a different answer:

> In presence of the most tragic circumstances, represented in a work of Art, the feeling of enjoyment, as is well known, may still subsist: the representation of the most utter calamity, of the liveliest anguish, is not sufficient to destroy it: the more tragic the situation, the deeper becomes the enjoyment; and the situation is more tragic in proportion as it becomes more terrible.
>
> What then are the situations, from the representation of which, though accurate, no poetical enjoyment can be derived? They are those in which the suffering finds no vent in action; in which a continuous state of mental distress is prolonged, unrelieved by incident, hope, or resistance; in which there is everything to be endured, nothing to be done.[14]

Neither Aristotle nor Arnold had a psychology adequate to the problem, but the insights of both are sound, as far as they go. Translated into modern terms, they are describing our fourth pattern: painful events can give pleasure in tragedy because the work of art provides defensive ways of escaping the pain and somehow turning it into meaningful pleasure. Aristotle, typically Greek, stresses intellectualization as a defense. Arnold, typically Victorian, stresses action.

What is not clear at this point is whether psychoanalysis can go much farther. The psychoanalytic critic can generalize Arnold's and Aristotle's disparate explanations into the single notion of defensive management, but the question as to how a defense can reverse pain into pleasure reaches to the edges of psychoanalytic knowledge. My sketchy and empirical observations on literary affect seem to suggest that affect can arise as a kind of by-product from the application (by the literary work) of a certain kind of defensive maneuver. Denial can turn anxiety into reassurance. If so, then we would have to think in terms of two separate sources for affect: one the fantasy, the other the defense. Which dominates would depend on their relative strengths.

This, however, would be a quite unsatisfactory solution, contrary to what psychoanalytic theory of affect there is. Freud regarded affect as a "motor (secretory and vasomotor) discharge resulting in an (internal) alteration of the subject's own body without reference to the external world," to be contrasted to motor actions leading to changes in that external world.[15] Affect, then, is to be associated with drive discharge, not defense. In the fullest working out of this point of view, David Rapaport suggests the existence of "inborn affect discharge-channels"; as the ego develops, it is able to direct affects into different channels so that the feelings we experience change.[16] What this model does not explain, however, is precisely our fourth case—why should an anxiety-arousing fantasy, strongly managed by the literary work, create an affective response that is rather like those from drive gratification? Particularly since a drive-gratifying fantasy, strongly managed, seems to lead only to a general muting of affect.

I would like to suggest a different model, one patterned after the psychoanalytic explanation of the anger we feel when we are frustrated. That is, it is well known that frustration of libidinal drives leads to anger and aggression. This is not an easy phenomenon to account for, though it has been almost endlessly demonstrated. For example, the aggression cannot simply be a transformation of the drive for pleasure; if it were, satisfying the anger would silence the sexual drive. But it doesn't. The psychoanalytic explanation is: all drives are made up of libidinal and aggressive components. Should the libidinal side be frustrated, the aggressive side stands out in isolation. The aggression is not the transformation of sexual drives, but a residue after the sexual drives have been turned back.

In the same way, we could regard our more puzzling category of fantasies and affects as a combination. The top half of our chart represents fantasies of drive gratification. Weakly managed, we experience the affects of gratification. Strongly managed, we experience the affects appropriate to frustration. If the aggresssive side of the drive is managed, we feel a general muting of affect. If the libidinal side is denied satisfaction, the flawed rhyme, the unresolved plot, we feel the anger from the aggressive component. Now, if we consider the bottom half of the chart as dealing with fantasies which combine drive gratification with the arousal of anxiety (just as drives mingle libidinal and aggressive elements), the table would look like this:

CHARACTEROLOGICAL ALTERATIONS VS.

AESTHETIC INTROJECTION

FANTASY	MANAGEMENT OF FANTASY	
	WEAKLY DEFENDED	STRONGLY DEFENDED
Drive-gratifying	I. Positive satisfaction appropriate to the drive	II. a. Muted affect of type I b. Frustration, anger
Drive-gratifying with anxiety arousal	III. Anxiety	IV. Varying from zero toward affect of type I

An anxiety-arousing fantasy, weakly managed, elicits the anxiety one would expect. But the anxiety-arousing fantasy, strongly man-

aged, now ceases to be a mystery: the formal defensive management operates against the anxiety (that is, after all, what defenses
are for). But the affect we experience is what is appropriate for the
residual drive-gratifying side of the fantasy.

We are, in effect, applying the maxim that what one wishes, one
also fears; what one fears, one also wishes. Fear and wish combine
in fantasy as libido and aggression do in drives. Cases I and II,
then, must represent situations where the fear is minimal; cases III
and IV where it is noticeable. Such an explanation does not call
for transformations or redirections of affect, only selection among
possible affects. Further, if this explanation be sound, it tends to
confirm one of the basic positions of this book, that form in literature is like defense in a person: it serves to prevent or allay anxiety.
Our explanation of affect suggests that form is like a defense even
in its selectivity: it acts against only those elements in a fantasy
that arouse anxiety, letting drive-satisfying elements impinge on us
directly.

This explanation gets some confirmation from one of the inset
stories of *Pickwick Papers*. An old law-copyist is recalling tales of
the Inns of Court:

> "I knew another man—let me see—forty years ago now—
> who took an old, damp, rotten set of chambers, in one of the
> most ancient Inns, that had been shut up and empty for years
> and years before. There were lots of old women's stories about
> the place, and it certainly was very far from being a cheerful
> one; but he was poor, and the rooms were cheap, and that
> would have been quite a sufficient reason for him, if they had
> been ten times worse than they really were. He was obliged to
> take some mouldering fixtures that were on the place, and,
> among the rest, was a great lumbering wooden press for papers,
> with large glass doors, and a green curtain inside; a pretty use-
> less thing for him, for he had no papers to put in it; and as to
> his clothes, he carried them about with him, and that wasn't
> very hard work, either.
>
> "Well, he had moved in all his furniture—it wasn't quite a
> truck-full—and had sprinkled it about the room, so as to make

the four chairs look as much like a dozen as possible, and was sitting down before the fire at night, drinking the first glass of two gallons of whiskey he had ordered on credit, wondering whether it would ever be paid for, and if so, in how many years' time, when his eyes encountered the glass doors of the wooden press. 'Ah,' says he. 'If I hadn't been obliged to take that ugly article at the old broker's valuation, I might have got something comfortable for the money. I'll tell you what it is, old fellow,' he said, speaking aloud to the press, having nothing else to speak to: 'If it wouldn't cost more to break up your old carcase, than it would ever be worth afterwards, I'd have a fire out of you in less than no time.'

"He had hardly spoken the words, when a sound resembling a faint groan, appeared to issue from the interior of the case. It startled him at first, but thinking, on a moment's reflection, that it must be some young fellow in the next chamber, who had been dining out, he put his feet on the fender, and raised the poker to stir the fire. At that moment, the sound was repeated: and one of the glass doors slowly opening, disclosed a pale and emaciated figure in soiled and worn apparel, standing erect in the press. The figure was tall and thin, and the countenance expressive of care and anxiety; but there was something in the hue of the skin, and gaunt and unearthly appearance of the whole form, which no being of this world was ever seen to wear. 'Who are you?' said the new tenant, turning very pale: poising the poker in his hand, however, and taking a very decent aim at the countenance of the figure. 'Who are you?'

" 'Don't throw that poker at me,' replied the form; 'If you hurled it with ever so sure an aim, it would pass through me, without resistance, and expend its force on the wood behind. I am a spirit.'

" 'And, pray, what do you want here?' faltered the tenant.

" 'In this room,' replied the apparition, 'my worldly ruin was worked, and I and my children beggared. In this press, the papers in a long, long suit, which accumulated for years, were deposited. In this room, when I had died of grief, and long-deferred hope, two wily harpies divided the wealth for which I had contested during a wretched existence, and of which, at last, not one farthing was left for my unhappy descendants. I terrified them from the spot, and since that day have prowled by night—the only period at which I can re-visit the earth—

about the scenes of my long-protracted misery. This apartment is mine: leave it to me.'

" 'If you insist upon making your appearance here,' said the tenant, who had had time to collect his presence of mind during this prosy statement of the ghost's, 'I shall give up possession with the greatest pleasure; but I should like to ask you one question, if you will allow me.'

" 'Say on,' said the apparition, sternly.

" 'Well,' said the tenant, 'I don't apply the observation personally to you, because it is equally applicable to most of the ghosts I ever heard of; but it does appear to me somewhat inconsistent, that when you have an opportunity of visiting the fairest spots on earth—for I suppose space is nothing to you—you should always return exactly to the very places where you have been most miserable.'

" 'Egad, that's very true; I never thought of that before,' said the ghost.

" 'You see, sir,' pursued the tenant, 'this is a very uncomfortable room. From the appearance of that press, I should be disposed to say that it is not wholly free from bugs; and I really think you might find much more comfortable quarters: to say nothing of the climate of London, which is extremely disagreeable.'

" 'You are very right, sir,' said the ghost, politely; 'it never struck me till now; I'll try change of air directly.' In fact, he began to vanish as he spoke: his legs, indeed, had quite disappeared.

" 'And if, sir,' said the tenant, calling after him, 'if you *would* have the goodness to suggest to the other ladies and gentlemen who are now engaged in haunting old empty houses, that they might be much more comfortable elsewhere, you will confer a very great benefit on society.'

" 'I will,' replied the ghost; 'we must be dull fellows, very dull fellows, indeed; I can't imagine how we can have been so stupid.' With these words, the spirit disappeared; and what is rather remarkable," added the old man, with a shrewd look around the table, "he never came back again." [17]

From the point of view of a regular critical analysis, the story builds its plot on a contrast between the ritualized, ghostly, stereotyped habit of returning to the same place in the first half and a somewhat unexpected but nevertheless rather prosy and common-sensical resolution: the ghost decides to "try change of air." A re-lated set of incidents and images has to do with possessing—holding on as against letting go. The ghost lost his wealth; the tenant holds onto the poker, but would get rid of the press if he could. Both ghost and tenant want to hold onto the apartment. The ghost finally vanishes: perhaps all ghosts cease haunting. In short, the story contrasts two kinds of realness. That which is solid and undeniably there is also dreary (the apartment), ugly (the press), or fearful (the ghost). That which vanishes (the ghost; the "wealth") or is elsewhere (the young diner-out in the next cham-ber; "the fairest spots on earth") is much more desirable. In a way, the poker sums it up. Solid, substantial, heavy, it is also quite in-effective. By contrast, the tenant's insubstantial reasoning, his "presence of mind," exorcises the spirit. Indeed, the ghost even says, "It never struck me till now," while the poker could not have struck him at all.

So far as affect is concerned, the story, for me, at least, turns mildly anxious feelings about ghosts and the uncanny into mild amusement. The old, damp, rotten chambers, the mysterious press, the groan, the unearthly figure—these produce in me, anyway, the anxiety I usually experience in ghost stories. There is one jarring note—the poker. I feel that somehow the tenant's aiming it and the ghost's disquisition upon its uselessness are out of place. In-deed, I have a curious feeling that I don't quite believe the ghost, that he is protesting too much, that the poker might very well dent him a bit.* The spirit's tale of his woes, though, brings me

* See how the story would feel to you if Dickens had omitted the poker. Read it to the point where the ghost appears; then supply this revision:

> " 'Who are you?' said the new tenant, turning very pale. 'Who are you?'
> "Replied the form, 'I am a spirit.'
> " 'And, pray, what do you want here?' faltered the tenant.
> " 'In this room,' replied the apparition, 'my worldly ruin . . .

then return to the story as given. If you are responding as I am, you will feel the revised version is smoother and neater. A jarring note has been taken out.

back to my ordinary ghost-story response. Then the tenant's response to the "prosy statement" of the ghost's, his carefully stated
reasoning, the ghost's "Egad," his final departure, all seem hu-
morous—precisely in Freud's sense: affect (anxiety) I was expecting
to supply turns out to be unnecessary.

The question this chapter asks is, Can we, by analyzing the fantasy content, particularly in terms of anxiety-arousing and drive-
gratifying components, explain the affect? The fantasy in this story
has to do with that which is "old, damp, rotten," "shut up and
empty for years," "poor," "cheap," "mouldering," "ugly," "beggared," and the like. It deals with law in its most obsessional aspect, delays, dusty papers, a *res* which ultimately disappears. It
deals with possession—of furniture, of an apartment, but most of
all, of money, wealth, and credit. The story contrasts ritualized,
stereotyped behavior with an unpredictable escape from ritual. It
mixes up the living and the dead, most obviously in the ghost's
deadly and lively behavior, but also in the tenant's addressing the
press as "old fellow" or speaking of "your old carcase." In short,
the fantasy is an anal one, the first we have considered. The wish is
to hold onto something; the fear is that a parental figure will force
it away.

There are oral elements: the whiskey, the warm, snug fire, the
diner-out next door. But these are all distinctly less important than
the anal imagery. The fire is mentioned, then ignored. The diner-
out is elsewhere. The whiskey was bought on credit, scarcely
owned. At the oral level, the fantasy involves fear about a parent-
figure who comes, the ghost, also uncertainty about what is there
and what is not there, real and unreal. The fantasy is managed by
the parent-figure's going away in a non-threatening way, and the
child's establishing his own power.

Much more significant, however, is the anal level of fantasy. It
involves the fear—and wish—that a parent-figure will overpower a
child and force him somehow. The tenant is forced into the apartment by his poverty. He is also " 'obliged to take that ugly article
[the press] at the old broker's valuation.' " The two old harpies get

the wealth forced out by the lawsuit. But the important parental forcing is the ghost's trying to take the tenant's apartment. There is something of a reversal of the usual anal fantasy in that the tenant is not to give up something dirty in himself but to go out of something dirty he is in. The parental overpowering takes the form of frightening the tenant out: " 'If you insist upon making your appearance here,' said the tenant . . . 'I shall give up possession with the greatest pleasure.' "

The wishful side of the fantasy is gratified in that someone is indeed put out of the dirty apartment, but the objects are reversed: the tenant becomes active instead of passive. The fear evoked by the ghost's appearance is handled by reversal: I am not thrust out —he is, and perhaps not only he, but all ghosts. It would be possible for the reversal to arouse anxiety: a fear of overpowering someone else, but this is avoided by having the tenant pose a question rather than force a decision and the ghost rationally decide rather than, perhaps vengefully, accept defeat.

In short, one can see that the oral and anal fantasies act as unconscious nuclei for transformation into the conscious, intellectual idea that informs the story: that which is substantial and present is also dreary and ineffectual; that which is insubstantial or vanishing gives pleasure. One can also see that the affect (if you feel as I do when you read the story) can be understood as coming from a defensive reversal which takes out anxiety but gratifies the wish-fulfilling component of the story. The story arouses anxiety. Then the shift from passivity to activity (though not overpowering activity) gratifies the wish to evict something but does not arouse the fear of overpowering someone. These are, of course, dominant themes all through *Pickwick Papers*, the most notable instance being Mrs. Bardell's efforts to coerce Mr. Pickwick into marrying her and his subsequent confinement in prison. The affective pattern, too, runs all through this novel as so many of Dickens': the horror of the inset stories becomes absorbed in the cheery opposite represented by the sentimental doings of the principal characters, here, the Pickwickians.

One can even see, I think, why that poker sits so oddly in the story. The basic defensive maneuver is to shift from activity to passivity after the ghost has made his threat. The tenant's aiming the poker makes him active too soon—and too ineffectively. My own, perhaps quite idiosyncratic, reaction is that I don't believe the spirit when he says the poker won't hurt him. His description of the poker's passing through him and striking the wood is altogether too solid and concrete for a purely verbal demonstration from an already "unearthly" figure. In terms of the fantasy level, that which is substantial is ineffective, that which is insubstantial has power. The ghost's verbal argument, because it is so concrete, reverses this pattern or at least blurs it.

In general, though, the story supports the model I am suggesting for the affective side of our response. The fantasy has an anxiety-arousing side and a drive-gratifying side. The story manages the fantasy in such a way as to allay the anxiety but to satisfy the drive. Thus, we begin by feeling anxiety. We end with humor and a mild sense of triumph. These latter emotions do not represent transformations of anxiety, but rather components of the original fantasy that stand clear once the anxiety-ridden part has been taken care of.

Affect is the most cherished core of our response, but the least understood. Whether our quadrilateral explanation will stand the test of time is, of course, problematical, probably a matter better left to psychoanalytic theorists than to literary critics. It does, however, point the way for future investigation. What is needed is quite simple: more study of the ways people feel as they read various works embodying various types of fantasy and defense—works which are primarily drive-gratifying; works which mingle anxiety arousal with wish fulfillment; works in which the fantasy is strongly managed; works in which the fantasy is weakly managed. The results may lead not only to a firm explanation of our affective response to literature, but also to a deeper understanding of our emotions in life.

12 The Model Moralized

This book has not been a book of literary criticism, not even of psychoanalytic criticism, and perhaps that is just as well. "The history of criticism," writes I. A. Richards, "is a history of dogmatism and argumentation rather than a history of research. And like all such histories the chief lesson to be learnt from it is the futility of all argumentation that precedes understanding." [1] If this book has succeeded at all, it has added something to that understanding without which there can be no meaningful dialogue.

In human culture, we can distinguish two strands. In one, men add to the store of human knowledge. In the other, men seek experiences. These two strands reflect one of the deepest polarities in man's mind, that between activity and passivity, phallicly working on the environment as against asking from that environment nurturing and satisfying sensations. Nevertheless, C. P. Snow's phrase, "the two cultures," misleads because it establishes a false division. Most cultural activity has something of both strands. Literature, music, and art would seem to be almost purely experiential, yet it is a cliché as old as Aristotle that literature and music and painting enable men to gather the meanings of things. The "hard" sciences would seem wholly devoted to adding to the sum of man's knowledge. Newton's discoveries, however, were as much an aesthetic experience to men of the eighteenth century as they were a source of knowledge.

Literary criticism occupies an especially ambiguous position in this dual culture. At his best, the literary critic reveals possibilities and relationshps in literary works that were not seen before. In that sense, he adds to human knowledge. But he does this in hopes of adding to men's experience of the literary work he is talking about. In this sense, criticism is handmaiden to the muse, and this, to me, is literary criticism at its best. Most of what fills our quarterlies and fortnightlies, though, is a kind of general talking about books without adding much to our understanding of them. This, too, has its place—literate, urbane chatter can be a highly satisfying art-form in itself, and also a useful social and moral discourse. Yet much confusion results when people apply the standards of *causerie* to explication or vice versa.

This book perhaps adds to that confusion by being neither explication to enhance response nor conversation as an end in itself. This book is simply not literary criticism in any usual sense. It is an attempt to develop a theory about our response to books, to stand both inside and outside that response so as to observe and understand it.

What should a "theory of literary response" do? It should, I take it, explain why we respond to literary works as we do. "Explain" is, of course, a philosophically tricky word, but, for our purposes, we can say, simply, to explain a phenomenon is to relate it to principles more general than itself. For example, to explain why a magnet attracts a bar of iron, we say the molecules in the magnet are all lined up one way, appealing to more general notions of molecular structures and the electrical forces associated with them. Similarly, we explain the "willing suspension of disbelief" by saying we introject literary works, because the word "introject" draws on general psychological principles about our relations to people and things. At the outset, I assumed that literary experiences were continuous with other experiences, that they could be analyzed the same way. But to say one can analyze literary experiences by principles applicable to all human experience is simply to say one can "explain" literary experiences. The deepest premise on which this book rests, then, is simply that literary experiences can be explained.

Given this assumption, I have developed a theory—or model—of literary response. The basic datum is the organic unity of the literary work: poems, plays, and stories are series of words; but in each of these series there are implicit groupings into themes and meanings. As readers, we make these implicit groupings more or less explicit, possibly along themes that are of particular concern to us, Marxist, Christian, social, moral, and so on. Among these possible groupings of the elements of the text, there is one with a special status: a psychoanalytic reading will arrive at a central or nuclear fantasy, known from clinical evidence, in which all the separate elements of the text play a role. Because we know these fantasies clinically, because they have to do with the primitive, unconscious part of our mental life, we can safely say they are what give literature its astonishing power over us. Literature transforms these nuclear fantasies toward meaningfulness and thereby allows them to elude the censoring part of our minds and achieve an oblique expression and gratification. In effect, a literary text has implicit in it two dimensions: one reaches "up," toward the world of social, intellectual, moral, and religious concerns; the other reaches "down," to the dark, chthonic, primitive, bodily part of our mental life.

The text itself is only a series of words—it is we who stretch it in these two directions. Unconsciously or half-consciously, we introject it, taking it into us as, at the most primitive level of our being, we long to incorporate any source of gratification. Consciously, however, we perceive the text as separate, think about it, judge it, and, most important, supply coherence if it is not built in. Thus, either the literary work itself embodies, or we supply, a transformation of fantasy toward meaning. It is this transformational process, this management of fantasy, that we take into ourselves, feeling it as though it were our own mental activity—which, indeed, it in part is. Further, we not only contribute meaning, we analogize, enriching the central fantasy with our own associations and experiences that relate to it. Thus, the text transforms not only its fantasy but ours as well.

Within the literary work itself, what establishes the central fantasy is plot in the very broadest sense: the sequence and significance of images or events portrayed. The author's hand shapes this plot toward meaningfulness; we experience his shaping and ordering as the transformation of our own fantasy. We can distinguish two other important agents of transformation. The first is structure or form (in a large sense), that which determines what we are aware of at any given moment as we are seeing the text. Form acts to manage the underlying fantasy in a way that, if it happened in a person rather than on a page, would look very like a defense mechanism. Form in this larger sense tends to operate like denial or regression or splitting or condensation or displacement or isolation.

A second agent of transformation is what we have called "the displacement to language." Present to some extent in any literary text, it becomes particularly important when a text calls attention to its own language, as, for example, poetry does. The displacement to language handles the fantasy content by transferring our involvement with the text (in technical terms, shifting our cathexis) from the fantasy to the language in which the fantasy is expressed. The language then seems to manage the fantasy content—partly by a kind of pseudo-logic that gives the illusion of mastery; partly by enlisting us kinesthetically in muscular actions that seem to manage the fantasy; partly by gratifying or violating our formal expectations about the language. Gratifying our formal expectations about language gives us a satisfying sense of mastery. Violating our expectations binds our attention (or cathexis) still more tightly to the verbal texture.

Put in its very briefest form, the theory says that literature is an introjected transformation. The literary text provides us with a fantasy which we introject, experiencing it as though it were our own, supplying our own associations to it. The literary work manages this fantasy in two broad ways: by shaping it with formal devices which operate roughly like defenses; by transforming the fantasy toward ego-acceptable meanings—something like sublimation. The pleasure we experience is the feeling of having a fantasy of our own and our own associations to it managed and controlled but at the same time allowed a limited expression and gratification.

Given such a model, what can we explain with it? I have tried to show that it tells us something about our value judgments of literature. We get the feeling "this is good," when a literary work successfully balances fantasy and its handling of the fantasy, neither over-managing nor under-managing it. Such a model supplies reasons for our evaluations of literary works in terms of specific properties of the work—the presence or absence of transformation toward meaning (as in the two Fellini films); the acceptability or unacceptability of the defensive maneuvers built into its formal structure (the two Lovelace poems). It asks us to look specifically at all the factors in the dynamic balance of forces which is our experience of any given literary work. In a larger sense, such a model enables us to compare quite disparate experiences of literature in a way which I think is not possible without some such explanatory or generalizing system.

The notion of literature as a balance of fantasy and management of fantasy relates literary works to the psychoanalytic concept of character: libidinal level and habitual patterns of defense. Thus, the model enables us to relate the style (in both a broad and a narrow sense) to the man. One can see connections between a man's life and his work and between his various different works, even those which seem as special as *The Secret Agent* does in Conrad's total *œuvre*. The model also enables us to explain the somewhat puzzling role of myth in literature. Where we are aware of a mythic substructure in a literary work and where the work plays into its myth, it strengthens our introjection of the transformational process because the myth feels like a nurturing other both within and in addition to the text itself. Where the literary work plays against its myth, we feel the opposite—a sense of distance and parody, a weakening of our introjection.

Similarly, the model enables us to see what is meant by "identification" with a literary character. It is not exactly identification but rather an introjection, just one part of our introjection of the whole work. The work itself is a total economy of drive and management of drive. Some characters, like Romeo, we introject as vicarious satisfiers of drives. Others, like Mercutio or the Nurse, we introject because they embody defensive maneuvers for dealing with the anxiety-arousing aspects of the central fantasy. In short, we do not identify with *a* character so much as with a total interaction of characters in which some satisfy needs for pleasure and others satisfy our need to avoid anxiety. Further, our concept of literature as a balance of fantasy and management of fantasy leads us to at least a tentative understanding of the sources of the affects we experience, not only in books but perhaps in life as well. That is, the literary work transforms a fantasy which has both drive-satisfying and anxiety-arousing aspects. If not much in the fantasy arouses anxiety, we feel the affects appropriate to drive-satisfaction if the fantasy is not over-managed; we feel the affects appropriate to lack of satisfaction or even frustration if the fantasy is heavily managed. If the fantasy has a good deal of anxiety implicit in it, we feel that anxiety if the fantasy is weakly controlled. But if an anxiety-arousing fantasy is strongly managed, the defensive operation of literary form operates selectively against the anxiety, leaving the drive-gratifying side of the fantasy relatively uncontrolled. We feel the affects appropriate to drive-satisfaction, not because anxiety has been transformed into other affects, but because anxiety has been subtracted out, leaving affects it would otherwise have masked.

Evaluation, the links between a man and his style, the role of myth, the nature of our relation to literary characters, the sources of affect—these are some of the specific questions about literature to which this model suggests answers. There are, of course, larger issues which any theory of literary response ought to at least clarify and preferably settle. One is the complex role of meaning in literary response. This theory, by saying literature is a transformation, gives meaning a central role. The pleasure we seek in literary experience is feeling our fantasies managed and controlled so they become acceptable to our conscious ego. Form is one way literature does this, but the act or process of meaning is at least as important. Confronted by works that seem to lack this transformation to meaning, audiences search almost frantically for it. In the lobby of a theater where the latest Antonioni or Bergman is showing, there is almost a chorus of "What does it mean?" "What is it all about?" Evidently, meaning is central to our experience, for we demand it and feel frustrated if we cannot find it. Meaning must therefore be an essential ingredient in our pleasure, whether it be readily available in the work or whether we have to work to find it. This model accounts for both possibilities.

The model also suggests a relationship between form and meaning as the two major modes of managing fantasy content. Meaning works somewhat like a sublimation—it allows disguised and partial satisfaction of the fantasy. The process of meaning works in the same direction as the push for expression. By contrast, form tends to work against the fantasy, omitting, splitting, reversing. A small change in the phrasing of a joke or a lyric without altering the meaning nevertheless makes a big change in the effect—why? Because, in our minds as we introject the work, form balances off pressures from the fantasy. As in any other balance of forces, a slight change on one side produces a much bigger change in the final position of the balance. Thus, form must be much more precise than meaning. We need meaning, but we can accept a wide variety of possible meanings to achieve literary pleasure. Almost any kind of interpretation we derive from a text will get it past the censor and permit our egos to enjoy the fantasy content. Form, however, must be more artfully chosen, as beginning poets to their sorrow find.

In general, any literary theory ought to account for the presence and function of different literary forms. This theory explains form as a quasi-defensive management of the fantasy content. Form can control what we are aware of at any given moment; it can split the psychological issues involved, omit (or repress) them, displace our involvement from the fantasy to a purely verbal resolution of it, and so on. Thus, our model can account for the differences between prose literature and verse: in one, the displacement to language is an important part of the defensive handling of the fantasy; in the other, it is not.

Similarly, our model accounts for the existence and relation of genres by considering them as different defensive modes. For example, Swift's "A Modest Proposal" represents a distinctive type of satire, one which advocates one proposition by reducing its opposite to absurdity. Having realistically explored the possibility of treating the Irish like cattle, we come away from the satire convinced that we should treat them like human beings and identify with them in some way other than eating them. Psychologically, Swift uses a reaction-formation that already exists in his reader, the horror and revulsion we feel at the idea of eating babies. One could define this kind of satire psychologically, then, as presenting a highly unpleasant fantasy and using, to manage it, a reaction-formation the reader already has.

One could define allegory as a genre that handles fantasies by making the transformation into meaning quite explicit. Angus Fletcher has suggested allegory resembles obsessional or compulsive behavior.[2] Tragedy, I have suggested elsewhere,[3] involves the failure of a defense (the death of Mercutio, for example), leading to punishment for an impulse toward pleasure. Comedy builds up a defense, leading to gratification of an impulse toward pleasure without punishment. And so on. It seems unlikely that these psychological definitions could ever be phrased as exactly as definitions based on the formal properties of the various genres. Nevertheless, these psychological definitions do suggest the reason different genres exist: they represent different ways of managing fantasy materials. We seek out different genres because they supply a variety in the psychological experiences we get from literature. The different genres are related, then, as different defensive patterns—one could have a comedy, a tragedy, a satire, each a different way of managing the same core fantasy, and they would each feel like a quite different experience.

In short, our model supplies answers for a variety of fundamental questions about literature. Whether those answers are correct or, indeed, whether the model itself is, are matters for—ultimately —experimentation. The model does, however, gain some confirmation in that it returns us finally to the very things literary critics have always talked about—though with a difference. Form, language, character, plot, genre, sound—these are all important, but we can only talk intelligently about them if we recognize that they shape and balance a core of fantasy material. Many statements about literature seem dogmatic or impressionistic because they deal only with one end of a total process of transformation and balance. It is as if literary critics have been looking at a group of children on one half of a somewhat mysterious see-saw, the other half being screened by a wall. They have been trying to explain why this board should rise or fall or stand out horizontally from the wall by examining only the weights and positions of the children on the end they can see. Similarly, one can analyze very, very precisely the sound of a line of poetry, but that analysis only makes sense when we understand the sound as a way of transforming and managing the fantasy content of the line.

Correct or not, the model does at least meet some of Robert E. Lane's rather telling objections to the usual statements about literature: that they lack classification, theory, methodology, or test procedure; that they are as unverifiable adn poetic as the very texts they seek to explain.[4] Whatever other virtues this model may have, it is at least testable. For example, the model says, when we willingly suspend disbelief, we are introjecting the literary text as a child (orally) fuses with a source of passive gratification of his oral needs. Similarly, Brenman and Gill found that easily hypnotizable people had more than their share of oral conflict and fixation. If the model is correct, one should be able to establish the same thing for the "willing suspension of disbelief": people who easily become absorbed in reading or play- or movie-watching should show more orality than those who don't. One should be able to correlate oral

issues, discovered by projective tests or interviews, with literary absorption, observed directly or by interview.

Similarly, the model suggests that a reader will respond "I like
it" to literary works whose formal or defensive techniques match
his own. One should, then, be able to correlate different readers'
preferences among a collection of more or less equally good short
stories with the different readers' characteristic patterns of fantasy
and defense, discovered by interview or projective test. One could
use two versions of a given story or a line of poetry to explore the
balance between form and fantasy content the model points to.
One could, for example, ask readers to explain their preference for
one of two versions of the same line of poetry to get at the way the
sound of the line manages the fantasy. We have already seen
something of this kind of test in the chapter on myth: texts in
which we strongly sense mythic resonance have images of oral fusion; texts which are based on a myth, but in which we do not get
a sense of resonance, lack images of oral fusion. One could test the
role of meaning in the same way, by using different versions of a
story in which the plot is made more or less meaningful and listening to the responses of readers.

That is, ultimately, what the model tells us: the things to tune
into in the responses of readers. If one listens with the analyst's
"third ear," one should be able to hear free associations to the fantasy content of, say, a story and perhaps also some indication of the
defensive management. Thus, a particularly powerful way to test
what the model tells us about any given fiction would be to ask a
reader or readers to retell the story in their own words. Here is a
free retelling by a freshman:

> Why and how can a book (the words) be more real than the
> actual experience? Because . . . for me sometimes the words
> bring the experience closer—it makes you aware of things you
> wouldn't have noticed—perhaps for me this is because I don't
> have a very critical eye, and many times words describe some-
> thing & make it more *real* for me. . . . My most favorite
> passage that I've ever read is in *One Flew Over the Cuckoo's*

Nest, when the guy in the asylum is looking out the window and sees a dog playing and jumping in the moonlight—then the dog gets run-over by a car as he chases some geese high in the air. This is more *real* to me than *reality* because when I read it I feel like the dog, the grass, the dew, the moon, the geese, and the car. If I just saw this, I probably wouldn't see anything but the dog getting hit—I would have missed the dog's life and action and his (for me) joy at just being outside and free to jump and bay at the moon and chase the geese and the beauty of the moon and the wetness of the dew beneath him. The words bring all the little pieces of the larger reality to me magnified, and the total experience, although I only read it, is closer and more real and more meaningful to me than it would have been if I had *only* seen it.[5]

Beginning student he may be, but his remarks make a handsome instance of the introjection process our model posits, particularly the introjection of a total economy of several elements interacting in different psychological ways ("I feel like the dog, the grass, the dew, the moon, the geese, and the car").

On the other hand, "My most favorite passage that I've ever read" is being rather dimly recollected. If one turns to the Kesey novel itself,[6] one finds that the dog does not bay at the moon and does not chase the geese. "He was still standing with his paw up; he hadn't moved or barked when they flew over." Moreover, the novel only implies the dog is hit by the car; it does not show the event which, indeed, may not have happened at all. "I watched the dog and the car making for the same spot of pavement. The dog was almost to the rail fence at the edge of the grounds when I felt somebody slip up behind me," and that is the last we hear of either dog or car.

If we listen to the student's comments for the psychological issues involved, we hear him contrast the weakness of his "critical eye" with the way words make things realer than reality: "makes you aware of things you wouldn't have noticed." "If I just saw this, I probably wouldn't see anything but the dog getting hit." "The words bring all the little pieces of the larger reality to me magnified." He is expressing both a wish to see the event and a wish not to see but to be told about it instead. We can guess what it is he wishes to see and not see from some remarks I omitted in quoting him earlier:

> . . . many times words describe something & make it more *real* for me. Like at the first chapter, he is lonely at night and *hears sounds that a ghost who couldn't communicate would say*—this brings another dimension, another type of definition that I never would have thought of but will think of again. Maybe the next time I'm alone at night a noise will become more than a noise for me. My most favorite passage . . .

One can guess that what this student wishes to be told about has to do with sights and noises at night—certainly his "most favorite passage" does.

Curiously, though—or not so curiously—he omits from his recollection of the passage precisely the part that has most to do with investigating nighttime activities:

> I saw it was a dog, a young, gangly mongrel slipped off from home to find out about things went on after dark. He was sniffing digger squirrel holes, not with a notion to go digging after one but just to get an idea what they were up to at this hour. He'd run his muzzle down a hole, butt up in the air and tail going, then dash off to another . . . . Galloping from one particularly interesting hole to the next, he became so took with what was coming off—the moon up there, the night, the breeze full of smells so wild makes a young dog drunk—that he had to lie down on his back and roll. He twisted and thrashed around like a fish, back bowed and belly up, and when he got to his feet and shook himself a spray came off him in the moon like silver scales.
>
> He sniffed all the holes over again one quick one, to get the smells down good, then suddenly froze still with one paw lifted and his head tilted, listening.

The passage contains much genital symbolism: the dog poking his nose down holes; his phallic body, ultimately fish-like; the smells; phrases like, "Things went on after dark," "what were they up to at this hour," "what was coming off," or "a spray came off him." All this presented as a sight seen suggests that we are confronting a primal scene fantasy, most of which the student omits or blurs in remembering the passage.

The flight of the geese continues the primal scene symbolism, now, though, in as eerie a fashion as the silent, motionless wolves in Wolf-Man's primal scene dream.[7] "Then they crossed the moon—a black, weaving necklace, drawn into a V by that lead goose. For an instant that lead goose was right in the center of that circle, bigger than the others, a black cross opening and closing, then he pulled his V out of sight into the sky once more." During this flight, the dog stands motionless and silent. Then, "he commenced to lope off in the direction they had gone, toward the highway, loping steady and solemn like he had an appointment." The novel continues to a third version of primal scene material, the implicit collision of the dog and the car.

If we look at this section of the novel as a transformation, it is reworking the primal scene fantasy at its core into a meaningful theme: the inevitable spoiling of—everything. The dog's innocent curiosity about the squirrels becomes his wonder at the geese and his apparent wish to join them and is ended by the danger that he will be struck by a car when he tries to. Kesey's novel deals throughout with the issue of contact and contact observed: here, dog-squirrel, dog-grass, dog-geese, dog-car, and finally the attendants who grab the narrator from behind. Contact destroys in this novel. Here, so long as the dog does not actually touch a squirrel or a goose, all is well. Trouble comes when the dog tries to contact the geese or when the car nears the dog or the men grab the speaker. Kesey handles the primal scene fantasy at the core by disguising it symbolically and splitting it into three distinct episodes, each with a different tone representing different possible responses to the primal scene: curiosity, awe and wonder, fear.

The student responded to the passage by omitting (repressing?) the first, most explicit statement of the fantasy and coalescing the second and third into a noisier, boisterous image with something of the security of a cliché. Further, he makes the dog, not a silent watcher of the goose opening and closing in the circle of the moon, but an active, phallic dog "outside and free," jumping and baying at objects impossibly distant. So far from the words bringing him "all the little pieces of the larger reality . . . magnified," he has converted the words back into a picture that leaves out the little holes and changes the fear of passively experiencing a primal scene into solitary, phallic activity followed by punishment. Or so we can surmise. Actually to know what was going on in his mind, we would have to talk it over with him.

Even so, the model tells us what to listen for, both in the novel and in the student's response to it. Understanding literature as a transformational process leads us to the fantasy material and the relation between the novel's way of handling it and the reader's. Here, we can guess that the fantasy material and the symbolic disguise of it matched something in the reader; it is his "most favorite passage." But we can also surmise that the first statement of the primal scene fantasy was insufficiently disguised for him and the second and third unsatisfyingly so, for he omits the one and supplies noise, violent activity, and disastrous contact to the others. We can also guess that no small part of his pleasure in the passage comes from his own mastery of the threatening material, not the novel's.

Knowing what to listen for in people's responses means we can confirm or deny our model, establishing its truth or falsity. If it is a true statement of the dynamics of literary response, then it has consequences for anyone concerned with literature: critic, teacher, writer, stage or film director, or those most matter-of-fact men of letters, propagandists and advertisers.

The propagandist seeks to use literature (or sub-literature) to encourage a certain opinion or conduct. Quite directly, our model tells us that literature can encourage an opinion or conduct only as a way of managing the fantasy material a literary text sets forth. The propagandist, then, must begin with a fantasy and offer the resolution for it. The most usual strategy, as in simple hate-literature or caricature, is projection: I am not dirty, avaricious, lazy, or whatever; *they* are. This opinion easily becomes conduct in that if I can project my own inner sense of insufficiency outward onto another, I can deal with it by acting on him without having to confront it in myself.

Projection is the most common mechanism for propaganda, but different cultures require variants. Shame being a major factor in Chinese life, the Nationalist Chinese, reports Lucian Pye,

> in trying to stimulate patriotism never felt it odd to establish "National Humiliation Days," a concept about what is the proper theme for a national holiday that is unknown to any other country. In giving expression to what is assumed to be patriotism Chinese publicists and political leaders have been tireless in recounting the innumerable ways in which others have taken advantage of China.

Out of "the apparent sense of satisfaction Chinese have in recounting publicly how they have been hurt, 'exploited,' and humiliated by others," the state was able to generate hatred for foreign political powers, which was seen as a "political awakening." [8] Such a strategy is highly particular. More generally, of the two modes for transforming fantasy, the pressure toward meaning and the defensive modes of form, propaganda relies more heavily on a readily accessible meaning. As art, propaganda tends to lack form.

If propaganda be a broadside, the television commercial is a triolet. Working within a much more limited form with a more restricted aim, the advertising industry occasionally produces a work of art of small, gem-like charm. The genre requires that the advertiser establish the name of a product in his audience's memory, but aside from this, the techniques fit the model as those of propaganda do: a favorable opinion of the product serves as a solution to the psychological issue embodied in the fantasy. Since the advertiser mostly wants to create a hunger for his product, the great majority of American commercials, at least, build on oral fantasies. Often the commercial develops an oral wish aggressively tinged with frustration or pain to which the product brings fast, fast relief. Many times a commercial will start with a little drama ("Everybody treats me as though I had bad breath"). The product then satisfies an (essentially oral) wish to end the suspense and take in a solution to the problem.

Not all commercials, though, solve oral fantasies. Detergents and cleansers, for example, are symbolized by such things as a white knight thundering about on horseback who pokes his long magical spear at dirty clothes which flash into white; a washing machine which swells into a ten-foot column; a giant's fist sticking up out of the washer. Characters may include magical figures like Mr. Clean or an omnicompetent plumber. The products promise power, energy, strength. One would not ordinarily think of soap powder as a phallic symbol, but the advertiser identifies it as such (and I assume he has some research to support his symbolism). From the point of view of our model, there is considerable sense in what he does; he is offering a progressive rather than a regressive solution to issues of the prior developmental phase: phallic power will erase anal fears about dirt. It is probably also relevant that these ads with their promises of masculine strength are directed primarily to women: instead of a dirty mess, your femininity can have phallic power. Shades of the loathly lady and the Wife of Bath!

Put to commercial use, our model can tell an advertiser what he is doing psychologically and the kind of response to look for in his audience. Given two versions of the same commercial, the model can isolate the psychological differences between the two and suggest which will be more effective. This last use applies many steps up the literary ladder, to the director of stage or film: the model can help him in judgments and choices. It is, of course, no substitute at all for creative inspiration. It cannot make ideas come. The model speaks about, not with, the voice of the unconscious. Inevitably, blockings or conceptions of a character, unusual camera angles or color effects must come from "inspiration," but the director choosing between two or more possibilities can use the fantasy-and-defense model to make his choice an informed one. He can gain some clear idea of the probable effect of his choice on an audience.

To a limited extent, the writer can also use the model this way,

to make an informed choice among different possibilities he has arrived at intuitively. Consider, for example, some choices Stephen
Spender made in composing his well-known "The Express." We
can isolate three versions of a single line:

> It is now she begins to sing—at first quite low
> Then loud, and at last with a jazzy madness—
> The song of her whistle screaming at curves,
> Of deafening tunnels, brakes, innumerable bolts.
> And always light, aerial, underneath
> Is the tapping metre of her wheels.

> Goes the racing metre of her wheels.

> Goes the elate metre of her wheels.

Karl Shapiro suggests, in his study of Spender's revisions of this
poem,[9] "The perfect solution has been found to describe sen-
sorially and emotionally the condition of the train at top speed. By
repeating the word 'elate' by itself very rapidly one even awakens
in the ear the characteristic music of the train." Certainly, "elate"
is perfect, but a fantasy-and-defense approach can show why more
precisely.

Quite subjectively, "tapping metre" seems sing-song to me; "racing metre" seems pretty good, the almost right phrasing; while
"elate" is the choice of genius. Possibly, the changes in sound are
enough to explain my reaction. "The elate" adds strongly to the
series of ē sounds: aer*i*al, undern*ea*th, m*e*tre, wh*ee*ls. To my ear,
anyway, perhaps because I give "aerial" four syllables, the vowel
sequence of "ay-EHR-ee-ul" somehow matches "ee-LAYT-mee-
tur." More surely, a double "t" comes into play with "elate metre"
that "racing" does not offer (though "tapping metre" does). As
against the other two adjectives, "elate" gives an extra series of
what we have called economies, leading to a greater sense of control.

But what is this control controlling? Listening to sound alone
neglects the different meanings of the words. "Tapping" is simply
onomatopoetic. "Racing" drops the onomatopoeia to suggest a

wilder, continuing kind of speed. "Elate" puts aside both onomatopoeia and speed to attribute to the metre or the train an emotion: high spirits or elation or even, given its latinity, just "lifted
out of." The use of "elate" instead of "elated" itself suggests a special kind of elegance and control, that "racing" does not have.

This choice matches others in the middle section of the poem:

> It is then she begins to sing—at first low
> And then loud and at last with mad joy—
> The ~~strange~~ song of her whistle screaming round corners,
> And of drums in tunnels, of her innumerable bolts,
> And a swaying melody of tearing speed:
> And always light, ariel ...
>
> (Draft A)

Draft B's change of "mad joy" to "a jazzy madness" similarly produces more elegance and tones down "joy" to jazz. The abandon-
ment of, even the composition of, so prosy and blustering a line as
"A swaying melody of tearing speed" suggests Spender was having
trouble shifting from "luminous self-possession" to "madness,"
"screaming," and "wild." Choosing "elate metre" instead of "racing metre" introduces a limited, controlled kind of madness.

Why was this extra control needed? Why the attribution of a
feeling? To answer such questions one must understand "the poem
as transformation." What is its conscious content, and what unconscious material does that content derive from? If we look at the
whole poem on the conscious level, we find what Karl Shapiro describes as the theme: "praise of the beauty of the machine and the
ecstasy of its motion." More exactly, the poem is "about" transcending, specifically, transcending through movement, speed,
metre, and song—the poetic act itself—the dichotomy between
power and beauty. The express train with its "first powerful plain
manifesto / The black statement of pistons" can, by the end of the
poem, be compared to a comet "Wrapt in her music," bird song,
and, most startlingly, a bough "Breaking with honey buds."
Throughout, the poem commonly follows an earthy phrase with an
other-worldly one:

> without more fuss
> But gliding like a queen . . .
>
> Beyond the town there lies the open country . . .
>
> At last, further than Edinburgh or Rome . . .

The very passage we are considering moves from tunnels and brakes and bolts to "the elate metre of her wheels."

At the fantasy level, the striking thing is the gender of the train —introduced by the word "queen" (which is followed in the manuscript by a short, obliterated word—it could possibly be "king" —as though Spender thought of doing the train in masculine terms, then stuck to his first intuition). "Queen," notes Shapiro,

> raises the strange question of the sex of trains. The vehicle in the poem, with its blackness, iron, bolts, pistons, and power, argues for the male interpretation. The wheels, flight, song, "luminous self-possession," mystery, and of course the analogy of ships at sea, argue for the feminine interpretation. . . . [As for the obliterated word] The original impulse to make the symbol feminine Spender finds correct, and the poem acquires a pleasing dualism at the outset.

At the fantasy level, then, the poem feminizes the strongly masculine "powerful plain manifesto / The . . . statement of pistons" into an aloof queen who glides past houses humbly crowding near her, the gasworks, and the "heavy page" of gravestones. "She" becomes poetically and musically mad (a further unmanning), but still powerful and phallic in the lines just following our passage:

> Steaming through metal landscape on her lines
> She plunges new eras of wild happiness
> Where speed throws up strange shapes, broad curves
> And parallels clean like the steel of guns.

Finally, she is quieted and rendered other-worldly—

> Beyond the crest of the world, she reaches night
> Where only a low streamline brightness
> Of phosphorus on the tossing hills is white.

And then "she" can be compared to a comet, bird song, or a bough breaking with buds. Consciously, the poem transforms power into beauty. At the unconscious level, the poem transforms a masculine image into a phallic, frenzied madwoman, finally de-phallicizing her to a quiet, budding, but breaking bough.

Interestingly, Spender tried in the first four drafts to see the wildness from the point of view of passengers within the express. "The idea of travelers and passengers," notes Shapiro, "awakens the complexity of dark associations in the poet's mind, and as we shall see, it is only by eliminating people altogether that unity is maintained in the poem, and the express freed to establish itself in the cosmos." An awareness of unconscious content offers a more precise explanation: the "travelers and passengers" are within the body of this mad, phallic mother. To ask the reader to see the events of the ride from within the train would be to ask him to imagine himself inside the body of an altogether repellent mother.

In the same way, the madness of the womanly, motherly train needs to be mollified lest the reader himself reject the somewhat overpowering imagery of a woman with the style and strength of a locomotive. This is particularly true in our passage which shifts from rushing into tunnels, brakes, and "innumerable bolts" (phallic images) to what is light, aerial, and underneath. We can guess at a reversal: what is "underneath" is not "light" and "aerial" at all, but dark and earthy like the images the queen had glided past in the first stage of the poem or vaginal like the tunnels in the preceding lines. But these darknesses the speed of the train eludes and escapes. Speed throughout has been the agency of transformation (or feminizing). Thus, Spender changes the opening of our line so that we read "underneath / Goes" instead of "underneath / Is." And, thus, he chooses "elate."

The onomatopoetic "tapping" displaces the issues of gender and madness to a purely verbal level without resolving them or even seeming to. "Racing" offers a more appropriate solution, the speed that throughout has been the agent both of feminizing and transcending the earthy, black elements of the poem, but the word does not deal with the "madness" and "screaming." "Elate" does, and also provides a much more complicated continuation of the fantasy with phonemic and semantic managment of it. Semantically, we are "lifted out of" the tunnels, brakes, and bolts as by the substitution of "Goes" for "Is." "Elate" precisely states only a limited and elegant kind of frenzy, high spirits—the attributing of any kind of definable feeling mollifies the train's "madness" and "screaming," which suggest lack of limit or control. And perhaps the deletion of the *d* from "elated" does something, too, to control the feminizing of the masculine train. The emasculated word is missing a heavy, dangling end, but the word reassures us in that it means the same without its *d*. Finally, the *t*'s and other sounds of "elate metre" give some displacement to the level of pure sound —not so much as "tapping" which becomes sing-song—just enough.

In poetry no less than painting, E. H. Gombrich's maxim must hold: "making comes before matching." [10] Spender made his poem as he went along; he did not start with some Platonic "intention" for the poem which he then approximated. Rather, he began with a fantasy—here, of feminizing a phallic symbol or phallicizing a "queen"—and, in the writing, controlled and modified the original unconscious content. Given a fantasy-and-defense model, the critic can analyze his changes and the reasons for them. Whether such a model would help a writer choose among "tapping," "racing," and "elate" once inspiration has caused those three words to surface, only the writer himself can say.

The fantasy-and-defense model, however, clearly has something to tell teachers of literature. I realize that some use literature to teach morals, human nature, history, ideas, or what-have-you. If, however, we define the teacher's basic aim as enabling students to have fuller experiences of literature, then the model becomes relevant. Because it explicates the experience of literature, it enables the teacher to have some idea what his various pedagogical strategies will do.

A first glance at this model, however, suggests that there is rather little the teacher can in fact do. The psychological transformation in the work itself is fixed. The character structure the reader brings

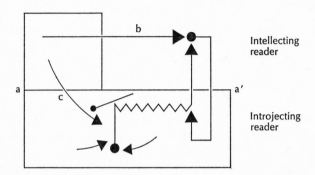

to the work is fixed. Nor can the teacher alter the analogies and associations his student brings to the work.

Conscious thinking about the work as a separate entity is marked off by line a-a' from introjecting and experiencing the work of art as part of oneself. To a large extent, a-a' is fixed by a reader's ability to be passive, but a teacher can also affect its position. If a-a' is higher, the reader is more engrossed; if a-a' is lower, it reveals a more active process of reading, one with more conscious effort. This may or may not be a good thing—even for Shakespeare and Milton, one would like to see not only intellectual response but also the kind of engrossment one feels with an "entertainment." For a very young child, one just learning to put letters together to form words, reading involves a lot of conscious effort: a-a' will be low; there will be less engrossment than when he is being read to. An older reader might experience the same putting off when he tries to read something for which his vocabulary, reading skill, or background is inadequate. Clearly, then, one thing a teacher can do is get reading skills to the point where they are automatic, be they the elementary skills or more advanced ones. If automatic, they will not interfere with the fusion and introjection that should be at least part of any literary experience.

Reading poetry calls for a special skill—one that many readers never acquire, namely, the ability to displace cathexis (or, loosely, commitment) from the fantasy level to a level of verbal play. Ultimately, this means the ability to take pleasures equal to those of fantasy gratification from the sheer play of language, the way young children enjoy nonsense rhymes like "hickory, dickory, dock." Quite possibly, only poets come by this ability naturally; for the rest of us, it is acquired and one may not be able to teach it. Nevertheless, an elementary school teacher who hopes to get his young charges to enjoy poetry in later life would do well to encourage them to play with such rhymes. For older readers, say, at the college level, I am not sure a teacher can do much more than get his students to read things like Edith Sitwell's early work, G. M. Hopkins's or Robert Bridges's metrical experiments, W. S. Gilbert's or Edward Lear's nonsense, or, at a higher quality, Byron's *Don Juan* and similar works in which sound plays an unusually strong part. Whether the teacher can do more than simply point to the verbal fireworks and say, "Have fun," I don't know. But neither do I know any other way to teach the ability to displace cathexis to a purely verbal level.

There is one point in our diagram where pedagogy clearly can affect the literary experience: line b, indicating meanings the reader supplies to supplement the transformation toward meaning embodied in the work itself. Meanings the reader supplies can be of many kinds: philosophical, political, religious, historical, psychological, and so on. Further, these meanings need not work out organic unity in any exact way, placing all the elements of the text in thematic relationships. Rather, to enhance the transformational process, these supplied meanings need only "make sense" of the text for the reader himself. It is for this reason that the teaching of literature can use so many different approaches with equal success or failure. During his college career, an English major may encounter professors who teach him to find historical significance in literary texts, "new critical" meanings, moral import, discernible textures, phenomenological space, or psychological truths. Any one of these that he finds congenial and that enables him to "make sense" of a text will enhance literary experiences for him. As Northrop Frye has said, we do not teach literature, we teach criticism, meaning, I take it, we teach students to make statements about literature. In terms of this model, we teach them to "make sense" of the text, thereby enhancing the experience of transformation, even though the "senses" may vary widely.

A given student may choose one or two of the methods he is taught, a classmate may prefer a different set, but all can serve the basic purpose equally well. For a teacher to assert that any one of these methods is erroneous or that one is essential and correct in a way that others are not is clearly absurd—at least as they apply to the enhancing of reader response to the literary transformation. All can "make sense" of a text. Of course, any one may have other claims on belief—as history, psychology, or philosophy—not, however, as anything essential to response.

Finally, there is another point at which a few teacher-critics have begun to affect the response to literature: analogizing. I am thinking of works like Bachelard's *The Poetics of Space* or *The Psychoanalysis of Fire* (quite unpsychoanalytic, despite its title), the recent writings of Norman O. Brown, and some of the insights of Northrop Frye.[11] Bachelard, for example, systematically explores the significances of different kinds of spaces in a great variety of poems: small spaces or large, spaces enclosing or unfolding, houses, seashells, and so on. To read a poem that uses space after reading Bachelard is an extraordinary experience: associations to each mention of space flood in, greatly enriching the poem. Less systematic but perhaps more effective therefore are Norman O. Brown's associations to classical myths. After hearing his "Daphne" or "Actaeon," listening to his associations, being forced to supply connections and echoes (for Brown makes a point of leaving much unsaid), one cannot ever again read a poem concerning trees or wood or horns complacently. The key terms become electric, charged with a rich aura of allusion and association. Something of the same sort goes on with Northrop Frye: startling juxtapositions of seasons and genres, science-fiction and cosmic myth, detective story and scapegoat ritual carry over into one's associations while reading.

All these critics affect their readers' response as indicated by arrow c. That is, they add materials with which we can analogize. Without attempting to change our private associations to a given literary fantasy, they give us new intellectual associations which we then preconsciously or unconsciously add to our analogizings to a given literary work, much as we use conscious knowledge ("day residue") to express unconscious wishes in dreams. Such an approach has wide implications for teaching and criticism, since heretofore teachers and critics have felt confined to b, that is, to helping their readers have thoughts about literary texts as entities separate from themselves. Bachelard and, in particular, Brown have opened up a radically new critical possibility: helping the reader precisely in his fusion with the work.

All in all, though, the possibilities for both critics and teachers to change a reader's pattern of responses are quite limited. Much the greater part of response depends on the reader's own character, which only a therapist—at best—can alter. One's whole ability to become engrossed, for example, depends on the capacity to regress and be passively receptive; one of the deepest of human traits, no pedagogy can touch it. Most teachers, I think, believe they can "improve" their students' tastes. As we have seen, though, preferences depend on character; a reader will respond "I like it" to those literary works that match his own patterns of fantasy and, particularly, defense. What a teacher may be able to do is get his student to accept more complex or exotic works within his established pattern of preferences. It seems very doubtful that he can change a characterological preference for one kind of defense or adaptation over another. Ultimately, the model insists, response depends on us, not our critics or teachers.

The teaching of literature thus inevitably raises another, more profound question: Does literature have any moral effect? Plato first raised the issue, banning poetry that would consist of untruths over-stimulating the emotions. Aristotle, supposedly, laid the issue to rest with his statement that catharsis or purgation of the emotions is healthy.* Literature has a moral effect, but it is a good one. Thus, Northrop Frye writes today: "There is no reason why a great poet should be a wise and good man, or even a tolerable human being, but there is every reason why his reader should be improved in his humanity as a result of reading him." [12] Yet, if this were true, English departments would be filled with saintly men, whereas, in fact, English departments are widely thought to be the most cantankerous of all.

To be sure, a literary work can implant an idea in us. Just as the television commercial offers a product as a solution to the psychological issue it raises, so other kinds of literary work can provide an idea or an attitude as a solution to fantasy content. Satire typically does or, as we have seen, propaganda, such as the muckraking novels or the films of World War II in which nasty Nipponese menaced blond American nurses. The films offered combat—activity—as the way to erase the passive primal scene threat. But those who claim a moral effect for literature usually imply something more than the moral effect of a newspaper editorial—some kind of deeper change in character, an improvement in a man's humanity, to use Frye's phrase. Does literature "improve" a man "in his humanity"? That would seem to be a psychological question, but, as Robert E. Lane drily remarks, "I am not aware of great attention by any of these [psychiatric] authors or by the psychotherapeutic profession to the role of literary study in the development of conscience—most of their attention is to a pre-literate period of life, or, for the theologians of course, to the influence of religion." [13] Frye is only the latest in the long tradition of critics who have put aside psychological evidence to claim a moral value for literature.

Our model suggests an explanation at least for the subjective feeling that many readers have that they have been improved in

* Instances of critical views calling for psychological backing, the appropriate passages are quoted in the Preface.

their humanity by literature. We have seen that, in introjecting the literary work, we partially regress. The work thus evokes in us a larger, deeper, richer self than the one we bring to everyday life. Moreover, within that larger self, the literary work embeds a fantasy or impulse which it—and we—then transform toward social, moral, or intellectual meaning. Transformed along with it are our own associations and analogizings to that fantasy. The condensations and displacements, both large and small, both in linguistic details and large segments of action, give us a feeling that we have mastered something—the fantasy content and our associations to it—which would ordinarily be repulsive to our egos. Literature has something in it of the saturnalia: the superego permits the ego to transgress all kinds of taboos for a limited time, then re-establishes control; and the re-establishment of control itself comes as a kind of relief and mastery.[14]

This, however, is a subjective feeling of moral mastery that comes during and after the reading of some particular work. Do these short-term effects result in a permanent change in character, an improvement in our humanity? From a purely psychological point of view, it seems highly unlikely, for we know that character is formed largely in the oedipal and pre-oedipal stages. By the time we get round to reading books, we bring to them a rather firmly structured personality. On the other hand, we have all seen adolescents become, for a month or two, Hamlet or Raskolnikov or Julien Sorel under the influence of some reading experience. In effect, there is a change of character for a period much longer than just the reading itself. But this is precisely the task of adolescence in human development: to achieve an identity separate from the family unit by trying out a variety of identities. The adolescent can just as well imitate a teacher or a peer or a movie star as a literary character. In other words, the possible character changes a particular book might evoke in an adolescent have more to do with his adolescence than the nature of the literary experience.

Nevertheless, adolescence provides a clue to the changes in character literary experiences might cause. For all of us, not just adolescents, literature lets us try on a different identity. That is, with literature, we introject an experience of fantasy and (more important, morally) defensive modes we would not ordinarily have, namely those the writer has embodied in the text. For the long moment of the work of art, we experience his character-traits as our own, especially his defenses and adaptations.

Thus, the writer becomes willy-nilly a transmitter of cultural values, for he has been shaped, as all men have, by the culture in which he matured. This book has been relatively silent about the role of culture in an individual's literary response.* My reason has been that the individual's own psychic structures make much more of a difference in response. A reader may adopt totally or totally reverse and reject the values embodied in a given writing, depending on his own character-traits, his attitudes toward authority, for example, or his sexuality or aggression. Nevertheless, culture has an effect and there is a kind of feedback loop: culture shapes the writer's character, his patterns of fantasy and defense; the reader introjects the writer's character for the time he is absorbed in the writer's writing; the reader may then modify the culture around him as a result of his literary experience. The human links in this feedback are quite unpredictable, however. The writer may radically modify the defenses or adaptations he has absorbed from his culture. The reader may change or reject the defenses and adaptations he takes in from the writer. And, of course, the motor inhibition of the aesthetic experience makes it quite problematic whether or not he will act on his culture as a result of his reading.

Even so, we can distinguish two opposite situations: where a writing closely conforms to cultural values; where it directly challenges them. Totalitarian governments, as Plato himself prescribed, have insisted their citizens get a steady diet of literature confirming the values of the state. It seems unlikely, however, that, say, the socialist realism of the Stalinist era and after played much part in brainwashing the Russian citizen. After all, the entire social and informational apparatus was engaged in this effort—art and literature

* But see pp. 209–11.

can have been only a few among a great many experiences shaping
the citizen's character toward a proper socialist state of mind. A
much more likely effect of political censorship, it seems to me, is
the elimination of literary experiences that might possibly loosen
the rigidity with which the citizen applies culturally sanctioned
patterns of defense and adaptation. Totalitarianism controls literary
response not so much to teach as to avoid unteaching.

The pithy remarks of Marshall McLuhan, however, suggest a
more accidental totalitarianism in art. The medium is the message:
that is, in our terms, television, film, radio, books—any medium,
"hot" or "cool"—gets us to introject and experience as our own the
defenses and adaptations appropriate to that medium. McLuhan
seems to be saying that sheer force of habit inculcates these defensive modes in us. A society in which all literature is in books will
necessarily embody in its citizens linear, sequential modes of
thought; the members of a television-oriented society will be more
adept at projection and regression.

McLuhan may be right—I think he is—but it is well to recognize the limitations of what he says. If the medium is the message,
then all works in that medium transmit the same message. All the
books ever written encourage only one value: linear, sequential
thought. Clearly, McLuhan is using the word "message" to mean
something radically different from the "message" conveyed by particular poems, stories, or plays, which may enact pros and cons on a
great variety of psychosocial issues. What McLuhan describes as
"the message" is a pervasive structure (or, more fashionably, infra-
structure) of the kind anthropologists like Kluckhohn or Lévi-
Strauss discover. Such a structure all aspects of a society—especially
all the technological aspects—tend to reinforce. The artistic totalitarianism McLuhan implies is no more than the tyranny of history.

The polar opposite of totalitarianism in art is the dissenting
writer in a free society. Yet here, too, one can wonder if he works
deep changes in those who read him, whether his "No! in Thun-
der" is really loud enough to muffle all the other cultural voices in

the mind of his audience. Deep in the American grain is the defensive use of phallic activity as an escape from, or pseudo-solution of, needs for dependency—this is our Puritan and revolutionary heritage; it has been called "the American neurosis." Reading Leonard Cohen or any of the other good writers currently expounding a "love ethic" with its emphasis on giving in to dependency needs seems hardly likely to overcome the older adaptation in any given reader. One in whose character the Protestant work-ethic is deeply engrained may toss aside *Beautiful Losers* in outrage and disgust. Another reader, in whom the phallic solution has failed, may embrace the gospel. But such a "conversion" comes not so much from the novel itself as from the character the reader brings to the novel. The best a writer like Cohen can hope for from a reader with "the American neurosis" is that he will loosen the rigidity with which he applies his typical defense. In short, a free literature seems not so much to teach for or against a given set of cultural values as to keep open, at least for the time of reading, the possibility of change. Like the adolescent, we try on roles.

So, at least, say a group of psychological writers we have considered before.* We have seen how the "willing suspension of disbelief," that partial, encapsulated regression, creates a richer, longer kind of self than our ordinary one. We become a "rind" of higher ego functions around a "core" regressed to the very deep, primary at-oneness with a nurturing other—the text. As a result, we respond to literature in more complex, larger ways than we can to reality. According to Marion Milner, illusions such as art and play let us relax those early established boundaries between self and not-self. We regress preparatory to future growth, taking one step backward to gain two forward. "Regressive adaptation," Heinz Hartmann calls it, "precisely because of the detour through the archaic."

Literature, these writers suggest, may have two adaptive modes: it opens up possibilities of fuller response to the text itself; perhaps it also opens up possibilities of growth once we have put the text aside. Whether growth will in fact come is questionable—unless

* See pp. 100–103.

we make the quite unwarranted assumption that a momentary loosening of boundaries during reading will carry over to other activities. And even if growth comes, it will very likely come from quite unliterary experiences. The moral effect of literature, then, is really to create not long-term change in itself, but a possibility of change. Art, in Mrs. Milner's more optimistic phrasing, "is a making of new bottles for the continually distilled new wine of developing experience." [15]

Mrs. Milner, however, goes further, suggesting that art may specifically break down in us the primal aggression from the frustrations inherent in the infant's early total dependence on a nurturing other: "this hate that is inherent in the fact that we do have to make the distinction between subject and object," "the primitive hating that results from the inescapable discrepancy between subjective and objective, between the unlimited possibilities of one's dreams and what the real world actually offers us."

> It is surely through the arts that we deliberately restore the split and bring subject and object together into a particular kind of new unity. What I had not seen clearly before was that in the arts, although a bit of the outside world is altered, distorted from its "natural" shape, to fit the inner experience, it is still a bit of the outside world, it is still paint or stone or spoken or written words or movements of bodies or sounds of instruments. It is still a bit of the outside world, but the difference is that work has been done, there has been a labour to make it nearer one's inner conception, not in the way of the practical work of the world, but in an 'as if' way. Thus it seemed that the experience of outer and inner coinciding, which we blindly undergo when we fall in love, is consciously brought about in the arts, through the conscious acceptance of the as-if-ness of the experience and the conscious manipulation of a malleable material. So surely it comes about that in the experience which we call the aesthetic one the cause of the primary hate is temporarily transcended.

She is reaching the same conclusion that the courtesy-books of the Renaissance did: art ennobles in the same way that being in love does. She, however, takes still another step:

Not only is it [the primary hate] temporarily transcended, surely also it is permanently lessened. For in the satisfying experience of embodying the illusion there has in fact been an interchange. Since the object is thereafter endowed with a bit of the "me," one can no longer see it in quite the same way as before; and since the "me," the inner experience, has become enriched with a bit more of external reality, there is now a closer relation between wishes and what can really exist and so less cause for hate, less despair of ever finding anything that satisfies.[16]

She states, in effect, that affection for works of art one has created or experienced persists, but whether this relation to certain bits of the outer world carries over to all the not-self—I wonder.

Either mode, though, seems worth encouraging, either permanent or temporary transcending of primal hate, toward particular objects or more generally. But "our whole traditional educational procedure tends to perpetuate this hate, by concentrating so much on only one half of our relation to the world, the part of it to do with intellectual knowing, the part in which subject and object have perforce to be kept separate."

Observations of problems to do with painting had all led up to the idea that awareness of the external world is itself a creative process, an immensely complex creative interchange between what comes from inside and what comes from outside, a complex alternation of fusing and separating. But since the fusing stage is, to the intellectual mind, a stage of illusion, intoxication, transfiguration, it is one that is not so easily allowed for in an age and civilisation where matter-of-factness, the keeping of oneself apart from what one looks at, has become all-important. And this fact surely has wide implications for education. For it surely means that education for a democracy, if it is to foster that true sanity which is necessary in citizens of a democracy, foster the capacity to see the facts for oneself, rather than seeing only what one is told to see, must also fully understand the stages by which such objectivity is reached. In fact, it must understand subjectivity otherwise the objectivity it aims at will be in danger of fatal distortion.[17]

Mrs. Milner's "surely's" suggest a certainty about the possibility of reducing man's primal aggression or of educating for democracy that I share only partly, at best. But I can surely agree that almost all education as we know it does far too little to nourish and understand subjectivity. Education in art and literature should seek to encourage the fusion of self and object in aesthetic experience, even though, as our model suggests, the ability to fuse stems from deep traits of character and there may be severe limts on what a teacher in a classroom can do. It is still undeniably worth a try.

In sum, literature seems to have two, in a way opposite, possibilities for moral effect. First, literature may reinforce or counter the defenses and adaptations our culture builds into us. Second, literature lets us experience those and other values in a more open, "as if" way; it breaks down—for a time—the boundaries between self and other, inner and outer, past and future, and it may neutralize the primal aggression bound up in those separations. Yet, given the firmness of cultural structures and individual character, it is very hard to see how the effects of literature can be more than small, local, and transient. All our inferences about the dynamics of literary response suggest that the experience of literature is but one experience among many to which we react, that other cultural and familial forces shape us much earlier and much more forcefully, to say nothing of our own heredity. Without experimental evidence, the best information we have suggests that we should make no claim of a long-term moral effect for literature. At most, literature may open for us some flexibility of mind so that growth from it and other kinds of experience remains possible.

A free literature makes for free men and an open society—that statement is perhaps true, perhaps only a little bit true, or, as seems most likely, it states a wish and illusion. What is not illusory is the especially deep psychic pleasure literature offers us. Having understood that pleasure somewhat, having through psychoanalysis seen its dark origins and its moral and social limitations, we need now the courage to accept literature, not for what we wish it were but for the one thing we can be certain it is—a source of rich and special pleasures, good in themselves, needing and perhaps having no further justification. In the deepest sense, to accept, understand, and enjoy literature for what it is, we must also accept, understand, and enjoy ourselves for what we are. Whatever psychoanalysis says about literature, it shows us how irreducibly human it is. As we respond, its glories become ours. As for its limitations, they have always been our own.

Notes

The following notes are for reference only. All notes that make substantive comments on the text appear as footnotes in the text itself.

I have used only one abbreviation: *The Standard Edition of the Complete Psychological Works of Sigmund Freud* (trans. by James Strachey, Anna Freud, Alix Strachey, and Alan Tyson), ed. James Strachey, 24 vols., The Hogarth Press and the Institute of Psycho-Analysis, London, 1957–   , is hereafter referred to simply as *Std. Edn.*

1 LITERATURE AS TRANSFORMATION

1. Adapted from *Playboy Magazine*, March 1964, p. 94, copyright © 1964, reprinted here by permission of the publishers, HMH Publishing Co., Inc. I am grateful to Mr. Stanley Mackenzie for calling the joke to my attention.
2. *Writers at Work: The Paris Review Interviews*, ed. Malcolm Cowley, Viking Press, New York, 1958, pp. 180–181.
3. "The Creative Writer and Day-Dreaming" (1908), *Collected Papers*, ed. Ernest Jones (trans. Joan Rivière), 5 vols., Hogarth Press and the Institute of Psycho-Analysis, London, 1956–57, IV, 183.
4. *Anatomy of Criticism: Four Essays*, Princeton University Press, Princeton, N.J., 1957, p. 158.

5. *The Aims and Methods of Scholarship in Modern Languages and Literatures,* ed. James Thorpe, Modern Language Association of America, New York, 1963, "Literary Criticism," pp. 63–65.
6. Erik H. Erikson, *Young Man Luther: A Study in Psychoanalysis and History,* W. W. Norton, New York, 1962, p. 118. See also Sigmund Freud, *Civilization and Its Discontents* (1930 [1929]), Ch. I, *Std. Edn.,* XXI, 64–73.
7. *The Works of Geoffrey Chaucer,* ed. F. N. Robinson, Houghton Mifflin Co., Boston, 1961 (2nd edn.), pp. 84–88.
8. "The Wife of Bath," *The Works of John Dryden,* ed. Sir Walter Scott, 18 vols., London, 1808, XI, 376.
9. Personal communication, 25 November 1965.
10. D. W. Robertson, Jr., *A Preface to Chaucer: Studies in Medieval Perspectives,* Princeton University Press, Princeton, 1963, pp. 317–331.
11. *Preface to Chaucer,* Ch. I.
12. Sigmund Eisner, *A Tale of Wonder: A Source Study of the Wife of Bath's Tale,* John English and Co., Wexford, Ireland, 1957, pp. 37, 38, 104, and 141. See also B. J. Whiting, "The Wife of Bath's Tale," in *Sources and Analogues of Chaucer's Canterbury Tales,* eds. W. F. Bryan and Germaine Dempster, University of Chicago Press, Chicago, 1941, pp. 223–268.
13. *Preface to Chaucer,* p. 330.

2 A DICTIONARY OF FANTASY

1. A fine contemporary statement of this developmental theory is Erik Erikson's "The Theory of Infantile Sexuality" in his *Childhood and Society,* W. W. Norton, New York, 1963 (2nd edn.), pp. 48–108. Development is related to literary works by Lilli E. Peller in "Libidinal Phases, Ego Development, and Play," *Psychoanalytic Study of the Child,* IX (1954), 178–198; see particularly the chart on p. 183.
2. Sigmund Freud, *Civilization and its Discontents* (1930 [1929]), *Std. Edn.,* XXI, 65–68.
3. Ibid.
4. Otto Fenichel, *The Psychoanalytic Theory of Neurosis,* W. W. Norton, New York, 1945, pp. 62–66. Karl Abraham, "The Influence of Oral Erotism on Character-Formation" (1924), *Selected Papers,* The International Psycho-Analytic Library, No. 13, Hogarth Press, London, 1927, pp. 393–406. Edward Glover, "Some Notes on

Oral Character Formation," *International Journal of Psycho-Analysis*, VI (1925), 131–154.

5. Karl Abraham, "Restrictions and Transformations of Scoptophilia in Psycho-Neurotics; with Remarks on Analogous Phenomena in Folk-Psychology" (1913), *Selected Papers*, pp. 169–234. Otto Fenichel, "The Scoptophilic Instinct and Identification" (1935), in *Collected Papers: First Series*, W. W. Norton, New York, 1953, pp. 373–397.

6. Edmund Bergler, *The Writer and Psychoanalysis*, Doubleday, New York, 1950.

7. The classic paper is Freud's "Character and Anal Erotism" (1908), *Std. Edn.*, IX, 167–177, greatly expanded by Karl Abraham in "Contributions to the Theory of the Anal Character" (1921), *Selected Papers*, pp. 370–392.

8. Joseph J. Michaels, *Disorders of Character*, Charles C. Thomas, Springfield, Ill., 1955, particularly Ch. VII. See also Fenichel, *Psychoanalytic Theory of Neurosis*, pp. 68–69.

9. Fenichel, *Psychoanalytic Theory of Neurosis*, pp. 74–91.

10. *Ibid.*, pp. 92–93 and 214–215.

11. Freud, "On the Sexual Theories of Children" (1908), *Std. Edn.*, IX, 205–226, particularly 220–222. See also, "From the History of an Infantile Neurosis" (1918 [1914]), *Std. Edn.*, XVII, 48–60.

12. Maxwell Gitelson, "Analytic Aphorisms," *Psychoanalytic Quarterly*, XXXVI (1967), 260–267.

13. Fenichel, *Psychoanalytic Theory of Neurosis*, pp. 98–101.

14. See Peller, "Libidinal Phases, Ego Development, and Play," and, by the same author, "Daydreams and Children's Favorite Books: Psychoanalytic Comments," *The Psychoanalytic Study of the Child*, XIV (1959), 414–433, and "Reading and Daydreams in Latency: Boy-Girl Differences," *Journal of the American Psychoanalytic Association*, VI (1958), 57–70. See also Kate Friedländer, "Children's Books and Their Function in Latency and Prepuberty," *American Imago*, III (1942), 129–150.

15. A much fuller listing of defenses occurs in Grete Bibring *et al.*, "A Study of Pregnancy (Appendix B: Glossary of Defenses)," *The Psychoanalytic Study of the Child*, XVI (1961), 62–71.

16. Freud, *Jokes and Their Relation to the Unconscious* (1905), *Std. Edn.*, VIII, particularly Ch. II.

17. Ernst Kris and Abraham Kaplan, "Aesthetic Ambiguity," in Kris, *Psychoanalytic Explorations in Art*, International Universities Press, New York, 1952, pp. 243–264.

3 THE "WILLING SUSPENSION OF DISBELIEF"

1. *Biographia Literaria* (1817), Ch. XIV, ed. J. Shawcross, 2 vols., Oxford, 1907, II, 6.
2. Irving Singer, *The Nature of Love: Plato to Luther*, Random House, New York, 1966, p. 17.
3. Tyrone Guthrie, "Is Lady Macbeth Really Walking in Her Sleep?" *The New York Times*, 28 August 1966, Section 2, pp. 1, 8.
4. Bernard Berenson, *Aesthetics and History in the Visual Arts*, Pantheon Books, New York, 1948, p. 84.
5. Gaston Bachelard, *The Poetics of Space* (trans. Marie Jolas), Orion Press, New York, 1964, p. xviii.
6. Marion Milner [Joanna Field], *On Not Being Able to Paint*, International Universities Press, New York, 1957 (2nd edn.), p. 154.
7. Siegfried Kracauer, *Theory of Film: The Redemption of Physical Reality*, Oxford University Press, New York, 1960, p. 159.
8. Gustav Janouch, *Conversations with Kafka* (trans. Goronwy Rees), Derek Verschoyle, London, 1953, p. 89.
9. *The Defense of Poesy* (1595), in *The Renaissance in England*, eds. Hyder E. Rollins and Herschel Baker, Boston, 1954, p. 617.
10. Northrop Frye, *Anatomy of Criticism: Four Essays*, Princeton University Press, Princeton, 1957, p. 345.
11. Morse Peckham, *Man's Rage for Chaos: Biology, Behavior, and the Arts*, Chilton Books, Philadelphia, 1965, pp. 68, 220, and 71.
12. Berenson, *Aesthetics and History*, p. 22.
13. Simon O. Lesser, *Fiction and the Unconscious*, Beacon Press, Boston, 1957, p. 194.
14. *Std. Edn.*, V, 565–566. See also, David Rapaport, "The Conceptual Model of Psychoanalysis," *Journal of Personality*, XX (1951), 56–81, for a systematization of these "primary" and "secondary" models of need-gratification.
15. *Std. Edn.*, V, 567.
16. Ralph J. Berger, "Tonus of Extrinsic Laryngeal Muscles during Sleep and Dreaming," *Science*, CXXXIV (1961), 840.
17. Herman A. Witkin, and Helen B. Lewis, "The Relation of Experimentally Induced Presleep Experiences to Dreams: A Report on Method and Preliminary Findings," *Journal of the American Psychoanalytic Association*, XIII (1965), 819–849.
18. Susan Isaacs, "The Nature and Function of Phantasy," in *Developments in Psycho-Analysis*, by Melanie Klein, Paula Heimann, Susan

Isaacs, and Joan Rivière, Hogarth Press, London, 1952, pp. 67–121, 109.

19. Otto Fenichel, "The Scoptophilic Instinct and Identification" (1935) in *Collected Papers of Otto Fenichel: First Series*, W. W. Norton, New York, 1953, pp. 373–397, 376. This is an extremely important paper for anyone attempting to apply psychoanalysis to literature.

20. *Civilization and Its Discontents* (1930 [1929]), *Std. Edn.*, XXI, 66–68.

21. Erik H. Erikson, *Young Man Luther: A Study in Psychoanalysis and History*, W. W. Norton, New York, 1962, p. 118.

22. Erik H. Erikson, *Childhood and Society*, W. W. Norton, New York, 1963 (2nd edn.), pp. 248–249.

23. D. S. Winnicott, "Theory of the Parent-Infant Relationship," *International Journal of Psycho-Analysis*, XLI (1960), 585–595.

24. Edmund Bergler, *The Writer and Psychoanalysis*, Doubleday, New York, 1950, Ch. III.

25. Avery D. Weisman, "Reality Sense and Reality Testing," *Behavioral Science*, III (1958), 228–261, 239.

26. Singer, *Nature of Love*, pp. 17–18.

27. Weisman, "Reality Sense and Reality Testing," p. 258.

28. Lesser, *Fiction and the Unconscious*, p. 161.

29. James R. Squire, *The Responses of Adolescents While Reading Four Short Stories*, N.C.T.E. Research Report No. 2, National Council of Teachers of English, Champaign, Ill., 1964, p. 31.

30. For this description of the analytic setting, I am relying heavily on Ida Macalpine's classic paper, "The Development of the Transference," *Psychoanalytic Quarterly*, XIX (1950), 501–537.

31. Ibid., p. 519.

32. Preface to the translation of Bernheim's *Suggestion* (1888 [1888–9]), *Std. Edn.*, I, 82.

33. Otto Fenichel, *The Psychoanalytic Theory of Neurosis*, W. W. Norton, New York, 1945, p. 561.

34. Merton M. Gill and Margaret Brenman, *Hypnosis and Related States: Psychoanalytic Studies in Regression*, International Universities Press, New York, 1961. I have quoted from pp. 98, 244, 306, and 84; this entire book, however, suggests many interesting analogies to our engrossment in literature, particularly in Chapter V, "The Metapsychology of Regression and Hypnosis," pp. 212–218.

35. Ibid., pp. 185 and 181.

36. Ibid., p. 191.
37. *The Interpretation of Dreams* (1900), *Std. Edn.*, V, 571.
38. See, for example, Bertram D. Lewin, "The Forgetting of Dreams," in *Drives, Affects, Behavior*, ed. Rudolph M. Loewenstein, International Universities Press, New York, 1953, pp. 191–201.
39. Maxwell Gitelson, "Analytic Aphorisms," *Psychoanalytic Quarterly*, XXXVI (1967), 260–270.
40. Roy M. Whitman, "Remembering and Forgetting Dreams in Psychoanalysis," *Journal of the American Psychoanalytic Association*, XI (1963), 752–774, 771.
41. Edward Bullough, " 'Psychical Distance' as a Factor in Art and an Aesthetic Principle," *British Journal of Psychology*, V (1913), 87–98.
42. Gordon Globus and Roy Shulman, "Considerations on Affective Response to Motion Pictures," unpublished report, Department of Psychiatry, Boston University School of Medicine, Boston, Mass., p. 17.
43. Ibid., pp. 18–19.
44. Weisman, "Reality Sense and Reality Testing," pp. 247–248.
45. Marion Milner, "The Role of Illusion in Symbol Formation," in *New Directions in Psycho-Analysis: The Significance of Infant Conflict in the Pattern of Adult Behavior*, eds. Melanie Klein, Paula Heimann, and R. E. Money-Kyrle, Basic Books, New York, 1957, pp. 82–108, 98.
46. Ibid., pp. 101–102.
47. Heinz Hartmann, *Ego Psychology and the Problem of Adaptation* (1937) (trans. David Rapaport), International Universities Press, New York, 1958, pp. 77–78.
48. Erikson, *Childhood and Society*, p. 222.

4   FORM AS DEFENSE

1. John Crowe Ransom, *The World's Body*, Scribner's, New York, 1938, pp. 301–302.
2. See "Glossary of Defenses" in Grete Bibring *et al.*, "A Study of Pregnancy," *The Psychoanalytic Study of the Child*, XVI (1961), 62–71.
3. Sigmund Freud, "On the Sexual Theories of Children" (1908), *Std. Edn.*, IX, 205–226, particularly 220–222.
4. Lascelles Abercrombie, *The Idea of Great Poetry*, Martin Secker, London, 1925, pp. 177–178.

5. Hardin Craig, *An Interpretation of Shakespeare*, Dryden Press, New York, 1948, p. 265.
6. Mark Van Doren, *Shakespeare*, Doubleday-Anchor Books, Garden City, N.Y., 1953, p. 227.
7. Elder Olson, *Tragedy and the Theory of Drama*, Wayne State University Press, Detroit, 1961, pp. 117–118.
8. My text comes from *The Poetical Works of Matthew Arnold*, eds. C. B. Tinker and H. F. Lowry, Oxford University Press, Oxford, 1950.
9. C. B. Tinker, and H. F. Lowry, *The Poetry of Matthew Arnold: A Commentary*, Oxford University Press, London, 1940, pp. 173–178.
10. Paull F. Baum, *Ten Studies in the Poetry of Matthew Arnold*, Duke University Press, Durham, N.C., 1958, pp. 85–97; Louis Bonnerot, *Matthew Arnold, Poète: Essai de Biographie Psychologique*, Imprimerie F. Paillart, Paris, 1947, p. 203; *The Case for Poetry*, eds. Frederick L. Gwynn, Ralph W. Condee, and Arthur O. Lewis, Jr., Prentice-Hall, Englewood Cliffs, N.J., 1954, pp. 17, 19, and "Teacher's Manual," pp. 14–15; Rodney Delasanta, *The Explicator*, XVIII (October, 1959), 7; Elizabeth Drew, *Poetry: A Modern Guide to Its Understanding and Enjoyment*, W. W. Norton, New York, 1959, pp. 221–223; Gerhard Friedrich, "A Teaching Approach to Poetry," *English Journal*, XLIX (February, 1960), 75–81; Frederick L. Gwynn, *The Explicator*, VIII (April, 1960), 46; Wendell Stacy Johnson, "Matthew Arnold's Dialogue," *University of Kansas City Review*, XXVII (Winter, 1960), 109–116; Wendell Stacy Johnson, *The Voices of Matthew Arnold: An Essay in Criticism*, Yale University Press, New Haven, 1961, pp. 90–94; J. D. Jump, *Matthew Arnold*, Longmans, Green, London, 1955, pp. 67–68 and 81; J. P. Kirby, *The Explicator*, I (April, 1943), 42; Murray Krieger, " 'Dover Beach' and the Tragic Sense of Eternal Recurrence," *University of Kansas City Review*, XXIII (Autumn, 1956), 73–79; Gene Montague, "Arnold's *Dover Beach* and *The Scholar Gypsy*," *The Explicator*, XVIII (November, 1959), 15; Frederick A. Pottle, *The Explicator*, II (April, 1944), 45; Norman C. Stageberg, *The Explicator*, IX (March, 1951), 34; C. B. Tinker and H. F. Lowry, *The Poetry of Matthew Arnold: A Commentary*, Oxford University Press, London, 1940, pp. 173–178.

I do not know of any psychoanalytic explications except Professor Morrison's, referred to in note 13.

11. Otto Fenichel, "The Scoptophilic Instinct and Indentification" (1935), *Collected Papers: First Series*, W. W. Norton, New York, 1953, pp. 373–397, especially sec. III.
12. Tinker and Lowry, *Matthew Arnold: Commentary*.
13. Theodore Morrison, "Dover Beach Revisited: A New Fable for Critics," *Harper's Magazine*, CLXXX (Feb., 1940), 235–244, 240–241. Professor Morrison offers his insight in the whimsical spirit of a *Pooh Perplex*, but it seems to me sound nevertheless. This essay contains the only other psychoanalytic explication of the poem I know.
14. *New Poets of England and America: Second Selection*, eds. Donald Hall and Robert Pack, Meridian Books, Cleveland and New York, 1962, p. 230.
15. Note 10 gives full citations for the commentators referred to.

5 THE DISPLACEMENT TO LANGUAGE

1. Noam Chomsky, "Some Methodological Remarks on Generative Grammar," *Word*, XVII (1961), 219–239; reprinted as "Degrees of Grammaticalness" in *The Structure of Language; Readings in the Philosophy of Language*, eds. Jerry A. Fodor and Jerrold J. Katz, Prentice-Hall, Inc., Englewood Cliffs, N.J., 1964, pp. 384–389. See also, in the same collection, Jerrold J. Katz, "Semi-sentences," pp. 400–416.
2. *The Idler*, Nos. 60, 61 (1759); reprinted in *Selections from Samuel Johnson, 1709–1784*, ed. R. W. Chapman, Oxford University Press, London, 1955, pp. 220–224.
3. "The Life of Pope," in *Lives of the English Poets* (1777), 2 vols., Everyman Library, London, 1925, II, 219.
4. *Anatomy of Criticism: Four Essays*, Princeton University Press, Princeton, N.J., 1957, p. 258.
5. Morse Peckham, *Man's Rage for Chaos: Biology, Behavior, and the Arts*, Chilton Books, Philadelphia, 1965, p. 140.
6. *Anatomy of Criticism*, p. 251. The possibility of a transformational model is developed by Morris Halle and Samuel Jay Kayser, "Chaucer and the Study of Prosody," *College English*, XXVIII (1966), 187–219.
7. *Man's Rage for Chaos*, p. 254.
8. Morse Peckham, "Art and Disorder," *Literature and Psychology*, XVI (Spring, 1966), No. 2, 62–80, 77.
9. *Man's Rage for Chaos*, p. 220.

10. Ibid., p. 199.
11. Simon O. Lesser, *Fiction and the Unconscious*, Beacon Press, Boston, 1957, pp. 210-11n. See also my "Psychoanalytic Criticism and Perceptual Psychology" (an article-review of Peckham's book), *Literature and Psychology*, XVI, Spring, 1966, 81–92.
12. Matthew Arnold, "The Function of Criticism Today," in *Lectures and Essays in Criticism*, ed. R. H. Super, University of Michigan Press, Ann Arbor, 1962, III, 269-70. I have repunctuated the passage slightly to indicate syntactic breaks more clearly.
13. In general, in discussing this passage, I am relying heavily and with much gratitude on personal consultations with Professor Ohmann as well as on his essays: "Methods in the Study of Victorian Style," *Victorian Newsletter*, No. 27 (Spring, 1965), pp. 1–4; "Generative Grammars and the Concept of Literary Style," *Word* (December, 1964), XX, 423–439; "Literature as Sentences," *College English*, XXVII (January, 1966), 261–267; "A Linguistic Appraisal of Victorian Style," *Victorian Prose as Art*, eds. George Levine and William A. Madden, Oxford University Press, New York, 1968.
14. See my own essay, "Prose and Minds: A Psychoanalytic Approach to Non-Fiction," *Victorian Prose as Art*, eds. George Levine and William A. Madden, Oxford University Press, New York, 1968.
15. W. H. Auden, "Byron: The Making of a Comic Poet," *The New York Review of Books*, VII (August 18, 1966), No. 3, 12–18, 16–17.

6 MEANING AS DEFENSE

1. Arthur Schlesinger, Jr., "When the Movies Really Counted," *Show*, III, No. 4 (April, 1963), 125.
2. Marshall McLuhan, quoted in *The New York Times*, 19 March 1967, Section 2, p. 1.
3. Leslie A. Fiedler, "A Night with Mr. Teas," *Show*, I, No. 1 (October, 1961), 118–119.
4. Sigmund Freud, "On the Sexual Theories of Children" (1908), *Std. Edn.*, IX, 205–226, particularly 220–222.
5. See, for example, Joseph Bennett, "The Essences of Being," *Hudson Review*, XIV (1961), 432–436; or, in general, Ian Cameron, "Michelangelo Antonioni," *Film Quarterly*, XVI, No. 1 (Fall, 1962), Special Issue, 1–58, particularly 37–58.
6. Martha Wolfenstein and Nathan Leites, *Movies: A Psychological Study*, Free Press, Glencoe, Ill., 1950, p. 289.

7. I am taking Brecht's and Ionesco's statements about their theory and practice from *Brecht on Theatre*, ed. and trans. John Willett, Hill and Wang, New York, 1964, and Eugène Ionesco, *Notes and Counter Notes*, Grove Press, New York, 1964.

8. Ernst Kris, "On Preconscious Mental Processes," *Psychoanalytic Explorations in Art*, International Universities Press, New York, 1952, p. 310.

9. Simon O. Lesser, *Fiction and the Unconscious*, Beacon Press, Boston, 1957, pp. 203–204 and 242–247.

10. Elizabeth R. Zetzel, "The Theory of Therapy in Relation to a Developmental Model of the Psychic Apparatus," *International Journal of Psycho-Analysis*, XLVI (1965), 39–52, particularly Figs. 1 and 2.

11. Erik H. Erikson, "Toys and Reasons," in *Childhood and Society*, W. W. Norton, New York, 1963 (2nd edn.), pp. 209–246.

12. T. S. Eliot, "The Metaphysical Poets, *Selected Essays*, Harcourt, Brace, and Co., New York, 1950 (2nd edn.), p. 247.

13. "Creative Writers and Day-Dreaming" (1908 [1907]), *Collected Papers*, trans. and ed. Joan Rivière, 5 vols., Hogarth Press, London, 1924–1950, IV, 183.

14. Kris, "On Preconscious Mental Processes," p. 63.

15. Lesser, *Fiction and the Unconscious*, generally.

7 EVALUATION

1. The best exposition I know of Moore's argument as it applies to literary evaluation occurs in Monroe Beardsley's *Aesthetics*, Harcourt, Brace, New York, 1958, Ch. X, "Critical Evaluation" and Ch. XI, "Aesthetic Value."

2. Edmund Wilson, "The Historical Interpretation of Literature" (1941), reprinted in *Modern Criticism: Theory and Practice*, eds. Walter Sutton and Richard Foster, Odyssey Press, New York, 1963, pp. 234–242, 240.

3. *Civilization and Its Discontents* (1930 [1929]), *Std. Edn.*, XXI, 145.

4. Margaret Macdonald, "Some Distinctive Features of Arguments Used in Criticism of the Arts," reprinted in *Problems in Aesthetics*, ed. Morris Weitz, Macmillan, New York, 1959, pp. 683–696, 696.

5. Irving Singer, *The Nature of Love: Plato to Luther*, Random House, New York, 1966, pp. 3–6.

6. T. S. Eliot, "The Perfect Critic," in *The Sacred Wood*, London, 1928, p. 11.

7. T. S. Eliot, "The Frontiers of Criticism" (1956) in *On Poetry and Poets*, Farrar, Straus, and Cudahy, New York, 1957, pp. 113–131, 131.

8. Robert E. Lane, *The Liberties of Wit: Humanism, Criticism, and the Civic Mind*, Yale University Press, New Haven and London, 1961, p. 73.

9. Northrop Frye, "Literary Criticism" in *The Aims and Methods of Scholarship in Modern Languages and Literatures*, ed. James Thorpe, The Modern Language Association of America, New York, 1963, pp. 57–69, 58–59.

10. My text is taken from *The Poems of Richard Lovelace*, ed. C. H. Wilkinson, Oxford University Press, Oxford, 1930. The line indicated by the superscript is, in the 1649 edition, "Thou prov'st the pleasant she." The line as I have given it makes better grammar and more sense—Wilkinson admits this reading as "a possibility."

11. Professor Beardsley criticizes this "affective" statement of the problem from a number of points of view. See Beardsley, *Aesthetics*, Chapters X and XI.

12. Erik H. Erikson, *Childhood and Society*, W. W. Norton, New York, 1950, pp. 185–195, referring to Freud, "Beyond the Pleasure Principle" (1920), *Std. Edn.*, XVIII, 14–17. See also Freud, "Creative Writers and Day-Dreaming" (1908), *Std. Edn.*, IX, 143–153.

13. Freud, "A Special Type of Choice of Object Made by Man" (1910) and "On the Universal Tendency to Debasement in the Sphere of Love" (1912), (Contributions to the Psychology of Love I and II), *Std. Edn.*, XI, 163–190. I am referring particularly to pp. 166–168, 169, 187–188, 190.

14. Norman Holmes Pearson, *The Explicator*, VII (June, 1949), 58. In the explication of "To Lucasta," I have also drawn on: Mark Van Doren, *Introduction to Poetry*, William Sloane Associates, New York, 1951, pp. 21–26; John Ciardi, *How Does a Poem Mean*, Houghton-Mifflin Co., Boston, 1960, pp. 929–934; Richard R. Kirk and Roger P. Mc.Cutcheon, *An Introduction to the Study of Poetry*, American Book Co., New York, 1934, pp. 12–14; George F. Jones, "Lov'd I not Honour More: The Durability of a Literary Motif," *Comparative Literature*, XI (1959), 131–143.

15. Pearson, *The Explicator*, 58.

16. Scenario by Federico Fellini, Tullio Pinelli, Ennio Flaiano, and Brunello Rondi. Directed by Sr. Fellini; produced by Guiseppe Amato; released in this country by Astor Films. Marcello Rubino is finely played by Marcello Mastroianni, and his photographer-

sidekick by Walter Santesso. In addition to the actors identified in the text, the men are: Steiner—Alain Cuny; Marcello's father—Annibale Ninchi. The women are: Emma—Yvonne Furneaux; Maddalena—Anouk Aimee; the nightclub chorine—Megali Noel.
17. 8½. Screenplay by Federico Fellini, Tullio Pinelli, Ennio Flaiano, and Brunello Rondi. Music by Nino Rota. Directed by Sr. Fellini and produced by Angelo Rizzoli.
18. Dwight Macdonald, "Films," *Esquire* (January 1964).

8. STYLE AND THE MAN

1. Otto Fenichel, *The Psychoanalytic Theory of Neurosis*, W. W. Norton, New York, 1945, p. 467.
2. In my coments on *The Secret Agent*, I am drawing in a general wav upon a great many studies of Conrad, but most notably Albert Guerard's discussion of the ironic "voice" in this novel in his superb *Conrad the Novelist*, Harvard University Press, Cambridge, Mass., 1958.
3. My references are to page numbers in *The Secret Agent: A Simple Tale*, Doubleday-Anchor Books, Garden City, N.Y., 1953.
4. Claire Rosenfield, *Paradise of Snakes: An Archetypal Analysis of Conrad's Political Novels*, University of Chicago Press, Chicago and London, 1967, Ch. III.
5. Ibid., Ch. IV, pp. 166–168.
6. Marion Milner [Joanna Field], *On Not Being Able to Paint*, International Universities Press, Inc., New York, 1957 (2nd edn.), pp. 150–151.
7. For a further discussion of the types of inference involved in reading from a writer's texts to his life, see my *Psychoanalysis and Shakespeare*, McGraw-Hill, New York, 1966, p. 141n.
8. Bernard C. Meyer, *Joseph Conrad: A Psychoanalytic Biography*, Princeton University Press, Princeton, N.J., 1967, pp. 69, 60, 33–34, 8, and 10. Dr. Meyer's study appeared, partially, in article form in the *Journal of the American Psychoanalytic Association* after I had formulated for myself the ideas in this chapter. Dr. Meyer probes Conrad's mind primarily from biographical data and secondarily from the works—the opposite direction from this study of Conrad's style. Nevertheless, we arrive at the same "myth" for Conrad, though Dr. Meyer shows many more of its particular ramifications in Conrad's life; particularly interesting and persuasive is his explanation of the failure of Conrad's creativity after 1910.

9   MYTH

1. C. L. Barber, "From Ritual to Comedy: An Examination of *Henry IV*," *English Stage Comedy*, ed. W. K. Wimsatt, Jr., English Institute Essays, Columbia University Press, New York, 1955, p. 50.
2. Sherman Hawkins, "Mutabilitie and the Cycle of the Months," *Form and Convention in the Poetry of Edmund Spenser*, ed. William Nelson, Columbia University Press, New York, 1961, p. 93.
3. *Civilization and Its Discontents* (1930 [1929]), Ch. I, *Std. Edn.*, XXI, 64–73.
4. My quotations are from the Penguin edition, Penguin Books, Baltimore, 1952.
5. Richard Ohmann, *Shaw: The Style and the Man*, Wesleyan University Press, Middletown, 1962, p. 153.
6. J. I. M. Stewart, *Character and Motive in Shakespeare*, Longmans, Green, London, 1949, pp. 132–139. Philip Williams, "The Birth and Death of Falstaff Reconsidered," *Shakespeare Quarterly*, VIII (1957), 359–365. My quotations are from the Signet Classic edition, ed. Norman N. Holland, New American Library, New York, 1965; the Introduction provides a longer study of the play developing further the interpretation suggested here.
7. My quotations are from the Pelican edition, Penguin Books, ed. Ralph M. Sargent, Baltimore, 1959.
8. See the film but, if necessary, *Four Screenplays of Ingmar Bergman* (trans. Lars Malmstrom and David Kushner), Simon and Schuster, New York, 1960, pp. 1–94.
9. My text is from *The Portable D. H. Lawrence*, ed. Diana Trilling, Viking Press, New York, 1947, pp. 147–166.
10. W. D. Snodgrass, "A Rocking-Horse: The Symbol, the Pattern, the Way to Live," *Hudson Review*, XI (1958), 191–200.
11. Claire Rosenfield, *Paradise of Snakes: An Archetypal Analysis of Conrad's Political Novels*, University of Chicago Press, Chicago and London, 1967, Ch. III. As in Ch. 8, my text is the Anchor edition.

10   CHARACTER AND IDENTIFICATION

1. Maxwell Gitelson, "Analytic Aphorisms," *Psychoanalytic Quarterly*, XXXVI (1967), 260–270, 266.

2. Freud, *New Introductory Lectures on Psycho-Analysis* (1933 [1932]), Lecture XXXI, *Std. Edn.*, XXII, 63.

3. Margaret Cavendish, Marchioness of Newcastle, *Sociable Letters* (1664), Letter CXXIII, in *Shakespeare Criticism: A Selection*, ed. D. Nichol Smith, Oxford University Press, London, 1916, p. 14.

4. "Preface to Shakespeare" (1765) in *Samuel Johnson on Shakespeare*, ed. W. K. Wimsatt, Jr., Hill and Wang, New York, 1960, p. 27.

5. *An Essay on the Dramatic Character of Sir John Falstaff* (1777) in Smith, *Shakespeare Criticism*, pp. 171–172.

6. Review of William Hazlitt, *The Characters of Shakespeare* (Wiley and Putnam's Library of Choice Reading, No. XVII) in *Broadway Journal*, 16 August 1845. *The Complete Works of Edgar Allan Poe*, ed. James A. Harrison, 17 vols., George D. Sproul, New York, 1902, XII, 225.

7. *Explorations*, Chatto and Windus, London, 1951, pp. 16–17 and 4.

8. G. Wilson Knight, *The Wheel of Fire*, Oxford University Press, London, 1930, p. 16.

9. Kenneth Muir, "The Jealousy of Iago," *English Miscellany II*, Rome, 1951, pp. 65–83, 67.

10. Kenneth Burke, "Othello: An Essay To Illustrate a Method," *Hudson Review*, IV (1951–52), 187–188.

11. Edmund Wilson, "J. Dover Wilson on Falstaff" in *Classics and Commercials*, Farrar, Straus and Company, New York, 1951, pp. 162–163.

12. F. R. Leavis, Introduction to *Towards Standards of Criticism*, reprinted in *The Importance of Scrutiny*, ed. Eric Bentley, Grove Press, New York, 1948, p. 401.

13. Northrop Frye, *The Well-Tempered Critic*, Indiana University Press, Bloomington, 1963, pp. 148–149.

14. My quotations are from the Pelican edition, ed. John E. Hankins, Penguin Books, Baltimore, 1960.

15. Harley Granville-Barker, *Prefaces to Shakespeare*, 2 vols., Princeton University Press, Princeton, 1947, II, 337.

16. Fritz Heider and Marianne Simmel, "An Experimental Study of Apparent Behavior," *American Journal of Psychology*, LVII (1944), 243–259.

17. Marcel Proust, *Remembrance of Things Past* (trans. C. K. Scott Moncrieff and Frederick A. Blossom), 2 vols., Random House, New York, 1927–1932, II, 1024.

18. Johnson, "Preface to Shakespeare," p. 39.

19. William Hazlitt, "Hamlet" in *Characters of Shakespear's Plays* (1817), ed. Catherine M. Maclean, J. M. Dent and Sons, London, 1960, p. 232.

20. Harry Levin, "Form and Formality in *Romeo and Juliet*," *Shakespeare Quarterly*, XI (1960), 3–11. See also my *The Shakespearean Imagination*, Macmillan, New York, 1964, pp. 72–84.

21. *Std. Edn.*, XVIII, 107–108.

22. See *Std. Edn.*, XXII, 63.

23. Edith Buxbaum, "The Role of Detective Stories in a Child Analysis," *Psychoanalytic Quarterly*, X (1941), 373–381. Fenichel states, "The typical neurotic symptom expresses drive and defense simultaneously," *The Psychoanalytic Theory of Neurosis*, W. W. Norton, New York, 1945, p. 193. See also Freud, "Splitting of the Ego in the Process of Defence" (1940 [1938]), *Std. Edn.*, XXIII, 273–277.

11 AFFECT

1. Franz Alexander, *et al.*, "Experimental Studies of Emotional Stress: I. Hyperthyroidism," *Psychosomatic Medicine*, XXIII (1961), 104–114.

2. Sigmund Freud, *Civilization and Its Discontents* (1930), Ch. I, *Std. Edn.*, XXI, 65.

3. Gordon Globus and Roy Shulman, "Considerations on Affective Response to Motion Pictures," unpublished report, Department of Psychiatry, Boston University School of Medicine, Boston, Mass. See the discussion above, pp. 94–96.

4. Sigmund Freud, "The 'Uncanny' " (1919), *Std. Edn.*, XVII, 217–252, especially 247–252.

5. Sigmund Freud, *Jokes and their Relation to the Unconscious* (1905), *Std. Edn.*, VIII. See also Theodore Reik, *Psychology of Sex Relations*, Farrar and Rinehart, New York, 1945, p. 141, for a discussion of the factor of suddenness.

6. Harold G. Henderson, *An Introduction to Haiku*, Doubleday-Anchor, Garden City, N.Y., 1958, pp. 3–4.

7. Sigmund Freud, "Humour" (1927), *Std. Edn.*, XXI, 161–2; Bertram D. Lewin, *The Psychoanalysis of Elation*, W. W. Norton, New York, 1950.

8. Edward Young, *Night Thoughts* (1742–1745), "Night V," *Complete Works*, ed. J. Mitford, Houghton Mifflin, Boston, n.d., pp. 91–93.

9. Leonard Berkowitz, "The Effects of Observing Violence," *Scientific American*, CCX (1964), 35–41, with bibliography at p. 152.

10. J. D. Jump, *Matthew Arnold*, Longmans, Green, London, 1955, p. 81.

11. Franz Alexander, *Fundamentals of Psychoanalysis*, W. W. Norton, New York, 1963, pp. 185–186 and 190.

12. Freud, "The 'Uncanny,' " p. 251.

13. Aristotle, *Poetics*, Ch. IV (trans. W. D. Ross) in *Introduction to Aristotle*, ed. Richard McKeon, Modern Library, New York, 1947, p. 627.

14. Matthew Arnold, Preface to *Poems* (1853), *The Portable Matthew Arnold*, ed. Lionel Trilling, Viking Press, New York, 1949, p. 187.

15. Sigmund Freud, "The Unconscious" (1915), sec. III, *Std. Edn.*, XIV, 179n.

16. David Rapaport, "On the Psychoanalytic Theory of Affects," *Psychoanalytic Psychiatry and Psychology, Clinical and Theoretical Papers*, Austen Riggs Center, Vol. I, International Universities Press, New York, 1954, pp. 274–310, especially 307. See also Otto Fenichel, *The Psychoanalytic Theory of Neurosis*, W. W. Norton, New York, 1945, p. 164.

17. Charles Dickens, *The Posthumous Papers of the Pickwick Club*, The Modern Library, New York, n.d., Ch. XXI, pp. 287–289. I have re-paragraphed the passage to make it easier to read as a separate story.

12   THE MODEL MORALIZED

1. I. A. Richards, *Practical Criticism*, Harcourt, Brace, and Co., New York, 1951, p. 8.

2. Angus Fletcher, *Allegory: The Theory of a Symbolic Mode*, Cornell University Press, Ithaca, N.Y., 1964, especially Ch. VI.

3. Norman N. Holland, *Psychoanalysis and Shakespeare*, McGraw-Hill, New York, 1966, p. 339.

4. Robert E. Lane, *The Liberties of Wit: Humanism, Criticism, and the Civic Mind*, Yale University Press, New Haven and London, 1961.

5. *Freshman English Review*, Vol. I, No. 4, January 1967 (mimeographed publication of the Department of English, State University of New York at Buffalo).

6. Ken Kesey, *One Flew Over the Cuckoo's Nest*, Viking Press, New York, 1964, pp. 155–157.

7. *Std. Edn.*, XVII, 30.
8. Lucian W. Pye, "The Dynamics of Hostility and Hate in Chinese Political Culture," Center for International Studies, Massachusetts Institute of Technology, Cambridge, Mass., June 1964.
9. Karl Shapiro, "The Meaning of the Discarded Poem," in *Poets at Work*, ed. Charles D. Abbott, Harcourt, Brace, and Co., 1948, pp. 83–121—I am quoting from pp. 95–100. Six drafts of "The Express" occur in Spender's workbook in the Lockwood Collection, State University of New York at Buffalo. I have occasionally combined alterations from two drafts to make comparison easier. The finished poem is reprinted in many anthologies—one reason for my choosing it to discuss.
10. E. H. Gombrich, *Art and Illusion*, Bollingen Series xxxv.5, Pantheon Books, New York, 1960, p. 116.
11. Gaston Bachelard, *The Poetics of Space* (1958) (trans. Marie Jolas), The Orion Press, New York, 1964; *The Psychoanalysis of Fire* (trans. Alan C. Ross), Beacon Press, Boston, 1964. I have heard Professor Brown give these two essays publicly; at the time of writing they are not yet in print. Northrop Frye, *Anatomy of Criticism: Four Essays*, Princeton University Press, Princeton, 1957.
12. Frye, *Anatomy of Criticism*, p. 344.
13. Lane, *Liberties of Wit*, p. 113.
14. Simon O. Lesser discusses this point at length in *Fiction and the Unconscious*, Beacon Press, Boston, 1957, Ch. V.
15. Marion Milner [Joanna Field], *On Not Being Able to Paint*, International Universities Press, New York, 1957 (2nd edn.), p. 132.
16. Ibid., pp. 68 and 131–132.
17. Ibid., pp. 68 and 146–147.

Glossary

This glossary provides definitions only for those psychoanalytic terms of importance in this book. For other psychoanalytic terms, the reader should consult Otto Fenichel's *The Psychoanalytic Theory of Neurosis*, New York, W. W. Norton and Co., 1945.

Affect. The subjective experience of emotion, in contrast to its behavioral signs.

Aggressive drive. A drive (*q.v.*) to destroy or eliminate.

Cathect. Cathexis. (German: *besetzen, Besetzung*) The act of attaching mental energy (libidinal or aggressive) to structures, processes, or objects in the mind like an electric charge.

Condensation. The representation in a single image, word, thought, symptom, or act of several unconscious wishes or objects.

Defense. Defense mechanism. An organized reaction of the ego automatically and unconsciously applied after a signal of inner or outer danger, typically, anxiety or guilt associated with forbidden wishes.

Denial. A defense mechanism (*q.v.*) which excludes from consciousness perceptions of outer reality. Cf. *Repression.*

Displacement. The shift of mental energy from one entity in the mind to another.

Drive. (Sometimes the term *Instinctual drive* is used.) A demand of the body upon mental life, as contrasted with the demands of external reality. A drive comprises a source (a state of excitation within the body), an aim (satisfaction, which is to remove the excitation), and an object (the means by which the drive can achieve its aim). All actual drives combine libidinal (*q.v.*) and aggressive (*q.v.*) components.

Ego. An organized portion of the total personality, derived from the id (*q.v.*) under the pressures of external reality, and having conscious, preconscious, and unconscious sectors. Its primary function is the synthesizing and unifying of man's responses to the demands of inner and outer reality. Thus, the ego is the repository of consciousness, judgment, intelligence, affects (*q.v.*), perception, motor control, defense mechanisms (*q.v.*), and identifications (*q.v.*) with early objects.

Ego-syntonic. In conformity with the demands of the ego.

Fantasy. "Thinking not followed by action" (Fenichel); it may be creative or simple daydreaming. In this book, the word is associated more with the imagined fullfillment of wishes that cannot be fulfilled than with creative planning for action. Fantasies, in American usage, may be conscious or unconscious. Cf. *Wish.* A fantasy usually combines several wishes.

Father-figure. See *Parent-figure.*

Fusion. In this book, becoming one with an object of drive-gratification.

Id. A theoretical construct—an unstructured "reservoir" in the mind containing the primitive, unmediated drives (*q.v.*) pressing for immediate gratification; thus, the source of mental energy. The id can be known only by inference from primitive operations of the ego (*q.v.*).

Identification. Introjection (*q.v.*) of another person with an alteration of the subject's ego to imitate the person identified with. A primitive and early way of dealing with others, identification is a developmental precursor of object choice. Object choice is to *have* the other; identification is to *be* the other. The three modes of internalizing (incorporation, introjection, and identification—*qq.v.*) form a developmental continuum, incorporation being the most primitive.

Incorporation. Physically taking an object (*q.v.*) into one's body, typically, by eating or inhaling it. Fantasies of incorporation are particularly common in early infancy. Cf. *Identification.*

Instinct. Used by Freud's early English translators to render his "*Trieb.*" Drive (*q.v.*) would have been more accurate. "Instinctual drive" is often used today.

Instinctual drive. See *Drive.*

Introjection. Mentally taking an object (*q.v.*) into one's mind, often with the fantasy that it has been physically incorporated through eyes, ears, nose, mouth, or skin. Cf. *Identification, Incorporation.*

Isolation. A defense mechanism (*q.v.*) in which the ego cuts an idea or fantasy off from affects or other thoughts that would ordinarily be associated with it.

Klang associations. Associations based on similarities of sound, e.g. "A wise soldier cares more for bottles than battles." German *Klang* = sound.

Latency. A developmental phase between the repression of the oedipus complex and the onset of puberty, characterized by a lessening of genital drives.

Libidinal drive. A drive (*q.v.*) "to establish ever greater unities" (Freud), to unite with and preserve some object. Cf. *Aggressive drive.*

Libido. Mental energy associated with libidinal drives.

Mania. A psychosis characterized by lack of restraint, heightened and excited mental and physical activity, often alternating (in manic-depressive psychosis) with periods of depression.

Mother-figure. See *Parent-figure.*

Motor inhibition. Limitation by the ego of muscular actions—it may be normal or pathological.

Narcissism. Libidinal attachment to the self, normally present at all stages of development, but mixed with object-love, except in earliest infancy ("primary narcissism").

Object. A means external to the self of gratifying a drive (*q.v.*), usually but not always another person.

Onanism. Masturbation.

Oral frustration. The non-gratification of oral drives, typically leading to massive infantile reactions of aggression.

Orality. The cluster of drives (*q.v.*) associated with the lips, mouth, tongue, and nostrils, with eating, drinking, or breathing, or, in general, with the fondling, warmth, and total environment of maternal nurturing in the early months of life.

Parent-figure. A person toward whom the subject has the emotions and attitudes appropriate to a parent.

Primal aggression. In this book, massive reactions of aggression (*q.v.*) resulting from oral frustrations (*q.v.*) inherent in the newborn child's total dependency.

Primary-process thinking. Irrational and unrealistic thought processes like those in dreams or psychoses. Ideas are associated without regard to logic, consistency, contrariety, or the limitations of space and time, usually by pictures rather than words (though words may be linked as puns or by sound—see *Klang associations*), with much use of condensation (*q.v.*), displacement (*q.v.*), and symbolization. Cf. *Secondary-process thinking*.

Projection. The perception of an inner reality as though it were outside the self, typically, attributing one's own wishes, traits, or ideals to another. Usually, but not always, a defense mechanism (*q.v.*).

Psychopath. A personality type marked by a lack of conscience (defective superego) and an inability to think conceptually and to delay.

Reaction-formation. A defense mechanism (*q.v.*) that usually becomes a permanent alteration of character in which the ego turns the *aim* of a drive (*q.v.*) into its opposite, for example, when impulses to mess become an obsessive concern with cleanliness. Cf. *Reversal*.

Regression. Displacement of the aim or object of a drive (*q.v.*) to one that would normally occur earlier in development, for example, from a mature, loving relationship with another person to a childish dependency. Regression can be pathological, a defense mechanism, normal behavior (as in dreaming), or a prelude to new, creative adaptations ("regression in the service of the ego").

Repression. A defense mechanism (*q.v.*) which excludes from consciousness inner realities—wishes, fantasies, memories, or affects. Cf. *Denial*.

Reversal. A defense mechanism (*q.v.*) in which the ego turns the *object* of a drive (*q.v.*) into its opposite, often taking the self as object instead of another person or turning a passive position into an active one. Cf. *Reaction-formation*.

Scoptophilia. Pleasure in looking, especially at genitalia.

Secondary-process thinking. Rational and realistic thought processes like those used in problem-solving. A function of the conscious ego (*q.v.*). Cf. *Primary-process thinking*.

Self-object differentiation. That stage in development at which the infant ceases to regard his own ego as including everything and recognizes the external world, typically the nurturing parent, as separate (an "object" as against a "subject"). Usually, self-object differentiation occurs around the eighth month of life.

Sexuality. In psychoanalytic usage, behavior to obtain pleasure from any particular zone of the body (hence, "oral sexuality," anal, phallic, etc.); the "sexuality" of ordinary speech is referred to as "genital sexuality." Cf. *Libidinal drive.*

Splitting. Dividing the aim or object of a drive (*q.v.*) into two or more aims or objects.

Sublimation. The "normal" defense mechanism (*q.v.*) in which the subject's ego alters the aim of a drive (*q.v.*) to make it acceptable to the ego (also, usually, acceptable to society), for example, the transformation of infantile sexual curiosity into scientific research.

Superego. An organized portion of the total personality, largely but not wholly unconscious, derived from the ego (*q.v.*) through the child's identification with parents (or their substitutes) whose prohibitions and idealizations defined the conditions for love in his early external environment. In the adult, the superego enforces these old external demands by internally threatening the ego with guilt.

Taboo. The conventional or social prohibition of certain forms of behavior; the term is derived from the study of primitive societies but now applied to all.

Transference. A patient's relationship toward and fantasies about his psychoanalyst during therapy, typically recapitulating early object-relations.

Transformation. In this book, a generalized term for the alteration of an infantile fantasy (*q.v.*) into a meaningful series of words acceptable to the ego; analogous to the action of a combination of defense mechanisms on a drive.

Wish. An impulse to re-evoke a perception previously associated with gratification of a drive (Freud).

Wish fulfillment. The reappearance of a perception previously associated with gratification of a drive (Freud).

Index

The titles of particular works are indexed under their authors' names or, for films, their directors' (unless, of course, the work is anonymous).